37.50

Dance Rhythms
OF THE
French Baroque

Music: Scholarship and Performance
Thomas Binkley, General Editor

Typical Close of a Dance Facing the Presence

Dance Rhythms
OF THE
French Baroque
A HANDBOOK FOR PERFORMANCE

BETTY BANG MATHER

With the Assistance of Dean M. Karns

INDIANA UNIVERSITY PRESS
Bloomington and Indianapolis

Publication of this book was assisted by a grant from the Publications
Program of the National Endowment for the Humanities, an independent
federal agency.

An early version of portions of chapter 15 appeared as "The Performance of
Trills in French Baroque Dance Music," in *Concerning the Flute*, edited by
Rien de Reede (Amsterdam: Broekmans & Van Poppel, 1985).

Frontispiece courtesy Dean M. Karns and Helen Chadima

Library of Congress Cataloging-in-Publication Data

Mather, Betty Bang.
Dance rhythms of the French Baroque.

(Music—scholarship and performance)
Bibliography: p.
Includes index.
1. Dance music—France—17th century—History and
criticism.   2. Dance music—France—18th century—History
and criticism.   3. Music—Performance.   I. Karns, Dean M.
II. Title.   III. Series.
ML3427.M37   1987   785.4'1'0944   86-45991
ISBN 0-253-31606-5
1   2   3   4   5   91   90   89   88   87

To Roger

Contents

PREFACE

Our study of the dance rhythms of the French Baroque centers around the dance music in Lully's theatrical works and, more broadly, around the rhythms of the dance music composed at the court of Louis XIV. Louis's great support of the arts and of the classical heritage produced a magnificence of achievements that has caused the period of his personal reign (1661–1715) to be called the *grand siècle* (the great age). During the *grand siècle*, French dances reached the height of excellence and popularity. They were copied in ballrooms all over Europe and the New World, and composers of many nations included French dance movements in their instrumental suites.

Our chief goal is to help modern performers give life and soul to French Baroque dance music through understanding why French dancing masters, librettists, composers, dancers, singers, and instrumentalists created and articulated the dance rhythms as they did. Although we direct the book chiefly toward performers—professional musicians and dancers, college performance majors, and serious amateurs—we also discuss matters of interest to musicologists and dance scholars, and therefore cite specific references throughout. We make no attempt to teach readers to dance, but only to perform certain step rhythms and to appreciate the larger rhythms of the floor patterns. Admirable books by Wendy Hilton and Anne Witherell, listed in the Bibliography, provide more detailed instruction.

In identifying dance rhythms, tempos, articulations, and so forth, we have found that no one practice applies to all dances or even to all pieces having the same dance title. As a result, words such as "usually," "normally," "often," "tends to," and "for the most part" appear many times in the text, indicating that a certain feature applies generally but not always. If readers recognize the most characteristic practices in the music they play, they will be able to perform dance music as dance music—a sarabande as a sarabande, a rhythmic subject as a rhythmic subject—as well as to identify and bring out the features that make one dance piece, sarabande, or rhythmic subject different from another.

Part I of this book describes the development of the dance rhythms at the court of Louis XIV. It begins with the principles of classical antiquity and continues with dance rhythms of the late sixteenth and early seventeenth centuries. Next it discusses the dance rhythms of Lully and his followers. The last chapters relate how French dancers, singers, and instrumentalists of the seventeenth and early eighteenth centuries brought out the dance rhythms in their performances. Part II describes the fifteen dances most often encountered and identifies their typical performance in light of the discussion in Part I.

Citations. Complete citations are listed in the Bibliography. In the text, only the last name of the author, the date of the source, and the page numbers are given, often within parentheses. The author's initials are included if two authors have the same surname. Two books written by the same author in the same year are differentiated by letter, e.g., "P. Rameau, 1725a"; "P. Rameau, 1725b."

For a modern facsimile edition, the publication date of the original work is cited: "Mersenne, 1636" (the facsimile edition was published in 1963); and for a modern translation, the letter "t" is added to the book's original date: "Mersenne, 1636t" (translation published 1957). When a second or later edition of an original work is cited, the letter "e" follows the publication date: "Grimarest, 1760e" (work first published 1707). Citations from the sections within the modern facsimile edition of Mersenne's treatise are explained in the Bibliography.

All Greek and Latin quotations are taken from modern translations, and the standard procedure for identifying classical citations is followed; that is, the numbers of the original volumes and lines are given, but no dates.

If a musical example comes from a source cited in the Bibliography, the caption gives only the date. If the source is not in the Bibliography, the caption includes the full identification.

Acknowledgments. Especial thanks go to Dean M. Karns, who did most of the research into the classical sources for chapter 1 and into the dance sources for chapters 2, 8, and 9 and Part II. He also helped with the analyses of musical structures in chapters 3 and 7, of tempo in chapter 10 and Part II, and of harpsichord fingerings in chapters 14, 15, and 16. He designed a number of the examples, helped with many critical points, and thoroughly checked the final draft. The "we" in this book is not the usual editorial term but often refers specifically to Karns and myself.

I am exceedingly grateful to Patricia M. Ranum, modern authority on the declamation of French Baroque dance songs, recitatives, and *airs de cour*, for her generously offered, as yet unpublished collection of dance songs, her guidance in matters of seventeenth-century France, her lively criticism of several early drafts, and for allowing me to see in advance of publication her two recent articles on the declamation of French dance songs. I am also thankful to Dorothy Parker for making available to me, through Ranum, the dance parodies she discovered.

I should like to thank Geneviève Prévot Smith for her suggestions on translating dance lyrics; David Lasocki for his help with the Bibliography and his suggestions on an early draft; Sven Hansell for his careful reading of an early draft and for his suggestions regarding several other drafts; Helen Chadima for her early reading of the chapters on the dance; Amy Gibson for checking all the French sources and commenting on the text; Elizabeth Sadilek for help with the final draft and the German sources; Susan Bennett for reviewing especially the examples of the final draft; Holly Carver for her guidance on preparing the manuscript for submission to publishers; John Dowdall for his help in deciphering guitar and lute tablatures and for reviewing the sections on these instruments; and Leopold La Fosse, Lynne Day Denig, Margaret Wilmeth, and Diane Theobald for their assistance in matters of string bowing. Also, I greatly appreciate the advice of Marilyn Somville on the chapters dealing with lyrics and wish to express my special thanks to her for supporting my applications for grants and assistantships.

I am extremely grateful to The University of Iowa for giving me the time to prepare this book, through a Senior Faculty Fellowship in the Humanities and a Faculty Development Leave. The University made available a graduate research assistant to help me with this project for one semester and three undergraduate scholar assistants for a total of six semesters. For four years it supplied me with office space and the outstanding resources of University House. My particular thanks go to its director, Jay Semel, and his right hand, Lorna Olson, for their help, friendship, and support. I should also like to thank The University of Iowa Libraries (including the former head music librarian, the late Rita Benton, and the present one, Joan Falconer); the Library of Congress; and the Bibliothèque Nationale of Paris for making their materials available.

In the final preparation of this book, I am most grateful to Thomas Binkley for his support, his overall suggestions, and his special advice on the guitar chapter. I deeply appreciate George Houle's enthusiastic backing and his suggestion that I read and use some of the material in the chapter on *rhythmopoeia* from his forthcoming book, *Meter in Music, 1600–1800*. I thank The University of Iowa Foundation and Coe College for their help toward financing the examples of the book, and Mark Johnson for his careful and artistic notation of them.

Finally, special thanks are due my husband, Roger Mather, for his help in developing a writing style intended to make my findings both accessible to performers and acceptable to musicologists; for his editorial aid; and for his always ready, generous, and loving support.

Iowa City   BETTY BANG MATHER
January 1986

INTRODUCTION

And the manner so esteemed
Of our ancient poets,
Verses [set] with music,
[And] the complicated measured dance,
Demonstrating from the blue sky
Harmony with a mystical effect.[1]

—Baltasar de Beaujoyeulx (1581)

The "tragedies in music" of Jean-Baptiste Lully were said by contemporary observers to unite music, song, and dance in ways that closely resembled the tragedies of Greek antiquity. Without question, the "harmony with a mystical effect" described by Beaujoyeulx reached its apex in the operas of Lully, the favorite composer of Louis XIV. To achieve this "mystical" union, Lully worked closely with a librettist and a choreographer—usually the poet Philippe Quinault and the dancing master Pierre de Beauchamp. When a piece in a ballet or opera was both danced and sung, the music had to fit both renditions.

The poet wrote the lyrics first. Then Lully composed music to those lines, adjusting the words as necessary to fit the traditional dance rhythms. Finally, being himself an excellent dancer, he worked with the dancing master on the choreography. Because Lully was able to take part in shaping not only the music but also the verse and the dance, the harmony so admired in Greek drama was attained as closely as the French language, musical conventions, and dancing style allowed.

Both Louis XIII (1601–1643) and his son, Louis XIV (1638–1715), loved to dance. Dancing was an important ingredient in many aspects of court life, and courtiers practiced daily to promote their health and polish their technique. Dance was featured at all court entertainments. It dominated the court ballets of the late sixteenth and early seventeenth centuries and the comic and tragic operas of the late seventeenth and the early eighteenth centuries. Much of the concert music played at court bore dance titles.

Lully began his service at the French court in 1653, during Louis XIV's minority, and immediately began writing ballets. After Louis achieved his majority in 1661, Lully continued with the king's full backing to compose increasingly grand stage works. In many ways Lully was a traditionalist who looked back to the dance rhythms of the sixteenth century. But he was also an innovator who explored new and better ways to achieve the harmony of verse, music, and dance so admired by the French classicists. In his classical leanings, Lully was enthusiastically supported by Louis XIV's academies of Literature, Music, and the Dance. Lully died in 1687 at the height of his creative powers.

Louis XIV danced exceptionally well. During his younger years, he performed the principal role in many ballets staged at court, where he was joined by proficient dancers among his courtiers and by a few professional dancers. Toward the end of the seventeenth century, however, theatrical dancing had become so demanding that only professionals could execute the intricate steps.

Many dance pieces performed in the theater were "pieces of character," that is, dances that depicted people from the French provinces or from other countries. They were choreographed for one, two, sometimes four, or even eight dancers, who wore costumes indicating their province, country, or stage personality. Originally each characteristic dance had its own steps and floor patterns. But by the eighteenth century most dances were performed with similar steps and patterns and in the elegant style called *la belle danse* (the beautiful dance), which led to the classical ballet of the nineteenth century.

Lully's ballets and operas contain bourrées, canaries, chaconnes, courantes, gavottes, gigues, loures, menuets, passacailles, passepieds, and sarabandes; and his horse ballet, *Le Carousel*, includes a folies. His immediate successors added forlanes, rigaudons, and a new type of allemande. Unfortunately, no choreographies survive from the original productions of Lully's works, but we do have many choreographies composed for eighteenth-century revivals of his works and for the original productions of those of his followers.

Concert pieces bearing dance titles include all the characteristic dances used in ballets and operas during the *grand siècle* as well as an occasional branle or contredanse. In addition, many instrumental suites contain a "stylized" allemande, in which the traditional dance rhythms are divided into quick notes or dotted figures. All these pieces, being performed without dancing to hold the audience's attention, rely on instrumental techniques to suggest the character of the dance and add variety to the performance.

The basic rhythms of the characteristic dances are found in theatrical, ballroom, and concert pieces. But, since little ballroom music of the period remains, and because the music written to accompany theatrical dancing is simpler and more standardized than most of that composed for concerts, in this book we look especially at the dance music in the operas and ballets of the *grand siècle*. And, because most choreographies for the ballroom are simpler and more standardized in their steps than those for the theater, we discuss chiefly the simplest and most common dance steps of the ballroom choreographies.

Much of the information in this book applies also to other kinds of Baroque music—to all French music, to dance music composed in other countries, and even to much metered music of the period. For instance, the French organist André Raison told church organists to base the movement of the music they played on dance pieces having similar rhythms, though he recommended moderating the tempo somewhat, "due to the sanctity of the place" (1688, Preface). As late as 1778, the German violinist, theorist, and composer Johann Philipp

Kirnberger—a student of J. S. Bach—considered understanding the rhythms of the characteristic dances vital to good performance in pieces of all kinds:

> To achieve the necessary qualities for good performance, the musician can do nothing better than to play industriously all kinds of characteristic dances. Each of these dance types has its own rhythm, its rhythmic subjects [*Einschnitte*] of equal length, [and] its accents in the same place in each phrase. [The musician] thereby recognizes these easily and, through frequent practice, becomes accustomed subtly to differentiate each rhythm, and to mark the phrases and accents, so that the varied and mixed rhythms are readily perceived even in a long piece. He also gets into the habit of giving each piece its particular expression, since each kind of dance melody has its own characteristic beat and note values.[2] (1778, Preface, pp. 1–2)

Kirnberger found practicing the characteristic dances helpful even for composing and performing fugues, and he blamed what he considered a deterioration in the musical art of his day on its lack:

> It is impossible to compose or to perform a fugue well if one does not know all the different [dance] rhythms; and therefore, because this study is neglected today, music has sunk from its former worth, and one can no longer endure fugues, because, through miserable performance that defines neither phrase nor accents, they have become a mere chaos of notes.[3] (1778, Preface, p. 2)

In fact, many of the principles governing the characteristic rhythms apply equally to much nineteenth- and even twentieth-century music and its performance. If these rhythms are overlooked, the characteristic movement that many Baroque authors called the soul of the music is lost.

Dance Rhythms
OF THE
French Baroque

Prologue:
The King's Grand Ball

I believe there is no better way to . . . draw
attention to the ceremonies, and the rules of
the particular dances, than to begin with a
small description of the king's grand ball; because it ranks first [among balls] and should be
imitated at private balls; as much for the order
to be followed, as for the respect and decorum
to be observed.[1]

—Pierre Rameau (1725b, p. 49)

Ten years after the death of Louis XIV, the dancing master Pierre Rameau gave
an account of the conduct and decorum observed at a royal grand ball, which he
said should also be followed at private balls. While this information is not essential for understanding the dance rhythms, it gives a view of their cultural
setting. In Louis XIV's later years, according to Rameau, balls opened with traditional branles, continued with *danses à deux*, and finished with contredanses.
The following protocol was observed:

In the first place, no one is admitted to the royal circle except the princes and princesses of royal blood; then the dukes and peers, and the duchesses, and afterwards
the other lords and ladies of the court according to their rank. The ladies are seated
in the front row [around the edge of the room], and the gentlemen behind. . . .
Every one being thus placed in order, when His Majesty wishes the ball to begin
he rises, and the whole company does likewise.
The king takes his position at the place where the dancing is to begin (which is
[at the end of the room] near the musicians). In the time of Louis XIV, His Majesty
danced with the queen or with the first princess of the blood. Behind the king and
his partner, the other couples took their places according to their rank. . . . The
lords are on the left side, and the ladies on the right: and in this order, they make
their bows one before the other. Then the king and queen lead the branle, which
was the dance with which the court balls began; all the lords and ladies follow Their
Majesties, each on their own side. . . . After they dance the gavotte [the last
branle], . . . they make the same bows on parting, as those they made at the start.[2]
(1725b, pp. 49–51)

The branles, originally from the French provinces, had been refined at court.
Basically round dances, they were performed by an unspecified number of
couples who faced the inside of the circle and took most steps to the side. Usu-

ally the dancers reiterated a single step pattern throughout the piece, stepping first to the left and then to the right. In one of the favorite dances, the _branle à mener de Poitou_ (leader-dance from Poitou), the leader broke the ring and led the others in an S-shaped pattern around the floor.

After the branles, a number of _danses à deux_ (dances for two) were performed. Only one couple danced at a time, while the rest of the company looked on. These dances were choreographed in the elegant style of the theater, but most of the motions were simpler. Although the courante was the favorite _danse à deux_ in the early part of the seventeenth century, by the latter part the menuet had replaced it in popularity. According to Rameau, the king and his partner danced the first menuet of a ball, with the following protocol:

> When the king has danced the first _Menuet_, he goes to his seat, and everyone sits down, for while His Majesty is dancing all stand; then the prince who is to dance next, after His Majesty is seated, makes him a very deep bow, and then comes to the queen or the first princess, and together they make the bows one makes before dancing. Thereafter they dance the menuet, and after the menuet they make the same bows again. Then this lord makes a very deep bow to this princess on leaving her. . . .
>
> At the same moment he takes two or three steps forward, to address the princess or lady whose turn it is to dance next. . . .[3] (pp. 52–53)

Other characteristic dances such as the bourrée, sarabande, passepied, and rigaudon were also performed in the ballroom, usually as _danses à deux_ but sometimes as solo dances. "But if His Majesty desires another dance to be performed, one of the first gentlemen of the bed chamber announces his wish, which does not prevent the same bows being observed" (pp. 53–54).[4]

Contredanses, which closed the balls of Louis XIV's late years, were adopted from English country, or longways, dances. The dancers formed two parallel lines, as in the Virginia reel. While ballroom dancing at the French court had grown increasingly technical and theatrical during the seventeenth century, social dancing among the nobility in England had remained stylistically closer to folk dancing. Contredanses were slow to catch on in France, however, because the democratic arrangement of the dancing couples prevented protocol from being adequately observed. Dancing masters expressed strong disfavor with the design of and decorum in these dances, which Rameau complained "are not to the taste of those who love _la belle danse_" (p. 107):

> It is true that there are many [contredanses] that have neither design nor taste, because the figures are always the same, without any fixed steps. The greatest perfection of the contredanses is to torment the body, to extricate oneself in turning, to stamp the feet as with sabots [wooden clogs], and to assume attitudes that are not decent.[5] (p. 108)

Despite the rhetoric of embittered dancing masters, the contredanses found favor with young courtiers, and by the early eighteenth century they were well established at court balls. At the start of the eighteenth century, the French invented their own form of contredanse, the cotillon, which was performed by four couples arranged as in modern square dancing. (Perhaps the square rooms common in France, in contrast to the oblong English ones, required a change from the English longways dances.) Most contredanses were set to English tunes, though some carried the name of a French dance, such as "menuet" or "bourrée." By the mid-eighteenth century, the contredanses had replaced all *danses à deux* except the menuet, and the menuet of that day had replaced the branle as the traditional way to open the ball.

After setting down the protocol and the order of dances, Rameau described the way a gentleman or a lady should invite another person to dance and the courtesy with which the proposed partner should respond (pp. 55–59). Even at private gatherings, attended only by family and friends, essentially the same ceremonies were observed: "I recommend above all to young people, for whom these sorts of gatherings are often made, to observe the rules that their [dancing] masters have taught them, in order to give honor to the education they receive" (p. 59).[6]

I

Features of
the Dance Rhythms

1

Reason and the Passions

The notion of beauty is double. . . . [That is,]
I discern two kinds of perceptions [of the
beautiful]; I call one *ideas* and the other
feelings. . . .
    Ideas occupy the mind, feelings interest the
heart.[1]

—Jean Pierre de Crousaz (1715, pp. 7–8)

Following the philosophers of ancient Greece and Rome, classical thinkers of the
Renaissance and Baroque eras considered music one of the mathematical disci-
plines, and thus to deal with ideas. At the same time, they believed mathematical
proportions could stir the feelings. Beauty in music was therefore "double,"
because music both occupied the mind and interested the heart. Jean Grimarest,
for instance, described vocal music as

a kind of language, in which men agree to communicate with more pleasure [than
in speech] their thoughts and their sentiments [that is, ideas and feelings, or reason
and passions]. Thus he who composes this sort of music should be considered a
translator, who in observing the rules of his art, expresses these same thoughts and
these same sentiments.[2] (1760e, p. 120)

In the early seventeenth century, as composers returned to the homophonic,
word-based musical style of the ancient Greeks, classical thinkers related both
vocal and instrumental music to rhetoric, the art of oratory. Rhetoric could be
pleasing or persuasive. Pleasing rhetoric was intelligent, reasoned, and regular:
its divisions exhibited simple mathematical proportions. Persuasive rhetoric,
on the other hand, was at times impassioned, irregular, and "baroque" (that is,
extravagant, bizarre).

Phérotée de La Croix recognized the classical alliance of reason and the passions in the rhetoric of the French music of his day:

In the art of speaking and singing, one calls number [meaning also measure, meter, and time] everything that the ears perceive as proportioned . . . , whether following the proportion of the measures of time, or a just distribution of the intervals of breathing; this is what the Latins call *Numerosa oratio* [timed, metrical, or rhythmic oratory] and the French, *Discours harmonieux* [harmonious, or musical, discourse]. St. Augustine remarks that there is a marvelous alliance between our mind and the numbers [of time]. . . . And Cicero . . . says that numbers [that is, rhythmic proportions] are marvelously suited to excite the passions.[3] (1694, pp. 652–53)

Perhaps more than any other art form, French Baroque dance music as developed at the French court by Lully and his colleagues carefully balances firm control (reason) with strong releases of feeling (the passions).

REASON

The French philosopher René Descartes was the foremost exponent of reason, and Frenchmen of the *grand siècle* took rational thought as a maxim—whether they were dealing with philosophy, science, the arts, or affairs of state. The poet Nicholas Boileau revealed how much Frenchmen respected reason:

> Aimez donc la raison; que toujours vos écrits
> Empruntent d'elle seule et leur lustre et leur prix.

> 1673, Canto I, lines 37–38

In 1683 Sir William Soame translated this couplet into English verse:

> Love reason then; and let whate'er you write
> Borrow from her its beauty, force, and light.

The French love for reason, logic, and an orderly, rational life prompted Louis XIII and Louis XIV to create the French royal academies: the Academy of Literature in 1635, of Painting and Sculpture in 1648, of Dance in 1661, of Music in 1669, and of Architecture in 1671. The academies investigated and attempted to codify their respective fields of knowledge, in keeping with the principles of reason, the mathematical relationships, and the artistic models of classical antiquity.

Reason and the passions were linked so inextricably in classical thought that Jean-Pierre de Crousaz had to strain credibility to divide them for separate discussion (1715, pp. 12–15). Yet he was able to discern five qualities of beauty that exist independently of feelings. These rational attributes, which he called the "real and natural qualities of beauty," are uniformity, variety, regularity, order, and proportion—in that sequence. And proportion, he said, includes the other four.

On the surface, Crousaz's first and second qualities of beauty—uniformity and variety—seem to contradict one another. But Bernard Lamy, in his book on oratory, quoted St. Augustine on the way that equality and diversity can coexist in music: "The Ear cannot receive a greater contentment than what it feels when it is charm'd by diversity of Sounds, and yet is not depriv'd of the pleasure that equality gives it" (1675t, pp. 138–39). Descartes, after praising the virtues of uniformity in the first seven "preliminaries" of his *Compendium musicae*, extolled variety in the eighth and last: "Finally, it must be observed that variety is in all things most pleasing" (1650t, pp. 11–13).

The variety that the classical authors esteemed so highly is always pleasing, rather than persuasive or passionate. In no way is it discordant (nonuniform), irregular, disorderly, or ill proportioned. Lamy used a flower garden to demonstrate that variety is pleasing and at the same time uniform, regular, orderly, and well proportioned:

> In appearance, [equality and variety] are incompatible, and destructive the one of the other; but they agree very well, and equality and variety may coexist without any confusion. There is in nothing more variety, than in a Garden of Flowers, [where] there are Tulips, and Violets, and Roses, Etc. The Borders or Compartments are different, some round, some oval, some square, some triangular. Yet if this Plot be consider'd by a skilful man, the equality agrees well enough with the variety, being divided into Beds proportion'd one to the other, and adorn'd with regular Figures. (1675t, p. 138)

Lamy later declared that the "sweetness of the Equality" must be tempered by the "salt of the Variety" (p. 181). A similar balance of uniformity and variety is apparent in the texts of dance songs, the steps of dancers, and the ornaments of instrumentalists playing dance music.

Crousaz's third and fourth qualities of beauty—regularity and order—are closely related to uniformity. St. Augustine probably referred to regularity as "similitude" when he said that number, the basis of rhythm, "has beauty by equality and similitude" (*De musica*, Bk. VI, xvii. 56). As examples of the regular, Crousaz cited geometrical figures having some or all of their sides equal, such as an equilateral triangle, an isosceles triangle, a rectangle, and an equilateral regular polygon. "The equalities of these figures form a regularity that we esteem and love" (1715, p. 14).

Crousaz saw regularity in the sections of gardens, in the stories of buildings, and in the rooms of each story. Regularity is also apparent in the dance figures traced by the choreographies of the early eighteenth century, in the mirror images formed by a dancing couple, and in the near or exact repetition of rhythmic subjects and refrains in Lullian dance pieces.

Order was considered similar to regularity. According to St. Augustine: "All nature requires order. It seeks to be like itself, and it possesses its own safety and its own order, in spaces or in times or in bodily form, by methods of balance" (*De musica*, Bk. VI, xvii. 56).

Crousaz described order as gradual change from one item to the next in a regular sequence: "To go by order is not to jump suddenly from one extremity to another, it is to advance with a difference accompanied by much equality, [and then to progress] to a third item strongly approaching the second, but a little further away than the first" (1715, p. 14).[4] He contended that it is natural for the human spirit to love order, because order "extends the light, that is, it sheds light on objects or actions that would otherwise be obscure."

An example of order that can hardly be surpassed is the rigid protocol observed in the sequence of dancers at the king's grand ball, cited in the Prologue. Order can also be seen in the succession of step-units in dance figures and of dance figures in whole choreographies. Lyrics arranged into stanzas and stanzas into whole dance songs, and rhythmic subjects organized into musical reprises and musical reprises into whole pieces follow a certain order—as do the movements of the melody and the harmony toward each musical cadence and of lesser cadences toward more final ones.

Proportion, the fifth of Crousaz's "real and natural qualities of beauty," is related etymologically to reason in both English and French. The English word *ratio*, meaning proportion, comes from the past participle of the Latin verb *reri*: to reckon, calculate, think. And the French word *raison* means both reason and ratio, or proportion.

Since the time of the Pythagoreans, musical intervals have been expressed as mathematical proportions. The length of a string or pipe that produces the upper pitch of a given interval was found to be in fixed proportion to the length that produces the lower pitch. By extension, the simple proportions of musical intervals were thought to apply to all things in the universe. Aristotle gave the Pythagoreans initial credit for this notion, which underlies all the artistic philosophy of ancient Greek and later classical thinkers:

> [The Pythagoreans believed] that the properties and ratios of the musical scales are based on numbers, and since it seemed clear that all other things have their whole nature modelled upon numbers [that is, proportions], and that numbers are the ultimate things in the whole physical universe, they assumed the elements of numbers to be the elements of everything, and the whole universe to be a proportion or number. (*Metaphysics*, Book I, 986a)

Proportions for the consonances of early Greek music were called "simple" because they were made up of small whole numbers: $2:1$ for the octave, $3:2$ for the fifth, and $4:3$ for the fourth. These simple proportions were considered perfect. In *Problems*, Aristotle claimed that the octave is the most beautiful consonance because its $2:1$ proportion expressed as a fraction is $\frac{2}{1}$ or as a whole number is 2 (Book XIX, 920a).

The notion that simple proportions are the best and that the "elements of numbers" pervade all things in the universe led many Greek and later classical thinkers to see proportion as the main organizing force also in the arts other than music. For instance, the Italian architect Leone Battista Alberti, whose *Ten Books on Architecture* of 1485 influenced Western architecture well into the eighteenth century, based his architectural principles on Pythagorean proportions:

> I am every Day more and more convinced of the Truth of *Pythagoras*'s Saying, that Nature is sure to act consistently, and with a constant Analogy in all her Operations: From whence I conclude, that the same Numbers, by means of which the Agreement of Sounds affects our Ears with Delight, are the very same which please our Eyes and our Mind. We shall therefore borrow all our Rules for the finishing our

Proportions [that is, proportions for length, breadth, and height] from the Musicians. . . . (1485t, pp. 196–97)

Simple proportions pervaded all aspects of the French dance music and dance motions of the early seventeenth century. Descartes pointed out that the two types of mensuration used in the music of his day are based on the proportions of 2:1 and 3:1, namely, on divisions of the measure into two or three equal units (1650t, p. 14). In today's terms, a measure of duple time is divided into two equal units and a measure of triple time, into three.

French composers of the period also chose simple proportions for the rhythms and forms of dance melodies. For instance, the main long and short notes in many dance melodies—like the long and short syllables in Greek metrical feet—have time values in the proportion of 2:1. That is, the long note is twice the length of the short one: L = SS. Descartes in addition allowed the 3:1 ratio of note values: L = SSS (ex. 1.1). He claimed that only these two relationships can be readily distinguished by the ear (1650t, p. 13).

EXAMPLE 1.1.
Distinguishable relationships of note values. Descartes, 1650t, p. 13. a. 2:1; b. 3:1.

Descartes stated further that the entire melody of a piece often exhibits the 2:1 proportion (p. 14); that is, it consists of 8 (2 x 4), 16 (2 x 8), 32 (2 x 16), or 64 (2 x 32) units, especially in dance pieces having two reprises of equal length. This simplest of all proportions (2:1) helps listeners distinguish the components of a composition as they listen to it: "While hearing the end of one time unit, we still remember what occurred at the beginning and [can anticipate what will occur] during the remainder of the composition" (1650t, p. 14).

PASSIONS

The reasoning by which classical philosophers related numbers and mathematical proportions to the "passions of the soul" may surprise modern readers. Yet, like Cicero, classical thinkers of the seventeenth century held this relationship to be appropriate.

Descartes explained that a proportional relationship must exist between music that excites a certain emotion and the emotion itself (1650t, p. 11). In his last work, *Passions of the Soul*, he hypothesized that human emotions, or passions, are aroused by certain "animal spirits" that circulate through a person's nerves and bloodstream in response to such external stimuli as thoughts or musical figures. He described more than 30 passions, ranging from generosity to disgust (1649, part II). Other authors had their own lists. For instance, Marin Mersenne mentioned love, desire, hate, sadness, flight (aversion), hope, audacity, boldness, anger, fear, and despair (1636, IIb, p. 367), but pointed out that the main passions expressed in French airs are sadness, sorrow, joy, love, and hope (IIb, p. 371). Grimarest added envy, jealousy, indignation, and compassion (1760e, pp. 81ff.).

In France, intense passions were never allowed to rule for long. A basic social premise that developed under Louis XIV was that man is civilized, and therefore his feelings ought always to be controlled through the force of reason. The difference between the Italian and the French expressions of the passions in the early eighteenth century was stated emphatically by François Raguenet, a supporter of the Italian musical style. Of an Italian musical performance, he wrote approvingly:

> Everything is so brisk, sharp and piercing, so impetuous and affecting, . . . that the imagination, feelings, soul, and even the body are swept along in a common transport. . . . The violinist who performs . . . torments his violin, his body, . . . he is agitated like one possessed. . . .[5] (1702, pp. 43–44)

But the tamer, French operas "are regular, coherent designs. . . . Love, jealousy, anger, and the other passions are treated with infinite art and delicacy" (pp. 5–7).[6]

Lully was said to have excelled in setting the passions of lyrics to music. Some twenty years after Lully's death, Grimarest wrote that a singer who performs Lully's songs has no difficulty in expressing the various passions and enjoys singing them; and that listeners easily grasp the sentiment of a song the first time they hear it "because it is natural." That is, its rhythmic and melodic inflections are the natural ones for the passion expressed in the text.

That rhythms and melodies could excite the various passions is a belief dating back at least to Aristotle, who pointed out that "rhythms and melody supply imitations of anger and gentleness, and of courage and temperance" (*Politics*, Bk. VIII 1340a). According to Mersenne, a variety of rhythmic patterns called "rhythmic movements" were used to excite or calm the passions: "Rhythm is an Art that concerns itself with rhythmic movements and regulates their course and their combination in order to excite the passions, and also to support them, or augment, diminish or calm them" (1636, IIb, p. 374).[7] Music must follow and imitate the movement of the passion it wishes to excite in listeners (IIa, p. 99). In fact, Mersenne called his rhythmic patterns "movements" because they "imitate the movement of the passions"; that is, they are proportioned to the passions they are intended to arouse.

For instance, Mersenne pointed out that metrical feet of two equal units (LL) are appropriate for "minds that love tranquility and peace, and that are friends of rest and solitude." For a "more turbulent expression," one of the units must be twice as long as the other, as in the trochees (LS) and iambs (SL) of Greek poetry. The iambic foot incites listeners to war, while the anapestic foot (SSL) excites their anger (IIb, p. 402).

George Houle (1987, chap. 3, "*Rhythmopoeia*") discusses in detail the relationship of the rhythms of the Greek metrical feet to the passions. He shows that Isaac Vossius, a Dutch scholar who taught in England during Lully's heyday in France, matched the greatest number of metrical feet with the passions they elicit. Vossius's *De poematum cantu et viribus rhythmi* of 1673, a treatise on the alliance of music and poetry, was important enough to be mentioned by Johann Mattheson (1739) and Jean-Jacques Rousseau (1768). Vossius related metrical feet to the passions as follows:

Rhythms	*Passions*
pyrrhic (SS) and tribrach (SSS)	light and voluble, as in dances of satyrs
spondee (LL) and molossus (LLL)	grave and slow
trochee (LS) and sometimes the amphibrach (SLS)	soft and tender
iamb (SL) and anapest (SSL)	fierce, vehement, violent, and warlike
dactyl (LSS)	cheerful and joyous
antispast (SLLS)	hard and rugged
anapest (SSL) and, still more powerful, the 4th paeon (SSSL)	furious and mad

Mersenne believed that the chief purpose of rhythm is to please or to excite some passion in the audience:

> Those who use [rhythm] on drums and trumpets, at dances and ballets, in songs, and in poetry, etc. have no other intent than to please the listeners and the spectators, or to excite them to some passion or affection, be it joy or sadness, love or hate, etc.[8] (1636, IIb, p. 374)

In giving pleasure to the listeners and spectators, the music makes agreeable rhetoric. To the extent it excites them to some passion, it makes persuasive rhetoric.

PLEASING AND PERSUASIVE RHETORIC

The Roman historian and moralist Plutarch likened the dance to mute poetry, while the French cleric Arbeau compared it to mute rhetoric (1589t, p. 16). The purpose of classical rhetoric was to fashion and deliver orations that pleased people, as with a eulogy; or that persuaded people to a particular point of view, as through a discourse in the senate, pulpit, or court of law.

Pleasing rhetoric was agreeable to listen to. It appealed to the intellect and exhibited Crousaz's five "real and natural" qualities of beauty. The Roman orator Cicero said that a pleasing oration

> indulges in a neatness and symmetry of sentences, and is allowed to use well defined and rounded periods; the ornamentation is done of set purpose, with no attempt at concealment, but openly and avowedly, so that words correspond to words as if measured off in equal phrases; frequently things inconsistent are placed side by side, and things contrasted are paired; clauses are made to end in the same way and with a similar sound. (*Orator*, xii 38)

Pleasing choreographies, dance lyrics, and dance music of the *grand siècle* exhibited the same qualities of neatness and symmetry.

Persuasive rhetoric, on the other hand, stirred the hearts of listeners. It grasped their attention because it excited their passions. To move the audience, some extravagance of expression was necessary, and the greater the distortion the more intense the passion. Thus the heartfelt expressions of persuasive rhetoric are quite unlike the abstract quality of variety found in pleasing orations. Discord, irregularity, disorder, odd proportions, and sometimes even a lack of pleasing variety are hallmarks of a persuasive utterance.

All classical oratory includes persuasive as well as pleasing elements. For instance, although long, "classical" sentences are carefully balanced to include clauses of equal length, Lamy showed that many speeches mingle short, emotional sentences with the long, dispassionate ones:

> Equal periods should not follow one another immediately; it is better for the discourse to flow more freely. A too exact equality of the intervals of breathing would become monotonous. . . . A discourse with equal periods can be uttered only with coldness. These periods . . . are only good for speaking of majesty or to please the ear. One cannot run [be passionate], and at the same time walk in cadence [be controlled].[9] (1701e, pp. 242–44)

In a dance air, as in a classical oration, a change in rhythm or phrase length reveals a new "movement of the animal spirits." For instance, the opening measures of a dance piece, which characterize the dance, are fairly predictable in their rhythmic subjects and in the way these are organized into musical periods; and the standard cadential formulas used at the end of reprises are pleasing rather than passionate. But the middle section of a piece tends to be more passionate and persuasive and thus more irregular than the beginning and the end.

Because the middle sections of dance airs vary greatly, they can be discussed only in a general way. Therefore this book dwells more on the "real and natural," or characteristic, elements of dance rhythms than on the less consistent, more passionate qualities. If performers examine each dance piece to find its regular and characteristic elements, they will find that the irregular and persuasive features stand out in relief.

Classical thinking was an important factor in the artistic creations of Lully and his contemporaries in France. Classical works were read widely, and classical principles were upheld by the French academies. Their influence can be seen in the many principles, described in subsequent chapters of this book, that can be traced back to Greek antiquity.

2

Arbeau's Dance Rhythms

The noun dance comes from the verb to
dance, which in Latin is called *saltare*. To
dance is to jump, to hop, to skip, to sway,
to stamp, to tiptoe, and to employ the feet,
hands and body in certain rhythmic movements. These consist of leaping, bending the
body, straddling, limping, flexing the knees,
rising upon the toes, twitching the feet, with
variations of these.[1]

—Thoinot Arbeau (1589t, p. 14)

Dancing, or saltation, is both a pleasant and
a profitable art which confers and preserves
health; proper to youth, agreeable to the old
and suitable to all provided fitness of time and
place are observed and it is not abused.[2]

—Ibid., (pp. 15–16)

In using the Latin word *saltare*, in relating dancing to health, and in requiring
"fitness of time and place" for dancing, Arbeau spoke as a Renaissance human-
ist. That is, he used the tenets of classical antiquity to explain such human activities as jumping, hopping, skipping, and swaying in the dance.

In Arbeau's day, social dances were performed for health and recreation.
People enjoyed dancing to the fullest at communal events such as village fetes,
weddings, masquerades, and religious festivals, as well as at court entertainments. Even in court guise, the dances described by Arbeau exude a large measure of their original ebullient, peasant flavor.

The frontispiece of Arbeau's dance treatise, the *Orchésographie* of 1589, reflects the importance of dancing in people's lives. Dancing is here equated with
joy, as opposed to sorrow, in the Latin subtitle taken from the third book of
Ecclesiastes: *Tempus piangendi, & tempus saltandi* (A time to mourn, and a
time to dance). On a decorative seal just below this biblical adage are the
French words *Telle est la gloire des hommes* (Such is the glory of mankind).

The joy and glory of Arbeau's dances lie in the vitality of the step rhythms and in the pleasing, dynamic, and often dramatic shapes of the choreographic units. These rhythms and shapes also influenced the musical accompaniment, both in Arbeau's day and during the *grand siècle*.

In this chapter we look especially at the features of Arbeau's dances that developed into the rhythms and forms favored by Lully, Beauchamp, and their successors. Other chapters in Part I utilize the general rhythmic and structural principles presented here; and Part II gives Arbeau's basic footwork and timings for dances that carried over into the *grand siècle*. Throughout this chapter and also in chapter 8, readers are advised to try the dance steps for themselves while singing the tunes of the dance tablatures. The joy and glory of Arbeau's and later dance rhythms cannot be adequately described on paper but must be experienced through one's own movements.

COMMON FOOTWORK AND ITS TIMING

The simplest step is a single step that moves one foot forward, to one side, or to the rear. In Arbeau's and later dances, most steps are taken on the ball of the foot, as when running in place—not on the heel and then the ball, as in ordinary walking.

In what we here call a "weighted step," the dancer's weight is transferred to the moving foot. A weighted step usually carries the dancer from one place to another. For a *pas du gauche* (step with the left foot), the dancer steps onto the left foot—L; for a *pas du droit* (step with the right foot), onto the right one—R.

In a "weightless step" the dancer advances the free foot without shifting weight onto it and remains in the same place. Arbeau called the weightless step having no ornamentation of any kind the *pied joint* (feet together). We show it in our diagrams with the designation (r) or (l), depending on the foot that takes the weightless step.

A "step-unit" is an integrated group of two or more individual (weighted or weightless) steps. Step-units discussed in this chapter are the "simple" (single step-unit) and the "double" (double step-unit), which are used in many of Arbeau's dances; and the *cinq pas* (five steps) of the galliard, the most popular dance of his day.

What modern scholars call the "closed" simple is the most elementary step-unit in Arbeau's dances. It consists of a weighted step followed by a weightless one. For a *simple à gauche* (simple to the left), the dancer steps onto the left foot, placing the weight upon it, and then brings the right foot to join it. The reverse, stepping onto the right foot and then bringing up the left, is a *simple à droite* (simple to the right). Most weighted and weightless steps take the same amount of time, namely, a whole note in Arbeau's slow dances and a half note in his quick ones. The duple-meter courante in example 2.1 (modern notation in ex. 2.2) starts with a closed simple to the left—L(r)—followed by one to the right—R(l).

The "closed" double is the step-unit used most often in Arbeau's dances. It

EXAMPLE 2.1.

Two simples and a double in a duple-meter courànte. Arbeau, 1589t, p. 124 (photograph of music from 1888 printing, p. 66 bis).

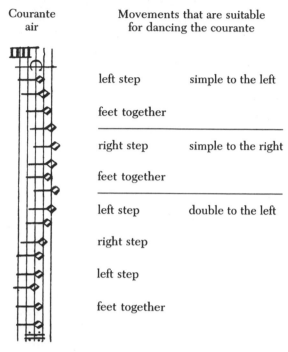

Courante air	Movements that are suitable for dancing the courante
	left step simple to the left
	feet together
	right step simple to the right
	feet together
	left step double to the left
	right step
	left step
	feet together

consists of four individual steps, the first three weighted and the last not. A *double à gauche*—LRL(r)—begins with a step onto the left foot; a *double à droite*—RLR(l)—with a step onto the right. A closed double takes the time of two closed simples. The step sequence for the courante in examples 2.1 and 2.2 ends with a closed double.

The "open" double occurs in a few of Arbeau's triple-meter dances. It has only three steps, all weighted and all taking the same amount of time—LRL or RLR. For instance, an open double begins the branle from Poitou (ex. 28.1b).

In contrast to earlier dance writers, Arbeau specified exact timings for most dance motions by writing each motion directly opposite its respective music. The vertical printing of the courante in example 2.1 is typical (1589t, p. 124). Example 2.2 gives the same music with round note heads and in the usual horizontal layout. This step sequence, one of the most common in Renaissance dances, strongly influenced the rhythmic structure of Lullian and later dance music. If readers practice these steps while singing the tune, they will feel in their bodies the rhythms of "two simples and a double." In this particular piece, each individual step requires two notes of the music.

The timing of the weighted steps in Arbeau's dances recalls the metrical feet of ancient Greek poetry. A weighted step followed by another weighted step

EXAMPLE 2.2.
Rhythmic feet in the two simples and a double of example 2.1.

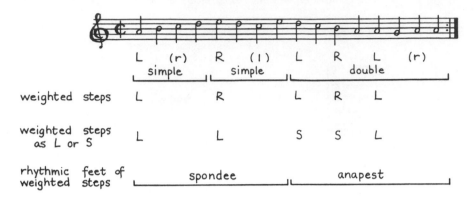

falls on a short note value (S). A weighted step followed by a weightless one falls on a long value (L). The weighted steps of a pair of simples thus make the metrical foot called a spondee (LL). The weighted steps of a closed double make an anapest (SSL).

Steps may be "low" or "high." Low steps are taken *par terre* (on the ground). High steps are springs made *en haut* (into the air). Springing steps are more energetic and thus more dramatic and "passionate" than low ones.

The basic step-unit of the galliard, the *cinq pas*, is unrelated to simples and doubles. It consists of five individual steps. The first four are performed with small leaps not indicated in the tablature and with *grèves*, or simulated kicks. The fifth step consists of a large spring, or *saut majeur*, followed by the dancer's return to the ground and posing momentarily in place, the *posture*. The dancer lands slightly sooner on the back foot, which then keeps most of the weight. Arbeau's illustration of the right and left *postures* (ex. 2.3) shows this step bringing the dance to a complete though momentary halt. In the right *posture* the right foot is in front and bears little weight, while in the left *posture* the same is true of the left foot.

In example 2.4 the timing of the five steps as well as the rhythm of the galliard music is SSSLS. Although we have been unable to find the SSSLS rhythm among the Greek metrical feet, Mersenne called it a "hegemeole" and said it typified sarabandes (1636, IIb, p. 165). The L of the hegemeole, written in most galliard music as a whole note, includes the fourth half note plus the half-note rest of the dance tablature.

Arbeau's galliard tablature shows the footfalls of five weighted steps. In actuality, the rhythm is closer to that shown in example 2.5, though the quarter note might be more like an eighth note, as in the practice today called *notes inégales* (discussed in chapter 5). The rhythm in example 2.5 is common also in sarabande music.

EXAMPLE 2.3.
Right and left *postures*. Arbeau, 1589t, p. 90 (1888, p. 47).

EXAMPLE 2.4.
Tablature for the five steps of the galliard. Arbeau, 1589t, p. 100.

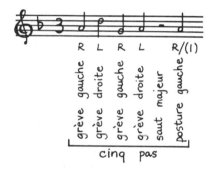

EXAMPLE 2.5.
Actual timing of the footfalls in example 2.4.

Ornamentation and division of individual steps characterize many dances. *Petits sauts* (little springs) are a common embellishment. They may be hops, leaps, or jumps. In a hop the dancer springs off one foot and lands on the same foot. In a leap he springs off one foot and lands on the other. In a jump he springs off one foot and lands on both feet, with the feet joined at the heels.

Because Arbeau did not indicate ornamental springs in his tablatures, the kind of spring intended is often open to question. For instance, the little springs

EXAMPLE 2.6.
Simulated kick. Arbeau, 1589t, p. 87 (1888, p. 45 bis). a. *pied en l'air droit* or *grève droite*, step with the left foot—L—and kick with the right; b. *pied en l'air gauche* or *grève gauche*, step with the right foot—R—and kick with the left.

a.   b.

of his courante, described in his text but omitted from his tablature, are interpreted differently between Evans's translation (1589t, p. 123) and Sutton's editorial notes to that translation (ed. note "a"). Evans implies that the weighted steps are executed as little leaps and that the weightless steps are performed as jumps, but Sutton claims that Arbeau meant that a hop preceded each weighted and weightless step.

Another common embellishment is the simulated kick, called *pied en l'air* (foot in the air) or *grève* (strike). For this kicking pose the dancer steps with one foot and raises the free foot "as if to kick someone" (Arbeau, 1589t, p. 86), as shown in example 2.6. The kicking pose may embellish the final weightless step of a double, as in Arbeau's allemande (ex. 18.1). Or it may accompany weight changes made with small leaps, as in the galliard.

Another way of varying a step-unit is to divide two individual steps into three, as occurs in the divided double to the right—RLR(r)—in Arbeau's branle double, a round dance (ex. 2.7). For the first step, *pied droit largi*, the right foot takes a large step to the right, the dancer moving in a counterclockwise direction around the circle. For the second step, *pied gauche approché*, the left foot takes a smaller step, also to the right. The three *pieds en l'air* (simulated kicks: RLR) and the "pause" divide, or ornament, the final weighted and weightless steps—R(l)—of a closed double.

Even a *saut majeur* (large spring) can be ornamented, as happens in the *capriole* that often ends a gavotte reprise. In example 2.8, the dancer moves his feet quickly backward and forward during a large spring. (Arbeau's complete tabulation for a gavotte is shown in ex. 25.1.)

EXAMPLE 2.7.
Divided double in a branle double. Arbeau, 1589t, p. 131, m. 2.

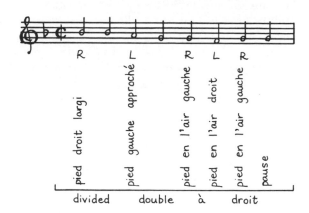

EXAMPLE 2.8.
Capriole. Arbeau, 1589t, p. 91 (1888, p. 48).

RHYTHMIC ORGANIZATION WITHIN STEP-UNITS AND THEIR SEQUENCES

Arbeau's step-units are interesting not only in their rhythms of metrical feet and in their ornamentations of footwork but also in their internal and external organizations.

The rhythmic organization of individual steps within a step-unit and of step-units within a sequence of step-units may be viewed from three standpoints. Paired elements make pleasantly symmetrical patterns; traveling steps moving to momentarily stationary poses create patterns of arsis and thesis (elan and repose); and occasional climaxes followed by greater reposes conclude longer choreographic units.

Because, as mentioned in chapter 1, a unit of two equal parts produces a feeling of tranquility and peace, a matched pair of individual steps or of larger elements gives the sense of calm and pleasing order so admired in sixteenth- and seventeenth-century France. Because of the bilateral symmetry of the human body, it is natural for paired step-units to start on opposite feet. Even a sequence of step-units, such as two simples and a double, is often repeated starting with the opposite foot. Arbeau displayed the reasoning of classical philosophers when he pointed out that the five steps of the galliard should not begin twice on the same foot, since "variety delights and repetition is odious" (1589t, p. 92).

Step-units and sequences of step-units may also be paired by coupling the dancers' movements in the forward and backward directions. In Arbeau's pavane, a processional dance shown in example 2.9, each half of the piece is repeated. In each reprise, the pattern of two simples and a double, begun with the left foot, is performed in the forward direction. In the repetition, the same pattern is begun with the right foot and performed in the backward direction. Thus the symmetries of left and right and of forward and backward are set to exact repetitions of the music. The individual steps in this dance are performed without embellishment. (Because people naturally take larger steps forward than backward, the pavane progresses slowly forward.)

Many of the steps and larger units in Arbeau's pavane make not only pleasantly symmetrical pairs but also arsic-thetic pairs. The notion of *arsis* (raising) and *thesis* (laying down), today often called elan and repose, also comes from ancient Greece. When a dancer takes a weighted step, lifting the foot is arsic; placing it and shifting weight onto it is thetic.

Arsis and thesis may also be applied to a pair of individual steps. The first step of a left-right pair initiates the motion of the pair and is thus arsic; the second step concludes the motion and is thetic. Arbeau apparently assumed an arsic left foot and a thetic right one when he reported that marching soldiers, whom he called "military dancers," always step first with the left foot "because most men are right-footed and the left foot is the weaker, so if it should come about that the left foot were to falter for any reason the right foot would immediately be ready to support it" (1589t, p. 21).

Arsis and thesis are also evident in the footwork and battle cries of soldiers charging into battle. As the drummer beats pyrrhic feet (SS), the soldiers close ranks and "lower their halberds and pikes" to attack the enemy. On the first note of the drumbeat each man moves his left foot forward, and on the second note he brings his right foot close behind the left to brace it. Thus, "leaping and dancing, they start to fight." Meanwhile, the drumbeats seem to be saying, *Dedans, dedans* (Within, within), probably a battle cry to force entry through the enemy's line. *De-* is the arsic prefix and *-dans* the thetic final and stressed syllable. In example 2.10 drumbeats, footwork, and the battle cry have been added to Arbeau's illustration of two soldiers charging with their halberds and pikes.

EXAMPLE 2.9.
Dance steps for a complete pavane piece. Arbeau, 1589t,
music, pp. 60–64; steps, p. 65. Mm. 1–8 and 9–16: first
time, dancers move forward; on the repeat, dancers move
backward.

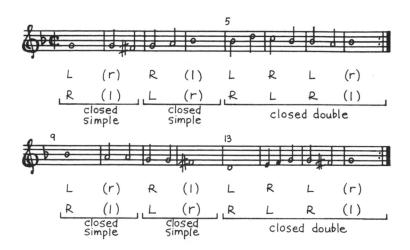

EXAMPLE 2.10.
Arsis and thesis in soldiers' charging steps. Arbeau, 1589t,
p. 38 (1888, pp. 17, 18). (L, R, and arsis-thesis signs added
by the present authors.)

Arbeau also recognized the advantage of soldiers' keeping in step when marching, so that their shoulders "incline first to one side and then to the other without jostling or hindering one another" (1589t, p. 37). Swaying from left to right
enhances the arsic-thetic pairing of the steps. In the same way, motion leads to
repose in each step-unit of Arbeau's recreational dances. For instance, the movement of the weighted step in the closed simple is arsic, and the repose of the
weightless step is thetic.

Arbeau's longer step-units tend to finish with a more definite repose. The
three traveling (weighted) steps of the pavane's unornamented double conclude
with a static (weightless) step. The double of the allemande finishes with a simulated kick. The divided double of the branle double ends with a pause. The five
steps of the galliard and many gavotte reprises conclude with a *posture*. With
all these step-units, a longer elan leads to a more final repose.

As shown in chapter 7, most musical periods of the *grand siècle* end with
conventional formulas today called "perfect authentic cadences." Though endings of choreographic units are often less formalized, Arbeau related the large
spring and landing of the galliard to a musical cadence:

> You have observed in a musical composition how musicians pause for a moment
> after the penultimate chord before playing the final chord in order to make an
> agreeable and harmonious ending; thus, the *saut majeur*, which is almost like a
> silence of the feet and a pause in movement, enhances the grace of the succeeding
> *posture* and creates a more pleasing effect. (1589t, p. 92)

In fact, some kind of compression or enlargement of the action intensifies the
movement to the final repose of many choreographic units. For instance, the
quick weight changes in Arbeau's two simples and a double and in his branle
double compress two or three weight changes into the time of one and thereby
increase the heart rate; and the large spring of the galliard and the virtuosic
capriole of the gavotte call forth a surge of blood pressure. Whether the intensification is created by weight changes at twice the speed or by a dramatic spring,
the dancer thereafter resumes the earlier pace or returns to the ground to conclude the choreographic unit in relative tranquility. In fact, the final repose is
enhanced by the flurry of excitement that immediately precedes it. Example
2.11 shows the arsis, the thesis, and (where applicable) the dramatic intensification in five of Arbeau's step-units and in his sequence of two simples and a
double.

A similarly dramatic event often takes place in the third of four equal parts in
dance music. In both eight-measure reprises of Arbeau's pavane (ex. 2.9), for
instance, the melody climaxes in the third pair of measures, where dancers
speed up their weight changes. In the first reprise, the melody reaches there its
highest pitch (mm. 5–6); in the second, its lowest (mm. 13–14). On the other
hand, if the piece is viewed as four phrases, each having four measures, the
most dramatic pitches make up the melodic descent of the third phrase (mm.
9–13), where dancers step again as at the start of the dance. This piece, like the
steps danced to it, can be viewed in three ways: as symmetrical pairs of four-

EXAMPLE 2.11.
Arsis and thesis, sometimes with a penultimate climax, in five
choreographic units. a. simple; b. double; c. galliard step;
d. branle de Poitou; e. two simples and a double. An asterisk
indicates a climax before the final repose.

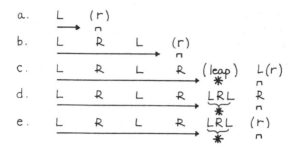

measure phrases and eight-measure reprises; as arsic-thetic pairs of two-, four-,
eight-, and sixteen-measure units; and as eight- or sixteen-measure rhetorical
periods (discussed in chap. 7).

As will be seen in chapter 8, both low and high steps continued to be used in
ballroom and theatrical dances of the *grand siècle*. Weighted steps continued to
be timed to rhythmic feet. Many steps continued to be ornamented and divided. Many choreographic units continued to be paired. Dance motions still
combined arsis and thesis. And some kind of choreographic climax increased
the excitement and announced the coming repose of longer units. In addition,
Lullian and later dance music continued to exhibit many rhythmic features of
the earlier dance steps.

Dance Rhythms from Early Guitar Sources

The sarabande . . . is danced to the sound of
the guitar, or of castanets, and this with several couplets of any number.[1]

—Marin Mersenne (1636, IIa, p. 165)

The rhythms of the so-called Spanish dances—the sarabande, chaconne, folie,
and passacaille—came to France from the New World via Portugal, Spain, and
Italy. Because no original steps survive, the numerous dance accompaniments
published during the first half of the seventeenth century in Italian books for
the Spanish guitar contain the earliest evidence of these rhythms.

Some evidence also exists about the early character of the dances. In an article on the origin and evolution of the sarabande, Kent Holliday cites many
sources of the sixteenth and early seventeenth centuries that reflect the sensuous motions of its dancers. For instance, Ben Jonson (*The Diuell is an Asse*,
1616; *The Staple of Newes*, 1625) called it a "bawdy dance"; Giambattista Marino (*L'Adone*, 1623, XX: 84) described it as "obscene" and "a barbarous usage introduced from New Spain"; and Padre Juan de Mariana (no date) told how "the
children of a Spanish gentleman, by means of the lascivious sarabande, . . .
made ruins of their part of the city" (Holliday, 1980, pp. 26–27). Marino was
also more specific:

> The girls with castanets, the men with tambourines, exhibit indecency in a thou-
> sand positions and gestures. They let the hips sway and the breasts knock together.
> They close their eyes and dance the kiss and the last fulfillment of love. (*L'Adone*,
> 1623; Holliday trans., p. 24)[2]

The *ciaccona* and *folia* were similarly sensuous and wild dances. Marino and
others equated the *ciaccona* with the *sarabanda*; and the *folia* presumably re-
ceived its name because of its wild, "crazy" motions.

At Italian courts of the late sixteenth and the early seventeenth centuries, the Italian *sarabanda, ciaccona*, and *folia* were danced and sung to the accompaniment of the Spanish five-course guitar. (Each course included two strings tuned to the unison or octave.) Between the stanzas of a song, an interlude made up of two *passacalli*, also from Spain, entertained the company (Hudson, *The New Grove*, article, "Passacaglia"). During the early seventeenth century, the sarabande, chaconne, folie, and passacaille spread to France and to other European courts.

The Spanish five-course guitar was played by strumming and plucking the strings; strumming was the more common. The Spanish guitarist Gaspar Sanz (1674) called strumming *rasgueado*, and Italian guitarists of the early seventeenth century called it *battente*. Plucking, called *punteado* and *pizzicato* in Spain and Italy respectively, was more characteristic of the lute. It did not appear in guitar books until 1629, but may have been used earlier (Tyler, 1980, p. 41).

Italian guitar books of the early seventeenth century include many strummed tablatures for the *sarabanda, ciaccona, folia*, and *passacallia*. Those discussed in this chapter and in Part II come mainly from books by the Italian guitarists Benedetto Sanseverino (1620, 1622) and Carlo Calvi (1646). Mersenne's few guitar examples of 1636 are similar to the Italian ones but use *punteado* tablatures. The many Spanish dance pieces by the Italian guitarist Francesco Corbetta, who was favored at the French and the English courts during the mid-seventeenth century, include both strumming and plucking. Sanz's book (1674), the only one by a Spaniard, contains both strummed and plucked tablatures; his strummed pieces have many of the rhythms, strumming patterns, and harmonic progressions found in early Italian tablatures.

The tablatures used to notate the strumming patterns and harmonic progressions in Italian guitar books of the early seventeenth century slightly resemble the "charts" of modern rock and folk guitarists. For each piece, they give the basic rhythmic pattern strummed by the right hand and the harmonic progression produced by stopping the strings with the left. This notation was called the *alfabeto* (alphabet) system because it used chiefly letters to indicate the left hand formations.

To some extent the *alfabeto* tablatures were intended as teaching tools, but they could also serve as a basis for improvisation. The early books begin with *passacalli* that function as elementary study pieces in an assortment of major and minor keys. After a good number of these tablatures, others appear mainly in *punteado* style, often with both strummed and plucked notes.

The simple rhythmic and harmonic skeletons given in the *alfabeto* tablatures for the *passacallia, sarabanda, ciaccona*, and *folia* reveal the underlying rhythmic and harmonic organization of the music, even though the basic rhythms and harmonies were varied in the stanzas of a song. The repeated rhythm of downward and upward strums and the continuous repetition of four- or eight-measure progressions must have furnished dancers and singers a strong rhythmic drive.

Little is known about the rhythms that early dancers played with their tambourins and castanets. But the castanet rhythm found most often in Raoul-Auger Feuillet's *belle danse* examples (1700, pp. 101–102), all in triple meter, is the iamb (SL, with the S on the downbeat). The iamb was also the most typical rhythm for the downward strums in the Spanish character pieces of the early seventeenth century.

Besides versions of the Spanish dances, Sanz's book and the Italian ones of the early seventeenth century include the *alemana* (allemande) of Germany, the *corrente* (courante) of Italy and France, and the *canario* (canarie) from the Canary Islands. Of these, only the *corrente* has a characteristic strumming pattern, and only the *canario* has a characteristic harmonic progression.

STRUMMING PATTERNS

The arrangement of downward and upward strums in each measure of a guitar piece creates a pattern of accents that, if repeated continually, defines the rhythm of the piece. The weight of the hand makes downward strums naturally stronger than upward ones. The downward ones are also more forceful because they are sounded with the back of the fingernails, while the upward ones use the pad of the fingers. Thus downward strums are the primary guitar strokes and upward strums the secondary ones.

In the *alfabeto* tablatures, the downbeat of almost every measure is played with a downward strum. (The downbeat of the second measure of a hemiola rhythm is strummed upward.) Downbeats in the simplest accompaniments are also marked by a change of harmony. In the first three *passacalli* of example 3.1, each measure begins with a chord change. In these as in other early *alfabeto* tablatures, short vertical strokes below a horizontal "staff" represent downward strums, and short vertical strokes above the staff indicate upward ones. Longer vertical lines that extend both above and below the staff designate bar lines, and note values above the staff indicate the timing of the strums. If a piece begins with quarter notes, it continues with these values until a new value appears above the staff. Then that value continues until another is shown.

In this book we adopt the practice introduced by Richard Hudson (1971, p. 200) and replace the *alfabeto* signs with Roman numerals that give the scale step of the root of a chord. Upper-case numerals (I, IV, V, VI) designate a major harmony; lower-case ones (i, iv, v, vi), a minor one. Like Hudson, we do not specify the inversion of a chord, because the notes of the *alfabeto* tablatures are distributed on the guitar's five courses without consideration for a melody or bass line. Thus "I" or "iv" may represent a chord in root position or in the first or second inversion. (See the Bibliography for Hudson's writings on the dances in the guitar tablatures.)

Besides having a downward strum on the downbeat, the strumming patterns in example 3.1 have further features in common with other pieces in *alfabeto* notation. Like most pieces in triple meter, the *passacallia* in example 3.1a is performed with a second downward stroke on the second quarter note of the measure and with an upward stroke on the third quarter. An upward second

EXAMPLE 3.1.
Tablature for four easy *passacalli*. Sanseverino, "Passacalli facili variati," 1622, p. 18. a. primo modo; b. secondo modo; c. terzo modo; d. quarto modo.

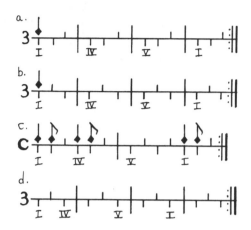

EXAMPLE 3.2.
Rhythmic feet articulated by downward strums in triple-meter dances. a. double iamb (more common); b. double trochee (less common).

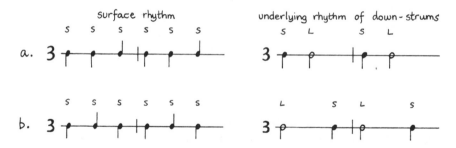

stroke and a downward third one are also possible, as in example 3.1b. The surface rhythm of both these triple-meter patterns is that of the tribrachic foot (SSS), but downward strums articulate iambs (SL) or trochees (LS), as shown in example 3.2. The turbulent iambic rhythm is the more common of the two.

The rhythms of most dances in duple meter are less regimented than those in triple meter. "Good" quarter notes (the first and third of a measure) are played with downward strums, as in example 3.1c. "Bad" quarter notes (the second and fourth of a measure), unless divided into eighth notes, are strummed in either direction. Regardless of the meter, a good eighth note is strummed downward, a bad one upward.

Although all Sanseverino's *passacalli* of 1622 in 3 meter begin on the downbeat, Calvi's of 1646 start on the second quarter note of the measure. That

EXAMPLE 3.3.
Calvi, "Passacalli sopra tutto l'alfabeto," first example, 1646,
p. 7.

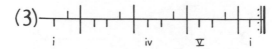

EXAMPLE 3.4.
Two concert passacailles for guitar. Corbetta, 1671. Repro-
duced from Richard T. Pinnell, *Francesco Corbetta and the
Baroque Guitar*, Vol. II, by permission of the author and
UMI Research Press. a. p. 9; b. p. 17. D = downward direc-
tion of the hand; U = upward direction of the hand.

causes the last two strums of the measure to lead to the first strum of the next:
the last two strums of one measure are arsic to the first strum of the following
one. As a result, the strumming pattern overlaps the bar line. (Even when the
first strum falls on the downbeat, as in ex. 3.1a, the following strums tend to be
perceived as grouped with the next downbeat.) Example 3.3 shows a typical
passacallia that begins on the second pulse of the measure.

The tendency of strumming patterns to emphasize the second quarter note in
the measure and to cross the bar line was carried over into many Spanish character pieces of the *grand siècle*. Composers for harpsichord, lute, viol, and guitar
often placed chords or ornaments on notes in the positions of those strummed
downward in the *alfabeto* tablatures, and composers for all instruments gave
longer values to many of them. For instance, in two of Corbetta's plucking and
strumming passacailles (first reprises shown in ex. 3.4), the second note of the
measure is always long, and chords or ornaments emphasize the first and second
quarter notes in almost every measure. The D and U in example 3.4 replace
respectively the upward and downward arrows in Pinnell's and most modern
transcriptions, which point in the direction of the sequential sounding of pitches

EXAMPLE 3.5.
Note groupings in Spanish guitar pieces.

in the chord rather than in the physical direction of the hand. Chords not marked with D or U are plucked. Chord symbols below the staff give evidence that the original i, iv, V, i progression for a *passacallia* in the minor mode is elaborated in these two later pieces.

Sanseverino's *passacallia* shown in example 3.1d is a little more sophisticated than the three above it. Each new harmony is sounded a quarter note before its usual measure. Here the harmonic rhythm groups the strums across the bar line, starting with the third note of each measure: down–|down–up. Perhaps this practice accounts for the upbeat note that begins some Spanish character pieces of the *grand siècle*.

In short, the three quarter notes in triple meter are grouped in one of four ways in Spanish pieces (see ex. 3.5). The first two make up a musical measure. The other two cross the bar line. All four continued to be employed in Spanish pieces of the *grand siècle*.

The stroke patterns used by French violin and viol players of the *grand siècle* are similar to those shown in the *alfabeto* tablatures, but they differ in one important regard: Instead of repeating a primary bow stroke, these later players preferred alternating primary and secondary strokes or making two secondary strokes in succession. Such patterns produce a smoother, less accented performance. Even many of Corbetta's guitar pieces written during the *grand siècle* avoid consecutive downward strums on the first and second pulses of the measure, as found in example 3.4.

HARMONIC PROGRESSIONS

In the Spanish character pieces in early guitar books, harmonic progressions are usually confined to four basic chord changes, set to four measures of triple meter. However, many *folia* progressions contain eight chord changes, set to eight measures of triple meter or to four measures of what today is called "compound-duple meter." All progressions begin with the chord built on the first degree of the scale, though it may not be in root position.

The chords of each progression fuse into an indivisible unit. Thus a four-measure progression in triple meter closely resembles a measure of $\frac{12}{4}$. This unity is effected in part by a slight repose in the middle of the progression and a greater repose at its end. Yet each repose is only temporary. The inner one is on chords IV, V, or VII; the final one is on V except in the *passacallia*, where it is on the major or minor tonic.

At the end of the repetition of a progression, the penultimate harmonies are

EXAMPLE 3.6.
Reposes in harmonic progressions that begin on the downbeat. a. passacalle; b. sarabanda; c. ciaccone; d. folia.

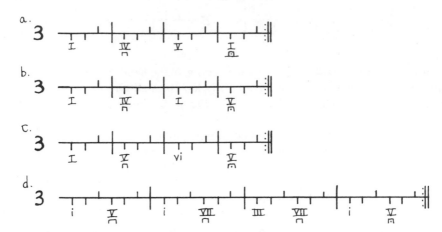

sometimes compressed into a single measure, so that the progression finishes
conclusively on the major or minor tonic. Even the more usual ending on the V
chord seems more final the second time, so that each pair of progressions is
heard as a unit.

Example 3.6 shows the reposes in the most characteristic harmonic progressions that begin on the downbeat. The symbol ⌐⌐ indicates the momentary
interior repose; ⌐·⌐ designates the principal repose at the end of a four-measure
progression; and ⌐·⌐ represents a final repose on the major or minor tonic.

When the progression starts on the downbeat of what today is called "simple-
triple meter," the inner repose falls on the downbeat of the second measure; the
principal repose, on the downbeat of the fourth. In examples 3.6a-c the reposes
occur on the downbeats of even-numbered measures; thus the first measure is
arsic to the thetic second measure, and the third is arsic to the fourth. The reposes in the *folia* progression that would become standard in the *grand siècle*
fall on the second half of each six-pulse measure (ex. 3.6d).

In most Spanish pieces that begin with the second note of a three-pulse measure, reposes still fall on the downbeats of even-numbered measures (exx. 3.7a
and b). But reposes in the six-pulse measures of the *folia* fall at the beginning of
each one (ex. 3.7c).

During the seventeenth century, harmonic progressions gave way to bass
melodies composed of the roots of the chords of each progression. Sometimes
the harmony and the bass line united to form a progression to which varied
couplets were set. Of the Spanish dances that flourished during the Baroque
period in Italy and France, the *sarabanda* and sarabande soon came to be written in binary form, and their original harmonic progression was forgotten.

EXAMPLE 3.7.
Reposes in harmonic progressions that begin on the second
quarter note of the measure. a. passacalle; b. ciaccone; c. folia.

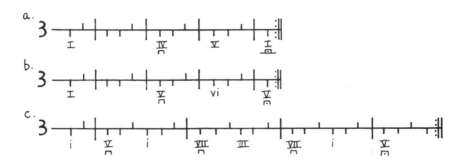

ORGANIZATION OF COUPLETS AND
WHOLE PIECES

Just as harmonic progressions organize the strumming patterns into larger units, so couplets organize the harmonic progressions. Harmonic progressions function as "members" of the couplets, a term Baroque musicians borrowed from classical rhetoric. A member is the shortest unit that concludes with a definite cadence. Presumably couplets were so named because they were set originally to a pair of lines of lyrics, and each line ended with a poetic cadence.

Although little is known about the performance of whole pieces from *alfabeto* tablatures, an early chaconne for lute and the many slightly later pieces for strummed and plucked guitar probably represent somewhat tamed versions of the early guitar accompaniments. In these concert pieces, often the music set to each two statements of the basic progression makes a couplet.

The members of each couplet are always related in some way. Frequently they are identical, or the second differs only in the finality of its cadence. Sometimes the second member differs considerably from the first but is still related. The later couplets of a piece stray further from the music and passion of the first, though a return at the end of the piece to some features of the opening material concludes the form.

"La chaconna" (ex. 3.8), a concert dance based on four-measure progressions, is the earliest French arrangement of a Spanish piece that we found. It illustrates many characteristics of the variation dances of the *grand siècle*.

Couplet 1 (mm. 1–8). The first couplet of "La chaconna" has two members, each set to the basic four-measure progression. In the first member (mm. 1–4), chords in root position progress along the scale degrees 1, 5, 6, 2, 5 in the E-flat Lydian mode. That is, the fourth degree of the scale, A, is natural. Here a combination of two characteristic bass-line progressions for chaconnes—1, 5, 6, 5 and 1, 5, 2, 5—furnishes both the principal harmonic framework and the principal bass line of the piece.

EXAMPLE 3.8.
Vallet, "La chaconna," for lute, 1615 (transcription by André
Souris, in Nicolas Vallet, *Le secret de muses,* vol. 1, repro-
duced by permission of Éditions du Centre National de la
Recherche Scientifique).

Chords in the first member enunciate four rhythmic feet: two trochees (each LS), an iamb (SL), and another trochee. Thus the relentless iambic rhythm of chords in the *alfabeto* tablatures is softened; only the chords in the third measure retain the traditional rhythm. At the same time, the bass line exhibits the iambic rhythm in three of its four measures. Most later passacailles and chaconnes, like this early one, begin with some bow to tradition in their melodic or chordal rhythms and in their bass progression.

The second member (mm. 5–8) begins in the same way as the first but has some minor changes. The chorded iamb in m. 3 is replaced by continuous quarter notes that move toward and enhance the final cadence. The final cadence is pitched lower than the first and thus gives a greater feeling of repose.

This couplet resembles the first couplet of many chaconnes and passacailles of the *grand siècle* in which the initial member is repeated without change. But in sixteen-measure folies of the 1670s and later, the penultimate chords of the second eight-measure member are compressed to finish on the first degree, giving the sense of a complete stop at the end of each couplet.

Couplet 2 (mm. 9–16). The second couplet begins in the same way as the first, but its melody becomes more active. In addition, the first member ends deceptively on G minor (m. 12) instead of on the expected B-flat major. Both factors increase the intensity of the music. The G-minor cadence is arsic to the one on B-flat that ends the couplet.

In later chaconnes and passacailles, the second couplet—or sometimes the second pair of couplets—is more active than the first. One or more cadences in related keys can also be expected somewhere in the middle of long examples of these pieces.

Couplet 3 (mm. 17–28). This couplet has three members; such an extension normally signals an intensification of the passion. Here, however, the first member is exactly the same as that of the first couplet, and its chords bring out the basic trochee–trochee–iamb–trochee rhythm. But the second and third members forsake the initial rhythm for a graceful quarter-note movement, punctuated by full chords only at cadences (mm. 24 and 28).

Lully and other later composers often shaped a chaconne or passacaille in similar fashion. Their pieces begin with a salute to tradition in the opening rhythmic feet and bass progression, but other rhythms appear in the middle of the piece.

Couplet 4 (mm. 29–36). Almost continuous eighth notes delay the chordal accents until the last measure of the couplet (m. 36). The eighth notes in the fourth measure (m. 32) cover the cadence, leaving it barely recognizable. The bass melody in each member is simplified to a skeleton rhythm of dotted half notes that articulates a characteristic chaconne progression: 1, 5, 2, 5.

A similar masking of reposes in the middle of chaconnes and passacailles was also practiced by Lully and his followers. Most of these later dance pieces begin with a bass progression of only four notes, such as 1, 5, 2, 5 or 1, 5, 6, 5.

Couplet 5 (mm. 37–44). The skeleton bass line—1, 5, 2, 5—continues through the final couplet. The melody of the first member (mm. 37–40) descends in the continuous quarter-note motion first heard in mm. 21–28. The music of the final member (mm. 41–44) returns to the eighth-note motion heard in mm. 29–36. The iambic rhythm in the bass of mm. 43 recalls that of m. 2.

The music ends on the chord built on the fifth degree of the scale. The many repetitions of the progression 1, 5, 2, 5 in E-flat and the A natural of the Lydian mode cause the ear to be satisfied with the final repose on 5 (B-flat). Not until later in the century did dance pieces always conclude on the first degree.

During the *grand siècle*, the last couplet of a chaconne and passacaille always referred in some way to the opening of the piece. The last couplet of a late seventeenth-century or an early eighteenth-century folie is often a verbatim repetition of the first couplet. In all these pieces, the final return to beginning material helps unify the many varied couplets.

The melodies of chaconnes and passacailles of the *grand siècle* often cross the fourth bar line because the reposes of the poetic lines to which the music was set fall on the first downbeat of a new statement of a progression, that is, of a new member. In Lully's chaconne song from *Cadmus et Hermione* (app. ex. 6), the lines of the lyrics overlap the beginnings of the musical members, as determined by the bass progressions. This song, like most chaconne and passacaille songs of the *grand siècle* and most such pieces for harpsichord, is composed in what today is called "chaconne-rondeau form." The basic progression is heard in the refrain, but different bass lines underlie the contrasting couplets, in which new and often more intense passions are expressed.

In some later examples of variation dances today called "sectional variations," each varied couplet is a complete and isolated unit. (Most folies from the 1670s and later fall into this category.) Each couplet concludes on the first degree, features a completely different rhythm and melody from its predecessor, and expresses a contrasting passion.

Some of the large chaconne and passacaille pieces of the late seventeenth and the early eighteenth centuries, such as those in François Couperin's *Les nations*, are composed of large rhetorical sections, each of which contains several couplets. The large sections differ in their basic rhythms and melodies and sometimes even in their tonalities.

In all these variation pieces, arsis leads to thesis on a number of rhythmic levels. The first measure of a member leads to the second, and the third leads to the fourth. The first two measures of a member lead to the second two. The first cadence of a couplet leads to the second. In what is today called "continuous variation form," one couplet leads to the next, and often one group of couplets leads to the next. In chaconne-rondeau form, contrasting couplets lead back to the refrain couplet (or couplets). In sectional variations, all couplets lead to the final couplet, which repeats the first closely or exactly. Beneath all these levels of arsic-thetic organization lie the metrical feet of downward strums.

4

Rhythmic Movements in Mersenne's and Later Dance Music

As for the dances, there are several kinds that are part of metrical music because they are subjected to certain measures, or regulated and counted feet.[1]

—Marin Mersenne (1636, IIa, p. 164)

The most excellent metrical feet, which have given name and birth to the rhythm of the Greeks, are practiced in the *airs de Balets*, in dance songs, and in all the other actions that serve as public or private recreations, as will be proven when the [metrical] feet that follow are compared to the airs one sings or that one plays on violins, the lute, guitar, and other instruments.

Now these feet can be called "[rhythmic] movements" according to the manner of speech of our musicians and composers of airs. This is why I will use this term from now on, to join theory and practice.[2]

(IIa, pp. 177–78)

Marin Mersenne (1636) examined the application of the Greek metrical feet to dance music more deeply than any other French author. Taking the view that the rhythms of the Greek metrical feet underlay the recreational music of his day, he called the feet "rhythmic movements" and ascribed specific ones to the different character dances.

George Houle sets Mersenne's position in historical perspective in *Meter and*

Music, 1600–1800 (1987). In the third chapter, which he kindly shared with us in advance of publication, Houle describes the treatment of *rhythmopoeia* (poetic rhythm) by a number of authors. He begins with C. F. Abdy Williams's discussion (1911, p. 26) of Aristoxenus's views (ca. 330 B.C.). Aristoxenus defined *rhythmopoeia* as the art of applying the Greek rhythms to the intervals of melody to make song, to the syllables of speech to fashion poetry, and to the steps of a person walking or running to create dancing.

Houle continues with D. P. Walker's two series of articles on "musical humanism" and the revival of classical notions in music of the sixteenth century (1941–42; 1946, 1948–50). Sixteenth-century settings of Horatian *Odes* and of metrical Latin psalm paraphrases faithfully reflected the longs and shorts of the metrical feet for German school children and church goers. Houle also cites Athanasius Kircher's compendium of musical equivalents of Greek and Latin poetic feet, published in the *Musurgia universalis* of 1650. Isaac Vossius' description of the passions that relate to the metrical feet (1673) has been discussed in our chapter 1. In addition, the German theorist and composer Wolfgang Caspar Printz (1696) devoted several chapters to the *Pedum rhythmicorum* (rhythmic foot), and his compatriot Johann Mattheson (1739) included a chapter on the *Rhythmus* (rhythm[ic movement]), which he named the *Klangfuss* (sound-foot).

In spite of the heavy concentration of German sources, Houle points out that the development of *rhythmopoeia* as a theory of musical organization in the seventeenth century was French, and that it was particularly useful in analyzing the rhythms of dance music. He reflects the French viewpoint when he writes:

> The short and long elements of each musical foot seem to represent the pulses on which the dancers place their feet, and therefore they mark the underlying metrical structure of the dance music. The melody is sufficiently decorated that the dance meters [rhythmic movements] may not be evident without the clarification of *rhythmopoeia* [that is, without identification of the underlying rhythms in terms of metrical feet]. (Houle, chap. 3)

The same rhythms continued to underlie much of the dance music of Lully and his followers. Although, to our knowledge, the musical equivalents of the Greek metrical feet were not actually mentioned in any French source of that later period, Printz (1696) pointed them out in some of Lully's dances; Mattheson (1739) offered examples of them that resemble the rhythmic movements of Mersenne and the dance music of Lully; and Jean-Jacques Rousseau (1768) treated them rather thoroughly—though he related them to the duple, triple, and compound meters of his day.

Mersenne called the "longs" and "shorts" of the rhythmic movements "syllables." Yet he admitted that the French language is not suited to the rigid configurations prescribed by the Greek metrical feet but "requires complete freedom, without the constraints of regulated poetry" (1636, IIa, pp. 179–80). In this book we therefore discuss the rhythmic movements in the music only and imply no corresponding patterns of long and short syllables in the lyrics. Indeed, Mersenne wrote that these rhythms could equally well be called "the movement of the courante," "the movement of the sarabande," or be named for one of the standard drum rhythms of his day (IIa, p. 179). The accommodation of French lyrics to the dance rhythms is one of the principal subjects of this chapter and chapter 6.

THE RHYTHMIC MOVEMENTS AND THEIR VARIOUS GUISES

Mersenne explained that each short value of a rhythmic movement is like the point in geometry or the number 1 in arithmetic (IIa, p. 179): it is a primary value. In his table of rhythmic movements set to note values, "shorts" (S's) are written as quarter notes and "longs" (L's) as half notes (IIb, p. 376), showing that an L is normally twice as long as an S. In fact, the rhythmic movements represent both a numerical and an expressive arrangement of notes, whereby L's and S's in the proportion 2:1 are grouped in easily recognized patterns capable of arousing the passions discussed in chapter 1.

Example 4.1 lists the rhythmic movements cited by Mersenne (1636, IIa, pp. 163–80; IIb, pp. 376, 400–409) that also occur in Lullian dance music. They include both simple feet, which have only two or three notes, and compound feet, which have four or more and are often composed of two simple feet. For instance, a double trochee consists of two trochees (LSLS), each called "soft and tender" by Vossius (see chap. 1). A choriamb combines a trochee and a "fierce and vehement" iamb (LSSL: "choreus" is an earlier word for trochee). A choreobacchius consists of a trochee and a bacchius (LSSLL); Mattheson described the bacchius (SLL), named for the God of wine, as "drunk and staggering" (1739, p. 168). The movements marked with an asterisk in example 4.1 are the most common in Lullian dance music; all are compound movements.

Most of Mersenne's rhythmic movements are employed for music with exclusively binary or ternary beats. Rhythmic movements set to binary beats have SS, LL, SSL, or LSS groups. Those set to ternary beats have LS, SL, or SSS groups. For instance, the choreobacchius (LSSLL) is set only to binary beats, as

EXAMPLE 4.1.
Mersenne's rhythmic movements found in dance music. Asterisks indicate movements used most frequently in the dance music of the *grand siècle*.

simple feet	compound feet
pyrrhic (SS) ♩♩	procelematic (SSSS) ♩♩♩♩
iamb (SL) ♩♩	1st paeon (LSSS) ♩ ♩♩♩
trochee or choreus (LS) ♩ ♩	4th paeon (SSSL) ♩♩♩♩
tribrach (SSS) ♩♩♩	*choriamb (LSSL) ♩ ♩♩♩
dactyl (LSS) ♩ ♩♩	*antispast (SLLS) ♩♩ ♩ ♩
anapest (SSL) ♩♩♩	*double trochee (LSLS) ♩ ♩♩ ♩
scolien (SLS) ♩♩ ♩	epitrite ♩♩ ♩ ♩
bacchius (SLL) ♩♩ ♩	*hegemeole ♩♩♩♩ ♩
molossus (LLL) ♩ ♩ ♩	*choreobacchius (LSSLL) ♩ ♩♩♩ ♩

EXAMPLE 4.2.
Dactyls. a. binary beat; b. ternary beat.

EXAMPLE 4.3.
Dance rhythms derived from dividing an L into a dotted figure. a. divided hegemeole, common in sarabandes and menuets; b. divided choriamb, common in courantes; c. divided
antispast, found in some folies; d. divided choreobacchius,
found in some Lullian gavottes.

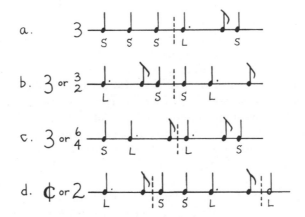

in **C** or **¢** meter; while the double trochee (LSLS), antispast (SLLS), choriamb
(LSSL), and hegemeole (SSSLS) are set to ternary beats, as in 3 or $\frac{6}{4}$ meter.

Mersenne showed the dactyl (LSS) to have two musical forms. The note values
of the first are set to a binary beat (ex. 4.2a); but the L and first S may also be
shortened to fit a ternary beat (ex. 4.2b), as in the canary shown in example 4.4a.
If the three notes are articulated in a single beat, binary and ternary dactyls
sound almost the same; both, as described by Vossius, express cheer and joy.

Rhythmic movements seem to have been so ingrained in the memories and
reflexes of early seventeenth-century musicians, dancers, and listeners that a
movement could be altered or replaced by another without the dance's losing its
identity. Mersenne stated that dividing the movements into quicker note values
"gives a different grace, and very different effects [yet] is taken for the same
thing as regards the space of time, or of movement" (IIa, p. 179).

One way of varying a rhythmic movement is to divide an L into two S's. For
example, Mersenne sometimes gave LSSSSL as the pattern of the choreobacchius, which is normally LSSLL. An L can also be divided into a dotted figure
consisting of a dotted note and a following quick note. Example 4.3 shows some
common dance rhythms derived by dividing an L into a dotted figure. Even S's
could be divided (Mersenne, IIa, p. 179). For further examples, see Mersenne's

EXAMPLE 4.4.
Divisions, contractions, and exchanges within rhythmic movements. Mersenne, 1636, IIa. a. "Canarie du dixiesme mode
transposé," p. 170; b. "La gavote de l'onziesme mode," p. 169;
c. "Allemande du second mode," p. 166.

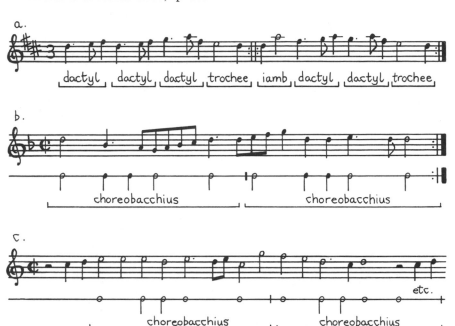

gavotte and allemande (exx. 4.4b and c) and Lully's menuet (ex. 4.12). Mersenne's two pieces contain many kinds of divisions and other alterations of the
L's and S's of their rhythmic movements. In the allemande, the first two notes
ornament the first L.

To provide a longer and more-final repose, many reprises are concluded with
a contraction of the last two or three notes of a rhythmic movement, which
reduces the motion and softens the passion. For instance, the reprises in example 4.4a end with the first two notes of the established cheerful and joyous
dactylic rhythm (LSS) contracted to a half note, making a soft and tender
trochee (LS). Both reprises of Lully's menuet in example 4.12 finish with contractions whose last note fills a whole measure.

Exchanges of rhythmic movements give variety to a piece. For instance, a
fierce and vehement iamb (SL) momentarily replaces the cheerful and joyous
dactyl (LSS) at the start of the second reprise of the canarie in example 4.4a.
Divided double trochees (LSLS: smooth and tender) and divided antispasts
(SLLS: hard and rugged) replace the divided hegemeoles (SSSLS) that characterize Lully's menuet melody in example 4.12. Although early sources do not
specify the hegemeole's passion, it is probably related to the sensuous nature of
the early sarabande.

EXAMPLE 4.5.
A single melodic rhythm extracted from three different rhythmic movements. a. hegemeole; b. double trochee; c. antispast.

It may seem strange to modern listeners and performers that a single melodic
rhythm can result from dividing different rhythmic feet, as shown in example
4.5. But Baroque performers, who knew the characteristic rhythmic movements of the various dances, could make the underlying rhythm and passion clear by emphasizing the notes and expression that typified the original
movement.

DANCE LYRICS SET TO RHYTHMIC MOVEMENTS

Setting dance lyrics to rhythmic movements presented certain problems. For
spoken tragedies, French playwrights employed mainly twelve-syllable lines
called alexandrines, which almost always broke in meaning after the sixth syllable; sometimes they used lines of ten syllables that broke after the fourth (or
occasionally the sixth) syllable. The fixed break was called the caesura; the two
resulting "halves" were called half lines, or hemistiches—regardless of whether
they were equal in length. These classical lines and their set caesuras that imitated Greek verse are found also in the recitatives of the musical tragedies of
Lully and his followers (Rosow, 1983, pp. 468–69).

Although Italian composers at the end of the sixteenth century had returned
to principles laid down by the ancient Greeks and Romans in writing vocal music that "almost speaks in tones" (Giulio Caccini, 1601, Preface), French composers of the early seventeenth century continued to set most dance lyrics to
rhythmic movements. For this they used *vers libres* (free verse), in which the
lines vary in length, and the principal breaks—except in lines of ten or twelve
syllables—are not fixed. Few alexandrines are found in the French dance songs.

Because rhythmic movements have only four or five notes, one or more L's in
French dance songs are usually divided into two pulse values or into a dotted
pulse followed by a quick note. Also, each of the first few lines of a song based
on rhythmic movements includes no more than six syllables. To make these
short lines less abrupt, song writers of the late Renaissance and early Baroque
began the lyrics with a pair of short lines that together function as a long one.
Each line is normally identified by a capital letter at its head and a rhyme at its
end. (The "rhyme," which is the final counted syllable of the line, of course
rhymes with the final counted syllable of another line.) Often two short lines
make up a clause of the text.

In Arbeau's pavane song (ex. 4.6), each reprise or its repeat includes two lines

EXAMPLE 4.6.
Lyrics for a pavane song. Arbeau, 1589t, words, p. 65; rhythms,
pp. 60–64.

| | |L S S S   S L |S
| | 1   2 3 4   5 6 –
| First reprise | Bel-le qui tiens ma vi-e
| | (Pretty [one], who holds my life)

|S   SS S   S L |
1   2 3 4   5 6
Cap-ti-ve dans tes yeulx
(Captive in your eyes,)

| | |L   S   S S S L |S
| | 1   2   3 4 5 6 –
| Repeat | Qui m'as l'a-me ra-vi-e
| | (Who has ravished my soul)

|S   S   S S S L |
1   2   3 4 5 6
D'un soubz-ris gra-ci-eux
(With a gracious smile,)

| | |L   S   S S S L |
| | 1   2   3 4 5 6
| Second reprise | Viens tost me se-cou-rir
| | (Come soon to save me)

|L S S S   S   L |
1   2 3 4   5   6
Ou me faul-dra mou-rir
(Or I shall have to die.)

| Repeat | (Repeat last two lines.)

of lyrics and two divided choreobacchii. The lines of the second reprise are repeated as a kind of refrain. The melody of this song is given in example 2.9,
where it can be seen that dancers set individual steps to L's and execute two
simples to the first line of each pair and a double to the second line. Each pair of
lines, each sequence of step-units, and each final cadence pair two divided
choreobacchii. In this example, a vertical "bar line" marks the beginning and
ending of each rhythmic movement, and a horizontal dotted line designates the
end of each line pair. L's and S's show the length of the note values, which in this
case are Renaissance breves and minims (whole and half notes), and numbers
above the syllables give the poetic scansion.

(Here, as elsewhere in this book, the lyrics have been translated as closely to
the original words and word order as possible to facilitate comparison of the
syllables with the note values. Obviously, these translations are not intended
for recitation or singing.)

The tendency for L's to divide into S's except at the end of a line is shown in example 4.6 and other dances set to choreobacchii, where two pulse values almost always divide the second L: namely, LSSLL becomes LSSSSL. In the first reprise and its repeat of example 4.6, the first L of the second choreobacchius is also divided: SSSSSSL. This course allows the feminine ending of the first line—the "mute" e—to join its line with the second in imitation of a twelve-syllable alexandrine. On the other hand, a masculine ending at the close of each second line (no "mute" e) noticeably separates each pair of lines from the next.

(The "mute" e is pronounced in French vocal music unless it is elided with a following vowel, but that never happens at the end of a line. An unelided "mute" e is always set to a separate note of the music. Within a line, this e is counted as a separate syllable; at the end, it is not. Modern linguists often indicate the final e of a line with a plus sign, to show it is added to the previous syllable; but we prefer to use a short dash, to avoid confusing this e with a trill marked by a plus sign—as occurs in some of our examples. Non-French speakers may prefer to sing the numbers of scansion given in the examples rather than use the French syllables; in that case, the feminine ending may be pronounced "uh.")

A characteristic of dance lyrics set to rhythmic movements is that an important word or pair of monosyllables is used at the beginning and the end of the initial lines and movements. In Arbeau's pavane song the vital words "Pretty one," "my life"; "Captive," "your eyes" give the sense of the lines and, by marking the boundaries of the rhythmic movements, establish the dance rhythm at once. Words in the middle of each line serve merely to connect the beginning word with the final one.

Two sarabande songs by Jean Boyer, published in 1642—some 50 years after Arbeau's pavane song but still well before the *grand siècle*—also begin with short lines set to rhythmic movements. (Patricia M. Ranum kindly shared these important songs with us when she discovered them in 1982; she has since discussed them in an article [1985].) The first of these songs (ex. 4.7) is set almost entirely to hegemeoles (SSSLS) whose L's are divided into a dotted pulse and a quick note. Again, the most important words of the two opening lines begin and end the rhythmic movements: "Cloris," "to know"; "The effect," "power."

The fact that the long final syllable of each of these lines falls on the last S of the rhythmic movement did not bother composers of the early seventeenth century, who were chiefly concerned with fitting lines to rhythmic movements. But this approach evidently did disturb Lully, for he wrote no sarabande songs after the one in the early *Ballet de la raillerie* (1659, VIII), which begins with this rhythm but immediately abandons it (see ex. 32.6).

Boyer's other sarabande song (ex. 4.8) anticipates the longer lines preferred during the *grand siècle*. It begins in the traditional way with two lines set to undivided hegemeoles (SSSLS), each of which covers two measures of 3 meter (mm. 1–4). But the third line (mm. 5–8) has eight syllables. Since it is too long to be set to a single rhythmic movement, two are employed: a hegemeole and a

EXAMPLE 4.7.
Hegemeoles at the start of a sarabande song. Boyer, 1642,
fol. 36v°-37. A diagonal slash indicates a textual break of the
poetry; a vertical one, a break between the rhythmic
movements of the music.

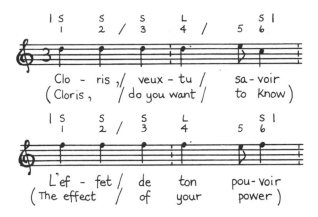

contracted double trochee (LSL[S]), which together cover four measures of music. Also unlike the earlier lines, the text does not break at the end of the first movement. This third line of lyrics shows that, once the rhythmic movements are established, the rhythm of the poetry is allowed to predominate.

The fourth line of Boyer's second song (mm. 9–12) has even more syllables—ten plus a feminine ending—but is still set to two rhythmic movements in four measures of music. In mm. 9, 10, and 11, the first of each group of three quarter notes is dotted and the second is shortened to an eighth, implying divided double trochees (LSLS). Again, breaks in the text do not agree with those between rhythmic movements.

(It is important to mention here that dance songs throughout the Baroque era rarely have more syllables than pulses in a measure. The syllables are set either to L's and S's or to continuous pulses often altered to a dotted quarter and an eighth. This insistence on no more than three syllables in a three-pulse measure, four in a four-pulse one, and six in a six-pulse one probably helped the dancers time their steps.)

The fifth and last line (mm. 13–17) is set to the longest phrase of the song, with ten syllables fitted to five measures of music. Although several S's are ornamented with quick and very quick notes, the syllables are set to an undivided hegemeole (SSSLS) and an unnamed three-measure rhythm (SSSSLL). Once again, the textual breaks differ from those of the rhythmic movements. Here the main break is a true caesura and so is marked with a double slash. The tendency to divide L's into S's and the usual mismatch of textual units and rhythmic movements continued as a structural principle in the dance songs of the *grand siècle*.

EXAMPLE 4.8.
Rhythms in the first stanza of a sarabande song. Boyer,
fol. 37v°.

RHYTHMIC MOVEMENTS IN THE BASS LINE OR HARMONIC RHYTHM OF THE ACCOMPANIMENT

During the early seventeenth century, the greatest number and most prominent rhythmic movements appeared in the highest voice of a dance piece (Mersenne, 1636, IIb, p. 213), while those in the bass usually contrasted with those
in the top part (IIb, p. 198). During the *grand siècle*, however, the natural

EXAMPLE 4.9.
Accompaniments that establish the characteristic rhythmic
movement. a. Chambonnières, allemande "La loureuse," livre
1, suite 2, 1670; b. Louis Couperin, "Gavotte de M.ʳ Hardel,"
late 1650s; c. Lully, menuet, from *Le Carousel*, 1686.

choreobacchius   in   the   bass   line

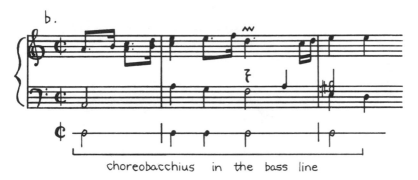

choreobacchius   in   the   bass   line

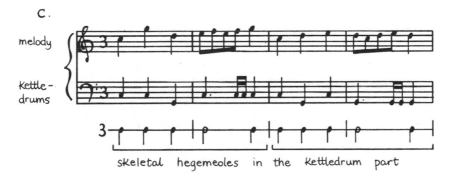

skeletal   hegemeoles   in   the   kettledrum   part

rhythms of speech (see chap. 6) or the more elaborate writing in concert pieces
sometimes masked the rhythmic movements in the highest voice; and those in
the bass line or harmonic rhythm often substituted for those missing from the
top part. In fact, accompaniment rhythms may follow one of the rhythmic movements that characterize a particular dance or may contrast with its typical form.

EXAMPLE 4.10.
Contracted rhythmic movements in accompaniments. a. Fran-
çois Duval, sarabande "Les castagnettes," sonata 6, from
Amusemens pour la chambre, 1718; b. Montéclair, "Le bal.
Menuet des mariés," from Concert VI for flute and bass,
1725; c. Lully, courante, from *Le mariage forcé*, 1664.

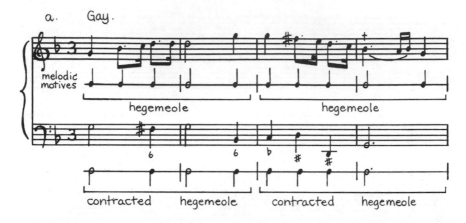

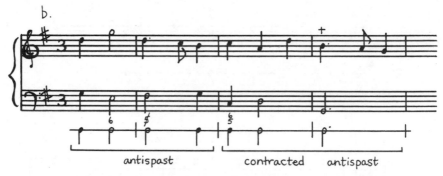

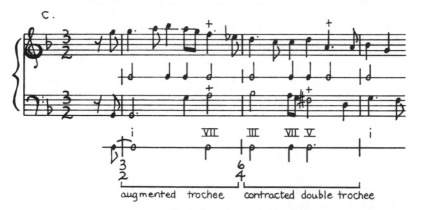

When divisions or other variations camouflage the rhythmic movement in the melody, the characteristic movement in the accompaniment often preserves the spirit of that dance. In all three dances in example 4.9, for instance, the bass line or the drum part in the opening measures states the characteristic rhythmic movement and passion of the piece.

The rhythmic movement in an accompaniment may be a contraction of the characteristic movement. For instance, the bass line of example 4.10a begins with a double trochee (LSLS), which is a contraction of a hegemeole (SSSLS), and ends with a contraction of the final LS of another hegemeole. In the bass line of example 4.10b, the final LS of an antispast (SLLS) is similarly contracted.

Sometimes the harmonic rhythm contracts the characteristic rhythmic movements of the melody. In example 4.10c, for instance, the choriambic melody (LSSL) is harmonized with two different rhythms. In m. 1, its initial LSS is set to a single tonic chord, making the final VII chord of the measure an S by comparison and implying $\frac{3}{2}$ meter. In m. 2, the final SL of the choriambic melody is set to a single V chord, making a contracted double trochee of the harmonic rhythm and implying $\frac{6}{4}$ meter. Many courantes, in fact, have only their harmonic rhythm to establish whether a given measure is organized as $\frac{3}{2}$ or as $\frac{6}{4}$ meter. Since the choriamb alone establishes neither the $\frac{3}{2}$ nor the $\frac{6}{4}$ organization, it functions as a softened hemiola.

Mersenne related some dance rhythms to well-known drumbeats of his day, some of which were probably accompaniment rhythms. For instance, the sarabande's "movement is hegemeolian" (SSSLS), but it also "follows the movement of the blacksmith's beat" (*battement du Mareschal*)—an iamb (SL). In example 4.11, the L (semibreve) of the second iamb of the accompaniment articulates the only pulse not sounded by the hegemeole of the melody.

Rhythmic movements in the melody, bass line, and harmony of a dance piece usually fit within a single measure or pair of measures, as in example 4.12. This menuet danced by two Spanish couples is built from divisions and contractions of the hegemeole (SSSLS), including divided and contracted double trochees (LSLS) and antispasts (SLLS). Since Mersenne identified the hegemeole with sarabandes, this emphasis probably gives the music its Spanish flavor. As usual, rhythmic movements in the bass occur mainly in their pure, undivided form.

EXAMPLE 4.11.
Sarabande melody and accompaniment. Mersenne, 1636, IIa, p. 166.

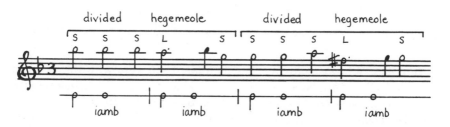

EXAMPLE 4.12.
Two-measure rhythmic movements. Lully, "Menuet pour
deux espagnols et deux espagnoles," *Le mariage forcé*, 1664.
$ = *petite reprise* (little repeat).

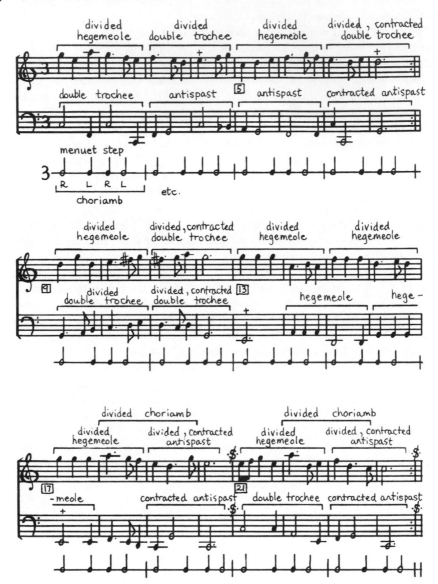

The interplay of hegemeoles reaches its highest intensity with the canon between the melody and bass in mm. 13–17. Here a divided hegemeole in the
melody is twice answered by a pure and undivided one in the bass.

The last eight measures contain a feature that often concludes a couplet or
reprise of a dance piece in triple meter. The usual procession of two-measure

movements in the melody is interrupted by a divided choriamb (LSSL) that spans the middle two measures of the four-measure unit and thus joins them. Had lyrics been set to Lully's Spanish menuet, each of the last two pair of rhythmic movements would have been set to a single four-measure line of lyrics.

Although no timing is available for the individual steps of Lully's menuet, later dancing masters (Feuillet, 1704, Preface; Pierre Rameau, 1725a) timed the weighted steps of the *pas de menuet* to the rhythm of the choriamb (LSSL). The dancers' steps would thus make rhythmic counterpoint to the second half of hegemeoles (SSSLS) and of double trochees (LSLS), to both halves of antispasts (SLLS), and to the central choriambs (LSSL) of the final four-measure members of this music.

In Lully's Spanish menuet, as in most other dances of the *grand siècle*, the downbeat of each measure is the only pulse sounded simultaneously by the rhythmic movements in the melody, bass line, and dance motions. Interior orchestral voices are less structured in their rhythms but they also articulate every downbeat; and, except in the final measure, each quarter-note pulse appears in at least one orchestral voice.

ARSIC-THETIC RELATIONSHIPS WITHIN RHYTHMIC MOVEMENTS

Because dance melodies of the *grand siècle* were composed to fit the speech rhythms of lyrics (chap. 6), the musical measure (chap. 5) replaced the traditional rhythmic movements as the primary measuring device. Conductors' beating patterns became particularly important as rhythmic regulators, and rhythms such as iambs (SL) and antispasts (SLLS), which did not fit the beating patterns, became less common than more suitable rhythms.

One result was the shift of the arsis (S) of the iamb (SL) from the downbeat to the preceding upbeat. This shift allowed the thesis (L) to fall on the downbeat, the stronger beat (chap. 11). Printz responded to this change by renaming the old iamb the *contrarius* (contrary foot), to make it clear that the S and L of this antiquated but still familiar rhythm go counter to the conducting pattern (1696, part II, p. 127).

Several other rhythmic movements listed by Mersenne begin before the bar line in Lullian and later dance music (ex. 4.13). Many eighteenth-century musicians, such as Freillon-Poncein (1700, pp. 55–57), identified a dance type by its upbeat notes and by the beats in its measures. For instance, the first L of the choreobacchius (LSSLL) precedes the downbeat in Lullian gavottes; and Freillon-Poncein identified the gavotte as a piece that begins on the second beat of a two-beat measure. Similarly, the S's of the ternary anapest—an anapest (SSL) adjusted to fit ternary beats—precede the beats in Lullian gigues in $\frac{6}{4}$ meter; and Freillon-Poncein described gigues as starting with the final two notes of the measure—an eighth and a quarter. Also, many rigaudons of the *grand siècle* begin with the epitrite (SLLL); according to Freillon-Poncein, they start on the last pulse of the measure.

In fact, the downbeat and upbeat in French dance music divide duple meter

Example 4.13.
Rhythmic movements that in the *grand siècle* begin before
the downbeat. a. choreobacchius (gavotte); b. ternary anapests (gigue); c. epitrite (rigaudon).

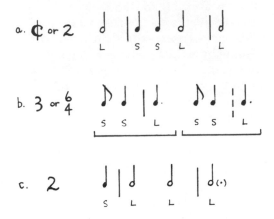

into tranquil spondees (LL), cheerful dactyls (LSS), or pairs of light and voluble
pyrrhics (SS); and triple meter into tender trochees (LS) or flowing tribrachs
(SSS). But these patterns lack the "off-beat" accents and more intense passions
found in Mersenne's much larger store of rhythmic movements.

The final ascendency of the new duple and triple meters over the old rhythmic movements is shown in the article "Rhythme" in Jean-Jacques Rousseau's
dictionary (1768), in which the old rhythmic movements are related chiefly to
the downbeat and upbeat:

> They [the feet] were divided, as today, into two beats, one the downbeat, the other
> the upbeat; there were three or even four or more varieties, depending on the dif-
> ferent relationships of these beats. These varieties were the equal [duple meter],
> which was also called dactylic (LSS), in which the rhythm was divided into two
> equal beats; the triple, trochaic (LS) or iambic (SL), in which the duration of one of
> the two beats was twice that of the other; the sesquialter [$\frac{6}{4}$ meter], which they also
> called paeonic (SSSL or LSSS), in which the duration of the two beats related 3:2;
> and finally the epitrite (SLLL), less used, where the relationship of the two beats
> was 3:4.[3]

Lully was a master at composing dance music that blended the Baroque and the
Classical—the passionate rhythmic movements and the regular metrical proportions. After his death, French composers used rhythmic movements far less
often and less prominently; and beginning instruction books of the final years of
the *grand siècle* show that the musical measure had replaced the rhythmic
movements as the chief building block of dance music.

5

The Musical Measure

Several ways of beating the measure are used
to give diversity to the pieces of music, as
well as to accommodate the quantity [syllable
lengths] of the words, which require sometimes a measure of four counts, sometimes one
of two or three, etc.[1]

—Jean Rousseau (1710?e, p. 86)

The [musical] measure is the most beautiful
thing we have in music, since music is nothing
without it: because it is with the measure that
one can conduct four, five and six parts, each
with a hundred performers, without some ar-
riving at the end sooner than the others.[2]

—Jean-Pierre Freillon-Poncein (1700, p. 24)

Several ways of beating the measure were used during the *grand siècle* to differentiate the various kinds of pieces, to accommodate a range of lyrics, and to
help conductors keep a large number of performers together. These methods
developed out of the much simpler beating patterns of the early Baroque.

EARLY BAROQUE MEASURES

As shown in previous chapters, some bar lines of the early Baroque indicated
the ends of step-units, drumbeats, or strumming patterns, while others helped
musicians keep time by pointing out the downbeats, and sometimes also the
upbeats, of the music. In dance pieces having no bar lines, the beating pattern
was implied by the time signature.

In all French dance pieces of the early Baroque, the downbeats and upbeats
were of equal length. Example 5.1 shows the most likely beating patterns in
five of the pieces discussed in chapter 4. The bar lines in Arbeau's pavane (ex.

EXAMPLE 5.1.
Beating patterns of the early Baroque. a. Arbeau, pavane,
1589t, pp. 60–61. Mersenne, 1636, IIa: b. gavotte, p. 169;
c. allemande, p. 166; d. sarabande, p. 166; e. canarie, p. 170.

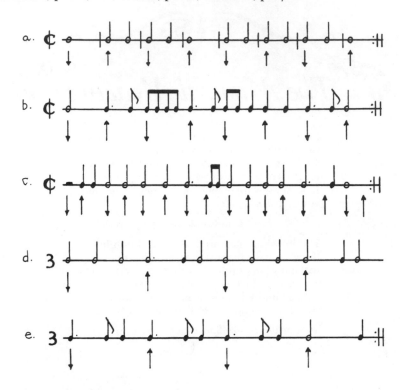

5.1a) mark off each beat, or semibreve (whole note), so that the first measure
was probably conducted with a downbeat, the second with an upbeat, and so
forth. Mersenne's dances have no bar lines, but his gavotte and allemande (exx.
5.1b and c) were in all likelihood conducted with minim (half note) downbeats
and upbeats. The ternary beats of Mersenne's sarabande and canarie (exx. 5.1d
and e) were conducted as downbeats and upbeats, though the note values of
this sarabande's beats (dotted semibreves) are twice as long as those of this canarie (dotted minims).

   The chief melodic notes within these equal downbeats and upbeats depended
on the rhythm of the step-unit, strumming pattern, or rhythmic movement,
rather than on any subdivision of the two beats. This freedom of note values
within the equal beats allowed the S of iambs (SL) to fall on the downbeat in a
variety of dances; dactyls (LSS) and anapests (SSL) to be either binary or ternary; and the notes of courantes to be grouped in several ways.

MEASURES IN MUSIC OF THE *GRAND SIÈCLE*

During the *grand siècle*, conductors refined the simple down-and-up motions of earlier times to help coordinate the playing with the singing and dancing of the soloists, ensembles, and choruses on stage. Lully's orchestra, one of the forerunners of today's opera orchestra, consisted of a fairly large body of string players, usually divided into five or six parts (rather than today's four), and assorted wind and percussion players, who were added as needed.

Presumably to fit the music better to the dancing and singing, downbeats were made to coincide with the first individual step of step-units and with the stressed syllables of lyrics. Also, to help coordinate all the parts, some upbeats and downbeats were divided into lesser beats, and bar lines were notated at regular intervals.

As the organization of the musical measure was codified, notes came to be considered relatively "good" or "bad" according to their position in the beating pattern. Good notes corresponded to the beats of the measure or their major divisions. Bad notes filled the spaces between good notes.

With the sign ₵, for instance, a downbeat half note was felt to be good in relation to the following upbeat half note. The first and third quarter notes of the measure were good in relation to the second and fourth; and odd-numbered eighth notes were good in relation to even-numbered ones.

With the sign 3, the downbeat quarter note was good in relation to the third, or upbeat, quarter note. But the upbeat quarter note was good in relation to the second one in the measure. Again, odd-numbered eighths were good in relation to even-numbered ones.

The German violinist, composer, and conductor Georg Muffat, whose preface to his *Florilegium secundum* of 1698 was intended to teach non-French players how to perform "in the Lullian manner," specified the good and bad notes in various rhythms. In example 5.2, the signs "n" and "v," the first letters of the Latin words *nobilis* (noble) and *vilis* (of little worth), designate good and bad notes respectively. Muffat advised violinists to play most good notes with the down-bow, their primary stroke; and most bad notes with the up-bow, their secondary one.

Muffat wrote that the "good, noble, or principal" notes of the measure are naturally more reposeful than the "weak or poor," that is, bad ones; and he implied that bad notes are arsic to good ones: "The good notes are those that seem naturally to give the ear a little repose. . . . The weak [bad] notes . . . , not satisfying the ear so well, leave a desire to go on"[3] (1698t, p. 239). That is probably why Muffat, in example 5.2, did not place in a good position any note value shorter than the next. For him, a good note had to be as long or longer than the following note, in order to suggest some repose. Clearly, the initial S on a good note in an iamb (SL) or antispast (SLLS) conflicted with his notion of good and bad positions in the musical measure.

Early in the eighteenth century, every musical tutor covered the subject of *la mesure*, citing all the characteristics indicated by each meter sign. Freillon-

Example 5.2.
Musical examples with good and bad notes indicated. Muffat,
1698t, p. 225. n = good note; v = bad note.

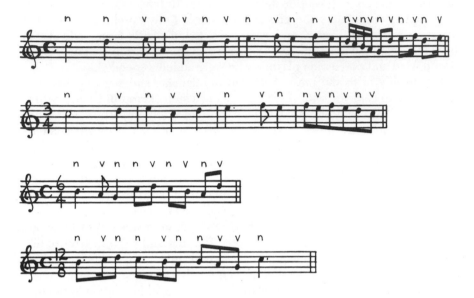

Poncein, who claimed that "it is rather difficult to beat time well," insisted that
the measure, or meter, "must be established as the foundation and the spirit of
the music [and that] the ear and the voice must follow and be regulated by it"
(1700, p. 24).

With the increased influence of the musical measure and its interior organization, composers of French sarabandes came to prefer a dotted note value on
the first (good) rather than on the second (bad) pulse of the measure. French
canaries and gigues came to be written exclusively with ternary beats. French
courantes became notated with the more rigid $\frac{3}{2}$ instead of the flexible 3 sign,
even though the music still included all the early rhythms.

By the end of the seventeenth century, *la mesure* had replaced the various
rhythmic movements, not only as a primary building block of dance music but
also as a leading regulator of the passions. Jean Rousseau's voice tutor of 1678
pointed out that the meters "serve mainly as a means toward the different kinds
of movement that are the pure spirit of the music" (1710?e, p. 86). And the
French musical theorist Charles Masson declared:

> Meter is the soul of music, since it makes a great number of persons react so specifi-
> cally, and since through the variety of its movements it can also arouse many differ-
> ent passions, being able to calm some and excite others, as has always been ob-
> served.[4] (1697, p. 6)

More succinctly, the harpsichordist Michel de Saint-Lambert said that the
meter of a piece "distinguishes its character" (1702, p. 14).

FRENCH METER SIGNS

French meter signs of the late seventeenth and early eighteenth centuries provide all the information given by meter signs today. They indicate the note values encompassed by a measure and show whether the measure and its beats divide into two or three smaller values.

But the French signs also imply considerably more about the characteristics of the music. Unless contradicted by descriptive words at the start of the music, these signs suggest the tempo, articulation, type of piece, and national style and whether the note values are performed freely, or "unequally." For example, the description the flutist Jacques Hotteterre le Romain gave of the meter indicated by the numeral 2 offers numerous clues to its use and character:

> Two-meter is marked by a simple 2; it is composed of two half notes or the equivalent; it is beaten in two equal counts. It is usually lively [*vive*] and sharply articulated [*piqué*]. It is used at the start of opera overtures, in *entrées de ballet*, marches, bourrées, gavottes, rigaudons, branles, cotillons, etc.; its eighth notes are performed unequally [*pointé*]. It is never used in Italian music.[5] (1719, p. 58)

The organization within the downbeat and upbeat is very important to the character of a meter. Both these beats divide into two or three pulses, which are normally the shortest "equal notes" found in the measure. Dancers, singers, and instrumentalists set the large majority of steps, syllables, and strokes to pulse values. Although the half-note pulses common in Mersenne's dances occur in a few sarabandes of the *grand siècle*, quarter-note pulses are usual in Lully's dances. Eighth-note pulses typify Italian music of the late seventeenth and early eighteenth centuries but also appear in many Italian-style dance pieces by French composers of the *grand siècle* and later.

Note values on the level immediately below the pulse serve to ornament the basic steps, syllables, and strokes of dance music and so are performed somewhat freely, or "unequally" (*inégales*). In this book we call these values "quick notes" rather than "unequal notes," since values on all levels below them may also be performed freely. Eighth notes are normally the quick notes of Lully's dances. The values immediately below the quick notes we call "very quick notes"; they are usually sixteenths. Lully used few notes quicker than a pulse in his dance music, except for a quick note or a pair of very quick ones after a dotted-pulse value.

The meter signs used in French dance music of the *grand siècle* fall into five categories: They signify measures consisting of two beats of two pulses; four beats of two pulses; essentially one beat of three pulses; two beats of three pulses; and three beats of two pulses. From the 1670s, the signs Lully used most often in dance music were 2, 3, and $\frac{6}{4}$, all with quarter-note pulses and freely performed eighth notes.

MEASURES OF TWO BEATS OF TWO PULSES

Whether the sign was **C**, **¢**, or 2, quarter notes were the pulses in the quick duple-meter dances of Lully's day, and eighth notes were performed freely

EXAMPLE 5.3.
Metrical proportions in measures of two beats of two quarter-
note pulses. Montéclair, 1709, p. 10. Names of note values
added by the present authors.

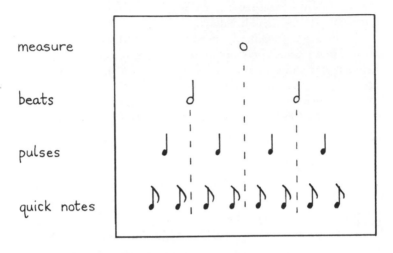

EXAMPLE 5.4.
The sign ₵ with quarter-note pulses. From Lully, *Ballet des
plaisirs*, 1655: a. bourrée; b. gavotte.

(ex. 5.3). Until the mid-1670s, Lully used ₵ for most dances in simple-duple
meter (see ex. 5.4); but thereafter he employed the sign 2. Example 5.5 gives
the three dance pieces cited by Hotteterre to demonstrate the use of the sign 2.

In the early eighteenth century, some French composers adopted the relatively new $\frac{2}{4}$ sign of the Italians for quick dances (see ex. 5.6). Here eighth notes
were the pulse values, and sixteenths were performed freely. Hotteterre pointed
out that a $\frac{2}{4}$ measure is nothing but a four-beat C measure divided into two.

MEASURES OF FOUR BEATS OF TWO PULSES

In the late seventeenth and early eighteenth centuries, many concert allemandes and some dance pieces in the Italian style kept the old C and ₵ signs but

EXAMPLE 5.5.
Dances with the sign 2. Hotteterre, 1719, p. 58. a. Lully,
bourrée, from *Phaeton*, 1683; b. Lully, gavotte, from *Roland*,
1685; c. Campra, premier rigaudon, from *L'Europe galante*,
1697.

EXAMPLE 5.6.
Bourrée with the sign $\frac{2}{4}$. Montéclair, 1711–12, p. 12.

made eighth notes equal and sixteenth notes the values to be performed freely.
As a result, four beats were conducted in each measure, eighth notes functioned as pulses, and sixteenths were the quick notes of the measure. As shown
in chapter 10, the four beats tended to be beaten more slowly in dances marked
C than in those marked ₵, unless the former had a word like *gay* or *allegro* at
the start.

Example 5.7 illustrates the metrical proportions in dance measures having
four quarter-note beats and equal eighth notes, whether the sign is C or ₵. The
principal dance of the *grand siècle* to use these metrical proportions is the so-
called stylized allemande, a polyphonic concert piece that commonly has some
dotted rhythms and numerous sixteenth or quicker notes. In the four-beat allemande in example 5.8, the sixteenths are to be *un tant-soit-peu pointées* (pointed
so much but no more), that is, played somewhat unequally.

Italian dances with the signs C and ₵ have equal eighths, according to Hotteterre. The first piece in example 5.9 is conducted in four beats; the second
and third, in four quick beats or two slow ones. All three examples are by Co-

EXAMPLE 5.7.
Metrical proportions in measures of four beats of two eighth-
note pulses. Format based on Montéclair's in ex. 5.3.

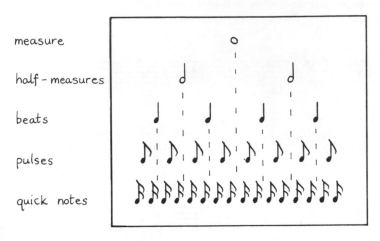

EXAMPLE 5.8.
F. Couperin, "Allemande la laborieuse," livre 1, ordre 2, 1713.

relli, but Hotteterre and other French composers of his day also used these signs
for their music in the Italian style.

French tutors of the late seventeenth and early eighteenth centuries offer
three ways of counting four beats in a measure. Étienne Loulié divided the
downbeat and the upbeat (1696t, p. 30). In each measure, he moved his hand
downward in two stages and then upward in two: down, down, up, up. The first
"down" marks the main downbeat of the measure; the first "up," the main upbeat. Montéclair used the modern pattern for four beats: down, left, right, up
(1709, p. 11). Saint-Lambert reversed the left and right directions of the modern pattern: down, right, left, up (1702, p. 17). Loulié's beating pattern is perhaps the best for concert allemandes, because their quarter-note beats are essentially divisions of the larger half-note beats of earlier, danced allemandes.
The two patterns in which the hand moves in four different directions might
better serve dance pieces in the Italian style.

EXAMPLE 5.9.
Italian dances by Corelli with four beats and equal eighth notes.
Hotteterre, 1719, p. 57. a. allemanda, op. 5/10, 1700; b. Tempo
de gavotta, op. 5/9, 1700; c. Tempo di gavotta, op. 4/9, 1694.

EXAMPLE 5.10.
Metrical proportions in measures with three quarter-note
pulses. Format based on Montéclair's in ex. 5.3.

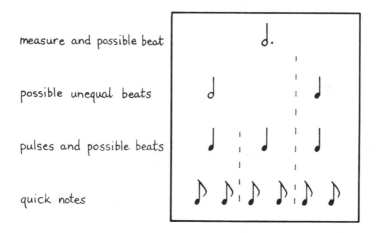

MEASURES OF THREE PULSES

The pulse in the triple-meter dance pieces of the *grand siècle* may be half
notes, quarter notes, or eighth notes. The organization with quarter-note pulses
(see ex. 5.10), called "simple triple" then as today, is the most common. The
usual French sign for simple-triple meter is the numeral 3, but the Italian fractional sign $\frac{3}{4}$ was sometimes used in France in the early eighteenth century.

EXAMPLE 5.11.
Dances in simple-triple meter. Hotteterre, 1719, pp. 58–59.
a. Lully, sarabande, from *Issé*, 1677; b. Lully, menuet, from
Roland, 1685; c. Lully, passacaille, from *Armide*, 1686;
d. idem., later couplet; e. Corelli, courante, op. V/7, 1700;
f. Corelli, sarabande (bass), op. V/8, 1700.

Example 5.11 presents several dances in simple-triple meter cited by Hotteterre. Because the number of beats per measure in triple meter varies with the
tempo, we do not show them in this example. Examples 5.11a and b have equal
quarters and freely performed eighths. Examples 5.11c and d demonstrate the
normally unequal and then the equal performance of eighth notes in a single
piece. Eighths are performed unequally in the first couplet and equally in a
later one. Hotteterre explained this change in the level of the freely performed
notes by saying that eighth notes in simple-triple meter are performed equally
if they leap or are mixed with quicker values, as in the later couplet.

Finally, according to Hotteterre, examples 5.11e and f demonstrate the equal performance of eighth notes in Italian-style pieces. The eighth notes in Corelli's courante leap, but those of his sarabande bass move mainly by steps. Hotteterre and other French composers of his day sometimes imitated Corelli in their courantes and sarabandes.

Some sarabandes of the *grand siècle* are composed with the sign $\frac{3}{2}$ in what Hotteterre called "major-triple" or "triple-double" meter; half notes are pulses, and quarter notes are performed freely. Montéclair's sarabande (ex. 5.12), unlike most of his day, is written partly in the so-called white notation of the sixteenth century: white eighth notes are the equivalent of black quarter notes and are the values that may be performed freely. Montéclair used black eighth notes for the very quick values, also performed freely.

Dances in "minor-triple," or $\frac{3}{8}$, meter are notated like those using the sign 3, except that their note values are halved: eighth notes are pulses, and sixteenth notes are performed freely. As examples, Hotteterre cited a canarie and a passepied, two of the quickest dances (ex. 5.13). As with the $\frac{2}{4}$ signature sometimes used for lively dances in simple-duple meter, the eighth-note pulse ensures a fast tempo.

Dance pieces with three pulses to a measure are conducted in one, in two unequal, or in three equal beats. Two measures of the quickest dances are sometimes paired and conducted as if in compound-duple meter, with one beat to each measure.

EXAMPLE 5.12.
White and black notation in a dance piece. Montéclair, sarabande, 1711–12, p. 15.

EXAMPLE 5.13.
Dances with the sign $\frac{3}{8}$. Hotteterre, 1719, p. 59. a. Lully, canarie, from *Issé*, 1677; b. Lully, passepied, from *Temple de la paix*, 1685.

Measures of moderately quick dances are conducted with "two unequal beats" according to Masson (1697t, p. 37), or with "one and a half beats" according to Freillon-Poncein (1700, p. 25). This inequality of the downbeat and upbeat articulates a trochaic rhythm (LS). The hand lowers on the first pulse and lifts on the third, making the downbeat twice as long as the upbeat. Whether this pattern should be altered to fit the notes of an iamb (SL) when that rhythm occurs in the music is not known.

The slowest dances are conducted with three slow beats. Loulié made downward motions on the first and second pulses, thus dividing the downbeat, and an upward motion on the third pulse (1696t, p. 29). Many writers recommended three beats in the triangular pattern used today: down, right, up-and-left.

MEASURES OF SIX PULSES

The sign $\frac{6}{4}$ and sometimes $\frac{3}{2}$ and 3 indicate six quarter-note pulses in the measure. Although with all three signs the pulses may be grouped in twos or in threes, the ternary arrangement prevails in $\frac{6}{4}$ and the binary arrangement in $\frac{3}{2}$. Example 5.14 shows the metrical proportions that result from the ternary and binary groupings. Hotteterre cited the loure (ex. 5.15a), gigue (ex. 5.15b), and forlane to illustrate $\frac{6}{4}$ meter.

Although many courantes of the early seventeenth century were written with the simple signature 3, bar lines measured off the equivalent of either three or six quarter-note pulses, normally grouped in threes. However, French-

EXAMPLE 5.14.
Metrical proportions in measures with six quarter-note pulses.
a. 3 + 3 pulses; b. 2 + 2 + 2 pulses. Formats based on Montéclair's in ex. 5.3.

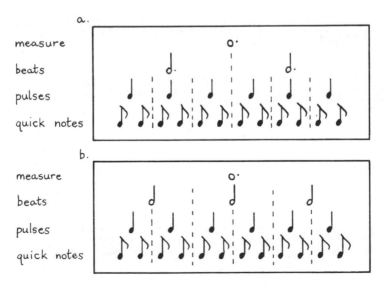

EXAMPLE 5.15.
Dances in $\frac{6}{4}$ meter. Hotteterre, 1719, p. 59. a. Campra, loure, from *Thetis*, 1708; b. Lully, gigue, from *Roland*, 1655.

EXAMPLE 5.16.
Similar melodic rhythms in courantes notated in three ways. a. Muffat, courante, 1698t, p. 228; b. Corbetta, courante, 1671, pp. 47–48 (Pinnell transcription; reprinted by permission of Richard Pinnell and UMI Research Press); c. Anonymous, courante "La Bourgogne," in Pécour, 1700.

style courantes of the late seventeenth and early eighteenth centuries were written with the sign $\frac{3}{2}$ and with quarter-note pulses whose grouping was often ambiguous. For instance, little differentiates the melodic rhythms of the three courantes in example 5.16, although the first two differ in the number of pulses in the measure and the third differs from them in its meter sign.

Some canaries, gigues, forlanes, and a few menuets are notated in $\frac{6}{8}$. Eighth notes are pulses and sixteenths are performed freely. This meter may be viewed as two measures of $\frac{3}{8}$, or as $\frac{6}{4}$ with the note values halved. Hotteterre and his contemporaries used this meter sign for both Italian-style and French-style gigues (ex. 5.17).

Most dance pieces with six pulses grouped 3 + 3 are beaten with two equal hand motions. The hand lowers on the first pulse of the measure and rises on

EXAMPLE 5.17.
Dances in ⁶⁄₈. Hotteterre, 1719, p. 60. a. Corelli, gigue, op. V/7,
1700; b. Lully, gigue, from *Persée*, 1682.

the fourth. But Hotteterre said that loures, in ⁶⁄₄ meter, are conducted with four
unequal beats because of their slow tempo (1719, p. 59). He did not specify the
exact hand motions, but Loulié did (1696t, p. 31). Loulié subdivided both the
downbeat and the upbeat, grouping the pulses 2 + 1 in each beat. Each first
downward or upward motion covers two quarter notes; each second one, only
one quarter note. With this conducting pattern, the beats on the "good" first and
fourth pulses of the measure are longer than those on the "bad" third and sixth.

In sum, tutors written after Lully's death called the musical measure the foundation, spirit, character, and most beautiful thing in music. But in fact it was
the poetic rhythms of dance lyrics—with a nod to traditional rhythmic movements—that formed the rhythmic subjects of many dance pieces with and without words. As the downbeat of the measure became its focal point, the final
stressed syllable of each line of a dance song was almost always placed on a
downbeat. Lesser stresses within the line also tended to fall on downbeats or
upbeats, the "good" notes of the measure. In addition, most syllables on bad
notes led to those on good notes.

6

Correspondence of Melodic and Poetic Rhythms in Lullian Dance Songs

It is necessary to examine a piece before undertaking to perform it, for two reasons: first, to try to divine its character, and to develop the intention of the composer; second, to find its regular rhythmic fall [*cadence*]. The rhythmic fall of an air is a certain number of measures that determine a melody: several of these melodies of two, three, four, or sometimes more measures determine the reprise of an air, or an entire air; so that if the air begins either on the first, second, third, or fourth part of a measure, each subsequent period begins the same, in such a way that one must lift all the fingers and stop the wheel [of the hurdy-gurdy] in order to differentiate each of these units. This is easy to understand in the measured airs, such as menuets, bourrées, rigaudons, chaconnes, contredanses and others, where a perceptible melodic ending occurs every two or four measures, after which the same melody begins again, or a different phrase begins: it is these closes that few people pay attention to, yet on them depends the perfection of the performance.[1]

—Jean-Baptiste Dupuit (1741, p. 8)

The expression of the melody in response to that of the words depends on the inventiveness and the careful discretion of the composer; this expression, being sustained and perfected by a judicious diversity of the movement of the measure, has the force and the virtue to make the spirit pass from one pas-

sion to another; such is the natural proof of a
work's perfection.[2]

—Charles Masson (1699e, pp. 27–28)

Lully and his principal librettist, the poet Philippe Quinault, worked out a
fairly simple way of matching the rhythms of French lyrics to those of the various dances: they fitted melodic endings to what the hurdy-gurdy player Dupuit
called the "rhythmic falls" of the music. Melodies set in this fashion to dance
lyrics became the typical rhythmic subjects of the dances. At the same time,
Lully managed to vary the rhythmic subjects of his dance songs to achieve the
"judicious diversity of the movement of the measure" so highly recommended
by the musical theorist Masson. Jean Grimarest attests to the success of Lully's
method when he commends Lully and his followers André Destouches and
Michel de La Barre for their excellent settings of words to music, and praises
especially Lully's dance songs (1760e, pp. 124–26). Although instrumentalists
"have no words under the notes to guide them" (Dupuit, 1741, p. 7), they can
nevertheless learn to recognize these subjects in dance pieces and to appreciate
the myriad rhythmic inflections within each subject.

RHYTHMIC SUBJECTS

Lully and his librettists seem to have followed four principles in composing the
lines and rhythmic subjects of their dance songs. The first two pertain only to
dance music. The last two, which derive from the spoken tragedy of French
classical poets (Rosow, 1983, pp. 468–69), affect Lullian recitative and dance
airs in somewhat different ways:

    1. Two-measure rhythmic movements (chap. 4) and the tendency of step-
units to be paired (chaps. 2 and 8) require most Lullian dance lines to be fitted
to two or four musical measures of equal length. (The lines of Lullian recitative
vary more in length, sometimes covering an odd number of measures, or two or
more of unequal length.)

    2. The variety of syllable lengths in the French language (chap. 13) calls for a
corresponding diversity of note lengths. Accordingly, Lully used half notes, dotted quarters, quarters, and eighths in the 2, 3, and $\frac{6}{4}$ meters favored in the
dance music of his day, along with free, or "unequal," performance of the
eighths. Most syllables in dance songs are thus set to S's or to divisions of the L's
of rhythmic movements. In some lines, an undivided L appears only at the
rhyme (app. ex. 3), and sometimes only where the ending is masculine (app.
ex. 2). At the same time, in order to make clear the pulses to which dancers
must set many individual steps, a minimum of extra syllables is used. As with
the dance songs discussed in chapter 4, rarely are more than three syllables set

to three-pulse measures, four syllables to four-pulse ones, and six syllables to six-pulse ones. (Recognition of the pulse movement is not important for recitative, where each measure may have a different number of syllables.)

3. Because the final counted syllable, or "end-accent," at the rhyme and principal break of a French line is normally the strongest of its hemistich, Lully usually placed it on a strong beat of the music. Wherever possible, he also gave it a longer note value than most other syllables. (Chap. 13 shows that in forceful declamation some important interior syllables are also long or strong.) Almost all end-accents of Lullian dance lyrics fall on downbeats of the music. (Those of recitative may fall on the second count of a two-beat measure or on the third count of a four-beat one.) The end-accent at the principal break of a line is usually masculine (i.e., has no final "mute" *e*). The one at the rhyme may be masculine or feminine.

4. The length of a line helps determine the musical rhythm. (In recitative, the composer adjusts either the number of pulses or the value of the notes in the measure, or both, to make the end-accents of unequal lines fall suitably. Rosow says that lines of eight, ten, and twelve syllables are the commonest there.) Short lines occur frequently in Lully's dance songs. Some have only three or four syllables (app. ex. 1, mm. 1–4). Lines of six or fewer syllables often function in pairs, as do the initial lines of earlier songs. In addition, isolated or paired lines of five syllables occur at the end of some sections in gigues and loures (app. ex. 4, mm. 14–15, 17–19, 21–23). Most bourrées begin with one or more six-syllable lines (app. ex. 5); most gavottes, with seven-syllable ones (app. ex. 2). In fact, lines of seven syllables predominate in duple-meter dances, and lines of ten syllables in triple-meter ones.

a. In menuets, sarabandes, gavottes, and many other dances, the regular rhythmic fall of the dance forces most feminine lines to be concluded with a half note plus a quarter note or with two quarters (app. ex. 1, first three lines; app. ex. 2, all odd-numbered lines). Recognizing the feminine endings in these dances is vital to instrumentalists, since the gender of the ending determines the phrasing.

b. The principal break in dance lines set to two measures of music usually falls after the note on the first downbeat. However, two-measure lines in triple-meter dances are too short for much of a break (app. ex. 1, mm. 1–8). Four-measure lines in triple-meter dances may divide into equal or unequal hemistiches. If they are unequal, the main break normally falls after the downbeat of the second measure (app. ex. 1, mm. 13–16, 21–24).

In an article on the characters of the Baroque dances to be cited throughout this chapter, Patricia M. Ranum (1985) points out that the passion of four-measure lines that divide equally tends to be majestic and placid. In other words, these lines are balanced in their expression as well as in the length of their hemistiches. In contrast, lines that divide unequally are more emotional and tender, that is, unbalanced. Ranum explains too that the shorter of two hemistiches in a line is by nature the more intense. In dance songs, the first hemistich is usually the shorter.

When the principles of end-accentuation and line length in lyrics are combined with the requisite paired measures and limited number of syllables in dance music, the typical rhythmic subjects of the different dances are born. The characteristic upbeat or downbeat start, the typical meter, and the regular stresses on all or alternate downbeats give each dance its particular rhythm.

Rhythmic subjects in simple-duple meter are characterized by their upbeat or double upbeat start. A bourrée line beginning with an upbeat pulse, continuing with four syllables in the measure, and ending with a feminine rhyme is typically scanned 1 |2/ 3 4 5 |6–(e.g., app. ex. 5, mm. 1–2). The numerals stand for syllables; vertical lines for bar lines; underlined numerals for end-accents; a slash for the principal break in the line; and a final dash for a feminine ending. A characteristic gavotte line starting with two upbeat pulses and ending with a feminine rhyme is normally scanned 1 2 |3/ 4 5 6 |7–(e.g., app. ex. 2, mm. 1–2). Later lines of bourrées often adopt the rhythm of a gavotte line having a masculine rhyme (e.g., app. ex. 5, mm. 3–4).

Rhythmic subjects in compound-duple meter typically have longer lines and at least a few gigue-like, ternary dotted figures that are begun with an upbeat eighth and quarter note. For instance, a gigue line with masculine rhyme is commonly scanned 1 2 |3// 4 5 6 7 8 |9 (e.g., app. ex. 4, mm. 1–2). The double slash shows the principal break in a line of eight or more syllables.

Dances in simple-triple meter are more varied in their scansion. Four-measure sarabande and menuet lines having two equal hemistiches, each concluded with the LS of a feminine ending, are usually scanned |1 2 3 |4 –//| 5 6 7 |8–(rather like the line pair that starts app. ex. 1). But most four-measure folie, sarabande, and menuet lines that begin on the downbeat and finish with a feminine rhyme are scanned |1 2 3 |4// 5 6 |7 8 9 |10–(e.g., app. ex. 3, mm. 1–4). In contrast, the end-accents of a twelve-measure chaconne line, whose bass begins on the downbeat but whose melody starts on the second pulse, fall on the third and fifth downbeats: 1 2 |3 4 5 |6// 7 8 |9 10 11 |12 (app. ex. 6, mm. 1–5).

Some menuets and a few other dance songs begin with and often continue with three-measure lines. When they start with an upbeat pulse in simple-triple meter, these pieces are likely to be scanned 1 |2// 3 4 |5 6 7 |8–; e.g., Un |coeur// qui veut |ê-tre vo-|la-ge (A |heart// that wants |to be |fickle) (Lully, menuet, from *Triomphe de l'amour*).

For instrumentalists, with no lyrics, a final long note or a notated rest may signal the end of a rhythmic subject. A few composers used breath marks to point out these endings and even the principal break within some subjects. Michel L'Affilard, for instance, placed a small "c" on the bottom line of the musical staff to indicate breathing places in his dance songs first published in 1694 (app. ex. 3 and the first lines of his songs in the tempo sections of Part II). François Couperin often inserted commas above the staff for the same purpose. In example 6.1 commas set off the first four-measure rhythmic subject in a sarabande and the first two two-measure subjects in a bourrée. Later two-measure subjects in that bourrée (not shown here) are either broken by a comma into the equivalent of

EXAMPLE 6.1.

Rhythmic subjects marked off by commas. F. Couperin, *Les
nations: L'espagnole,* 1726: a. sarabande; b. bourée. Parenthetical ornaments, slurs, accidentals, and breath marks added
by the present authors.

one-measure hemistiches or joined through the lack of one into the equivalent
of four-measure lines.

MUSICAL RHYMES

A dance is identified not only by its typical rhythmic subject but more specifically by the rhythm that represents its first hemistich. This rhythm is called the
musical rhyme. Although the poetic rhyme concludes its line of lyrics, the musical one initiates its rhythmic subject. The musical rhyme covers one to three
pulses plus the note on the following downbeat. It is usually distinctive enough
to be easily recognized.

Various musical rhymes typify the character dances (ex. 6.2). In simple-duple
meter, for instance, an upbeat pulse note followed by a note on the downbeat
characterizes bourrées and rigaudons; two upbeat quarter notes (or their rhythmic equivalent) followed by a downbeat note typify gavottes. In simple-triple or

EXAMPLE 6.2.
Musical rhymes. a. bourrée; b. gavotte; c. gigue; d. folie,
sarabande, or menuet.

compound-duple meter, an upbeat quick note, an upbeat pulse note, plus the note on the following downbeat characterize gigues and some loures. Three pulse notes (or their rhythmic equivalent) plus the note on the following downbeat typify the ten-syllable lines of many folies, sarabandes, and menuets.

Sometimes the same musical rhyme begins all rhythmic subjects in a dance piece. In Lully's gavotte song from *Atys* (app. ex. 2), for instance, the initial rhyme—dotted quarter, eighth, quarter—begins every two-measure rhythmic subject. In L'Affilard's menuet (app. ex. 3), three quarters plus a dotted quarter start every rhythmic subject but the last. On the other hand, the initial rhyme (basically quarter, half, half) of Lully's menuet from *Psyché* (app. ex. 1) marks the beginning of each pair of short lines.

The most impassioned dance songs may be expected to exhibit the greatest irregularity in their musical rhymes. The first three lines of the gigue and bourrée songs in the Appendix (app. exx. 4 and 5) begin with unlike rhythmic figures. In the gigue, the imitation in the bass supplies the musical rhyme. In the bourrée, the single upbeat note of the initial figure is replaced by two upbeat notes in the next two rhythmic figures. The two contrasting couplets of the emotional chaconne song from *Cadmus* (app. ex. 6) begin with the same rhythmic figure, but the other rhythmic subjects start with a variety of figures.

In many dance songs, only musical periods (app. ex. 4) or musical reprises start with the same rhythmic figure. The repetition points out the beginning of the next section. Of the five dance songs in two-reprise form in the Appendix (app. exx. 1–5), only the starts of the bourrée's reprises do not rhyme musically. This bourrée's departure from the general rule may result from the second reprise's beginning unconventionally in the middle of the first stanza of the lyrics.

In short, some musical rhymes, such as those in examples 6.2c and d, characterize the beginnings of several dance types. Some dance types, such as the menuet, are characterized by more than one initial rhyme. One dance type, the bourrée, characteristically includes a rhyme that typically begins another dance type, the gavotte. And some dances, such as the chaconne and passacaille, lack a characteristic rhyme.

DIVERSITY OF RHYTHM

Once the dance has been identified by a characteristic rhyme and subject, a greater diversity of rhythms follows. Some dance songs have lines of only one length (app. exx. 2 and 3). Others begin with short lines and end with long or at least somewhat longer ones (app. exx. 1 and 5). Still others start with long lines and finish with short ones (app. exx. 4 and 6).

Certain songs, such as gigues and chaconnes (app. exx. 4 and 6), are less regular in their line lengths than most menuets and gavottes (app. exx. 1, 2, and 3). Sometimes a masculine rhyme takes up only the first pulse of the measure, as occurs with "pas" in Lully's song from *Amadis* (app. ex. 4, m. 14), and the new line starts on the second pulse. In this particular example, the pitches of the melody also help define the start of the new line: the upward leap of a sixth, from "pas" to "Tout," leaves no doubt that the first line ends on the first pulse and the next line begins on the second.

The principal break of a line always follows the first note of the measure except when a special effect is desired. This happens in each of the last four lines of Lully's gavotte song (app. ex. 2, mm. 12–20) and in the second line of his gigue song (app. ex. 4, mm. 2–4) and of his bourrée song (app. ex. 5, mm. 2–4).

In the later lines of a song, an unusual variety of note values in the measure may declaim intensified passions. Uncommonly short values may express urgency, as do the two upbeat notes shortened to eighths at the start of the second period of Lully's bourrée song: "Let's renounce sadness" (app. ex. 5, upbeat to m. 5). An unusually long value may emphasize a particularly passionate word, for instance, the half note on the stressed syllable of "Souf-frons" (Let's suffer) in the first contrasting couplet of Lully's chaconne song (app. ex. 6, m. 12). For very excited lines, an extra syllable and note may be introduced; for example, the many extra eighths in the final period of Lully's bourrée song: "When heaven is favorable to our wishes, Let's banish the ennui, Let's bannish the ennui" (app. ex. 5, mm. 9–12). Alternatively, at very dramatic moments, the number of syllables in the measure may be reduced, as if the singer were holding his breath: "Ah! Ah!" (Lully's chaconne song, app. ex. 6, mm. 5–6).

TEXTUAL CELLS

Underlying Lullian dance lyrics are units determined by the pronunciation and "the sense of the words" (Bacilly, 1668, p. 374). Modern linguists call these basic units, articulated in a single thrust and finished with an end-accent, "phonetic words," "phonetic units," "measures," or "rhythmic units." We prefer to name them "textual cells" because, as Bacilly implied, they are based on the information given by the text as well as on the pronunciation. Examples are a verb and its object; a short subject, verb, and its object; a definite article and its noun; a prepositional phrase; an adverb or an adverbial phrase; an adjective and its following noun. (When the adjective follows the noun, Ranum [1985] considers each word a separate "rhythmic unit"—her name for "textual cell." That is because Lully and his followers often set the end-accent of such a noun to a dotted note, which of course musically separates the noun from the following adjective.) The textual cells in the dance songs of the *grand siècle* play a large part in the diversity of rhythm that "has the force and the virtue to make the spirit pass from one passion to another" (Masson, in the quotation at the start of this chapter).

Ranum shows that hemistiches and short lines contain one or more rhythmic units (textual cells) of one to six syllables, as in the first pair of lines in L'Affilard's menuet song (app. ex. 3):

[Single slashes mark the end of all but the final textual cell in each hemistich.]

|1   2   3 |4 //5 6 |7   8 9 |10 –   (4 + 6)
|Pour me van-|ger// de l'in-|grat-te Cli-|me-ne)
(To avenge myself// on the ungrateful Climene)

|1 2 /3 |4 //56 |7 /8 /9 |10 (2 + 2 + 3 + 1 + 2)
|Ba-chus/ est |prêt// à rem-|plir/ tous/ mes |voeux:
(Bacchus/ is ready// to fill/ all/ my wishes:)

The division of a line into textual cells is far less standardized than its division into hemistiches, and it sometimes allows several interpretations. Because the final syllable of a textual cell is usually the most stressed, it is likely to fall on a strong count of the music; many textual cells thus overlap the musical bar line. Yet cell lengths usually change almost continuously. Even the repetition of a melody is commonly varied in its word groups (e.g., app. ex. 3: "Pour me van-ger" and "Ba-chus/ est prêt"). The near repetitions of the first four very short lines of appendix example 1 are exceptions.

Ranum explains that the varying of rhythmic units (textual cells) in a song creates an ever-changing movement that reflects the passions of the lyrics. More specifically, she describes units of one or two syllables as "pressing and intense"; those of three syllables as usually "placid and equal"; and longer ones as "proper for streams of words pronounced in confusion, surprise, or unrest." Units of five or six syllables, which conclude many dance songs, "express a very strong emotion." However, no matter what the number of syllables in a unit, she points out that a predominance of long syllables (discussed in chap. 13) gives a slower, heavier, and more intense expression; while a predominance of short syllables makes it quicker, lighter, and more flowing.

To a large extent, the librettist determines the textual cells of the lines. Yet the composer can sometimes alter them. For instance, had L'Affilard (in app. ex. 3) set "Pour" and "-grat-" to dotted quarters or followed each syllable with a large melodic interval while the other syllables moved stepwise, the text of the first line of his menuet song would necessarily divide "|Pour/ me van-|ger// de l'in-|grat-/te Cli-|me-ne" (In order/ to avenge myself// on the ungrateful [one,]/ Climene): 1 + 3 + 3 + 3. In this case, the "mute" e of *ingratte*—as usually occurs with a feminine ending within a line—is separated from its word and begins the following cell. With this change, all the textual cells in the first line finish on downbeats. Sometimes, too, the singer can decide the cells through articulation, without changing the pitches or durations of the notes.

Lully often showed by his musical setting the way he wanted the cells to be divided. For example, the first two lines of his gigue song from *Amadis* (app. ex. 4) might be articulated "Les plai-sirs// nous sui-/vent dé-sor-mais" (Pleasures//

follow us/ from now on). But he emphasized the "mute" *e* of *sui-vent* by placing it on an unusually high pitch and long value, and on a strong count of the measure. This particular "mute" *e* thus declaims the joyous anticipation of pleasure expressed by the lyrics.

Instrumentalists have no words under the notes to tell them where to break a melody into the equivalent of textual cells. But Ranum advises players to assume that most rhythmic subjects should be performed somewhat differently on repetition.

STROPHIC STRUCTURE

The line lengths and rhyme schemes in the strophes, or stanzas, of Lully's and later dance lyrics created structures to which composers fitted their music. Similar structures appeared in many dance pieces without texts.

In Lullian dance songs, the number of syllables and the rhyme scheme of the lines vary from the most regular and thus rational to the most irregular and thus passionate. During the *grand siècle*, fairly regular structures identified serious subjects in the lyrics. Lully's rather regular menuet song from *Psyché* (charted in ex. 6.3c) is concerned with knowledge, and his very regular gavotte song from *Atys* (ex. 6.3b) discourses on the merits of perseverence; whereas his more erratic gigue song (ex. 6.3e), bourrée song (6.3f), and chaconne song (6.3g) extol respectively sexual pleasures, improved fortune, and romantic love. On the other hand, dance songs of the early eighteenth century—regardless of the message of their lyrics—commonly exhibit far greater regularity of strophic structure than do the songs of Lully and his librettists. The text of L'Affilard's menuet song (ex. 6.3a) speaks of vengeance, yet its structure is extremely regular.

Most lines of Lullian dance songs are paired by their relative length, their rhyme, or both. The basic pattern is that of the menuet and gavotte songs shown in examples 6.3a and b, in which all the lines are the same length and alternate lines are paired by their rhymes. Throughout both songs, the lesser repose of a feminine rhyme ("a" or "b") leads to the greater repose of a masculine one ("A" or "B"). The two stanzas of the menuet have the same masculine and feminine rhymes, but each stanza of the gavotte has its own rhymes.

Lully's menuet song from *Psyché* (ex. 6.3c) contains a more intriguing rhyme scheme and a pleasing pattern of short and long lines. The first stanza contains two pair of short lines. Each pair ends with the slightly longer and thus more reposeful line of the two, and the stanza concludes with the masculine rhyme of the second pair of lines. The second stanza contains two groups of three lines, with two short and one long line making up each group. The third line of each group is more conclusive than the other two because of its greater length and its masculine rhyme. The final line is the longest of the stanza and indeed of the whole song. In this song, the masculine rhymes of the two stanzas are the same, but the feminine rhymes differ.

The relationships of the stanzas in the first three songs in example 6.3 are relatively simple. The stanzas of the first song are in the proportion 1:2; those

EXAMPLE 6.3.
Strophic structures. Numerals in parentheses indicate the
number of syllables in each line. Lower-case letters signify
feminine rhymes; upper-case letters, masculine ones.

a. L'Affilard's menuet song (app. ex. 3)

(10) —————— a	Stanza 1 and Reprise 1
(10) —————— A	

1:2 proportion

(10) —————— a	
(10) —————— A	Stanza 2 and Reprise 2
(10) —————— a	
(10) —————— A	

b. Lully's gavotte song (app. ex. 2)

(7) ———— a	
(7) ———— A	Stanza 1 and Reprise 1
(7) ———— a	
(7) ———— A	

2:3 proportion

(7) ———— b	
(7) ———— B	
(7) ———— b	Stanza 2 and Reprise 2
(7) ———— B	
(7) ———— b	
(7) ———— B	

c. Lully's menuet song (app. ex. 1)

(3) — a	
(4) —— a	Stanza 1 and Reprise 1
(3) — a	
(4) —— A	

2:3 proportion

(3) — b	
(3) — b	
(9) —————— A	Stanza 2 and Reprise 2
(3) — b	
(4) —— b	
(10) —————— A	

d. Lully's menuet song (app. ex. 1) with short lines paired

(7) — a — a	Stanza 1 and Reprise 1
(7) — a — A	

1:2 proportion

(6) — b — b	
(9) —————— A	Stanza 2 and Reprise 2
(7) — b — b	
(10) —————— A	

EXAMPLE 6.3.
Continued   e. Lully's (gigue) song (app. ex. 4)

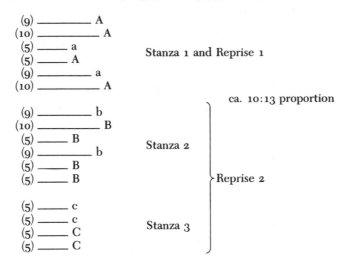

of the second, 2:3. The stanzas of the third song have the proportion 2:3 in terms of the number of lines, but 1:2 if each pair of short lines is joined to make a long line, as in example 6.3d.

The lyrics of the last three songs exhibit a great deal of exuberant irregularity in their structures. The pleasure-loving gigue text (ex. 6.3e) mixes long lines of nine and ten syllables with short ones of five—until the final stanza, which is repeated as the conclusion of the song. In the triumphant bourrée (ex. 6.3f) not only are the line lengths varied, but the reprises and stanzas do not match; and the incomplete sixth line is repeated and then finished as the seventh line. The structure of the chaconne text (ex. 6.3g), a call to love, is quite irrational until the final contrasting couplet, and even there each of the four-measure lines overlaps its bass progression by one note. In short, all strophic structures of Lully's songs in the Appendix follow the principle that the greater the irregularity the more intense the passion.

The strophic structures in these six songs are not exhaustive, and no single form is characteristic of a given dance type. Yet, even without words or breath marks, instrumentalists can often deduce most of the line lengths and a possible strophic structure by examining the musical rhymes, the masculine and feminine endings, and the musical reposes (discussed in chap. 7).

Lullian dance lyrics exhibit an endless variety of rhythmic subjects, textual cells, and strophic structures. Some are standard, while others represent expressive departures. The following points summarize the standard rhythms and structures of the dance songs of the French Baroque.

1. Most dance lines are set to two measures of four pulses each, or to four measures of three pulses each.

2. Most measures have the same number of syllables as pulses, though the syllables may be set to a variety of note values.

3. The principal stresses of most hemistiches and short lines fall on downbeats.

4. The musical rhyme that identifies the first rhythmic subject in a dance piece is likely to begin the next one or to announce the start of each musical period or reprise.

5. Textual cells tend to finish on a strong beat of the music, yet diversity is the rule rather than the exception.

6. All dance songs exhibit some regularity in their line lengths and rhyme schemes.

7

Rhetorical Proportions

> Airs in a way ought to imitate orations, in or-
> der to have members, parts and periods, and
> make use of all manner of figures and harmonic
> passages, as the orator does, so that the art of
> composing airs and writing counterpoint will
> not be second to rhetoric.[1]
>
> —Marin Mersenne (1636, IIb, p. 365)

Rhetoric is the art of oratory and, by extension, the art of speaking or writing effectively. Many of today's principles of rhetoric were formulated by the ancient Greeks and Romans and were practiced by preachers and lawyers of the seventeenth and eighteenth centuries. Among other rhetorical devices, an orator employs members (the clauses of oratory), periods (its sentences), and parts (the structural units that include one or more periods). On the highest level of organization, the parts are joined to form the whole speech.

During the *grand siècle*, rhetorical proportions were applied to the composition of poetry, music, and the dance. As a result, each dance song, dance piece, and dance choreography has the proportions of a miniature but complete speech. Patricia Ranum was the first to point this out (personal communication). More recently she has compared a seventeenth-century rhetorical description of a sarabande with the rhetorical parts in several sarabande songs of the Baroque era (1986).

Many writers of the seventeenth and eighteenth centuries discussed the rhetorical proportions of speech, poetry, and music. In 1668 Michel de Pure recognized there were rhetorical parts in the dance but was not specific about them. In the same year Bernard Lamy described the rhetorical structure of poetry; in 1675, that of oratory. In 1702 the harpsichordist Michel de Saint-Lambert and in 1739 the German organist, harpsichordist, singer, and conductor Johann Mattheson compared the proportions of oratory with those of music. Lamy, Saint-Lambert, and Mattheson agreed on all essential points. Saint-Lambert likened the whole of a musical piece to the whole of an oration and then showed the relationships between smaller units (1702, p. 14). His oratorical units correspond to those of Lamy and Mattheson, except that the latter related a whole menuet to only a paragraph rather than to an entire speech (1739, II, 13, para. 83). This difference is minor, since Mattheson's proportions are the same as those of Lamy and Saint-Lambert.

The most important structural unit in classical rhetoric and also in French Baroque dance music is the sentence, complete thought, or period. Two or more members make up each period of a dance piece; one or more periods make up the large rhetorical parts; usually three to five parts make up the complete composition. At the same time, the whole piece can be viewed as a large period of three to five members, each itself an ordinary period. The relative finality of the musical cadences within the piece determines the organization of musical members into musical periods and parts, and of musical periods and parts into musical reprises and whole dances.

For the purpose of this discussion, we divide the rhetorical proportions in seventeenth-century dance music into three categories: musical members and periods; rhetorical parts; and sentence structure and overall textual organization of complete lyrics.

MUSICAL MEMBERS AND PERIODS

Musical cadences define the ends of musical members and periods, just as nonfinal and final punctuation marks show the ends of clauses and sentences in written rhetoric and, according to Antoine Furetière's dictionary, in speech (1690, "Cadence"). As evidence that the musical cadences of the *grand siècle* were considered primarily melodic rather than harmonic formulas, we have the statement by the theorist Charles Masson that a vocal melody comes to rest "with the sense of the words" (1697, p. 21). César Pierre Richelet's dictionary adds that musical cadences occur "when the parts come together and end on a note that the ear is expecting to hear, in a way that seems natural [that is, that imitates speech]" (1710e, "Cadence"). Both Masson and Richelet were presumably referring to the cadence at the end of a musical period. Many French composers of the *grand siècle*, Montéclair among them, used the word "cadence" in music only for the conclusion that parallels the end of a sentence, or period (1739, p. 77). Saint-Lambert called the musical period a "complete thought," or "cadence," meaning that the standard musical cadence typically concludes it (1702, p. 14). On the other hand, the composer Marc-Antoine Charpentier said that the various musical cadences imitate the period, question mark, colon, semi-colon, and comma of prose (ca. 1693t, pp. 56–57). In this book, to help identify the members within periods, we consider the musical cadence to be the repose at the end of either a musical member or a period.

The following symbols are used in the examples in this chapter, in Part II, and in the Appendix:

⌐ harmonic repose weaker than a musical cadence
⌐· weak cadence at the end of a musical member
⌐·⌐ strong cadence at the end of a musical period
⌐·⌐ final cadence of a musical reprise
⌐ , ⌐· , ⌐·⌐ , ⌐·⌐ interrupted or extended repose or cadence

Although most reposes in Lullian dance songs are unambiguous, a few may be interpreted differently than shown here.

Most musical periods conclude with what musicians today call a "perfect authentic cadence." For a perfect cadence the melody ascends or descends by a scale step to the tonic note, or "final," of the passage. The final of periods may be on almost any scale step of the key; but the large period that is the whole piece must end on the first degree of the home key. For an authentic cadence, the bass leaps up a fourth or down a fifth to the final. French Baroque writers used the adjectives "final," "perfect," or "complete" for a perfect authentic cadence.

Although almost all musical periods in the dance songs end with such a cadence, a few finish differently. At the end of the first reprise of Lully's gigue song from *Amadis* (app. ex. 4), the bass concludes on the fifth degree and the melody on the seventh, making a "half" cadence. At the close of the initial reprise of Lully's menuet song from *Psyché* (app. ex. 1), the melody ends on the third degree, making an "imperfect authentic" cadence. (The first member of this reprise concludes with the same musical cadence as the second member, except that the bass of the second one is an octave lower. The lowered bass, along with the otherwise exact repetition of the music, is what makes the second cadence sound final.)

The musical cadences of members other than the final one of a period are in some way less final than the last: they give the impression that the passage will continue. Reposes of half-members are too transitory to be considered cadences.

Many musical members and periods of the early seventeenth century are extremely short by later standards. A principal cadence often occurs on every fourth downbeat and a lesser cadence on every second one. In these pieces, a pair of two-measure members—the equivalent of two short lines of lyrics—makes up a four-measure period. Though this period is brief, the finality of its last cadence causes it to be perceived as a complete thought. In example 7.1, a four-measure period is repeated with ornamental divisions of its notes to make a double period.

The rhythms in many members of these early dance pieces are based on traditional rhythmic movements. For instance, example 7.1 begins with a musical member (and rhythmic subject) whose skeleton rhythm is that of a choreobacchius (LSSLL) begun with two upbeat eighth-notes.

The rhythmic shape of the musical periods and double periods is based on the symmetrical, arsic-thetic, and rhetorical relationships exhibited by Arbeau's pavanne (ex. 2.9) and discussed in chapter 2. Paired measures make up members; paired members constitute periods; and paired periods create a double

EXAMPLE 7.1.
Relationships among rhythmic movements, members, and periods. Vallet, allemande "Fortune helas pourquoy," for lute,
1615 (transcription by André Souris, in Nicolas Vallet, *Le secret de muses*, vol. 1, reproduced by permission of Éditions
du Centre National de la Recherche Scientifique).

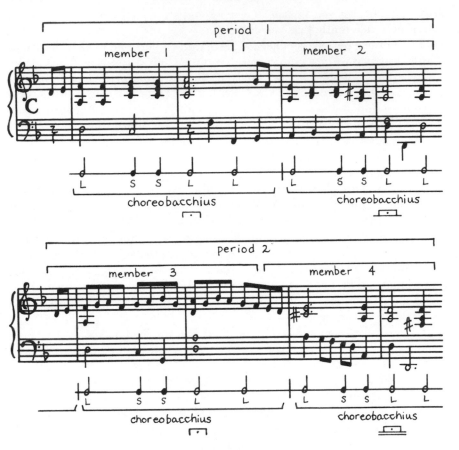

period. Each first measure, member, and period is arsic to the second. Within
each period, the third measure is more dramatic than the others, while the
third member is the rhetorical highpoint of the double period.

Also popular in the early seventeenth century were dance pieces with members of three measures and periods of six. Each measure had the skeleton
rhythm of an LS or SL foot; three feet combined to make a member. For instance, an LSSLLS underlies example 7.2.

In the dance songs of the *grand siècle*, musical periods also exhibited the
symmetrical, arsic-thetic, and dramatic structures of early dance songs. But
their musical members were more closely related to the lines of lyrics. Most
musical members were set to a rather long line or to a pair of short ones. This

EXAMPLE 7.2.
Three-measure members. L. Couperin, "Menuet de Poitou,"
for harpsichord, 1660?

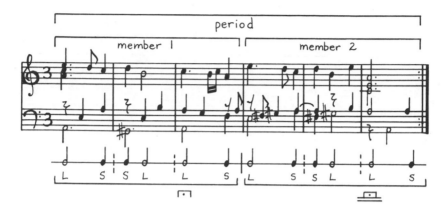

means that perfect authentic cadences occurred less frequently than in earlier dance songs and pieces, and that the repose at the end of a short line of lyrics might be so weak that a second line was needed to make a musical member.

In Lully's menuet song from *Psyché* (app. ex. 1), for instance, the musical repose at the end of the initial three-syllable line is far too weak to be considered a musical cadence. As a result, the first musical member finishes with the imperfect authentic cadence at the end of the second short line; together the two lines take the place of a seven-syllable line set to a four-measure member. Two of these members are needed for a musical period. On the other hand, each of the longer lines that end the second and third periods of this song covers four measures and concludes with a perfect authentic cadence; each long line combines with the two previous short ones to make a period.

The musical reposes at the ends of five- and six-syllable lines are not always conclusive enough to finish a musical member. A repose that is barely recognizable as a cadence ends the initial, six-syllable line of Lully's bourrée song from *Bellérophon* (app. ex. 5). The reposes that conclude the six-syllable lines of his chaconne song (app. ex. 6) are not at all cadential; the music flows right through them. In the second contrasting couplet of the chaconne song, each six-syllable line joins with the five-syllable one that follows, making the equivalent of an eleven-syllable line that lags one syllable behind the four-measure bass progression.

Musical members in dance pieces of the late Baroque, like the rhythmic subjects of the same era, usually cover four measures in simple-duple or simple-triple meter, or two measures in compound-duple meter. But some four-measure members in duple-meter dances are still composed of a pair of two-measure rhythmic subjects (ex. 7.3).

Five-measure members prevail in a few triple-meter dances. In the pieces we examined, these oddly proportioned members are set to the notes of two rhyth-

EXAMPLE 7.3.
Eight-measure period consisting of two four-measure members. Boismortier, rigaudon for flute and bass, op. 35/2, 1731.

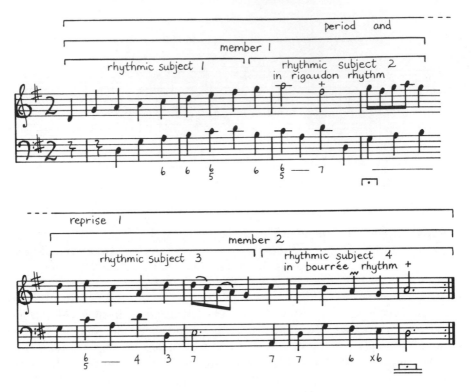

mic subjects, the first having three measures and the second, two (ex. 7.4). (For the scansion of a song with five-measure members, see ex. 28.5.)

As late as the 1730s, some older dance types began with, or at least hinted at, four-measure periods composed of two-measure members and rhythmic subjects. For instance, the bourrée in example 7.5, from the same suite as the rigaudon in example 7.3, begins and ends with four-measure periods whose interior cadences are however extremely weak. The second reprise starts with an eight-measure period made up of four two-measure members.

Even the eight-measure periods of French dance songs and pieces are far shorter than many sentences, or "periods," in the literature of the day, which often—like many quotations cited in this book—fill a half page or more. The relatively shorter musical periods of dance pieces suggest a light nature and at the same time make the overall proportions of the piece easy to identify.

Because the Greek word for "period" means "circuit," a classical period consisted of two to four equal members united into a single sentence. Between these equally balanced periods, it was considered good for the discourse to flow with more freedom, because "an overly exact regularity of the intervals between breaths could become boring" (Lamy, 1701e, pp. 240–241).

EXAMPLE 7.4.
Menuet with five-measure members. Lully, menuet "Troisième
air pour les pastres," from *Alceste*, 1674.

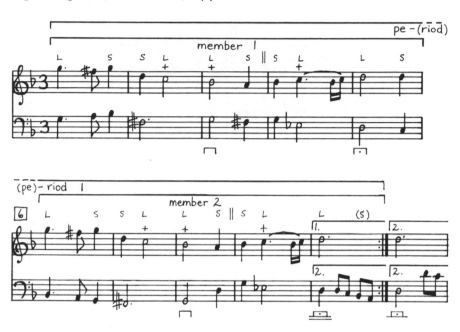

Many musical periods in dance songs are quite classical—that is, regular—in their proportions. Others are not. For instance, each ten-syllable line in L'Affilard's menuet song (app. ex. 3) is set to a four-measure musical member, and each sequence of two members makes an eight-measure musical period. Lully's menuet and gavotte songs (app. exx. 1 and 2) also have simple, or classical, relationships between their musical members and periods. In contrast, the relationships of members to periods in the other three dance songs in the Appendix are less regular and therefore more passionate. Not only are the lines of unequal length but also an extended member in the second reprise or in the first contrasting couplet upsets the simple proportions that characterize the other pieces.

A few musical periods have three or occasionally four members. Lully's gigue song (app. ex. 4) begins with a period of three members; the second reprise in example 7.5 starts with a period of four two-measure members; and the second reprise of Lully's Spanish menuet (ex. 4.12) has a period of four members of four measures each.

An orator uses pronunciation both to separate and to unite the two to four equal members of a period. The speaker's voice so to speak "rolls" (*rouler*) in uttering the period and, in so doing, "makes a sort of circuit that encloses all the members" (Lamy, 1701e, p. 242). The voice reposes briefly at the end of each member and stops more or less completely only at the end of the complete period. Each member is spoken with a rise and fall of the voice, that is, the

EXAMPLE 7.5.
Two-measure members. Boismortier, bourrée for flute and
bass, op. 35/2, 1731.

EXAMPLE 7.5.
Continued

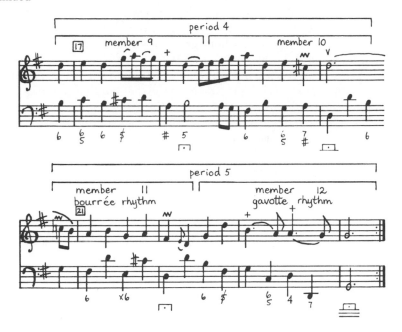

voice rises to the caesura of each long line and falls to the rhyme. Each member but the last is given the same amount of repose.

RHETORICAL PARTS

On a still higher level of organization, pieces of oratory, poetry, music, and dance are divided into "parts" in accordance with classical principles. The division is needed to help the listener remember the various points made in a long speech: "It is difficult for the memory to retain the various things and the infinite number of parts in a long harangue, if it is not relieved by something . . . that arrests them and causes them to be retained"[2] (De Pure, 1668, p. 230).

Saint-Lambert likened the musical reprise to the rhetorical "part" (1702, p. 14). Although Baroque writers called today's binary form "two-part form," rhetoricians from ancient to modern times have said that a speech has three basic parts: a beginning, a middle, and an end. A preacher or a lawyer introduces the subject at the start of an oration, argues the case in the middle, and sums up at the end. Together the three parts make a large period, or full circle, that expresses the orator's complete hypothesis.

Lamy called the three rhetorical parts of a poetic action the "proposition," "intrigue," and "denouement" (1668, pp. 143–51). Because dance songs are set to poetic lines, they may also be expected to have these three parts.

Thus the first reprise of Lully's menuet song from *Psyché* (app. ex. 1), with words by the poet Corneille, presents the proposition: "Is it wise not to fall in love when one is young?" Questions like this are the commonest rhetorical figures (Lamy, 1701e, p. 96). Repetition, as of the phrase "Is one wise," is another popular rhetorical device. Here, for emphasis, both music and lyrics are repeated exactly. Corneille's initial period fits Lamy's description of a proposition in a poetic action, namely, that the poet states the proposition in a "clear yet obscure" way, so that the reader both grasps the theme of the action and becomes curious about it (Lamy, 1668, p. 143).

The first period of the second reprise of this song represents the intrigue: "Let's hurry and enjoy today's pleasures." That the middle section of a poetic action is presented suddenly is borne out by Corneille's "unceasing hurry" and Lully's sudden leaps and two quick notes. The intrigue piques the reader's curiosity by delaying the poet's conclusion, which the reader has been eagerly awaiting (Lamy, 1668, p. 144).

The final period of this song represents its denouement, that point near the end of a poetic action where "things come out as the reader had hoped" (p. 144). Lully's strong final cadence and Corneille's conclusion satisfy the listener: "Youth has the sense to enjoy love's charms."

Many seventeenth- and eighteenth-century writers discussed a variety of other, smaller parts in orations. For instance, the proposition is often preceded or replaced by one or two parts. In the "exordium," the orator rises and addresses the listeners, alluding subtly to the coming theme. The "narration" adds a few details or tells a story, before the main proposition fully states the theme.

In fact, the proposition of this particular menuet song can be divided into three very small parts. The introductory "Is one wise" is a tiny exordium, which uses the word "wise" both to give the theme and to arouse curiosity. "In one's youth" adds the details of a narration. Only thereafter is the proposition proper revealed: "Is one wise not to love?"

Often the proposition has only two parts. The first reprise of one of Lully's gavotte songs from *Atys* (app. ex. 2) consists of an opening exordium ("Beauty, most severe, take pity on a long-suffering lover") and a narration ("Who is finally rewarded for his perseverence"). Together this exordium and narration present the main theme, or proposition.

The central section of an oration, in which the case is argued, may also be broken down into several parts, the most usual being the "confirmation" and the "confutation." In the confirmation the orator tries to convince the audience with various proofs. Often the confirmation of dance songs has a certain sweet softness, as in Lully's gavotte: "All is sweet and nothing is too costly for the heart one wishes to touch." In the confutation the orator aggressively counters all opposing arguments; here the discourse reaches its highest emotional peak. In the gavotte under discussion, the determined lover—by searching hard enough—finally forges his own path toward his goal.

The final section of an oration is the "peroration," or winding up, in which the orator restates the main theme. The peroration is equivalent to the denouement of the poetic actions mentioned above. In the peroration of Lully's gavotte song, the gratifying results of the lover's perseverence are proclaimed: "Water that falls, drop by drop, pierces the hardest rock."

Most dance songs have three, four, or five rhetorical parts, each a single musical period. In three-part forms, the intensity of feeling is relatively low in the proposition, mounts to its highest point in the intrigue, and wanes in the denouement. In four-part forms, it is low in the exordium, increases in the narration, reaches its climax in the confirmation, and falls away in the denouement or peroration. Five-part forms are of two kinds. In the first, the intensity rises during the narration and confirmation and peaks in the fourth part, the confutation. In the second kind, the confutation precedes the confirmation, so that emotion is highest in the third part.

For the songs in the Appendix that divide into three musical parts, we use Lamy's names for the parts in a poetic action: proposition, intrigue, and denouement. For those that divide into five parts, we employ his terms for oratory: exordium, narration, confirmation, confutation, and peroration. Ranum (1986) uses the terms exordium, narration, confirmation, and peroration for certain sarabande songs she analyzes to be in four parts. However a piece is analyzed, clearly the exordium and the narration in four- or five-part forms are the proposition of a three-part form, and the confirmation and confutation make up an intrigue; the peroration is of course the same as a denouement. Thus all dance songs have essentially three main parts, and their intensity mounts in the middle one and ebbs in the last. Many dance pieces without words also divide into the basic three, four, or five parts. For instance, the five couplets of Vallet's lute arrangement of "La chaconna" (ex. 3.8) exhibit characteristics of an exordium, narration, confutation, confirmation, and peroration. At the same time, couplets 1 and 2 join into a proposition that states the chaconne theme; couplets 3 and 4 add the slightly more dramatic events of an intrigue; and couplet 5, as a denouement, sums up.

SENTENCE STRUCTURE OF LYRICS AND OVERALL TEXTUAL ORGANIZATION

Although the rhetorical parts of French dance music are closely related to the periodic structure, the actual sentences in the lyrics of dance songs do not necessarily match the periods and the rhetorical parts of the music. In fact, the sentence structure is often arbitrary. Although a few sentences are set to musical periods, most are longer and cover two or three periods. Occasionally, a short sentence is set to a musical member.

Example 7.6 shows how the sentences in the six dance songs of the Appendix relate to the musical periods and reprises. Each sentence has been laid out as a single paragraph, with lower-case letters starting every line but the first—except where two sentences are included in a single musical period (exx. 7.6d and e). A Roman numeral in parentheses indicates the musical cadence at the end of a musical period. Solid horizontal lines divide the text into poetic stanzas and musical reprises. The dotted line in example 7.6e identifies the end of the first musical reprise, which in this unusual case does not correspond to the end of the poetic stanza.

Example 7.6.
Sentence structure and textual organization.

a. Lully's menuet (app. ex. 1)

Is one wise in one's youth, is one wise not to love? (I)

Let's not cease to hasten to taste the pleasures here on earth: (V) the wisdom of youth is to know how to enjoy [love's] charms. (I)

b. Lully's gavotte song (app. ex. 2)

Beauty, most severe, take pity on a long torment, (I)
and the lover who perseveres becomes a happy lover. (I)

All is sweet and nothing is too costly for a heart one wants to touch, (VI) the wave makes itself a route, when exerting to search one out. (ii)

Water that falls drop by drop, pierces the hardest rock. (I)

c. L'Affilard's menuet song (app. ex. 3)

To avenge myself on ungrateful Climene, Bacchus is ready to fill all my wishes: (V)

---

cruel Cupid, I am tired of your chain, the God of wine is going to break all my bonds; (V) he makes his juice flow into a full cup, I'll drink so much that I'll extinguish my fires. (i)

d. Lully's gigue song (app. ex. 4)

Pleasures follow us from now on(,) we're going toward our satisfied desires. Let's live without fears, let's all live in peace. (III)

Come back and revive all your charms(;) innocent games, come back forever. (V)

It is time that the dawn redden the sky (and) cede to the sun who walks in its steps(;) all shines on this earth(.) (v)

It is time that everyone awake; love does not sleep, all feel its charms(.) (III)

The amiable Zephire for Flore sighs(,) on such a fine day all talk of Love. (i)

e. Lully's bourrée song (app. ex. 5)

Let's show our happiness. Let's speak no more of sorrow: (V)

----

let's renounce sadness, our troubles are coming to an end. (IV)

When Heaven is favorable to our wishes, let's banish the ennui(,) let's banish the ennui that presses us, we will all be happy. (I)

f. Lully's chaconne song (app. ex. 6)

Let's follow, let's follow love(,) let's let it inflame us. (I)

Ah! Ah! Ah! how sweet it is to love! (I)

When love commands us, let's suffer its rigors, let's cherish its languors; (V) it exempts no one from its victorious arrows, (ii) what peril astonishes us? Let's let tremble the weak hearts. (I)

Two lovers can pretend when they are agreed, (vi) the more that love finds to fear, the more effort it requires; (V) when one has to constrain it [the love] is more strong. (I)

The relationship of sentences and text to musical members and periods varies from song to song and even from stanza to stanza. In example 7.6, only the lyrics of L'Affilard's menuet song (ex. 7.6c) consist of one long sentence. The lyrics of the other songs also express a single complete thought, but for emphasis their clauses have been cast as short sentences. The sentences, like musical periods, then serve as members of the large period that makes up the complete lyrics.

The menuet song from *Psyché* (ex. 7.6a) has two sentences, one for each poetic stanza and musical reprise. The first sentence covers one musical period; the second, two. Together the sentences make an arsic-thetic pair that work together as a large period, or complete thought. The first sentence poses a question; the second answers it. In the late eighteenth century, this question-answer relationship came to be called the "antecedent and consequent" of a musical period.

In the gavotte song from *Atys* (ex. 7.6b), the first two sentences each include two musical periods; the third, only one. The text forms one large period if the punctuation marks ending the first two sentences are regarded as colons.

In the single long sentence of L'Affilard's menuet song (ex. 7.6c), the first independent clause covers the first period and reprise of the music. The second, which actually includes several minor independent clauses, is set to the two musical periods of the second reprise.

Because many lines of the gigue song from *Amadis* (ex. 7.6d) have no punctuation, we have guessed at the sentence structure. We surmise that this song has six sentences, with the last one repeated (and therefore not given in the example). The first two sentences are set to a three-member musical period, the first sentence taking up the first two members. Each of the other four sentences covers a musical period. The text embraces a large period if the punctuation marks at the ends of sentences within musical periods are viewed as commas; those at the ends of musical periods, as semicolons; that at the end of the first reprise, as a colon.

In the bourrée song from *Bellérophon* (ex. 7.6e), the first sentence is set to a musical member; the second includes the second member of the first musical period and both members of the second. Quite eccentrically, the first reprise ends in the middle of this second sentence. The third sentence and the second reprise make up only one musical period. The complete text forms a large period if the punctuation marks following its four sentences are considered respectively a comma, semicolon, colon, and period.

The chaconne song from *Cadmus* (ex. 7.6f) is in rondeau form and has four dissimilar couplets—two refrain couplets and two contrasting ones. Each refrain couplet is composed of a rather short sentence, set to a musical member and repeated. Each contrasting couplet consists of a single long sentence, set to three unlike musical members and not repeated. The text becomes one large period with the same changes as noted for the gigue song above, except that all couplets but the last must be finished with a colon.

Poetic lines thus relate to musical members, and musical periods relate to the rhetorical parts of the music and to the texts of particular dance songs. *La belle danse*, the elegant style of dancing practiced at the court of Louis XIV, drew on the dance rhythms of the early Baroque but was strongly influenced by the dance poetry and rhetorical proportions of the *grand siècle*.

8

Step-units of la belle danse

Plato teaches us that dancing is not only an
honest recreation but that it is a type of study
and practice [that is] absolutely necessary for
regulating our [physical] movements. This is
indeed what gives a noble and free air to all
actions, and a certain grace that is rarely seen
among those who have not studied dancing.
Orators' gestures, [decorum at] public ceremonies, and [soldiers]' manual of arms call for
this practice in order to acquire that supple-
ness of body, that skill of movement, that elo-
quent appearance that Cicero and Quintillian
so strongly recommend.[1]

—Claude Ménestrier (1682, pp. 33–34)

Most sources on the rhythms of the French dance steps were written either
long before Lully's arrival at court or some years after his death. Unfortunately,
the lengthy description by François de Lauze (1623) of the smooth and graceful
steps he knew includes neither timings nor music; and Mersenne's (1636) scanty
explanation of the steps of his day contains music but no timings. Of the dance
steps practiced to Lully's music during his lifetime, only the information from
dictionaries remains. Dance entries in Antoine Furetière's posthumous dictionary of 1690 seem to have been written during the early years of the *grand siécle*
or slightly before.

The notation for the choreographies of the early eighteenth century was
worked out during the late seventeenth century, probably by Lully's choreographer Pierre de Beauchamp in collaboration with other dancing masters of the
Royal Academy of Dance. The system was first published in 1700 by an otherwise undistinguished dancing master, Raoul-Auger Feuillet, in a book called

Chorégraphie (Dance Writing; later the term "choreography" came to mean dance composition). Feuillet's book includes symbols for the steps, movements, and floor patterns used in ballroom dancing and for many of those used chiefly in the theater.

With the choreographic symbols, dancing masters could record their creations on paper and make them available in printed or manuscript form. From 1700 to 1722, Feuillet and his French successors published annual *recueils* (collections) of choreographies, which quickly made their way to other European courts. These could be practiced with a dancing master and danced at balls. Most *recueils* contained only two or three choreographies, some composed for special occasions. The character dances most often included were bourrées, passepieds, and two of the most popular new dances at court, rigaudons and forlanes. Some contredanses were also included. By 1700, new choreographies for the menuet and other earlier dances were rare. Many of the dances in the *recueils* were "figured," that is, steps and floor patterns from theatrical dancing were added to the customary ballroom steps.

Choreographies to be danced at a ball had to be practiced in advance and their complicated movements learned as thoroughly as for performing in the theater. The *belle danse* style was demanding both physically and mentally. Most individual steps were taken on the ball of the foot, with a stiff knee and an elegant, lifted carriage. A carefully stylized "bend and rise," called a *mouvement*, began most step-units. Springing steps, *pirouettes*, delayed weight changes, and other embellishments required considerable technical prowess; and the endlessly changing sequence of step-units and floor patterns challenged the memory of the dancers. In fact, *la belle danse* was a first-rate aerobic and mnemonic exercise, and the only invigorating exercise allowed women. Mastery of its techniques promoted good health, courtly manners, beautiful gestures, and an upright and stylish posture that gave young courtiers the self-confidence and bearing they needed to succeed at court.

Though dance writers of the seventeenth century provided too little information for modern scholars to trace exactly the development of the dance steps or their rhythms, a relationship can be observed between many step-units of *la belle danse* and their predecessors. The sequences of individual steps in Feuillet's step-units recall certain ones of Arbeau, and the timings of the individual steps in many step-units recall Mersenne's rhythmic movements. Above all, Crousaz's five "real and natural elements of beauty"—uniformity, variety, regularity, order, and proportion—can be seen in every aspect of *la belle danse*. Pierre Rameau advised, "Especially in Ball-room dances, . . . the steps should be executed with every regard for uniformity and proportion" (1725bt, p. 99).

Several other factors discussed in previous chapters are apparent in the step-units of *la belle danse*. The various meters are clearly defined by the step rhythms; the bend of the *mouvement* is arsic to the rise; and the *mouvement* that starts almost every musical measure—or every pair of measures in menuets and passepieds—carries the dancer smoothly onward, from one measure to the next, as do the rhythmic subjects of dance lyrics.

The step-units of *la belle danse* exhibit two principal rhythms: the timing of the individual steps and the timing of the *mouvements*. This chapter is concerned mainly with the rhythms of the step-units rather than with their execution in the appropriately elegant style. As Michel de Pure put it, a good teacher and good examples are needed to master this art, and even then many difficulties are encountered:

> *La belle danse* is a certain finesse in the movement, in the carriage, in the step, and in the whole person, that cannot be expressed or taught by words. Good eyes, good examples, and good teachers are necessary; and sometimes even with all these aids, one has difficulty in the conception, and even more in the execution.[2] (1668, pp. 180–81)

Despite de Pure's mistrust of written instructions, we refer readers to the 1700a and 1704 publications of Feuillet, the two books of 1725 by Rameau, and two modern treatises, *Dance of Court & Theater: The French Noble Style of 1690–1725* by Wendy Hilton and *Louis Pécour's 1700 "Recueil de danses"* by Anne Witherell. In this chapter and the next, we follow the practice of Hilton and Witherell in using modern spellings for step-units and for the titles of choreographies. The French words *pas* (step), *temps* (count), and *contretemps* (hop) can be either singular or plural. Thus a term like *pas de bourrée* may mean either "step" or "steps of [the] bourrée."

TIMING OF INDIVIDUAL STEPS

Crousaz's first and second qualities of beauty—uniformity and variety—are manifested in the arrangement and ornamentation of individual steps within the step-units of *la belle danse*. A step that typifies a particular character dance gives uniformity to a choreography, whereas other steps give diversity.

For instance, the large majority of step-units in menuet and passepied choreographies of the early eighteenth century are *pas de menuet* (menuet steps). Yet the number of *mouvements* in these step-units tends to vary, and a succession of *pas de menuet* is usually interrupted with one or two *contretemps de menuet* (menuet hops), *pas de menuet en fleuret* (see chap. 28), or other step-units.

Another dance having its own step-unit is the bourrée. *Pas de bourrée* make up about half the step-units in bourrée choreographies. Other step-units often used are *contretemps de gavotte* (gavotte hops), *contretemps de chaconne* (chaconne hops: one version of gavotte hops danced to the side), *temps de courante* (courante counts), *coupés* ("cut" steps), *jettés* (leaps), *pas de sissonne* (sissonne steps, named for the Count de Sissonne), *glissades* (gliding steps), and *contretemps ballonnés* ("ballooned" hops that cause the dancer's costume to spread out).

A third dance with characteristic steps is the courante. Courante choreographies normally begin with a *temps de courante* (courante count) and continue with a mixture of *demi-jettés* (small leaps) and *coupés* ("cut" steps). The combined *demi-jetté* and *coupé* is called a *pas de courante*, but other arrangements of these two step-units are also common in this dance. Most courante choreographies employ a *temps de courante* at some cadences.

The most characteristic step-units for each dance are given in the *belle danse* sections of Part II. But many dances—such as sarabandes, forlanes, and gigues—have no characteristic step-unit and employ a variety of *pas de bourrée*, *temps de courante*, *coupés*, *jettés*, and so forth. Francine Lancelot claims that, on the basis of step-units alone, a rigaudon choreography is indistinguishable from that of a forlane (1971, pp. 42–43). In these dances, uniformity is achieved in other ways.

The weighted and weightless steps in the choreographies of *la belle danse* are timed similarly to those of Renaissance simples and doubles. The relationships are shown in examples 8.1, 8.2, and 8.3. The *belle danse* timings come from Feuillet's *Chorégraphie*, from the preface to his 1704 collection of Louis Pécour's choreographies, and from Rameau's *Abbregé* of 1725.

In these examples, as throughout this book, R stands for a weighted step onto the right foot and (r) for a weightless step performed with the right; (R) indicates that the weight remains on the standing (right) foot and that the expected weight change is delayed. Similarly for L, (l), and (L). A verbal instruction such as "rise," "small leap," "hop," or "jump" indicates an action that embellishes the individual step. T, which accompanies a jump, shows a landing on both feet.

Example 8.1 relates the timing and footwork of nine of Feuillet's step-units in simple-duple meter to Arbeau's closed simple. The *coupé* with a single weight change is timed exactly like the closed simple; that is, the weighted step is taken on the first count and some kind of ornamentation—perhaps a small kick or a circling of the foot in the air—is performed by the free foot on the second count. The *temps de courante* is similar, but the "rise" of the *mouvement* and the forward slide of the stepping foot fill the whole first count and postpone the

EXAMPLE 8.1.
Belle danse timings that recall Arbeau's closed simple.

	♩		♩
closed simple	L		(r)
coupé with one weight change	L		(r)
temps de courante	(R)		L
	rise		
contretemps balonné	(R)		L
	hop		leap
pas de bourrée, or *fleuret*	L	R	L
coupé with two weight changes	L		R
pair of *jettés*	L		R
	leap		leap
pas de sisonne	T		R
	jump		leap
contretemps de gavotte or	(R)	L	R
contretemps de chaconne	hop		

EXAMPLE 8.2.
Belle danse timings that recall the open double of the
Renaissance.

	♩	♩	♩
open double	R	L	R
pas de courante	R	L	R
	small		
	leap		
pas de menuet	R	L R	L

weight change until the second. In the *contretemps balonné*, a hop on the standing foot delays the weighted step until the second count, and the weighted step—when taken—is executed with a leap. The *pas de bourrée*, or *fleuret*, is timed like the Renaissance *fleuret*. Its three weighted steps divide the single weighted step of the closed simple.

The *coupé* with two weight changes recalls the *coupé* with one weight change, except that the step on the second count is weighted instead of weightless. The timings of several other step-units resemble that of this kind of *coupé*; for instance, a pair of *jettés*, the *pas de sissonne*, and the *contretemps de gavotte* or *de chaconne*. The first weighted step of either *contretemps* is, however, ornamented with a hop, so that the change of weight is delayed until the second pulse of the measure.

To appreciate the relationship between Arbeau's and later timings, and to gain some acquaintance with *belle danse* step-units, readers should perform the step-units in example 8.1 to the time of two half notes. Each step-unit should be executed first on the left foot and then on the right, in order to practice a number of repetitions of a step-unit. In preparation for a step onto the left foot, the dancer's weight is on the right foot, and vice versa.

Example 8.2 relates two *belle danse* step-units to the open double of the Renaissance. Both are used exclusively in triple-meter dances. The weighted steps of the *pas de courante* recall the open double, except that the first step is taken with a small, gentle leap. (The second step is taken with a *mouvement*, to be discussed shortly.) The *pas de menuet* is also similar, except that its second weighted step is divided into two weighted steps.

Example 8.3 relates a single *belle danse* step-unit, a sequence of three step-units, and a pair of step-units to Arbeau's closed double. All four are used only in duple-meter dances. The *pas de gavotte* is an embellishment of the closed double. A hop ornaments and delays the second weight change, and a jump onto both feet replaces the final, weightless step. The group of three *glissades* forms a division of the closed double. Each *glissade* is a *coupé* with two weight changes, danced to the side in such a way that the ball of the foot glides along the floor in taking each second weighted step (Rameau, 1725bt, p. 84). For this group of step-units, each of the first two weighted steps of the double is divided into a *glissade*. The resulting four weighted steps are thus taken to quarter notes, that is, twice as quickly as the two weighted steps in the closed double.

EXAMPLE 8.3.
Belle danse timings that recall Arbeau's closed double.

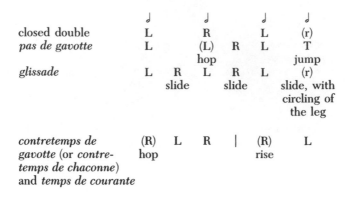

EXAMPLE 8.4.
Belle danse step-units timed to rhythmic movements.

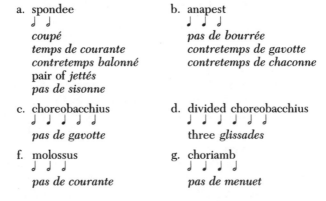

The third of the three *glissades* is at normal tempo, and its two steps are taken to half notes. The very last step corresponds to the weightless step of the closed double and may be performed as a simple weighted step or be ornamented with a *ronde de jambe*, a circling in the air of the free foot as the free leg is rotated outward from the hip. Certain pairs of step-units, such as the *contretemps de gavotte* or *de chaconne* and the *temps de courante*, are also timed like a division of the closed double.

The timings of the individual steps of *la belle danse* also recall Mersenne's rhythmic movements. In duple meter, for instance, the *coupé* and other step-units timed like it move to a spondee (LL); the *pas de bourrée*, *contretemps de gavotte*, and *contretemps de chaconne* move to an anapest (SSL); the *pas de gavotte* moves to a choreobacchius (LSSLL); and the three *glissades* move to a division (SSSSLL) of a choreobacchius (ex. 8.4a, b, c, and d). In one measure of compound-duple meter or in two of simple-triple meter, the *pas de courante* moves to a molossus (LLL) and the *pas de menuet* to a choriamb (LSSL) (ex. 8.4f and g). The timings of the individual steps in step-units look back to the "long-short" rhythms of the past but also reflect the new interest in musical meter.

FITTING THE INDIVIDUAL STEPS OF STEP-UNITS TO MUSICAL METERS

Like the syllables of Lullian dance songs, many individual steps of *belle danse* choreographies are set to pulse notes of the music, especially in simple-triple meter. Some sarabande choreographies, for instance, are set to almost continuous *pas de bourrée*, step-units that in triple meter have a weighted step on each pulse of the measure. By reducing the number of "longs" in a measure, this practice masks the relationships to Arbeau's step rhythms and to Mersenne's rhythmic movements. It also makes the musical downbeat essential for organizing individual steps into step-units.

The emphasis on musical meter in the seventeenth century made the individual steps of step-units fit squarely within one or sometimes two measures of music. In the process, many step-units of duple-meter dances—such as the *pas de bourrée*—were adjusted to fit dances in simple-triple or compound-duple meter. Example 8.5 shows how the individual steps of step-units were fitted within the bar lines of musical measures. Two or three steps in duple-meter step-units were always timed in the same way, but two individual steps in triple-meter units allowed some variety. According to Feuillet's "Examples for measures in duple and triple meter" (1704, preface), the two steps of a *coupé* or *temps de courante* in triple meter were set to an LS rhythm, the L being a half note and the S a quarter note. But his example in "On the measure or cadence" (1700a) shows an SL rhythm for one of the two *coupés* included. All three *temps de courante* in that example have the more usual LS rhythm.

Individual steps do however cross musical bar lines in three of the step-units that characterize specific dances. All three dances are holdovers from earlier times, before the musical measure had become so important. As shown in ex-

EXAMPLE 8.5.
Individual steps fitted within bar lines.

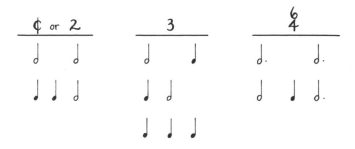

EXAMPLE 8.6.
Step-units whose individual steps cross bar lines. a. *pas de courante*; b. *pas de gavotte*; c. *pas de menuet.*

a. $\frac{3}{2}$ b. ¢ or 2   c. 3

ample 8.6, the *pas de courante* and *pas de gavotte* begin before the bar line, and the *pas de gavotte* and the *pas de menuet* cover the equivalent of two musical measures.

In all step-units, the final individual step serves as the repose, or cadence, of the unit. Furetière stated that a cadence in dancing occurs at the end of each dance measure (1690, "Cadence"), and Richelet called this cadence the "fall of the body's *mouvement*" (1710e, "Cadence"). The fall is the "bend" that initiates the next step-unit.

Most of Feuillet's step-units begin with a bend-rise, or *mouvement*, that emphasizes the musical downbeat. The bend, or *plié* in French, occurs before the first individual step; the rise, or *élevé*, takes place as part of the step.

TIMING OF THE *MOUVEMENTS*

In the quotation at the head of chapter 2, Arbeau mentions flexing the knees and rising onto the toes; but de Lauze was the first to describe this movement in any detail (1623, p. 29). By the late seventeenth century, a *mouvement* at the start of most step-units was a main feature of *la belle danse*. Furetière went so far as to define dancing in terms of the *mouvement*: "To dance is to bend and to rise in cadence, that is, at the beginning of the measure in an air" (1690, "Danser"). Rameau, knowing that *mouvements* make a dance "more pleasing," said they should always be well marked, especially when one is learning them, "whereas, if they be not marked, the steps can hardly be distinguished and the dance appears lifeless and dull" (1725bt, p. 100).

Example 8.7 shows the three stages of a dancer executing a weighted step initiated by a *mouvement*. Many hours of diligent practice were required to achieve a completely smooth and elegant rendition that would give just the right "lift" to the step. Readers can get some feeling for the effect of this elegant *mouvement* by lowering the heel to the ground at the end of a step, bending the knees, and then straightening the knees as they take the next one.

The *mouvement* at the start of almost all step-units of *la belle danse* not only emphasizes the start of the unit and of almost all musical measures, but also carries the dancer across the musical bar line and from one step-unit to the next. In fact, the initial *mouvement* evokes the upbeat start of many rhythmic subjects in dance melodies. Or perhaps the upbeat start of many rhythmic subjects imitated the dancer's *mouvement*.

EXAMPLE 8.7.
Dancer taking a weighted step initiated by a *mouvement.*
Rameau, 1725b, pp. 72–74. Reproduced by arrangement with
Broude Brothers Limited. a. With weight on left foot, bend
knees, holding right foot slightly off the floor. b. Carry right
foot forward, transferring some weight to it. c. Rise onto ball
of right foot; balance.

EXAMPLE 8.8.
Mouvement at the start of step-units.

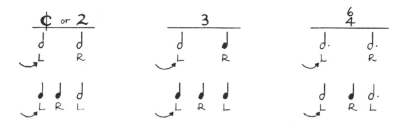

Example 8.8 shows the initial *mouvement* as it relates to the timing of individual steps in the three basic meters. A curved arrow indicates the bend and
rise. It also suggests the arsic-thetic nature of the bend-rise and graphically
conveys the overall lift of the motion. Ironically, the dancer rises from the
mouvement at the same time as a conductor's hand or a violinist's bow drops at
the start of a musical measure. To get a feeling for the effect of the *mouvement*
on the timing of the step-units in the three basic meters, readers should practice a sequence of each of the step-units in example 8.8, beginning with a step-
unit on the left foot and then alternating step-units between the right and
left feet.

Sometimes a second *mouvement* enhances an additional step in the step-unit
and an extra pulse in the musical measure, as shown in example 8.9. The addi-

EXAMPLE 8.9.
Mouvements in the middle of step-units or of musical measures. a. *pas de menuet*; b. *pas de courante*; c. *contretemps balonné*; d. pair of *jettés*; e. *pas de sisonne*; f. *pas de gavotte*; g. *pas de rigaudon*; h. *glissade*.

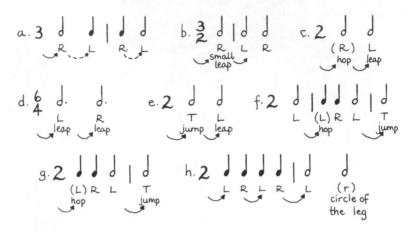

EXAMPLE 8.10.
Comparison of dance and musical measures. From Lully, "La bourrée d'Achille," 1700. a. bourrée; b. menuet.

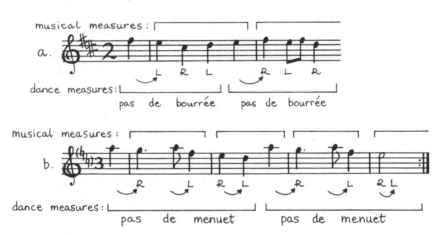

tional *mouvement* gives an extra accent to the measure. The *pas de menuet* (ex. 8.9a) is especially interesting, since one or two additional *mouvements* cause the dance motions to fit $\frac{3}{2}$ meter.

Dance measures that start with an initial *mouvement* begin about one pulse before the musical measure or measures to which the steps are set. Example 8.10 compares the musical and dance measures at the start of the bourrée and the menuet in "La bourrée d'Achille." The music for this choreography comes from the opera *Achille et Polixène*, which Lully was composing when he died. The choreographer was Beauchamp's successor, Louis Pécour. Here, as almost always, the dance measure begins before the musical measure.

SOME BASICS OF FEUILLET NOTATION

The symbols we have been using allow musicians to grasp the timing of *belle danse* steps without having to learn the eighteenth-century notation. However, the basics of Feuillet notation are not difficult, and a knowledge of the system will help readers understand some points in chapter 9.

Example 8.11 shows the Feuillet notation for the two *pas de bourrée* in example 8.10. The first symbols to look for in a choreographic plate are those giving the starting position of the dancer(s). The half moon at the bottom of example 8.11 shows this dancer to be male (an additional and smaller half moon within this one would signify a female dancer). The horizontal line atop the half moon indicates that the dancer is facing the "royal presence," the king's chair at a ball or at any entertainment where the king is present. The "presence" is represented by the top of the page. Two small circles with stems show the position of the dancer's feet at the start of the dance. Here the dancer stands in the so-called fourth position. The small dot beside the symbol for the left foot shows that only the ball of the left foot is on the ground; the dancer's weight is on the right foot. The horseshoe with stem, to the right of the tract, tells the dancer to take his partner's left hand with his own right hand. (At the end of the example,

EXAMPLE 8.11.
Feuillet notation of two dance measures. Pécour, "La bourrée d'Achille," 1700, p. 1, mm. 1–2.

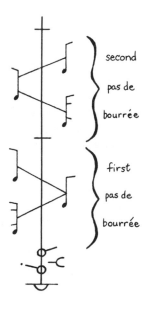

a perpendicular line through the stem of the same symbol tells the dancers to drop hands.)

For other symbols, the Feuillet system of "dance writing" borrows heavily from musical notation. A one-line staff, or "tract," leads from the half-moon symbol to show the dancer's direction of travel. In example 8.11, the dancer moves toward the "presence." Small horizontal lines across the tract signify bar lines at the starts of dance measures. Signs for individual steps resemble musical notes; a beam connects the individual steps of each step-unit.

The various parts of a choreographic "note" show the different features of the step. A black note head to the left of the tract indicates an individual step by the left foot; one to the right shows an individual step by the right. The stem of a note and the flags attached to it show actions of the foot as it takes the step. The stem indicates the path of the moving foot, while the flags show such actions as bends, rises, hops, and slides. In general, the closer a flag is to the note head the earlier is its action. For instance, a small diagonal flag near the note head designates the "bend" of a *mouvement*. A small flag perpendicular to the stem and further from the note head shows a subsequent "rise." The diagonal flag at the top of the stem indicates the position of the foot on the floor after the step has been taken.

RHYTHMIC CHARACTER OF CHOREOGRAPHIC ACTIONS

Besides the names, timings, and basic notation of the commonest step-units of *la belle danse*, the rhythmic character of various choreographic actions is important. One vital factor is the proportion of "high" (springing) to "low" (walking) step-units, which measures the energy of the dancing. For example, a sampling of bourrée choreographies shows that about 25 percent of the individual steps in bourrées are springing steps. But gigues, contredanses, and canaries include an even greater proportion of springing steps. For instance, Feuillet's "Gigue à deux" (1700b), Pécour's "Contredanse" (1700b), and Pécour's "Canary de Madame la Dauphine" (undated) consist of about 33 percent springing steps. Gavottes made up entirely of the *pas de gavotte* are even more energetic, but others are relatively calm. Balon's "Gavotte du Roy" (1716?), which is composed of continuous *pas de gavotte*, has 44 percent springing steps, but his "Gavotte de Seaux [sic]" (1714?), with 25 percent springing steps, resembles a bourrée in this regard.

Sarabande choreographies can be either energetic or calm, as is demonstrated in three different choreographic settings of Lully's "Serenade des Espagnols" from *Ballet des nations* (III): Feuillet's "Sarabande pour homme" (1700b) has 33 percent springing steps; his "Sarabande pour femme" (also 1700b) has 25 percent springing steps; and Pécour's "Sarabande pour une femme" (1704) has only 8 percent springing steps. Of course the ladies were not expected to spring as often or as high as the gentlemen, but Feuillet's sarabande for a lady is far more energetic than Pécour's for a lady, which is set to the same music.

Other dance motions contribute further to the rhythmic character of a choreography. One important indicator is the number of quarter, half, or full turns—the last-named being called *pirouettes*. *Pirouettes* are especially common in the triple-meter dances of Spanish origin—sarabandes, chaconnes, passacailles, and folies. In the sixteenth century, these fast, wild, and licentious dances had probably featured many full turns. In eighteenth-century choreographies, the fiery Spanish temperament is moderated by a slower tempo, but some of the exotic visual effect remains in the large proportion of turns—at least in relation to the much smaller proportion in most eighteenth-century choreographies for other dances.

Turning steps, particularly half or whole turns, cause a dancer's skirt or coat-tails to flare out. With a series of turns the skirt also undulates as it flares. If the turns are executed on a spiral floor pattern, the total effect probably suggests the old Spanish dances. Such an effect is made by the choreography for the fifteenth of the eighteen musical couplets in Pécour's "Chaconne pour une femme" (1704), which is set to the music of Lully's chaconne from *Phaeton*. In this couplet, each of a series of *pas de bourrée* is executed with half a clockwise turn, which enhances the initial *mouvement* of each measure by adding rotation.

Adding springs to turning steps gives further energy and dramatic effect to the turn. In fact, *pirouettes* with leaps and hops occur frequently in the Spanish dances of *belle danse* choreographies. That such turns were associated with chaconnes and passacailles is suggested by the "chaconne or passacaille step"—a complete turn executed by three springing steps—described by the English dancing master Tomlinson (1735, p. 83).

Both the characteristic timing and the characteristic actions of the step-units influence the rhythm of *belle danse* choreographies. The way the step-units are combined into larger units is also important. A step-unit to the right may be followed immediately by one to the left—as occurs in Arbeau's dances. But often the choreography is more varied. Forward units are frequently mixed with units to the side. Traveling units are interrupted with turns or with steps in place. Walking steps are mixed with springing steps; circling figures alternate with straight lines. The goal of the *belle danse* choreographer was to choose and arrange the step-units to achieve a perfect blend of uniformity and variety.

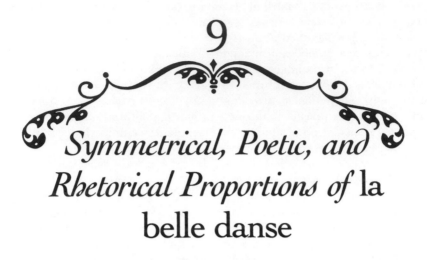

9

Symmetrical, Poetic, and Rhetorical Proportions of la belle danse

Dance is mute poetry, and poetry is spoken dance.

—Plutarch (1572, II, p. 439)

Dancing is a kind of mute rhetoric.[1]

—Thoinot Arbeau (1589t, p. 16)

Although Plutarch and Arbeau published these thoughts some years before the *grand siècle*, French authors continued to refer to dancing as "mute poetry" and "mute rhetoric." For instance, Claude Ménestrier compared ballroom dancing with lyric poetry and likened theatrical dancing, or ballet, to dramatic poetry (1668, p. 53). The ballroom dancing of that day had the symmetrical proportions of pleasing rhetoric; the theatrical dancing had the less regular but more dramatic proportions of persuasive rhetoric.

The "passion" expressed in the ballroom dancing of the *grand siècle* is that of elegant, courtly flirting. With his performance, the dancer persuades the spectators that he is "gallant and worthy to be acclaimed, admired and loved. . . . [He] pleads tacitly with his mistress, who marks the seemliness and grace of his dancing, 'Love me. Desire me'" (Arbeau, 1589t, p. 16).

Belle danse choreographies are usually highly symmetrical, a quality that makes them a pleasure to perform and watch. Most of the choreographies consist of paired step-units, paired pairs of step-units, and often paired floor patterns. Two rigaudons, two menuets, or two passepieds frequently make up a single choreography. In addition, the music of the two individual dances, with the reprises of each repeated, is often repeated again in full and the whole choreographed. Occasionally a choreography is set to a suite of dances. For instance, Louis Pécour's "La bourrée d'Achille" is set to the music of a bourrée, a menuet, a repeat of the menuet, and a repeat of the bourrée (including repetitions of all the reprises). Perhaps the poetic proportions and pleasing rhetoric of Lullian ballroom dances led in the early eighteenth century to the extreme regularity of *belle danse* choreographies and of many dance songs and pieces. On the other hand, the rhetoric of theatrical dancing is that of a [persuasive] oration (de Pure, 1668, p. 230). For example, Pécour's theatrical choreography of 1704, set to the continuous variations of Lully's passacaille from *Persée*, has the five rhetorical parts often used in an oration.

STEP-UNITS THAT PAIR MUSICAL MEASURES

Francine Lancelot (1971, p. 42) and Anne Witherell (1982, p. 153) note that *belle danse* choreographies often contain certain pairs of one-measure step-units, such as two *pas de bourrée*, a *pas de bourrée* and a *coupé*, or two *jettés* and a *pas de bourrée*. In fact the choreographies exhibit a large proportion of paired step-units in one of three forms. The first is the parallel relationship of two identical step-units. The second is the symmetrical relationship of two step-units that are identical except for the second unit starting with the opposite foot. The third form manifests an arsic-thetic relationship in that the first step-unit requires more energy than the second and thus leads to a repose on the second. For example, two *pas de menuet* make an identical pair since all *pas de menuet* begin with the right foot; two *pas de bourrée* form a symmetrical pair; and either a *pas de bourrée* and a *coupé* or two *jettés* and a *pas de bourrée* make an arsic-thetic pair.

The first step-units of "La bourrée d'Achille" are two *pas de bourrée*, a symmetrical pair. The third and fourth step-units are a *contretemps de chaconne* and a *temps de courante*, an arsic-thetic pair: the energy of the *contretemps*, or hop, is released in the long weight change of the *temps de courante*.

All existing eighteenth-century choreographies are accompanied by music with a continuous or almost continuous series of four- or eight-measure members to which pairs of pairs of step-units are set. The only irregularity is the occasional five- or six-measure member in a piece whose other members have four measures. In choreographing an irregular musical member, an extra step-unit or pair of step-units is normally added. (Because no choreographies remain for the theater dances—chiefly menuets—that have musical members of three or five measures throughout, the step-units that were arranged to these members are not known.)

Because no choreographies for Lully's original productions exist, it is impossible to compare the lyrics of his dance songs with the choreographies created under his supervision. However, some parody words written for Lullian dance melodies later choreographed in the annual *recueils* show how eighteenth-century lyrics relate to *belle danse* step-units. The drinking song set to the melody of "La bourrée d'Achille" was published only two years after the cho-

Example 9.1.
First two parody lines set to "La bourrée d'Achille." *Nouvelles parodies bachiques*, 1702, vol. III, p. 1.

> Peut-on jamais avoir du chagrin,   [two *pas de bourrée*]
> Quand on a de bon vin?   [two *pas de bourrée*]
>
> (Can one ever be melancholy,
> When he has good wine?)

Example 9.2.
First two parody lines set to the menuet of "La bourrée d'Achille." *Nouvelles parodies bachiques*, 1702, vol. III, p. 1.

> Bachus est aymable,   [one *pas de menuet*]
> Son empire est doux;   [one *pas de menuet*]
>
> (Bachus is friendly,
> His empire is sweet;)

reography appeared. It is typical of such parodies and seems to fit the overall structure of Pécour's dance motions particularly well. Each line of bourrée lyrics is set to a pair of one-measure step-units, and each pair of bourrée lines corresponds to a double pair of step-units. The pair of lines in example 9.1 starts the first bourrée (the melody and step rhythm for these measures are given in ex. 9.4). A few older dances such as the menuet have two-measure step-units that also pair the musical measures. Example 9.2 shows the start of the menuet of "La bourrée d'Achille," in which each line of lyrics is set to a two-measure *pas de menuet* (see the melody and step rhythm in ex. 8.10b).

DANCE PHRASES

On a higher level of organization, each double pair of one-measure step-units that begins "La bourrée d'Achille" and each pair of two-measure step-units that starts its menuet suggest a long line of lyrics or a rhetorical "member." These four measures form a choreographic phrase. Each dance phrase concludes with a repose similar in effect to that of a musical period.

Lancelot believes specific step-units have no particular places in a choreographic phrase, but she notes that a great number of *assemblés*, *pas de bourrée*, and *coupés* conclude dance phrases. She also observes that dances never finish with a *pas de sissonne*, *pas de rigaudon*, or *pirouette* (1971, p. 41). Clearly some step-units of *la belle danse*, like some French words, are especially suitable for relatively strong cadences.

Several factors cause certain step-units to give a feeling of repose. Step-units that require less muscular or mental effort than previous units are restful; thus an unornamented *coupé* is probably the most tranquil of all step-units. A step-unit having fewer weight changes than previous step-units allows some repose since the smaller number of weight changes retards the dancer's progress; for example, the single delayed weight change of the *temps de courante* produces a momentary "hold" as the dancer poses on the balls of both feet. Steps made more or less in place halt progress; one such step-unit is the *pas de bourrée emboité* (nested bourrée step)—the first step is taken backward, the next one joins it in the third position, and the last one moves forward again, resulting in no net advance. Concluding with both heels on the floor gives a sense of stability. Thus the step-unit at the end of a dance, usually the *coupé* with two weight changes, finishes with both heels on the floor. The *assemblé*, or jump onto both feet, ends a dance phrase with particular finality.

When a reposeful step-unit occurs at the end of a dance phrase, a step-unit that includes one or more springing steps often precedes it. Springing steps require extra effort, which is relaxed in the more tranquil steps that follow. Therefore any hop, leap, or jump heightens the drama and leads to the repose of steps taken on the floor. In "La bourrèe d'Achille," for instance, the first two *pas de bourrée* (shown in ex. 8.10a) are followed by a *contretemps de chaconne* and *temps de courante* (ex. 9.3). The relative effort required of the four step-units suggests the musical progression shown today as I, I, V, I—the dance equivalent of tonic harmony for the first two step-units, dominant harmony for the third, and tonic harmony again for the fourth. The two *pas de bourrées* can also be viewed as the proposition of the phrase (the two step-units constituting its exordium and narration). The *contretemps de chaconne* is then the confutation; the *temps de courante*, the peroration.

Half or full turns may also help shape a dance phrase. For instance, the fifteenth couplet of Pécour's "La chaconne pour une femme" (Feuillet, 1704), mentioned on page 105, is choreographed to three complete clockwise turns executed by eight successive *pas de bourrée* on the floor pattern of a counterclockwise spiral. The first two turns each require two *pas de bourrée*. The last turn is performed during the fifth, sixth, and seventh *pas de bourrée*, and the final *pas de bourrée* is made without turning. Thus the turns divide the choreographic phrase into 2 + 2 + 4 measures, the climax (confutation) occurring in mm. 5–7 with the longest and final turn.

Often a dance phrase is set to a musical period and the choreography requires twice as much time as the music to come to its cadential repose. Presumably a visual idea requires more time than a musical one. The first four-measure dance phrase of "La bourrée d'Achille" (ex. 9.4), for instance, reposes only at

EXAMPLE 9.3.
Climax and repose in a dance phrase. Pécour, "La bourrée d'Achille," 1700, p. 1, mm. 3–4.

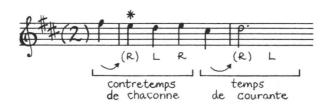

EXAMPLE 9.4.
Comparison of reposes in music and choreography. Pécour,
"La bourrée d'Achille," 1700, p. 1, mm. 1–4.

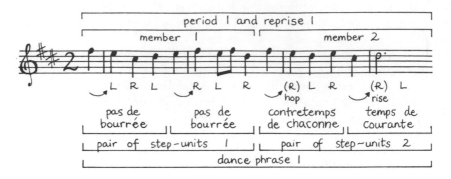

the *coupé* at the end of the second pair of step-units (m. 4); whereas the first four-measure period of the music has a cadence at the end of each of its two-measure musical members (mm. 2 and 4).

DANCE FIGURES

Dancers of *belle danse* choreographies were not restricted to traveling forward and backward, left and right, as were Arbeau's dancers, who shared the dance floor with a number of other dancing couples. The *belle danse* couple could also move in long paths that took advantage of the whole dance floor to evoke the lines of poetry and the structure of rhetoric.

According to Feuillet, a dance figure is a route "traced with art" (1700a, p. 2). Among the dance figures employed in *belle danse* choreographies are vertical lines, horizontal lines, diagonal lines, curved lines, half circles, ovals, and spirals. These figures are combined into regular, orderly, and well-proportioned floor patterns. Most figures made by a dancing couple are isometric in one of two ways: symmetrical or parallel. In symmetrical figures, the dancers' paths form mirror images. In parallel figures, the paths make identical images, side by side. Feuillet calls symmetrical figures "regular" and parallel figures "irregular" (ex. 9.5):

> The regular figure occurs when two or more dancers move in opposite directions. While one goes to the right, the other goes to the left. The irregular figure occurs when the two dancers . . . together go to the same side.[2] (1700a, p. 92)

In other words, symmetrical figures were customary in *belle danse* choreographies, and parallel figures were the exceptions.

Because the dance figures in *belle danse* choreographies are geometric designs, they are best seen from above. In the theater, viewers seated higher than the stage were placed most favorably. At the king's ball, the king sitting on his throne had the most advantageous position.

EXAMPLE 9.5.
Regular and irregular figures. Feuillet, 1700a, p. 92. Reproduced by arrangement with Broude Brothers Limited.
a. regular (symmetrical); b. irregular (parallel).

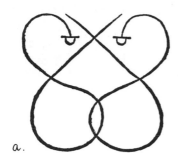
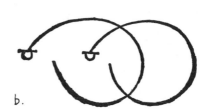

a.   b.

EXAMPLE 9.6.
Plate 1 of "La bourrée d'Achille." Pécour, 1700, p. 1. Reproduced by arrangement with Broude Brothers Limited.

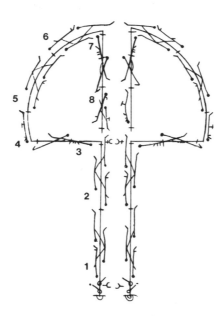

| 1 | 2 | 3 | 4 |
Peut-on jamais avoir du chagrin, Quand on a de bon vin?
Peut-on jamais avoir du chagrin, Quand on a de bon vin?
| 5 | 6 | 7 | 8 |

Example 9.6 shows the first choreographic plate for Pécour's "La bourrée d'Achille." The melody to which the choreography is performed appears at the top; for purposes of comparison, we have added the parody words of 1702 at the bottom. We have also placed numerals at the initial "bend" of each step-unit to show how the start of each dance measure relates to the music, choreography, and lyrics.

Each choreographic phrase tends to be set to a single playing or singing of a musical reprise. In "La bourrée d'Achille," for instance, the first playing of the first reprise accompanies the first choreographic phrase, and the repetition of that reprise accompanies the second choreographic phrase. The second reprise of the piece is, as usual, longer than the first. It is composed of an eight-measure musical period, and an eight-measure choreographic phrase is set to each playing or singing of the music.

DANCE PERIODS

Just as the two playings or singings of a musical reprise form a tightly knit unit, so do the two choreographic phrases set to them combine into a whole. We call these combined phrases a dance "period." Even though the dance periods in a choreography are usually twice the length of the musical ones in the accompaniment, the repose that ends each dance period resembles the repose of the perfect authentic cadence that finishes most musical periods. The reposes of the dance phrases and often the dance figures help identify the dance periods.

The dance periods of *belle danse* choreographies are of three kinds, depending on the relationship of their two phrases. In the first kind, the phrases have essentially identical or symmetrical step-units and isometric (parallel or symmetrical) floor patterns. The two dance phrases of this kind of period may be said to "rhyme." Rhyming phrases fit exactly or almost exactly the corresponding musical reprise and its repetition, because both the music and the choreography are repeated. Examples include the first dance period of Pécour's "Le passepied nouveau" (1700a, pp. 1–2), the first period of Pécour's "La bourrée" from "La Carignan" (1703, p. 7), and the first period of Dezais' "La Corsini," a bourrée (1718?, pp. 11–12).

The second kind of dance period corresponds only in part to the music. It has phrases that are similar either in their sequence of step-units or in their dance figures. Thus only the step-units or the dance figures match during the two repetitions of a musical reprise. A dance period having very similar step-units but unlike dance figures is the first dance period of Pécour's "La bourrée d'Achille," shown in example 9.6. In the second period of that choreography, shown in example 9.7, the step-units are again similar, and the geometric figures are more alike but not completely isometric. An example with dissimilar step-units but similar figures for its dance phrases is the second dance period of Pécour's "Le passepied nouveau" (1700a, pp. 3–4). The figures for both phrases of this dance period are based entirely on straight lines.

The third kind of dance period has practically no common elements between its two phrases. Identical music is used for the reprise and its repetition but is set to completely dissimilar choreography. For example, each of the two dance periods of the short bourrée from Pécour's "La nouvelle Bourgogne" (1707) consists of two unlike phrases, with different sequences of step-units and strikingly different dance figures.

Occasionally, one dance period is set to a musical reprise and another to its repetition. That may happen when the second reprise of a piece is long enough to include two musical periods. If the music is repeated, as is usually called for, the corresponding dance period becomes a double period. That is, while musicians play A–A–B–B, dancers execute a single dance period to A–A and a double period to B–B. (Each "A" stands for the first reprise or its repeat, each "B" for the second reprise or its repeat.) An example is Pécour's passepied from "La Carignan" (1703).

With double periods in the choreography, the four choreographic phrases have common elements. For instance, in the first and third phrases of the double period of Pécour's passepied from "La Carignan" the dancers perform in a parallel floor pattern, but in the second and fourth phrases they resume the usual symmetrical pattern.

Once in a while, the whole dance is repeated instead of just the second reprise. That is, the musicians play A–A–B–A–A–B, while the dancers perform four dance periods, one for each A–A and one for each B, as in Pécour's "La bacchante," a bourrée choreography (1706). In short, almost all dance periods embrace the two playings or singings of a musical reprise. Knowing this fact may help modern musicians connect the two playings of a reprise and choose suitable ornamentation for the repetition, especially when accompanying dancing.

Ingenious though Feuillet's choreographic notation is, it may mislead the eye as to the periodic structure and the complete floor pattern. In example 9.7, the second dance period of "La bourrée d'Achille" is divided between two plates, each showing one statement of the musical reprise and one phrase of the choreography. The step-units of the two phrases are identical.

At first glance, the two plates seem to represent distinct and somewhat dissimilar floor patterns. Yet each pattern consists of a partial spiral and some short straight lines. In performance, the two figures are superimposed, with somewhat larger spirals the second time. The two *pas de sissone* (each a jump plus a leap) are danced practically in place. In both phrases the partial spiral, executed with four *pas de bourrée*, leads directly to the springing steps of the almost stationary *pas de sissonne*. Because of the overlapping and doubling back of the dancers' tracts, Pécour could not have combined these plates to show the complete floor pattern.

For the same reason, one plate must sometimes illustrate only a half-phrase or less, while the next plate shows the rest of the dance period. Such a scheme quite masks the symmetry of the floor pattern and footwork and causes the mu-

EXAMPLE 9.7.
Plates 2 and 3 of "La bourrée d'Achille." Pécour, 1700, pp. 2–
3. Reproduced by arrangement with Broude Brothers
Limited.

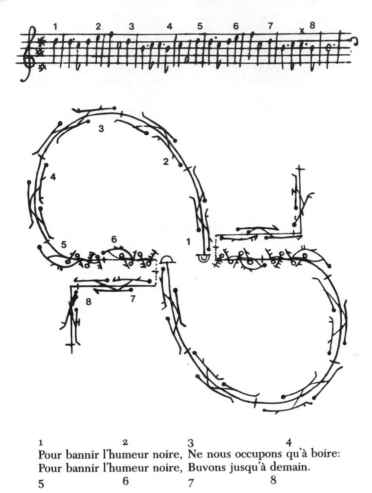

1   2   3   4
Pour bannir l'humeur noire, Ne nous occupons qu'à boire:
Pour bannir l'humeur noire, Buvons jusqu'à demain.
5   6   7   8

sic to appear unnaturally divided. Example 9.8 gives the final dance period of
"La bourrée d'Achille," which is set to essentially the same step-units as the
period in example 9.7. Plate 10 shows a spiral figure by each dancer; Plate 11
indicates three straight lines (beginning with two *pas de sissonne*), followed by
a spiral figure and two straight lines (again beginning with two *pas de sissonne*).
As before, each dance phrase consists of a spiral figure and some straight lines;
the two phrases of the dance period (mm. 1–8 and 9–16) are almost exactly
symmetrical, even though the two plates (mm. 1–4 and 5–16 respectively) appear quite dissimilar.

EXAMPLE 9.7.
Continued

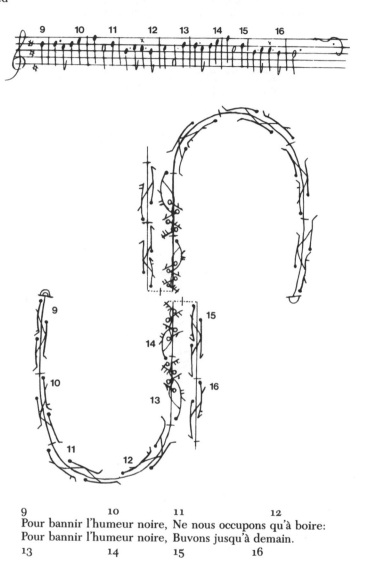

9   10   11   12
Pour bannir l'humeur noire, Ne nous occupons qu'à boire:
Pour bannir l'humeur noire, Buvons jusqu'à demain.
13   14   15   16

OVERALL PROPORTIONS OF CHOREOGRAPHIES

Dividing dance periods and floor patterns irregularly on the choreographic
plates, in order to delineate the dancers' paths, also obscures the overall proportions of the choreography, which on close examination can be seen to relate
to both poetry and rhetoric. If dance periods are viewed as poetic stanzas, whole
choreographies resemble whole poetic actions. Example 9.9 demonstrates that

Example 9.8.
Plates 10 and 11 of "La bourrée d'Achille." Pécour, 1700,
pp. 10–11. Reproduced by arrangement with Broude Brothers
Limited.

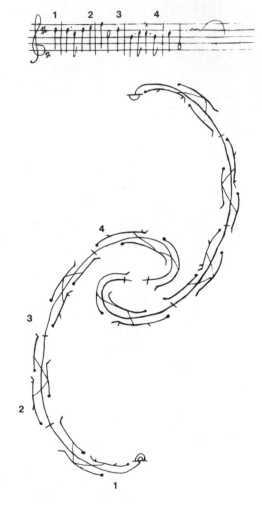

```
1        2    3          4
Le vin est ma folie; L'Amour me genne et m'ennuye;
```

the structure of the complete parody lyrics for "La bourrée d'Achille" and that
of Pécour's choreography are the same. The lyrics set to each dance period are
grouped into a poetic stanza. Each first stanza (and each first dance phrase) encompasses two poetic lines and their exact repetition. A single horizontal line
denotes the end of each first stanza. Each second stanza (and each second dance

EXAMPLE 9.8.
Continued

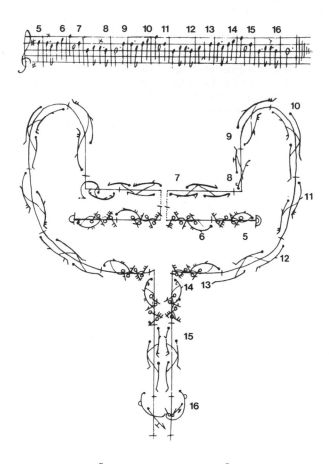

5   6   7   8
Le vin est ma folie, Le reste ne m'est rien.

9   10   11   12
Le vin est ma folie; L'Amour me genne et m'ennuye;
Le vin est ma folie, Le reste ne m'est rien.
13   14   15   16

phrase) encompasses four poetic lines and their exact repetition. A double horizontal line denotes the end of a second stanza.

Although "La bourrée d'Achille" may be viewed as the pleasingly symmetrical structure of a repeated pair of dances, it may also be perceived as a three-part action having its proposition set to the first bourrée music, its intrigue set to the two statements of the menuet music, and its denouement set to the repetition of the bourrée music. Because this choreography both begins and ends

EXAMPLE 9.9.
Parody words for "La bourrée d'Achille." *Nouvelles parodies
bachiques*, 1702, vol. III, p. 1.

Dance		Music/Poetry
	[Bourrée, 1st time]	
A	Peut-on jamais avoir du chagrin,	A
(plate 1)	Quand on a de bon vin?	
	Peut-on jamais avoir du chagrin,	repeat A
	Quand on a de bon vin?	

B	Pour bannir l'humeur noire,	B
(plates 2–3)	Ne nous occupons qu'á boire:	
	Pour bannir l'humeur noire,	
	Buvons jusqu'á demain.	
	Pour bannir l'humeur noire,	repeat B
	Ne nous occupons qu'á boire:	
	Pour bannir l'humeur noire,	
	Buvons jusqu'á demain.	
	==	
	[Menuet, 1st time]	
C	Bachus est aymable, Son empire est doux;	C
(1st half	Bachus est aymable, Son empire est doux;	repeat C
plate 4)	---	
D	Amant miserable, Que ne cherchez-voux;	D
(2nd half	Les plaisirs de table Qu'on prend parmy nous?	
plate 4, and	Amant miserable, Que ne cherchez-voux;	repeat D
plate 5)	Les plaisirs de table Qu'on prend parmy nous?	
	==	
	[Menuet, 2nd time]	
E	O l'humeur gaillarde, Qu'inspire les pots!	C
(plate 6)	O l'humeur gaillarde, Qu'inspire les pots!	repeat C

F	On rit, on hazarde Chansons et bons mots:	D
(plates 7–8)	On donne nazarde Aux pales Cagots.	
	On rit, on hazarde Chansons et bons mots:	repeat D
	On donne nazarde Aux pales Cagots.	
	==	
	[Bourrée, 2nd time]	
G	Soupire qui voudra pour de bien;	A
(plate 9)	Je veux boire de mien:	
	Soupire qui voudra pour de bien;	repeat A
	Je veux boire de mien:	
	==	
H	Le vin est ma folie;	B
(plates 10–11)	L'Amour me genne et m'ennuye;	
	Le vin est ma folie,	
	Le reste ne m'est rien.	
	Le vin est ma folie;	repeat B
	L'Amour me genne et m'ennuye;	
	Le vin est ma folie,	
	Le reste ne m'est rien.	
	==	

with bourrée music, set to essentially the same footwork and rather similar figures, its three parts form a complete circuit, or large period.

In fact, every choreography has three parts: a beginning, a middle, and an end, which together make a large period. At the start of the dance, the dancers face the "presence," the king's chair. At the end, they conclude where they had begun, in front of and facing the "presence" to make their closing bows.

According to de Pure, the division of a choreography into identifiable parts is especially important in theatrical dancing, because the theatrical choreography must be a "true whole," and its parts "must be distinguished truly and of themselves. . . . Since the ballet is a spiritual whole, [its] division must be artistic and regular, so that it pleases the memory by its appropriateness" (1668, pp. 230–31).

The majority of dances choreographed in Feuillet notation are set to music in two-reprise, or binary, form. Among the few set to music in rondeau form is Feuillet's passepied "La Gouastalla" (1709). It includes five dance periods, corresponding to the five sections of the music, A–B–A–C–A. In this particular choreography, the first dance period is introductory. The second might be considered a narration, as if an anecdote were being related. The third dance period suggests a confirmation in that the dancers circle each other, holding first right and then left hands. The fourth has choreography related to the second but might represent a confutation. The fifth, with choreography similar to the third period and music identical to the first, sums up as a peroration.

Passacaille and chaconne choreographies are set to music organized as a continuous variation. Many are quite long pieces, and their couplets may be grouped into three or five rhetorical parts. Pécour's "La passacaille de Persée" (1704, pp. 79–90) is set to music from Lully's opera *Persée* of 1682. Lully's music has twelve couplets, each set to two harmonic progressions. After the first couplet, the melodic phrases lag behind the bass progressions by one note (as do the lines of his chaconne song [app. ex. 6]). Pécour's choreography follows suit and, starting with the third couplet, lags one measure behind the harmonic structure. Because most melodic phrases in passacailles and chaconnes begin with two upbeat quarter notes, and all dance phrases begin with the "bend" of a *mouvement*, the dance and the melody carry the audience's eye and ear into the next phrase.

Example 9.10 shows the melody and bass line of Lully's music and the division of the dance into three parts (proposition, intrigue, and denouement); five parts (exordium, narration, confutation, confirmation, and peroration); and twelve choreographic plates. Measure numbers indicate the beginnings of dance phrases, and the symbols ⌞ and ⌟ below the bass indicate the start and finish of harmonic progressions.

The presence of the bass clef hints at the size of the musical forces, for when it appears, Lully used the six parts of his complete orchestra. When only the treble clef appears, the forces were reduced to the three top parts.

Viewed as a whole, "La passacaille de Persée" follows the usual plan of a fairly regular proposition, a much less regular intrigue, and a more regular denoue-

EXAMPLE 9.10.
Choreography for "La passacaille de Persée." Based on Pécour,
1704, pp. 79–90.

EXAMPLE 9.10.
Continued

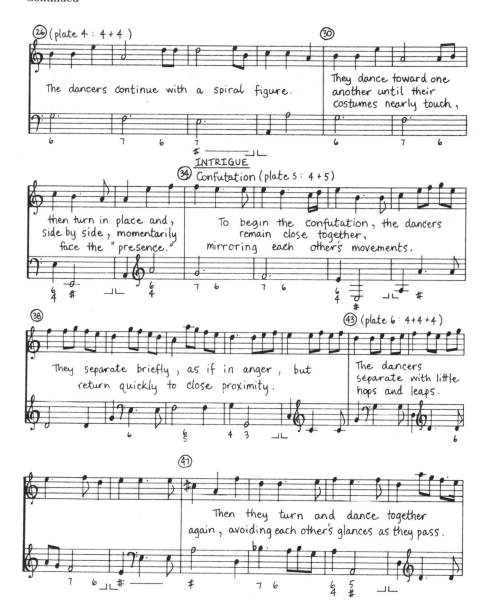

EXAMPLE 9.10.
Continued

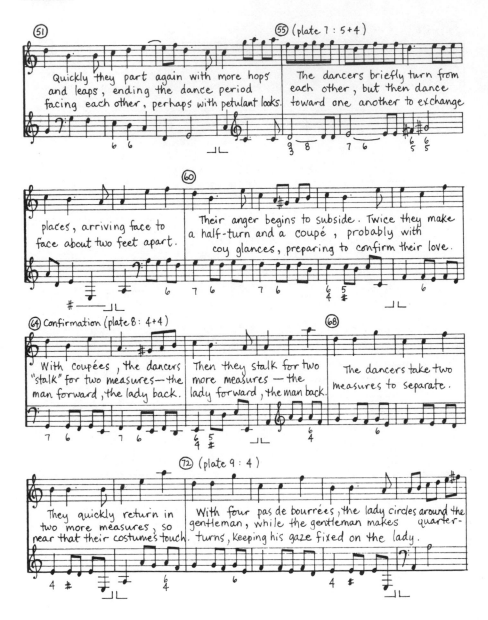

EXAMPLE 9.10.
Continued

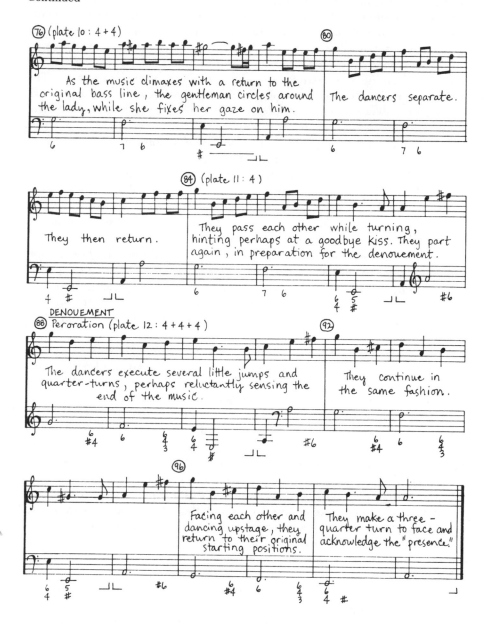

ment. The verbal description of this choreography takes many words but its performance lasts only three minutes.

In the proposition of "La passacaille de Persée" (mm. 1–33), the dancers execute a formal courtship dance while the musicians follow one of the traditional bass lines for passacailles: 1, 7, 6, 5. The exordium of this proposition (mm. 1–17) begins in a straightforward way with the full orchestra playing and the dancers performing their traditional acknowledgments to the "presence." The only irregularity is the final dance phrase, which is extended by one measure to allow all the following dance phrases to start a measure later than the corresponding harmonic progression.

The narration of this proposition (mm. 18–33) is announced in the music by the lower voices dropping out and the melodic motion increasing to almost continuous eighth notes plus a few sixteenths. In the choreography, the dancers no longer recognize the "presence" but maintain the discreet distance of a formal courtship. For the second dance period, the full orchestra returns (m. 25). At the end of the narration, the dancers momentarily face the "presence" again, as if to say, "We stand united at the end of our courtship."

The choreographic intrigue (mm. 34–87) departs from the traditional, formal, and regular to become far more passionate. The start of the music is again announced by a decrease in the size of the orchestra. Several rapid shifts from full orchestra to treble voices dramatize the strong feelings expressed while the dance suggests a lover's quarrel. Only the first and last phrases of the intrigue are set to the characteristic bass line.

The intrigue of this particular choreography seems to begin with its confutation (mm. 34–63), the quarrel between the lovers. The couple first becomes more familiar (mm. 34–37), and then their passion intensifies as the music moves to the relative major (m. 42). The dancers repeatedly turn away or move away from each other and then return. Springing steps further express their agitation. At the end of the confutation, their dispute begins to abate. All three dance periods of this confutation are irregular. The first and last have one phrase with five instead of the usual four measures, and the middle period is made up of three instead of the usual two dance phrases.

In the confirmation (mm. 64–87), which in this intrigue seems to follow the confutation, the dancers continue to act out their frustrations as they stalk around the dance floor. They finally make up as the lady circles around the gentleman and then the gentleman around the lady, while the full orchestra returns to the original bass progression.

Tradition, formality, and regularity are more or less revived in the denouement, or peroration, where the dancers are again united (mm. 88–99). Although the choreography continues to lag one measure behind the harmonic progression, the second musical member is played twice, verifying that peace and stability have returned, and the dancers conclude with formal bows.

Each of the first eight choreographic plates of "La passacaille de Persée" represents a dance period. Plate 9 combines with the first half of Plate 10 to make the ninth period; the second half of Plate 10 combines with Plate 11 to make the tenth period; and Plate 12 represents the eleventh and final dance period. Plates 6 and 12 include three dance phrases in their dance period.

The so-called sectional variations of folies are quite different from the continuous variations of passacailles and chaconnes. As shown in chapter 23, the poetic lines and choreographic phrases of folies are fitted exactly to the four-measure members of the music, from the beginning to the end of the piece.

Belle danse choreographies were set to preexisting music, not vice versa. Just as the flowing rhythms of Lullian dance lyrics draped themselves across the traditional rhythmic movements, so did the fluid floor patterns of *belle danse* choreographies often steal attention from the more static rhythms of the individual steps.

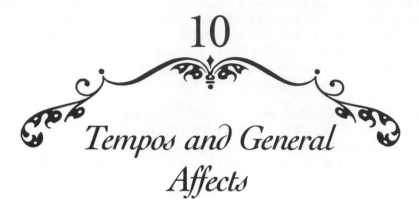

10

Tempos and General Affects

> Generally speaking there is a certain tempo
> that one must keep in all the *airs de ballet*, no
> matter what the [character] dance, especially
> with the French. I say French, because I have
> noticed much slower and more singable tem-
> pos among foreigners. . . . The dance air
> should not be as drawn out, nor as languorous
> as it would be if it were only sung. One must
> go a little further than the ornaments of the
> voice, and give [to these airs] a well-expressed
> passion, with a particular vivacity, and always
> with [a sense] of the heroic and the gay.[1]
>
> Michel de Pure (1668, pp. 264–65)

As de Pure makes clear in this quotation from his treatise on ancient and modern "spectacles," the tempo of most French character dances performed in the
theater was extremely quick, and the general feeling, or affect, was heroic and
gay. According to Descartes, the affect of a piece of music depends in large part
on its tempo:

> As regards the various emotions which music can arouse. . . , I will say that in gen-
> eral a slower pace arouses in us quieter feelings, such as languor, sadness, fear,
> pride, etc. A faster pace arouses faster emotions, such as joy, etc. (1650t, p. 15)

Dance pieces by Lully and his contemporaries have few descriptive words at
their start, but the tempo and affect of each dance were more or less standard,
and everyone who had danced a menuet or gavotte knew well their gay and
lively natures.

But soon after Lully's death many changes in musical and dance practices influenced the tempos and affects of dance music. Choreographers came to orna-

ment and divide the dancers' steps to the point that the choreographies of different types of character dance were indistinguishable, and musicians added a multitude of embellishments, divisions, and variations to the typical rhythms in concert pieces with dance titles. As a result, the tempo and affect of a dance piece could no longer be recognized from its name alone; other information was required to tell musicians how fast and with what general affect to perform each piece.

CONFLICTS BETWEEN THE TEMPO IMPLICATIONS OF TRADITIONAL AND MODERN METER SIGNS

To some extent the tempo implied by a meter sign is related to the mensural proportions, or time relationships, of the sixteenth century. Many writers of the late seventeenth and early eighteenth centuries provided tables showing the tempos suggested by the signs, but they did not always agree on the relationships between adjacent signs in the tables. Michel de Saint-Lambert still followed the principles of the sixteenth century and claimed that the sign ₵ indicated a tempo twice as fast as that indicated by C and that, by extension, the much newer sign $\frac{2}{4}$ showed a tempo twice as fast as ₵ (1702, p. 23). In contrast, the more progressive writers of his day gave essentially the same sequence of signs but said that the tempo of one sign was merely somewhat quicker than that of the previous one, rather than twice as fast.

The signs 3, $\frac{3}{2}$, and $\frac{6}{4}$ present further difficulties. Like the sign ₵, they originally indicated how the note values of one section of music related to the same values in the previous section. The sign 3 showed that each value moved three times as quickly as originally, and $\frac{3}{2}$ and $\frac{6}{4}$ showed that each value moved one and a half times as quickly as the original tempo. In other words, $\frac{3}{2}$ did more than designate three half notes in the measure, and $\frac{6}{4}$ six quarter notes.

By the end of the seventeenth century, 3, $\frac{3}{2}$, and $\frac{6}{4}$ were also viewed as fractional signs, like the $\frac{2}{4}$, $\frac{3}{8}$, and $\frac{6}{8}$ of the new Italian music. Fractional signs then as today indicated the number of notes of a given value in each measure: $\frac{2}{4}$ specified a measure having the equivalent of two quarter notes; $\frac{3}{8}$, one of three eighths. With these signs, a smaller denominator tended to suggest a slower tempo. For instance, the half-note pulses of sarabandes marked $\frac{3}{2}$ were slower than the quarter-note pulses of menuets, which were never given this sign; and the eighth-note pulses of passepieds marked $\frac{3}{8}$ were still quicker.

Saint-Lambert admitted that the meter signs of his day indicated tempo "only very imperfectly" (1702, p. 25), and he therefore urged composers to use descriptive words at the start of their pieces "to come to the aid of the impotent meter signs and express their meaning." Often these words indicate only the tempo: *lentement* (slowly), *modérément* (moderately), *vitement* (rapidly). At other times they give the general affect of the piece and suggest the tempo only indirectly: *gravement* (solemnly), *tendrement* (tenderly), *majestueusement* (majestically), *légèrement* (lightly), *gayement* (gaily).

GENERAL DESCRIPTIONS

During any one period, the tempo and affect of a given dance were described similarly in tutors, treatises, and dictionaries, and in the words at the start of most examples. However, most dances in triple meter whose popularity spanned many decades went through transitions in tempo and character, usually becoming slower. Dances new at court, such as the menuet in the 1660s, were described as gay and lively; but after they became established—for instance, the courante in the 1690s and the court menuet in the 1790s—they were usually depicted as slow and solemn. Similarly, French versions of the Spanish dances with the sign 3 were described as quick at the beginning of the seventeenth century but as slow and tender by the early eighteenth.

Many Baroque theorists ranked the tempos of the various character dances. Among dances usually written in compound-duple meter, gigues and canaries were said to be quicker than loures. Of the most popular dances in triple meter, menuets were said to be quicker than sarabandes, and passepieds quicker than menuets; French writers stated that the chaconne was quicker than the passacaille (German writers claimed the reverse).

The number of beats usually conducted in a measure, described in chapter 5, was also discussed in relation to tempo: in general, the fewer the beats the faster the tempo. Thus a canarie or passepied, normally conducted with one beat to the measure, is somewhat quicker than a menuet or chaconne, usually conducted in two unequal beats, and much quicker than a sarabande or passacaille, normally conducted in three beats.

NUMERICAL TEMPO INDICATIONS

Some Baroque treatises and dictionaries relate the tempo of a measure of music to the speed of heart beats or to a second of time. For example, Antoine Furetière, in his article "Mesure," claimed that a musical measure "normally contains a second of time, which is about the tempo of the beating of the heart." Although today's average human heart beats somewhat faster, the hearts of people who exercise regularly beat about sixty times per minute (MM 60). Since French courtiers were expected to practice riding, fencing, and dancing daily, their heart rates can be presumed to beat at this slower rate.

In any event, tempo markings derived from pendulum swings reveal that the measures of most dances of the early eighteenth century were still timed to a single, rather slow beat, in which the measure lasts about a second. The measures of faster dances moved to faster heart rates and those of slower dances to calmer rates, but only passacailles and most sarabandes of the early eighteenth century were slow enough that heartbeats related more to pulses than to measures.

Étienne Loulié was the first to use the swings of a pendulum to measure musical tempos systematically (1696t, pp. 84ff). When a weight is suspended from a fixed point by a cord and is allowed to swing freely under the influence of gravity, it forms a pendulum. The duration of the swings is determined only by

EXAMPLE 10.1.
Chronometer. Loulié, 1696, plate appended to p. 82.

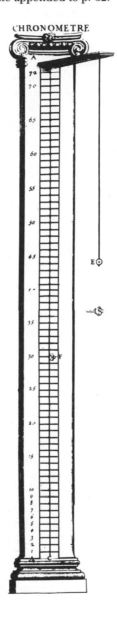

the distance from the fixed upper end of the cord to the center of the weight, or bob. The duration is independent of the mass of the bob or the width of the swings (provided the bob is far heavier than the cord and the swings are less than about ten degrees from the vertical). Loulié called his six-foot pendulum (ex. 10.1) a "chronometer" (time measurer) and defined tempos for various pieces according to the number of *pouces* (inches, approximately) between the top of the pendulum cord and the middle of the bob. Unfortunately, Loulié's tempos for dance pieces have not survived.

Michel L'Affilard in 1705 followed a slightly different course when he added pendulum indications to a new edition of his dance songs of 1694. Instead of designating tempos according to the number of *pouces* in the pendulum's cord, he specified the length of time, in *tierces*, required for one "vibration" of the pendulum. A *tierce*, or third, is equal to 1/60 of a second, just as a second is equal to 1/60 of a minute and a minute to 1/60 of an hour.

Most modern musical scholars, led by Neal Zaslaw (1970 and 1972), believe that by "vibration" L'Affilard meant a movement in one direction only (from left to right, or right to left). But, because the tempos that result from this calculation seem to make patter songs of some of L'Affilard's pieces and mandate very quick performances of the theatrical dances, many twentieth-century musical and dance performers have questioned the validity of his markings.

Eric Schwandt (1974) has suggested that L'Affilard may have intended a "vibration" to mean a full swing of the pendulum from left to right (or vice versa) and then back to the starting point. Some performers feel that this interpretation, which reduces the tempo to half, yields more satisfactory results for many of the songs; but only Zaslaw's interpretation brings L'Affilard's pendulum tempos close to the slightly later ones cited by Louis-Léon Pajot, comte d'Onzembray, and by Henry-Louis Choquel (to be discussed shortly). As further proof of the validity of the quicker interpretation, L'Affilard's slowest songs are much too slow to be danced at half the tempo. In any case de Pure warned readers against performing the French dance songs at the "slower and more singable tempos" of the dance songs of other nations (1668, p. 264).

The riddle of L'Affilard's tempos has not been solved to the satisfaction of all modern scholars and performers. Perhaps his tempos refer to the standard tempo for the character dances as performed in the ballroom and theater rather than to his songs. That would explain the fact that L'Affilard's tempos generally agree with the descriptions of the characteristic dances in other sources and with the pendulum markings of d'Onzembray for specific theatrical dances by Lully and his immediate followers.

In the early 1730s d'Onzembray invented a chronometer that included the mechanism of a grandfather clock (ex. 10.2). His device functioned like an inverted modern metronome: it allowed the pendulum to swing at different rates, and it used the ticking of the clockwork to mark the tempo audibly. Without question, d'Onzembray's "vibration" was a swing of the pendulum in one direction only, since each vibration produced a clear "tick."

In a report on his invention to the French Royal Academy of Sciences in 1732, d'Onzembray cited L'Affilard as his model for notating tempos in *tierces*. Thirteen of the twenty-two pieces for which d'Onzembray gave tempos are dances, many by Lully. As a young man, d'Onzembray had been close to Louis XIV and probably attended many court balls and theatrical productions, including revivals of Lully's works. Although the count was not a professional musician

EXAMPLE 10.2.
Two views of a clockwork chronometer. D'Onzembray, 1735,
plate appended to p. 195.

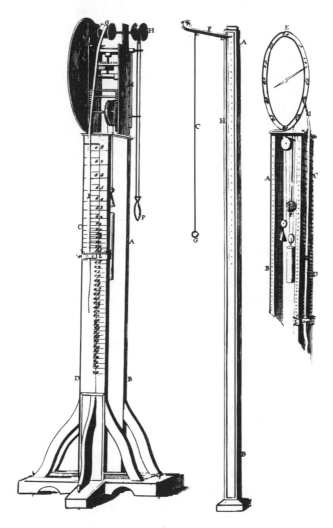

and he invented his chronometer long after Lully's death, his tempos for Lully's
and later theatrical dances are probably fairly reliable. Because d'Onzembray's
invention took advantage of technological progress not used by L'Affilard, his
tempos may be the more accurate of the two. Most of his markings are slightly
slower than L'Affilard's, yet the differences average no more than ten percent—
an amount psychologists say most people cannot perceive.

La Chapelle (1736) and Choquel (1759), like Loulié, calculated dance tempos
in terms of the length of the cord (in *pouces*). Choquel's tempo markings for
theatrical dances by Lully and his immediate successors are remarkably similar

to those of L'Affilard and d'Onzembray. But La Chapelle's markings for dance tunes apparently composed by himself vary more widely, perhaps reflecting the later date of his music.

The pendulum indications for tempo clearly support the observation that most measures of dance music were paced close to one heartbeat per second. In dance pieces with pendulum markings, half of those with the sign 2 have the tempo MM 120 for half notes, that is, MM 60 for the measures. Most of the other half fall within a slightly broader range: MM 56 to 65 for the measures, still suggesting MM 60 as the typical value. On the other hand, pendulum markings for the gigue-like dances marked $\frac{6}{4}$ or $\frac{6}{8}$ are somewhat slower: MM 50 to 58 for the measures (except for one very slow loure). The slightly slower range of tempos for compound duple meter is required for its ternary dotted figures, even when they move at the highest practical speed.

Dances in triple meter cover a wider range of tempos. The tempos given by L'Affilard, d'Onzembray, and Choquel for passepieds range from MM 86 to 100 for the measures—the tempo of a very fast heartbeat. For menuets, they prescribed tempos from MM 71 to 78 for the measures—a moderately quick heartbeat for courtiers of the day. Numerical indications of the tempo of later menuets (see chap. 28) corroborate the evidence of the pendulum markings and also show the gradual slowing of this venerable court dance during the eighteenth century. For courantes, L'Affilard and d'Onzembray gave tempos from MM 27 to 30 for the measures; in each measure of a courante, the heart of a healthy courtier would beat twice.

The four slowest of the pendulum indications—for three sarabandes and a passacaille—have one heartbeat per musical pulse (MM 63 to 73) rather than one per measure. Two faster sarabandes and two faster passacailles range in tempo from MM 86 to 133 for the pulses, or MM 29 to 44 for the measures. The three chaconnes with pendulum markings average still quicker tempos: MM 120 to 159 for the pulses, or MM 40 to 53 for the measures.

Among the dances with pendulum tempos, we found choreographies set to the music of only two, Lully's passacaille from *Persée*, described in chapter 9, and Destouches's sarabande from *Issé*. Both choreographies are well suited to their pendulum markings and certainly could not be danced twice as slowly, as suggested by Schwandt's interpretation of L'Affilard's markings. The choreography for Destouches's sarabande requires great skill and perfect balance to be performed even as slowly as d'Onzembray indicated.

In sum, the eighteenth-century pendulum markings are fairly consistent, and to some degree all are related to the speed of heartbeats. In general they agree with the descriptive words at the start of examples and with descriptions from other sources. The two pieces we found with both pendulum markings and extant choreographies are suitably danced at the tempos given by the chronometers. The more fully documented tempos of later menuets—the only character dances of the *grand siècle* that continued to be danced throughout the eighteenth century—show the customary gradual decline from those of the early eighteenth century.

DEVIATIONS FROM STANDARD TEMPOS AND AFFECTS

In practice, no single tempo or affect is suitable for all examples of a given character dance. A number of factors may suggest a tempo different from the standard one. The first such indication may be an uncharacteristic meter sign. For example, L'Affilard's three sarabandes, having the signs $\frac{3}{2}$, 3, and $\frac{6}{4}$ respectively, move at progressively faster tempos: MM 72, 86, and 133 for the pulses. And his two menuets, marked 3 and $\frac{6}{8}$ respectively, have progressively quicker tempos: MM 71 and 75 for the measures.

On the other hand, a sarabande marked $\frac{3}{2}$ was not necessarily slower than one marked 3, nor was a $\frac{6}{4}$ gigue necessarily slower than one marked $\frac{6}{8}$. As a result, the extent to which the meter sign indicates the tempo is often difficult for a twentieth-century performer to ascertain. The performers of the day had less difficulty, because they were often in close touch with the composer whose works they played, sang, and danced.

Sometimes a descriptive word or words at the start of a particular dance piece alerted the performer that the tempo or affect differed from the standard one for the character dance or for the meter sign. For example, though menuets were usually characterized as gay and lively, D'Anglebert indicated a slower tempo, *lentement*, for his keyboard arrangement of a menuet by Lully marked 3. It had been composed for *Le coucher du Roi*, the ceremonies in which the king said goodnight to his courtiers. The slower tempo probably suggested the slowing down and ending of the day's activities (ex. 10.3).

In any case, Saint-Lambert made the point that a dance piece is played more slowly in concert on the harpsichord than in the ballroom by an ensemble (1702, p. 19). Harpsichord pieces usually have many ornaments, some very quick notes, and one or more independent though fragmented inner voices. All these factors demand a slower pace than the simple melodies of French ballroom and theatrical dances.

De Pure, in the quotation at the start of this chapter, stated that dance airs in the theater should not be as "drawn out" or "languorous" as if they were "only sung." Bénigne de Bacilly, writing in the same year (1668), allowed singers to

EXAMPLE 10.3.
Harpsichord menuet with a slow tempo. D'Anglebert, menuet
"La jeune Iris," 1689, from Lully's *Trios pour le coucher
du Roi*.

perform certain dance songs that require special tenderness—such as some gavottes, menuets, and sarabandes—more slowly than if these pieces were danced. Although Bacilly recognized that some people objected to a slower tempo for these dance songs, on the grounds that they were intended for dancing, he believed that dancers should dance at their preferred tempos and allow singers to sing at theirs (pp. 106–108).

Still other factors may suggest a tempo different from the standard one. Dance pieces written for low-pitched voices or instruments may be expected to move more slowly than those for high-pitched ones. Theatrical dances may be performed more quickly or slowly than the standard dance, to show off the technical prowess of the professional dancers. And certain kinds of pieces prescribe their own tempos: A dance piece for a wedding party portrays merriment and is naturally fast, whereas an elegy—a dance song that describes sorrow—or a theatrical choreography that accompanies a sleeping hero or heroine is naturally slow.

With all these considerations, it is hardly surprising that precise tempos for French dance music are elusive. But more important than tempo is the affect. A gay menuet or a solemn sarabande may sound properly gay or solemn at a metronome marking considerably slower than the pendulum indications if the music includes a profusion of ornaments, a number of quick notes and perhaps some very quick notes, or an independent inner voice. Moreover, a menuet or sarabande choreography that must be performed more slowly than the standard tempo to allow the dancers to perform difficult "figures," or ornaments, may still express the characteristic affect. In any event, French musicians were more concerned with observing the affect and bringing out the "rhythmic cadence" of each dance piece than with finding its unequivocal tempo.

11

Marking the Musical Meter

Marked meter is that in which the beats are
strongly accented, as in *Airs de dances*.[1]

—Étienne Loulié (1696t, p. 64)

Music to accompany dancing is so composed and performed that dancers need
not strain to hear and feel the meter. Early seventeenth-century guitar accompaniments, dance melodies for Louis XIV's ballroom and theater, and dance
tunes in early eighteenth-century violin tutors have few quick notes and virtu-
ally no slurs, swells, elaborate trills, turns, mordents, or one-note graces to obscure the pulse movement. At the same time, tutors of the day tell musicians
accompanying the dance to bring out the meter more clearly and more forcefully than in their other playing—by strictly maintaining the tempo of pulses
and longer values and by emphasizing in some way the beats and pulses. Even
in dance songs and pieces that do not accompany dancing, a certain marking of
the meter identifies them as dance music.

STRICT TEMPO OF PULSE AND LONGER VALUES

The influence of the *cadence* on the composition of rhythmic subjects in dance
songs and pieces has been described earlier. (Both "rhythmic fall" and "rhythmic cadence" are valid translations of the French word *cadence*.) When the performance of a dance piece is well "cadenced," its downbeats, upbeats, and
pulses "fall" into place precisely and with their proper strength.

According to the lexicographer Sebastien de Brossard, an *air de mouvement*
is so called because of its regular and equal pulses (1703, article, "Motto"). The
dancing master Pierre Rameau said the rhythmic cadence "constitutes the soul
of the dance" (1725b, p. 6). The harpsichordist Michel de Saint-Lambert con-

sidered a well-marked rhythmic cadence the one indispensable element of a piece:

> [The rhythmic cadence] consists of passing over the notes of the same value with a great equality of tempo, and all the notes in general with proportional equality: because, whether one plays a piece quickly or slowly, he should always give it the rhythmic cadence that is its soul, and that is the thing it can least do without.[2] (1702, p. 25)

The German violinist, composer, and conductor Georg Muffat, who described in detail the "Lullian manner" of playing dance music on the violin, gave specific instructions for maintaining tempo throughout an entire dance piece (1698t, pp. 230–32). He advised players to keep the tempo "exactly constant" and not to slow down or rush "this measure or that note." Any deviation in tempo would of course unsettle dancers performing to the music.

In particular, Muffat pleaded that the downbeat and upbeat in duple meter, and the downbeat in triple meter, not be played too soon. That is, the previous bad pulse must not be hurried. The two pieces he used to illustrate this point are shown in example 11.1.

Besides being marked by equal performance, beats and pulses are usually detached from one another, making them stand out in relation to the flowing quick notes. In fact, many French writers identified the equal notes by separating them. Loulié said that playing notes equally "is called detaching the notes" (1696t, p. 29); and Pierre Dupont (see ex. 11.2) "detaches, or hops over" (*détache, ou sautille*) eighth notes and quarter notes in meters with eighth-note pulses (1718a, pp. 32, 35, 40, 43). (Since Dupont seems to have been a violinist, *sautiller* probably refers to a slightly bouncing bow stroke.)

Muffat described a more conscious "detachment" for note values longer than the pulse unit, "to mark dance movements more clearly" (1698t, pp. 239, 243–44). This detachment, which he classified as an ornament, was achieved by shortening the time that long values were sounded and increasing the length of the silence before the next note. It may be used on "notes of moderate length,"

EXAMPLE 11.1.
Bad pulses that are often rushed. Muffat, 1698t. a. gavotte in duple meter, p. 232; b. menuet-like piece in triple meter, p. 231. Asterisks mark the bad quarter notes that tend to be rushed.

EXAMPLE 11.2.
Detached eighth notes. Dupont, 1718a, p. 40. The notes
shortened by the separations Dupont specified in his text
are marked (⏐).

EXAMPLE 11.3.
"Detachments." Muffat, 1698t, pp. 243–44.

such as quarter notes in **C** and half notes in **¢**; or it may be employed on dotted
values that fill a measure of simple-triple meter or a half measure of compound-
duple meter (ex. 11.3). Muffat's notation indicates that undotted notes are shortened by one-half and dotted ones by one-third. In practice, the sound of the
strings would decay during part or all of the notated rest. Muffat advised that
the detachment should "always be expressed clearly, vigorously, and moderately, without affectation and without undue pressure on the strings."

Muffat also recommended maintaining the tempo at the end of musical periods. Here he differed from Bénigne de Bacilly, who allowed some stretching of

the final measures of tender gavotte songs (chap. 15). But even Muffat preferred slowing down to rushing the end of a piece.

MARKING THE BEATS AND PULSES

To Descartes, there was only one beat in the measure—the downbeat. Singers and instrumentalists of his day marked downbeats by exhaling more strongly or by increasing the pressure of their strokes, "so that at the beginning of each measure the sound is produced more distinctly" (1650t, p. 14). They did this instinctively, especially with tunes to which they were accustomed "to dance and sway." In Descartes' opinion, the increased sound on the downbeat "has greater impact on our spirits" and thus "rouses us to motion."

Although conductors of the *grand siècle* also marked other beats and pulses in dance pieces, Saint-Lambert emphasized that the downbeat is always more prominent than the other beats of the measure: "Those who beat time do so by striking their open palm or a table with a rolled-up piece of paper on [the downbeat]." This makes the first beat of the measure felt more than the others, which is proper "because the cadence of an air always falls on the downbeat." Even in concert performance, Saint-Lambert said the downbeat should be struck *avec éclat* (ostentatiously)—at least in the performer's imagination.

The words that French Baroque writers used for the downward and upward motions of the conductor's hand illustrate the far greater importance and vigor of the first. Descartes called the downbeat the *percussio* or *battuta*, both words meaning "beat" (1650t, p. 14fn). Loulié referred to the downward motion as the "good count," in contrast to the "false count," on which the hand is raised (1696t, pp. 61–62). By naming the downbeat the *frappé* (from *frapper*: to strike), Mersenne, Loulié, and others indicated that it was accented by the conductor. In turn, these writers demonstrated the relative lack of accent produced by the upward motion of the hand by naming it the *levé* (from *lever*: to raise). Thus the conductor's hand strikes on each downbeat and then is raised to prepare for the next.

Saint-Lambert warned that the conductor's hand motions should not be "effeminate," but should be "marked perceptibly and distinctly, as if the hand actually strikes a solid object." This is true even if the beats are made "only in the air." In beating time, the hand, so to speak, "dances" the rhythmic cadence (1702, p. 20).

Lully used a big conducting staff to keep his large force of singers, dancers, and musicians together. According to Rousseau's dictionary of 1768, the beats of the conductor at the French opera were audible even to the audience (article, "Battre la mesure").

Baroque dancers, singers, instrumentalists, and composers emphasized downbeats in their own ways. Dancers hopped, leaped, or rose onto the balls of their feet. Guitarists made downward strums, and violin and viol players used chiefly their primary bow stroke. Composers of dance songs placed the caesural and rhyme reposes of dance lyrics on downbeats; composers of dance music placed almost all melodic and harmonic reposes there; and composers of concert pieces with dance titles emphasized many downbeats with a thicker chord, a longer note value, or an ornament.

MARKING THE GOOD QUICK NOTES

In addition to setting off pulses by performing them equally and detached, French musicians made sure the pulse movement beneath a succession of quick notes was clear. They did so by lengthening or strengthening the good quick notes or by setting them up with an articulation silence (or at least a rapid decay of the previous note or chord).

French Baroque sources agree that in most cases good quick notes should be played at least slightly longer than bad ones. Loulié described the inequality of the notes as gentle (*louré*) or sharp (*piqué*) (1696t, pp. 29–30, 66–67). He notated the *louré* inequality as a 3:2 proportion by adding a dot to the good note and leaving the bad one unchanged (ex. 11.4a). He indicated the *piqué* inequality as a 3:1 proportion by dotting the good note and adding a beam to the bad one (ex. 11.4b).

Other Baroque writers were less specific about the degree of inequality used in performance. Jacques Hotteterre le Romain told woodwind players that the odd-numbered quick notes of the measure, that is, the good ones, should usually be "dotted" (1707, p. 28); and François Couperin complained in his harpsichord tutor that French composers expected performers to "dot" quick notes that are not dotted in the notation (1717, pp. 39–40). Probably both writers were referring to the approximately 3:2 ratio notated by Loulié. The violinist Muffat also avoided defining the ratio of inequality exactly, but pointed out that the bad quick note of each pulse unit must be shortened by the amount that the good one is lengthened (1698t, p. 232). Exact balancing of the lengthening and shortening of the quick notes within each pulse guarantees that all good ones sound exactly in time with the underlying pulses of the music.

A few Baroque writers differentiated between the execution of a good quick note on the downbeat and one elsewhere in the measure. The viol player Jean Rousseau "marked a little" only the downbeat quick note in *airs de mouvement* in triple meter, though he marked similarly all good quick notes in duple-meter airs (1687, p. 114). Dupont differentiated the first and third of four consecutive, stepwise quick notes by "giving weight" to the first and "reposing upon" the third (1718a, p. 9). Probably his "giving weight" implies extra length and loud-

EXAMPLE 11.4.
Gentle and sharp inequalities. Loulié, 1696t, p. 67. a. *louré*;
b. *piqué*.

Example 11.5.
Reversed inequality. Loulié, 1696t. a. gentle, p. 67; b. sharp,
p. 62.

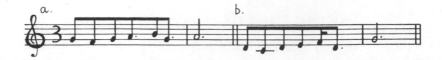

Example 11.6.
Various articulations in a single dance movement. Philidor,
gavotte, from *Suittes dessus et basse*, oe. 1/6, 1717. a. rondeau refrain, first phrase; b. first couplet, second phrase;
c. second couplet, last phrase.

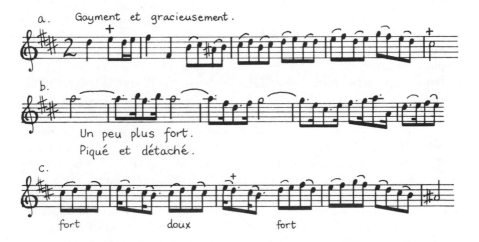

ness, whereas perhaps Rousseau's "marking" and certainly Dupont's "reposing"
imply extra length only.

    Although Loulié made clear that lengthening good quick notes was the usual
French practice, he also showed a reversed inequality (ex. 11.5) in one or two
pulse units of a measure. With this reversed inequality, the good note of the
pulse unit is shortened and the bad one is lengthened. For the gentler inequality of 2:3, Loulié merely dotted the bad note, but for a sharper execution, in
the ratio 1:3, he also added a beam to the good one (1696t, pp. 67, 62).

    Most composers left both the degree and the kind of inequality to the discre-
tion of the performer. This presented few problems in seventeenth-century
France, where the composer was often the performer or the conductor, but some
French composers of the early eighteenth century notated all unequal quick
notes as dotted figures, in the 3:1 ratio, to ensure an unequal performance.

    In a gavotte for flute, oboe, recorder, or violin, Pierre Philidor used a large
assortment of articulations (ex. 11.6). Unslurred quick notes are performed
with a sharply detached, 3:1 inequality; quick notes slurred in pairs are played

equally, or with normal or reversed inequality. Perhaps the majority of the dotted figures he notated with the 3:1 proportion should approach the 2:1 or 3:2 proportion; while those in the second phrase of the first couplet (b)—marked *piqué et détaché* (pointed and detached)—should be performed with a true 3:1 or even greater inequality.

Slurs occur in only one dance piece in a violin tutor. Michel de Montéclair (1711–12) slurred a few pair of good-bad quick notes in a pedagogical bourrée—presumably because of the speed of this dance. But quick notes in concert pieces with dance titles were often slurred in pairs (good-bad), as in Philidor's gavotte (ex. 11.6), or even in fours (good-bad-good-bad), as in many of the viol examples in Part II. Both ways of slurring bring out the good notes of the meter. Only occasionally, when the melodic contour identifies the underlying pulse movement, are the first or last three of four quick notes slurred (ex. 11.7).

Italian bowing practices introduced into France in the early eighteenth century go counter to French practices and allow the pulse movement to be more or less obscured, even in pieces with dance titles. For instance, staccato strokes or very long slurs often embrace all the pulses in one or two measures of music. Typical examples appear in a *corrente* for violin by Giovanni Antonio Piani, an Italian violinist who lived in France in the early eighteenth century and whose music was published there. In example 11.8a, a measure having French ornaments is followed immediately by a measure having a typically Italian run of

EXAMPLE 11.7.
Three-note slur in a concert dance. De Machy, gavotte, from suite 3 in *Pièces de viol*, 1685.

EXAMPLE 11.8.
Bowing practices that obscure the underlying pulse. Piani, corrente, from sonata, op. 1/4, 1712. a. mm. 44–45; b. mm. 71–74.

staccato strokes executed with a single bow stroke. In example 11.8b, a single slur covers two full measures. As French composers gradually adopted the Italian articulation practices, not only for the violin but also for other instruments, the underlying beats and pulses of their music too became blurred.

French musicians of the seventeenth and early eighteenth centuries kept a relatively strict tempo in dance music, emphasized good beats and pulses, and pointed up the good quick notes. Exact adherence to the tempo was needed to keep dancers in time; and even in concert pieces with dance titles, the tempo was followed more precisely than in other pieces.

12

Lullian Bowing of Dance Rhythms

The style of playing *airs de ballet* on string
instruments in the manner of the late, most
famous Monsieur Baptiste de Lully, here
understood in all its purity and acclaimed by
the best musicians in Europe, is so ingenious
a study that one can scarcely imagine anything
more precise, more agreeable, or more
beautiful.[1]

—Georg Muffat (1698t, p. 222)

The popularity of the violin in seventeenth-century France and Italy for accompanying dancing paralleled that of the Spanish guitar in sixteenth-century Spain. The variable strengths of the strokes on the violin and guitar—and in particular the difference between their upward and downward strokes—made these instruments especially suitable for bringing out the important pulses of the dance rhythms. According to Mersenne, the vigorous and high tones of the violin made it the instrument best fitted to accompany dancing. "And those who have heard the Twenty-four Violins of the King [Louis XIII, father of Louis XIV] avow that they have never heard anything more ravishing or more powerful [*puissant*]" (1636t, p. 235).

Most dance accompaniments in the operas and ballets of the *grand siècle* were scored for strings, sometimes with the addition of oboes and recorders. Lully tended to use five or six string parts, though he occasionally set entire dances—or contrasting sections of long dances—for three string or woodwind parts. Dancing lessons were often accompanied by the dancing master himself on a tiny violin that he could slip into his pocket while demonstrating a step.

French Baroque instruments of the violin family differed from their Italian counterparts in construction and in the way they were held. French violins were strung with lighter strings and played with shorter and lighter bows, which led to an intense and compelling but nevertheless light and flexible sound. Because the Italian instruments described by François Raguenet resemble the violins of modern orchestras, his words shed light on the differences between French Baroque and modern as well as Italian Baroque playing.

> The Italians have . . . the same advantage over us in respect of the instruments and the performers as they have in regard of the singers and their voices. Their violins are mounted with strings much larger than ours; their bows are longer, and they can make their instruments sound as loud again as we do ours. The first time I heard our band in the Opera after my return out of Italy, my ears had been so used to the loudness of the Italian violins that I thought ours had all been bridled.[2] (Raguenet, 1702t, p. 431)

At the same time, Raguenet commended the finesse and nicety of French string playing. By comparison, the Italians' strokes "sound harsh, if broken [detached], and disagreeable, if continued [sustained]" (p. 415).

For playing dance music, seventeenth-century violinists tended to hold the instrument to their chest rather than at their shoulder or neck (Boyden, 1965, plate 22). Since dance tunes of the day mainly required the left hand to be in the first or second position, a rigid hold on the violin was not necessary.

French violinists also used what later came to be known as the French bow grip, with the right thumb on the hair of the bow. This grip gives the player direct contact with the bow hair and "is very effective for the straightforward rhythmic and articulated bow stroke needed in dance music" (Boyden, pp. 152–53). In contrast, the viol bow is gripped from below rather than from above, and the middle finger of the right hand is on the bow hair. The player can thereby vary the tension of the bow hair as the articulation demands.

French bowing instruction comes from a variety of sources; that for the viol is the most descriptive generally and that for the violin best describes the articulation of dance rhythms. Many French viol players were aristocratic amateurs, so that French instructions in viol playing were often put down in detail, and rather complete bowings were given in concert music with dance titles. French violinists, on the other hand, were professionals hired to provide music for various court functions and entertainments, including balls and theatrical productions. They taught apprentices first hand and wrote down little, though several pedagogues gave beginners the normal violin bowings for the various dances.

No instructions on violin bowing survive from Lully's day, but his methods of playing dance music can be reconstructed from earlier and later violin and viol sources, all of which agree except for minor details. Mersenne (1636t) presented basic information on violin and viol bowing at the court of Louis XIII. Jean Rousseau (1687) and Étienne Loulié (unpublished manuscript, ca. 1690s) described the viol practices of Lully's final years. Muffat, in the prefaces to his *Florilegium primum* (1695) and *secundum* (1698), recollected Lully's practices when he (Muffat) had been a student in Paris some thirty years earlier. Michel Pignolet de Montéclair (1711–12) and Pierre Dupont (1718b), in tutors for beginning violin students, included bowings for specific dances, though few words of explanation. A general music tutor by Dupont (1718a) gave additional information. Concert pieces with dance titles by the viol players De Machy (1685), Marin Marais (1686–89, 1701, 1711, 1717, and 1725), and Jacques Morel (1709) included bowings and additional instructions.

In all these sources, two points concerning the bowing of dance accompaniments stand out: Most bow strokes are detached; and the strokes are ordered so as to differentiate the different meters and dance rhythms.

DETACHED BOW STROKES

The modern bow stroke called the "détaché" (separate stroke) does not detach a note from its neighbors. Rather, this term means that the player performs a single note with a single stroke. With the modern bow, the stroke tends to last throughout the value of the note, so that practically no silence or sound decay separates the notes. In practice, the modern détaché is similar to the sustained bow stroke of the French Baroque.

Although detached notes are rarely mentioned in seventeenth-century discussions of violin playing, most individual strokes in dance accompaniments were probably intended to be separated. The short violin bow of the French, along with the French Baroque manner of holding the violin and bow, practically dictated that pulse units and longer note values be detached.

The shortness and lightness of the French bow and the French hold and grip facilitated lifting the bow off the string or stopping the bow on the string at the end of a note. Lifting the bow leads to a decay of the sound: the string remains free to vibrate, but with steadily decreasing amplitude. Stopping the bow on the string, which Loulié in his unpublished viol tutor (ca. 1690s) called the "cut-off" or "dry" stroke (*coupé* or *sec*), halts the vibration of the string and creates silence except for room resonances. In a room with live acoustics, the sound of even a dry stroke reverberates appreciably.

The basic viol stroke is also well articulated. For the start of the stroke, the player presses the middle finger of the right hand firmly on the bow hair. In continuing the stroke, the pressure on the hair is decreased, causing the sound to decay rapidly, as if the string had been plucked. The bow is lifted at the end of the stroke (Hsu, 1981, p. 2). Hubert Le Blanc, in his defense of the viol, compared its simple bow strokes, "which strike the string as the jack plucks the harpsichord string," to the sustained strokes of the Italian violin of his day,

> where smooth and well-connected up-bows and down-bows, whose changes are imperceptible, produce an endless chain of notes that appear as a continuous flow, such as those emanating from the throats of [the famous opera singers] Cossoni [Cuzzoni] and Faustina.[3] (1740, pp. 23–24)

In short, French string players were able to articulate sensitively and cleanly because their instruments and playing techniques allowed considerable precision in the length of notes. Moreover, their bowing patterns were well regulated, so that all players on a given part bowed together and in a manner that clearly marked the meter and the dance rhythm.

BOWING PATTERNS FOR DANCE RHYTHMS

The so-called rule of the down-bow dominated the bowing of dance accompaniments in Europe through most of the seventeenth century and in France through the early eighteenth century. This rule broadly corroborates the strumming practices in Italian guitar books and French guitar pieces of the early seventeenth century. That is, the violinist uses the downward, or primary, stroke on most good notes of the measure, but never on quick bad notes; in addition, the primary stroke is used at most points of repose. The final downbeat of almost all musical periods is performed with a primary stroke.

Although viols were not normally employed in France to accompany dancing, they were used in many solo pieces with dance titles. Viol players followed bowing practices similar to those of violinists except that the downward and upward strokes were reversed. In other words, the viol's pushed stroke, or up-bow, was its strong, or primary, stroke and corresponded to the violin's down-bow. Concert pieces for viol included many expressive features not found in the simple tunes to accompany dancing: players tended to slur and ornament many more notes.

Our discussion of Lullian bowing patterns begins with Jean Rousseau's instructions for viol, which were conceived during Lully's most active years and so can be presumed to represent his practices. Rousseau began with a primary stroke on the first downbeat of a piece and then alternated the strokes until the flow was broken by a long note, rest, or melodic cadence (1687, pp. 108–109). After any of these points of repose he started again as at the beginning. Rousseau's stroke patterns for duple meter, shown in example 12.1, though not intended specifically for dance music, are the same as many in bowed dances. In our examples, we show viol bowings with the original signs in their original location beneath the notes. The letter p stands for *pousser* (to push), meaning the up-bow. The letter t stands for *tirer* (to pull), meaning the down-bow. Strokes are assumed to alternate until a new bowing sign appears.

Because violin bowings are more familiar to most modern readers than are viol bowings, and because violin bowings are the basic ones used for dance accompaniments, we give equivalent violin bowings in parentheses above the notes in all our viol examples. We indicate violin strokes with modern signs (⊓ for a down-bow, V for an up-bow) and include them for every note, as in most of the pedagogical examples for violin.

Alternating the bow strokes is natural for two, four, or eight notes of equal value in duple meter. Good notes receive primary strokes; bad notes, secondary ones. But groups of three notes require a more contrived ordering of the bow strokes. Several ways are discussed in the sources.

To accommodate three detached pulses in a measure of triple meter, Mersenne advocated using the secondary stroke for the downbeat of the second measure (1636t, p. 244). Similarly, Rousseau (1687, pp. 110 and 115) employed

EXAMPLE 12.1.
Alternated bow strokes in duple meter. Jean Rousseau, 1687,
p. 114. a. alternated strokes begun on a good note; b. alternated strokes begun on a bad note.

EXAMPLE 12.2.
Alternated strokes in triple meter. Jean Rousseau, 1687,
p. 115. a. bowing used by Mersenne and Rousseau; b. alternative bowing used by Rousseau.

EXAMPLE 12.3.
Slurring in *airs de mouvement* in triple meter. Jean Rousseau,
1687, p. 115.

the secondary stroke on either the second downbeat, as did Mersenne (ex.
12.2a), or the first (ex. 12.2b), and both practices are occasionally found in early
eighteenth-century violin tutors and viol music. However, the effects of the
two practices are quite different. Primary strokes on odd-numbered downbeats
support the rises of dancers at the starts of two-measure menuet steps. Primary
strokes on even-numbered downbeats evoke the lyrics of many menuet, sarabande, and folie songs, where the caesural repose falls on the second downbeat
and the cadential repose on the fourth.

For *airs de mouvement* in triple meter, Rousseau slurred the first two of three
pulses in a measure, emphasizing each downbeat (ex. 12.3). This practice is
common in viol and other solo music with dance titles, though it is not found in
pedagogical dances for violin.

The modern gambist John Hsu recommends that Loulié's *jetté* (thrown stroke)
be used for the last quarter note of each measure in menuets slurred as in example 12.3 (1981, pp. 15–16). Besides throwing the stroke for this final note,

the player reduces the pressure of the middle finger on the bow hair and thereby makes this note softer than the rest of the measure—even though the bow moves twice as quickly as before. The reduced pressure of the finger increases the feeling that the second stroke is thrown, or tossed lightly. A similar procedure could perhaps be effected when using the French grip on the violin, by lessening the pressure of the right thumb on the bow hair.

Another way that Rousseau and later string players accommodated a group of three notes was to play the first with a primary stroke and the second and third with a secondary one divided into two parts. The bow is lifted in the middle of the divided stroke and replaced immediately while the stroke is continued in the same direction (1687, p. 110). The string continues to vibrate between the two notes of the divided stroke, but the sound decays.

Hsu suggests that what Loulié called the stroke "with double expression" (*de double expression*) is a divided stroke that includes two sequences of press-and-release rather than a lifting of the bow to separate two notes (1981, p. 13).

Muffat called the practice of dividing the strokes on the violin *craquer* (to crack, upset, or throw into disorder), perhaps referring to the disruption of the flow of alternating strokes (1698t, p. 225). As illustrations, he cited a group of three equal pulses in triple meter and another of one pulse and two quick notes in duple meter (ex. 12.4). In both cases, the first note is played with a primary stroke and the second and third notes share a secondary one.

Muffat is the only Baroque authority who adopted different bowing signs for the two halves of a divided stroke: he used ∨ , his usual sign for the up-bow, for the first note of a divided up-bow, and a dot for the second note. He used ∣ for the down-bow.

Modern violinists use ⊓ for the down-bow and ∨ for the up-bow, and indicate a divided, or "hooked," up-bow by ∨ ∨ or by two dots joined by a slur. Because in performance the notes of a divided stroke are separated rather than joined, we do not use this last symbol. In Muffat's examples we use his ∨ for a

EXAMPLE 12.4.
Craquer, or divided stroke. Muffat, 1698t. a. groups of three
equal notes, p. 225; b. groups of one longer and two shorter
notes, p. 227.

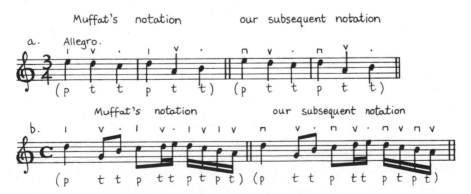

EXAMPLE 12.5.
Divided and retaken strokes in a sarabande. Dupont, 1718b,
p. 6.

divided up-bow, but because his ⎮ for a down-bow also means a detached note in Baroque music, we replace it with the modern ⊓ .

Example 12.4 shows Muffat's notation of two incipits, as well as the way we notate his examples later in this book. Equivalent viol bowings appear below the staff.

Other Baroque authorities did not differentiate the notation for two full up-bows from that for a single, divided up-bow (e.g., m. 1 of ex. 12.5). In most cases ⋁ ⋁ represents two separate notes played with a single divided stroke; occasionally it refers to two full up-bows.

Muffat and all French Baroque authorities seem to have recommended dividing only the secondary strokes, and even then only for a bad-bad or a good-bad pair of notes. That is, the last (bad) note of all or part of one measure and the first (good) one of the next never share a divided stroke, as often happens with today's "hooking." Such a division would make too large a separation at the bar line or at a smaller metrical break.

The silence, or sound decay, between the two notes of a divided stroke causes the first to be heard as the end of one group of notes and the second as the start of the next. For instance, the divided strokes in example 12.5 break each two-measure rhythm into two shorter, unequal units that simulate the syllable groups of sarabande lyrics described in chapter 6. Editorial strokes in the example indicate these small breaks.

Sometimes, instead of dividing a secondary stroke to make the bowing come out right, a full primary stroke is retaken. This resembles strumming twice in the downward direction. Muffat retook only primary strokes, and French violin and viol players of the period also followed that practice for the most part. In canaries and gigues, however, the quickness of the dotted figures may require repeated primary strokes to be divided rather than retaken. (See the bowed examples of these dances in Part II.)

Retaking a stroke generally requires more time and thus makes a larger separation than does dividing a stroke. The player must not only lift and replace the bow but also move it back into the starting position for the new stroke. Example 12.5 shows a stroke retaken on the downbeat of the third measure of a sarabande for violin. (In our examples retaken strokes are circled to make them more evident.)

Retaken strokes, like divided strokes, separate notes into groups. They also accent the start of a new group and thus help establish the particular character of a dance. For instance, the retaken stroke in example 12.5 breaks the four-measure melody into two equal, two-measure parts (each broken by a divided stroke into two unequal parts). Our editorial comma indicates the break caused by the stroke's being retaken.

According to Rousseau the bow may be retaken if necessary, provided the first of the two notes is "long enough," but he did not specify the criterion for length (1687, p. 109). The slight repose on the last quarter note in m. 2 of example 12.5 does in fact give a sense of length. Further examples may be seen in the triple-meter dances of Montéclair's and Dupont's violin tutors cited in Part II.

Muffat's description of Lully's art of playing dance music on the violin differs from all others in insisting that every downbeat be played with a primary stroke. Muffat complained that some German and Italian orchestras ignored this rule in triple meter, and that they alternated strokes throughout a menuet even though that led to secondary strokes falling on some downbeats (see Part II). He was especially concerned when the second note of the measure had a longer value than the first.

But the bowing pattern that Muffat rejected resembles Mersenne's and Rousseau's alternating pattern for triple meter (ex. 12.2a). Furthermore, Montéclair used a secondary stroke for the downbeat of the second measure of a softened hemiola rhythm in a loure (ex. 27.5), and Dupont showed a secondary stroke for the downbeat of the final measure of a sarabande (ex. 32.10b). Perhaps Lully did indeed require primary strokes for all downbeats in his ballroom and theatrical dances, or perhaps Muffat misremembered the Lullian practice. In any event, the rule of the down-bow evidently lost some of its power in France, as elsewhere during the 1720s and 30s, for the menuets in Corrette's violin tutor of 1738 have up-bows on alternate measures where convenient.

Violin concert solos with a figured-bass accompaniment, which were introduced into France by Italian virtuosi in the early eighteenth century, unfortunately include no bow markings other than the slurs and staccato indications of other Italian music of the period. However, dance rhythms at the start of many of these concert pieces should probably be stroked like their bowed counterparts in French tutors, but Italian figurations and articulations (such as runs of staccato or slurred notes) can deviate more from the rule.

To what extent French bowing practices also apply to orchestral suites by German composers such as J. S. Bach, Handel, and Telemann can only be surmised. If Lully's method was indeed "praised by the world's most eminent masters," as Muffat claimed, it must have been used by others. Muffat made clear that some German orchestras, including his own, followed Lully's practice. In any case, even the German and Italian players who performed downbeats of alternate triple-meter measures with the secondary stroke were following traditional principles.

What is indeed contrary to the French tradition of playing dance music is adding slurs to orchestral tuttis and dividing or retaking bow strokes inappropri-ately, as is done in some twentieth-century performances. Namely, modern players often divide primary strokes and sometimes divide a bad-good pair of notes. Both practices ignore the small breaks natural to the dance rhythms and so are foreign to the Lullian manner.

13

Forceful Articulation of Lullian Dance Lyrics

The familiar language, and that of singing, are
quite different, even as regards simple pronunciation; because what is done with weight,
that is, with the force necessary to the expression of the meaning of the words, is very different from what is practiced in the common
language. . . . In singing, which is a kind of
declamation, there is indeed a difference between [two utterances of the same letter, depending on the context], in order to make
sense of the words, and to give them the firm-
ness and the vigor that causes the singing to
have more variety, and not to be boring, as [an
actor] would be who simply recited the lines
in the theater, instead of declaiming them.[1]

—Bénigne de Bacilly (1668, pp. 253–54)

As Bacilly stated, there are many differences between declaimed singing and
ordinary speech. Some thirty years earlier, Marin Mersenne maintained that
"one of the great perfections of singing consists in pronouncing the words well,
and making them distinct, so that listeners do not lose a single syllable" (1636,
IIb, p. 356). But Bacilly did not consider it enough that each syllable of a song
be heard clearly. The singer had also to give each sound its necessary "force,"
so that the listener fully grasped the message contained in the words (1668,
p. 274).

Marilyn Somville suggests that one reason French opera took longer than
Italian opera to develop was that the French language created difficulties for the
singer, which had to be resolved before French singing could be forceful enough
for the theater (1967, p. 167). Bacilly (1668), Jean Grimarest (1707), and Jean-
Antoine Bérard (1755) gave suggestions for making French singing more power-

ful and projecting; and, because instrumental music "has no words under the notes to show the force and expression [each note] should be given," the hurdy-gurdy player Jean-Baptiste Dupuit told those who lacked a "sure and decided taste" not to play an instrument (1741, p. 7).

There was some disagreement during the *grand siècle* as to how far composers and performers of dance songs should exaggerate ordinary language. According to Bacilly (1668), these lyrics, being subject to the strict rhythms of the dance, are less influenced than other vocal music by the theatrical declamation of the words. The syllable lengths in serious songs are more important than the musical rhythm. But in airs in regular meter such as dance songs, he believed that the rhythm comes before the "quantity," or relative length, of the syllables—although the quantity must always be considered (pp. 354–55). Also, even though certain consonants generally omitted in everyday speech are normally sung for more solidity or to clarify the meaning, some of these may be dropped in "light airs," including dance songs (Bacilly, pp. 299, 316–17). In brief, Bacilly taught that "most airs such as gavottes, sarabandes and menuets" should be performed "in the common, or natural manner"; if sung in too affected a way, "they will have neither the pleasing quality, nor the tenderness that makes them so appealing" (p. 105).

Unlike Bacilly, Grimarest (1707) stated that declamation pertains not only to recitative and the "grand airs where passion reigns" but also to lyrics that "express only common thoughts, as in gigues, menuets or other quick pieces." Although some singers of dance airs paid attention only to the notes and did not bother with expression, "all lyrics have their particular character," whether they speak of tenderness, infidelity, constancy, or are drinking songs. A singer who does not animate every song according to the rules of declamation "sings not the words, but the notes" (Grimarest, 1760e, pp. 138–39). Even Bacilly allowed that, although dance melodies look very similar on paper, they are "distinguished by the adjustments the singer makes, and their agreeable performance." In the mouth of a good singer, these "little nothings" become "marvels" (1668, p. 106).

The rules of declamation apply also to the composing of music (Bacilly, 1668, p. 331). That is, the composer uses a variety of note values, melodic and harmonic accents, and positions in the measure to give each word exactly the right nuance. (The composer's use of especially long or short note values was mentioned in chap. 6.) As for melodic inflections, calm speech is represented essentially by diatonic steps in French vocal music. The melody ascends slightly to the end-accent of members, descends to that of periods. The final "mute" *e* of a feminine line drops an interval of about a third from the pitch of its end-accent. Any deviation from this normal melody signifies heightened emotion; the more noticeable the deviation the greater the intensity.

In the following discussion the composer's contribution is mentioned only in passing. For further information the reader is referred to the articles by Lois Rosow (1983) and Patricia M. Ranum (1985 and 1986) and to Ranum's forthcoming tutor on the declamation of Lullian lyrics.

BACILLY'S RULES OF QUANTITY

Bacilly explained that certain syllables are always long or at least somewhat long; but no syllable is so short that, depending on its relationship to the following one, it cannot "pass for long" (1668, p. 333) if the composer or singer finds it suitable (p. 339). A long syllable is merely somewhat longer than others (p. 338)—not twice as long, as are the L's in relation to the S's of rhythmic movements.

Bacilly pointed out that French poetry in its written form is not concerned with quantity; but when French lines are recited, sung, or declaimed, the long and short syllable lengths must be observed. He was therefore concerned not with the writing of French lines but only with their musical declamation, namely, with giving the syllables their proper significance and weight in singing (p. 328). A long syllable is usually set to a strong beat of the measure or to a relatively long note value. If not, the singer must perform the syllable so that it seems long.

Bacilly gave much information on and many examples of the length of syllables in vocal music. He explained which syllables are always long; and which are long, half-long, or short, depending on the context. Yet he advised that "often good taste must be the judge" (p. 386).

The following broad simplification combines Bacilly's rules, which cover seven chapters in his book. Although we do not account here for all the syllable lengths, we hope to show instrumentalists at least their general tendencies and arrangements in dance songs and to encourage singers to study Bacilly's 100 pages (pp. 327–428) for themselves. (Readers are advised if possible to use the modern facsimile edition rather than the English translation.) The examples in this section follow the method initiated in part by Ranum (1985 and 1986). Capital letters denote the "always long" or "always half-long" syllables, except for the final long one of a feminine line, which appears in bold type. Underlined letters designate the interior syllables that are long only because of the rules of "symmetry"—the alternation of long and short syllables. To show an elision, we replace the elided *e* with an apostrophe and join the previous consonant with the following vowel as in a single word, for instance, "gout-te à **gout**-te" becomes "gout-t'à **gout**-te" (app. ex. 2, mm. 17–18). We use Bacilly's spellings throughout and, unless otherwise indicated, all page references are to Bacilly.

1. This rule is perhaps the most important: Before a punctuation mark, at a caesura or a rhyme, or at a break in the meaning of a line, the last counted syllable is always long (pp. 369, 373; also, by implication, throughout chaps. 3 and 4 of his part III). These long syllables are the end-accents of their textual units.

> QUOY? vou-lez-VOUS. (p. 414)
> AH! qu'il est ma-lai-SÉ, // quand l'a-mour est ex-**trè**-me. (p. 422)

As discussed in chapter 6, the end-accents of the hemistiches and short lines in Lullian dance songs almost always fall on downbeats.

> Est-on |sa-ge (app. ex. 1, mm. 1–2)
> La beau-|TÉ/ la plus sé-|vè-re (app. ex. 2, mm. 1–2)

Although the end-accents of French recitation are brought out more by length and pitch than by loudness, the singer should perform the longest and most final syllables with a swell and then an ebb of the sound, that is, by increasing the volume "up to a certain point" and then gradually diminishing it (pp. 198–99). When the syllables *a, an, en, am,* or *em* occur on a very long note at a final cadence, they should be performed by opening the mouth gradually, so as to arrive at the ultimate quality and fullness of tone only after a while (pp. 258–59). In other words, the long final syllable at a principal cadence should never end suddenly, with what Bacilly called a "hiccup" (p. 194).

2. All syllables in a line of lyrics, and therefore all notes in the corresponding music, must have enough force to be clearly understood in the theater. For this reason, singers should pronounce the normally weak "mute" *e* more strongly than usual, namely, like the French *eu.* Although short syllables, such as many "mute" *e*'s, should be "passed over quickly and lightly with no mark of length" (p. 413), the *eu* pronunciation is recommended "as much to give strength to the expression as to make the *e* heard distinctly by the audience" (pp. 265–66). Care must be taken, however, not to lengthen a short syllable so much as to alter its meaning; for instance, *de* (of) should never be mistaken for *deux* (two).

3. Although a final "mute" *e* is often held at principal cadences, to give a sense of finality, many feminine lines of dances—notably in gavottes, sarabandes, and courantes—end with a short note value. Nevertheless, a truly short performance of these notes would be a "terrible error against musical good taste," which requires that all such notes be sustained (pp. 393–94). Therefore the "mute" *e* of, for instance, "SA-ge" (app. ex. 1) and "sé-vè-re" (app. ex. 2) should be made to seem as long as possible without disturbing the respective menuet and gavotte rhythms.

4. According to the rules of symmetry, the penultimate syllable at a masculine or feminine rhyme or caesura is normally short in relation to the last one. Even if that is not the case, the final accented note should at least seem somewhat longer than the penultimate one.

5. Also according to the rules of symmetry, the antepenultimate syllable at a rhyme or caesura can be long; and the syllable before that, short: "se <u>trop</u> flat-TER" (pp. 340–42); and "L'EAU qui |tom-be/ <u>gout</u>-t'à |gout-te" (app. ex. 2, mm. 16–18).

For whatever reason adjacent syllables are respectively short and long, the short one "yields" to the following long one (e.g., p. 424), and sometimes the short one is "thrown quickly onto" the long one (e.g., pp. 341, 374). In other words, the short syllable is at least somewhat arsic to the following long one, which is correspondingly thetic.

6. With three or more syllables in a unit, the rules of symmetry allow and encourage the composer to set one of two consecutive short syllables as if it were long; or, if the composer sets the two short syllables to the same note values, the singer may perform one of them like a long syllable (p. 416). Even a "mute" *e* within a line, although short in other contexts, may here be set or sung as a long syllable. The syllable "need not be absolutely long"; it is enough

for the sound to "cease being short" (p. 342): "ny de l'ai-MER" (p. 340); "de se ren-dre" (p. 341); also "L'ON-/de| se FAIT/ | u-ne |rou-te" (app. ex. 2, mm. 12–14). Instrumentalists too should avoid playing two consecutive notes of the same value in exactly the same way.

7. In Lullian songs, short and long syllables never alternate continuously. This is because certain syllables that often appear in nonfinal positions are long even if they precede another long syllable.

a. No matter where a feminine word occurs in a line, its final counted syllable is always long—unless the "mute" e is elided with a following vowel (p. 386): "u-ni-que" and "I-nu-ti-le" (p. 387); but, with an elision: "il EN ai-M'UN" (p. 389).

b. Nonfinal syllables are always long if an n (or m pronounced n) follows a vowel and precedes a pronounced consonant other than n or m: "DANS u-ne," "CENT au-tres," "SANS el-le" (p. 337); "CHAN-GER," "DAN-GER," "LAN-GUEUR," "SON-GER," "VAN-GER" (p. 407). Monosyllables that end with a single n are always long if the following word begins with a consonant: "BIEN," "BON," "C'EN," "D'UN," "EN," "FIN," "L'ON," "MON," "NON," "ON," "VIEN," "RIEN," "TON," "VAIN," "UN" (pp. 366–67).

In the theater, nasals lack power when they are pronounced as in everyday speech; therefore they should be sung by sustaining the vowel without a nasal quality for almost the full value of the note and then "stroking" the n only at the last moment (p. 262).

c. Most nonfinal monosyllables ending with s (or x or z, pronounced s), whether alone or in combination with another consonant, are long: "BEAUX," "CES," "CEUX," "DES," "DOUX," "EST," "FAIS" (from faire), "JEUX," "LES," "LIEUX," "LORS," "MES," "MAIS," "SANS," "SES," "TEMPS," "VOS," "YEUX" (pp. 356–58); "GOUS-TER" (p. 414). However, monosyllables such as the following are only half-long: "ILS," "LEURS," "NOUS," "PLUS," "SÇAIS," "SOUS," "SUIS" (from suivre), "TOUS," "TRES," "VOIS" (from voir), "VOUS" (p. 359); and so are the penultimate syllables of such words as "ES-POIR," "DES-TIN," "EX-trè-me," "ré-SIS-TER" (p. 410).

d. Nonfinal syllables that end with r or l followed by another consonant, or that precede a word or syllable that begins with a consonant, are half-long: "PERD," "SERT," "SORT" (pp. 367–68); "a-LAR-MER," "BER-GER," "CHAR-MANT," "CHER-CHER," "dé-SOR-MAIS," "PAR-LER," "PER-DU," "POUR-QUOY," "TIR-SIS" (p. 409); "MAL-GRÉ," "QUEL-QU'UN," "re-VOL-TER," "SIL-vi-e" (p. 410).

e. Monosyllables with the diphthong au are always long, as are the monosyllables voeu and noeud: "il VAUT MIEUX," "AU MOINS" (p. 371); "le NOEUD DAN-ge-REUX," "le VOEU so-lem-NEL" (p. 373).

Penultimate syllables having the diphthong au may be long: "AU-TANT," "BEAU-TÉ," "cru-AU-TÉ"; somewhat long: "AUS-SI," "BEAU-COUP," "CAU-SÉ," "é-CHAUf-FER"; or short: "au-RA," "au-RAY," "au-PRÈS," "sçau-RAY," "sçau-RA" (p. 413).

f. Monosyllables having diphthongs other than *au* and *oeu* may be short: "loy," "moy," "soy," "toy," "quoy"; "ou," "tout"; "peu," "lieu"; "luy," "fuit"; "vray," "ay" (pp. 372–73).

g. Penultimate syllables having the diphthong *ai* may be very long: "PLAI-SIR," "RAI-SON," "SAI-SON," "BAI-SER"; less long: "EN-CHAIS-NER," "MAI-SON"; or not at all long: "fai-SOIT," "trai-TER," "sou-hai-TER," "plai-SOIT" (p. 412).

h. Most penultimate syllables with the diphthongs *oi* or *ou* are not long: "moi-TIÉ," "choi-SIR," "loi-SIR," "cou-LER," "cou-RIR," "dou-CEUR," "dou-LEUR," "dou-TER," "mou-RIR," "sou-DAIN," "vou-LOIR," "cous-TER," "pous-SER," but: "GOUS-TER" (p. 414).

i. Most penultimate syllables that contain a single vowel and no following consonant are short. But a few are always long: "re-PO-SER," "O-SER," "re-FU-SER," "ex-CU-SER" (p. 415).

8. The penultimates at rhymes, caesuras, and other textual breaks are often long syllables that fall on bad notes of the music. Lengthening or suitably ornamenting these syllables usually emphasizes either the root of an important word or the first monosyllabic word of an important pair: "BEAU-|TÉ," "TOUR-|MENT" (app. ex. 2, upbeat to and first beat of m. 1, mm. 3–4); "VAN-|GER," "MES |VOEUX" (app. ex. 3, mm. 1–2, 7–8). Ranum (1985) points out that a series of long syllables often brings the music to a halt at important cadences; e.g., "PREND pi-|TIÉ/ D'UN LONG TOUR-|MENT" (app. ex. 2, mm. 3–5).

9. No matter where a syllable that is always long appears in a line, the previous syllable becomes relatively short—unless that syllable too is always long (p. 344). Even then, in the last example in the paragraph above, the syllables "D'UN" and "TOUR-" are somewhat short despite their final *n* or *r* before another consonant (pp. 352–53).

10. Not only are syllables that are always long, half-long, or long by symmetry sometimes set to short note values, but short syllables may be set to long ones. Some short syllables are even set to long values that fall on good pulses. In his menuet song (ex. 13.1 and app. ex. 1), Lully managed to set most long syllables to long note values or to downbeats. The few long syllables on shorter values have prominent pitches, such as an accidental or the highest note of a line (line 2, "le"), a noticeably low pitch (line 9, "la"), or a repeated pitch (line 7, "GOÛ"-[different spelling of "GOUS"-]); or the harmony is changed there, as indicated by the bass figures (line 10, "de"). Most short syllables are set to quarter or eighth notes; those on longer values make dramatic pauses, as the listener waits to learn what is to come: "L'ON se -?-" (line 6); "La sa- -?-" (line 8).

11. When the length of the syllable does not correspond to that of the note the composer has set to it, Bacilly expected singers to use their own skill and ingenuity to correct the discrepancy, and at the same time take care not to disturb the dance rhythm (pp. 331–32). Grimarest agreed with Bacilly: To sing well, the vocalist must know perfectly the rules of quantity. Grimarest went so far as to say that singers must make long syllables long and short syllables short,

EXAMPLE 13.1.
Long syllables in Lully's menuet song (app. ex. 1). Capital
letters indicate masculine end-accents and "always long"
syllables within the line; bold print designates feminine
end-accents; underlined syllables are those that can be long
by symmetry.

"regardless of the value of the notes to which they are set" (1760e, pp. 134–35). If a long syllable occurs on a short note, the note must be held as long as the rhythm allows, unless its initial consonants are emphasized by "doubling" them (see below). If a normally short syllable is set to a long note, the syllable may be lengthened somewhat if the meaning is not compromised, or the note may be cut short and followed by a silence.

12. Although Lully banned most ornaments from his stage works, Bacilly recommended they be used to clarify the syllable lengths of lyrics. His Part III states that the syllables that are always long allow the longest ornaments, such as a long *tremblement* (trill), *accent* (an upper grace note touched lightly after the principal note has been held almost its full value), or a more elaborate ornamentation. Often these syllables must be decorated in this way for the full impact of the word to be made. Syllables that are half-long permit only shorter ornaments, such as a short trill or a *doublement du gosier* (a single repetition of the pitch in the throat—probably something like a mordent or one pulse of a vibrato). In fact, Bacilly often determined the length of a syllable in a given context by the kind of ornament that would be suitable for it. To show how instrumentalists after Lully's death followed Bacilly's advice and expressed long syllables by means of ornaments, Ranum (1985) cites Jean-Henry D'Anglebert's sarabande arrangement for harpsichord (1689) of a piece by Lully.

D'Anglebert's gavotte arrangement of "Le beau berger Tirsis," an anonymous *air ancien*, is similar (ex. 13.2). (The words for this traditional song were included by Hotteterre in an arrangement for flute; see ex. 15.10.) D'Anglebert put ornaments of some kind on all the notes representing fully long syllables. For instance, "BER-" (m. 1) is only half-long and carries no ornament; whereas the first exclamation "AH" (m. 9) is decorated with four quick or very quick notes. D'Anglebert used trills in this arrangement also to emphasize a few short syllables set to long values: on the first downbeat ("Le"); on the penultimate syllable in mm. 4 and 6 ("r'An-" and "as-"); and on the final "mute" *e* in m. 8.

FORCEFUL CONSONANTS

Regardless of the spelling and the grouping into words, most French syllables begin with a consonant and continue with a vowel. The modern phoneticist Pierre Delattre explains that two consecutive sounds in French tend to divide into syllables when the mouth opens more for the first than for the second. Because the mouth is relatively open for vowels and closed for consonants, French syllables divide after a vowel if possible (1951, p. 18). Thus "Dans le bel age" (ex. 13.2, line 2) is pronounced in speech and song as if the words were divided "Dans le be la-ge," not "Dans leb el ag-e."

The initial consonants of a spoken or sung syllable in an important and emotional word are expressed forcefully. Stressing these consonants helps bring out the meaning and vitality of the text. Bacilly called the practice "sustaining the consonants" or, more dramatically, "snarling" (*gronder*). In impassioned utterances he especially sustained the soft consonant *m*, and often *f*, *n*, *s*, *j*, and *v* (pp. 309–11). The initial consonants of French syllables are normally sung be-

EXAMPLE 13.2.
Ornaments on long syllables. D'Anglebert's harpsichord arrangement of "Le beau berger Tirsis," 1689.

fore the beat, and the following vowel on the beat (Ranum, 1985). Thus a sustained initial consonant begins well before its indicated time; and it may last
through part of the following vowel.

Either the first or the root syllable of the intense words mentioned by Bacilly
begins with the snarled consonant (pp. 307–11): "mourir" (to die), "malheu-
reux" (unfortunately), "miserable" (miserable); "severe" (severe), "jamais"

(never), "v̲ous" (you), "v̲olage" (fickle); "in̲fidele" (unfaithful one), "enf̲in" (at last). These highly emotional renderings immediately fix the audience's attention on the vital words, wherever they fall in the measure. As examples, Bacilly cited a number of lines from his and others' songs. (Austin B. Caswell's 1968 translation includes the music for these lines.) Because these are not lines from dance songs, the number of syllables in a measure is highly irregular.

Je |m̲eurs/ vous le vo-yez.	(Caswell, p. 160)
I <u>die</u>/ you see.	

|Ah!/ qu'il |est m̲a-lai-|sé.	(Caswell, p. 160)
Ah!/ how <u>painful</u> it is.	

Ve-nez/ heu-reux m̲o-ment.	([no bar lines] Caswell, p. 161)
Come/ happy <u>moment</u>.	

|Puis-que Phi-|lis/ est in-f̲i-|de-le.	(Caswell, p. 162)
Since Phyllis/ is <u>unfaithful</u>.	

|N̲on,/ je |ne pre-tend |pas.	(Caswell, p. 162)
<u>No</u>,/ I don't intend.	

Bacilly used the term "doubling" for a similar but not always impassioned lengthening of the consonant *r*. He doubled the *r* when it begins a sentence or when it precedes or follows another consonant, but he enunciated it with increased intensity in a word that demands vehement expression (pp. 291–94).

Si l'n-|g̲rat-te.	(Caswell, p. 151)
If the <u>ungrateful</u> (one).	

La |C̲ru-el-le.	(Caswell, p. 151)
The <u>cruel</u> [one].	

Jean Antoine Bérard's extensive and dramatic "preparing," or "doubling," of consonants elongates the soft consonants that Bacilly sustained or doubled, but also "holds back" such hard consonants as *d*, *t*, and *c* (pronounced *k*)—making them more explosive than usual. Bérard indicated a doubled consonant of either kind by writing the letter a second time above the first. The size of the second letter indicated the intensity of the passion to be expressed (1755, pp. 93–99 of the text; pp. 1–8, 21–23, and 32–33 of the examples). Although Bacilly "snarled" or doubled only one letter in a prosodic unit, Bérard often doubled or held back two or more. In the following despondent couplet from a recitative in Lully's opera *Armide* (1686), Bérard "doubled strongly" and pronounced "with much harshness and gloom" the underlined letters (p. 13 of his examples).

Plus/ on c̲on-noit l̲'a\|-mour,// & p̲lus/ on le d̲é-\|tes-t̲e:
(The more/ one <u>knows</u> <u>love</u>, the <u>more</u>/ one <u>detests</u> <u>it</u>:)

Dé-t̲rui-\|sons/ son pou-voir f̲u-\|nes-te.
(Let's <u>destroy</u>/ <u>its</u> <u>funestral</u> <u>power</u>.)

In this song, as in all those quoted by Bérard, doubled consonants fall on more bad than good note values. Here the irregular disposition of the forceful consonants indicates passionate expression, and the clustering of stressed words at the ends of lines and hemistiches emphasizes the conclusion. Perhaps Bérard doubled more letters than Bacilly did because of the greater intensity and rhythmic variety in theatrical declamation of the eighteenth century (see Rosow, 1983, pp. 474–76).

In contrast, the much calmer "Joli air en brunette" from *Titon* has the rhythm of a gavotte and is uttered with an expression that lies "between a sweetness and an extreme clarity" (Bérard's examples, p. 32).

Vo-tre| coeur/ ai-ma-bl'Au-|ro-re
(Your heart[,]/ lovable Aurore)

Est sen-|si-/bl'a mes sou-|pirs,
(Is sensitive/ to my sighs,)

The doubled consonants in this song are "prepared only weakly," and the doubled letters are written much smaller than in Bérard's previous examples. In each of the two-measure rhythmic subjects that are typical of gavottes, the consonant in the stressed syllable of the first emotional word is doubled: *coeur* (heart), *sensible* (sensitive). (In fact, two consonants in *sensible* are doubled, though the "mute" *e* following the latter is elided with the vowel that follows.) These doubled consonants also emphasize the final syllable of the first hemistich in each line (*coeur* and *-si-*) and conclude the three-note musical rhyme that identifies the piece as a gavotte. At the end of each line, an off-beat consonant is doubled to emphasize the root syllable of the final emotional word: *-bl'Aurore* (the feminine ending of "lovable" elided with a girl's name) and *soupirs* (sighs). The doublings in this gavotte-like song are not only mild but also regular and rhythmic.

TONES OF VOICE

The tone of voice used by an actor or singer mirrors the passions of the character he is portraying. As pointed out by Ranum (personal communication), Grimarest discussed extensively the tones of voice used to express the passions (1760e, pp. 8off). For instance, love can have three expressions: When it is sweet, the voice is flattering and tender; when love gives pleasure, the voice is gay; and when the lover suffers, the tones are urgent and plaintive.

Desire also has several expressions: If love causes the desire, the voice is tender but urgent; if resistance heightens it, the tone is spiteful and angry; if the desire is moderate, a weak voice suffices to express it; if the lover languishes, the voice is sweet and broken by sighs.

Joy calls for a voice that is sweet, full, and easy. Sadness requires one that is weak, dragging, and plaintive but whose strength depends in fact on the power of the person speaking. (A king speaks in a strong voice; a peasant, in a weak one.) Hope is expressed in exclamatory, high-pitched, and precipitous tones.

Grimarest did not describe the melodic, rhythmic, and dynamic counterparts of the various tones of voice, which lie within the province of the composer and the performer; but they can be readily imagined. For instance, a flowing, unaccented execution, with few separations between notes, would seem suited to the tender and flattering tone of sweet love. A lively, leaping, somewhat detached performance would suggest the gay tone of pleasureful love. Descending intervals with a corresponding drop in loudness would represent the sighs of a languishing lover. Sharp accents, an erratic melody, and some separation of notes would express the spiteful and angry tone of desire resisted.

Modern singers wishing to recreate French Baroque dance songs must go more deeply into the texts of Mersenne, Bacilly, Grimarest, Bérard, and others than can be done here. And modern instrumentalists wishing to imitate the forceful articulation of French dance songs must study many more songs than can be presented in this book. Nevertheless, some guidelines to declamatory execution can be given:

1. Pronunciation even in dance songs is somewhat exaggerated.
2. Final syllables are lengthened to the extent the music allows.
3. Because of the rules of symmetry, short and long syllables tend to alternate, usually short-long, short-long.
4. However, several long syllables often fall on consecutive notes, especially at the ends of lines, hemistiches, and even some textual cells, where the long syllables help the singer bring out the most important word(s) of the unit.
5. Long syllables sometimes fall on short note values, and short syllables on long ones. In both cases, the singer is expected to make long syllables seem long, and short ones seem short by comparison.
6. Although Lully did not allow much ornamentation in his music, composers and performers before and after him often used embellishments to "correct" a long syllable set to a short note, or vice versa.
7. Forceful consonants may be used on good or bad notes, and on short or long note values. These consonants often bring out the initial or root syllable of an intense word or of a whole textual cell that expresses high emotion.
8. The tone of voice and its accompanying articulation mirror the emotion expressed.

14

Articulation of Dance Rhythms in Concert Pieces

> The bow is [the viol's] soul; since it is the bow
> that animates the viol, expresses all the pas-
> sions suitable to the voice, and marks the dif-
> ferent rhythms [*mouvements*] of the melody.[1]
>
> Jean Rousseau (1687, p. 107)

To the extent that the viol's bow is its soul, the souls of the guitar and the lute
are the player's strumming or plucking hand, and the soul of wind instruments is
the player's breath. For it is the strokes of the player's bow, hand, and breath
that animate the instruments, express the different passions, and articulate the
various rhythms in concert pieces of all kinds.

Some concert pieces with dance titles are almost indistinguishable from music to accompany dancing; others recall the rhythms and inflections of dance
songs. But, because these pieces lack dancing or singing to hold the audience's
attention, the composition and performance of many phrases rely on arresting
departures from customary practices. That is, the usual rhythms are altered
or divided so that the instrument's expressive and virtuosic capabilities can be
exploited.

EMPHASIZING IMPORTANT NOTES

Players of the viol, guitar, lute, and harpsichord had several ways of bringing
out significant notes. They used chords on some important notes, in partial imitation of early guitar accompaniments for the dance. They let certain notes continue to sound while going on to play less important ones; and they decorated
some notes with a variety of ornaments. Also, guitarists, lutenists, and harpsichordists chose fingerings that reflected the relative importance of the notes. In
short, the music for these instruments was more or less dominated by the *style*

brisé (broken style), which descended from the lute techniques in early French tablatures. As James R. Anthony describes it,

> The *style brisé* is a classic example of a musical style that exploited the very limitations of the instrument that created it. Chords are arpeggiated and inner voices shredded so that any linear writing is more implied than actual. Consecutive notes from different octaves pass freely in and out of the texture only to disappear in thin air. Ornaments help in sustaining a melodic line, and a constant thinning and thickening of the texture is apparent. (1978, p. 238)

Example 14.1 gives the first reprises of six concert dances, the first four of which are written in the *style brisé*. All these pieces start in characteristic ways, but the differing strengths of chords, long notes, ornaments, and slurs demonstrate the variety of inflections found in the concert dances of the *grand siècle*.

Chords are the most obvious way of making notes stand out. Where chords are few, they make powerful accents (exx. 14.1a, b, c, d). Where plucked chords are mixed with strummed ones, the latter are the loudest (ex. 14.1c). Where upward and downward strums are mixed, the upward ones yield to the stronger, downward ones (ex. 14.1c). Chords of some kind emphasize many salient downbeats, such as the first, last, or penultimate ones of a rhythmic subject, period, or reprise (exx. 14.1a, b, c, and d).

Rolled chords in harpsichord pieces imitate the strums of a guitar. Rolls that ascend in pitch mimic a chord strummed downward (since the stringing of the early guitars causes a downward strum to produce an upward sequence of pitches). In example 14.1b, in which ⸖ indicates a chord rolled upward, rolls define essentially $\frac{3}{2}$ and then $\frac{6}{4}$ meter (mm. 3–5).

Important rhythmic values in lute, guitar, and harpsichord pieces are often continued during later ones. Although lute and guitar tablatures do not specify the exact length of many notes, when a string is sounded it is usually allowed to vibrate until it is needed for another note. To some extent, therefore, the tablatures do indeed show the length of time that rhythmic values are heard. In m. 1 of example 14.1a, for instance, the three lowest pitches in the first chord are allowed to ring until their sound dies out (no letter appears after the "a" in the first, third, and fourth spaces of the tablature). The downbeat is strengthened both by the number of notes in the chord and by their longer ringing. On the other hand, the first three notes of the melody (a repeated A flat) sound only for the values indicated above the staff (the repeated pitches are produced by plucking the same string). The lower strings especially are often allowed to vibrate at the start or finish of a rhythmic subject, period, or reprise.

Ornaments, including slurs, emphasize important rhythmic values in several ways. Many mark downbeats, as do many trills, swells, and mordents in examples 14.1e and f. Others point up the notes of rhythmic movements, as do the slurred bow strokes in examples 14.1e and f and the trills (marked with commas) on the bad-note L's in example 14.1a (mm. 2, 4, 6, and 8). Some ornaments articulate a rhythmic movement that differs from the slurred one, as at the start of example 14.1e. There the slurring articulates an antispast (SLLS),

EXAMPLE 14.1.
Differing strengths of chords, long notes, ornaments, and
slurs. a. Mesangeau, courante for lute (Ballard's tablature,
1638, p. 9; transcription No. 24 by André Souris, in *Oeuvres
de René Mesangeau*, reproduced by permission of Éditions
du Centre National de la Recherche Scientifique), the symbol
i, indicating a note plucked by the index finger, added by the
present authors; b. Chambonnières, courante for harpischord,
1670, livre 1, ordre 1, #3; c. Visée, allemande for guitar, from
suite 6, "Tombeau de M.ʳ Francisque," 1682 (Strizich transcription; reproduced by permission of Heugel éditeurs);
d. Marais, allemande for viol, "La familière," #10, 1710;
e. Marais, sarabande for viol, #19, 1725; f. Marais, sarabande
for viol, #34, 1725.

EXAMPLE 14.1.
Continued

EXAMPLE 14.1.
Continued

but the mordent on the third pulse (marked with an x) divides the first L of the antispast, changing the rhythm to a hegemeole, which is characteristic of sarabandes (SSSLS). Some ornaments indicate the beginning of a new rhythmic subject, as do the swells (marked with an "e" over the notes) in mm. 2 and 5 of example 14.1d. Some mark the reposes of rhythmic subjects, as do the mordents and trills on downbeats in mm. 2, 3, and 5 of example 14.1d. The first two of these reposes are feminine; the last is masculine. Finally, as in the first four examples, cadential trills announce the imminent repose of many musical reprises.

Perhaps the most soulful ornament is the "swell," which imitates the *messa di voce* of singers. With a swell, players of bowed and wind instruments emphasize an important note by making it gradually louder and then softer. In an unpublished viol tutor, Étienne Loulié called the swell a "nourished" or "sustained" stroke (ca. 1690s). Marin Marais said the ornament "expresses" ("presses out") or "inflates" the note or stroke (1711, preface). Excellent illustrations of places where swells should be used are the dances in Marais's third, fourth, and fifth books of pieces for the viol (1711, 1717, 1725). In these pieces the letter "e," for *expresser* or *enfler*, indicates the ornament. If the "e" appears directly over the note head, the swell begins quickly and emphasizes the start of the note; if it comes after the note head, the swell begins slightly later and emphasizes the length of the note. Example 14.1f illustrates the two possible positions of the "e".

In a similar fashion the pedagogue Pierre Dupont, who was probably a violinist, told players to "lean upon" (*appuyer sur*) good quarter notes in $\frac{6}{8}$ meter (1718a, p. 40). This articulation is probably similar to Marais's "e" placed directly over a note. In addition, Dupont recommended "doubling the sound" (*redoubler la voix*) at the middle of a syncopated note (p. 13), an articulation probably similar to Marais's "e" placed after the note.

Fingerings in lute, guitar, and harpsichord pieces also reflect the rhythmic importance of notes. In the lute tablature in example 14.1a, for instance, the most-important notes of the melody are plucked with the longest, or middle, finger. Less-important notes are plucked with the main secondary one, the index finger (indicated with a dot in the tablature and an "i" in the transcription). Bass notes are plucked with the thumb. Often, as in this example, only the notes to be played with the index finger are indicated in the tablature. Except in the last measure of the example, where the index finger is one of three playing the final chord, the notes marked with a dot are bad notes.

Bénigne de Bacilly believed that the harpsichord, whose strings are plucked mechanically, could not be as expressive as instruments whose strings are sounded with the player's fingers, for only fingers that touch the strings can appreciably "mark and soften" the notes:

As regards marking and softening, . . . this is good on the lute, theorbo [bass lute], viol, and other instruments, whose strings can be sounded as much or as little as one wishes, to mark their difference from the harpsichord, over which those who touch [the strings with their fingers] have a great advantage, seeming by this means to make their instruments speak, and to express the passions of tenderness, or of anger, by means of [the strength of] the sound made in touching the strings lightly, or striking them with force. . . .[2] (1668, pp. 192–93)

Harpsichordists too seem to have used the middle finger for many good pulses of the meter. The only harpsichord pieces we found with complete fingerings are a menuet and a gavotte cited by Michel de Saint-Lambert (1702). In addition, François Couperin gave fingerings for a few isolated measures in some of his harpsichord pieces (1717, pp. 46–50, 66–71). The principal finger for harpsichordists, as for lutenists and guitarists, was the middle one, marked 3 in harpsichord music. The thumb, marked 1, and the little finger, marked 5, could substitute for the middle finger. Secondary fingers were the index finger (2) and the ring finger (4). In Saint-Lambert's menuet in example 14.2, primary fingers (1, 3, and 5) are used on most good notes in the first reprise, but on far fewer

EXAMPLE 14.2.
Saint-Lambert, menuet, 1702, p. 67; the symbol ○, indicating
an articulation silence, added by the present authors.

good ones and many more bad ones in the second. A silence (indicated by ○)
before a note makes that note stand apart. This silence may introduce an important note, or set off a group of notes.

ARTICULATION SILENCES THAT INTRODUCE
IMPORTANT NOTES

As discussed in chapter 11, pulse notes and longer values in the dance music of
the *grand siècle* are commonly detached to emphasize their regularity. In addition, repeated notes and leaping ones are normally more detached than stepwise ones. The silence or the decay in the sound that separates repeated notes
to prevent their running together enhances the melodic insistence on the same
pitch. The silence produced by the performer's crossing a string, moving the

EXAMPLE 14.3.
Saint-Lambert, gavotte, 1702, p. 68.

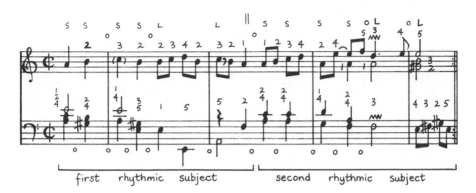

hand on the fingerboard or keyboard, or adjusting the embouchure or vocal cords in order to make a leap points up the drama of the interval.

Each family of instruments has its way of separating two notes. String players can readily lift a French Baroque bow between notes, and indeed they must do so to divide or retake a stroke. Wind players can hold a note at full volume until they wish to end it, and can then stop it as abruptly as they please. Lutenists and guitarists can stop a tone suddenly by lifting the finger of the left hand that holds down the vibrating string. Harpsichordists can end a note by lifting the finger that has sounded it.

Because a harpsichordist cannot make a vital note stand out by a stronger finger stroke, the player often shortens the previous note to set off the important one. If a note is repeated, if the same finger is used for consecutive notes, or if the hand is moved to a new position, the finger no longer holds down the key and an articulation silence results. For at least one of these reasons, the right-hand fingerings given by Saint-Lambert in examples 14.2 and 14.3 create silences at the places marked o.

During the first reprise of example 14.2, the silences enforced by the right-hand fingering divide the melody into two-measure units, each the length of a *pas de menuet*; and, in mm. 1 and 5, they mark off the iambs (SL) typical of many menuets. Leaps of a third or a fourth produce further iambs not indicated by o.

The enforced silences in the second reprise are, as expected, less predictable. Nevertheless, they accent the bad second pulse in mm. 1, 2, 3, 5, and 7, suggesting iambs (SL), and set up the caesural and rhyme reposes of imaginary lyrics on the downbeat of even-numbered measures. In short, they both hint at and contrast with the more straightforward articulation of the first reprise.

The fingerings for both hands in the first reprise of Saint-Lambert's gavotte (ex. 14.3) enforce silences before all downbeats and upbeats. They also articulate the notes of a divided choreobacchius (SSSSLL) in each two-measure rhythmic subject.

EXAMPLE 14.4.
Notations for the ornamental shortening. a. *détaché*, D'Anglebert, 1689, table of ornaments; b. *aspiration*, F. Couperin,
1717, table of ornaments.

Harpsichordists have an ornament that, like Muffat's "detachment" for string instruments (chap. 11), makes a more noticeable silence than the usual one. Jean-Henry D'Anglebert called it a *détaché* (ex. 14.4a) and indicated it by a rest directly over the note to be shortened; the "detached" pulse note is performed for half its written value. François Couperin called the same ornament an *aspiration* (ex. 14.4b). He used a vertical stroke over the note to be shortened and gave the "aspirated" pulse note three quarters of its written value.

Example 14.5 illustrates a few uses of the ornamental shortening in D'Angle-bert's and Couperin's dance pieces. In examples 14.5a, c, e, and f, for instance, a bad note is shortened more than usual in order to highlight the following beat, which is often a downbeat. In example 14.5b, silences prepare the syncopation in the melody and the final note of the bass. In example 14.5d, the L's of a hemiola (LLL) are separated noticeably.

Although French composers and performers of the *grand siècle* gave no wind syllables for whole pieces, woodwind tutors of the early eighteenth century show that wind players detached important pulse values. In example 14.6a Jean-Pierre Freillon-Poncein, an oboist in Louis XIV's wind band, used *tu* on most pulse and longer values that move by steps. But to vary the tongue strokes, he used *ru* for the less important second note in most measures, regardless of the length of the first note. If the second note was longer than the first, however, he employed *tu* for both.

In describing modern French pronunciation, Pierre Delattre indirectly explains the functions of the woodwind syllables *tu* and *ru*: The more tightly the mouth is closed for the initial consonant of a syllable, the more the syllable is detached from the one before (1951, p. 18). Since *t* is the most tightly closed of all the consonants, the syllable *tu* is prepared by a noticeable articulation silence. On the other hand, since the *u* of either syllable is one of the most closed vowels, and an *r* between two vowels is the most open consonant, practically no silence introduces *ru*.

The *t* is called an explosive consonant; the *r*, a liquid one. During the silence before the *t*, the tongue holds back the air while the lungs continue to contract, compressing the air. When the air is released to sound the *t*, a small explosion is produced. For the *r*, the air continues flowing, even though the *r* is not a slur. Bacilly told singers that *r* between two vowels (as in *tu ru*) is pronounced "simply, unaffectedly, very lightly, and not at all as a double *r*" (1668, pp. 291–92).

EXAMPLE 14.5.
Ornamental shortenings in dance pieces. D'Anglebert, suite
1, 1689: a. courante, m. 1; b. courante, first ending of first
reprise; c. second gigue, m. 1; d. second gigue, second ending
of second reprise. F. Couperin, Concert royale IV, 1714–15:
e. rigaudon; f. forlane.

EXAMPLE 14.6.
Woodwind syllables that separate and group notes. a. Freillon-
Poncein, 1700, pp. 16–17; b. Hotteterre, 1707, p. 29.

Although Freillon-Poncein followed *tu* with *ru* for consecutive pulse values, the flutist Jacques Hotteterre le Romain, writing only seven years later, used *tu* on all such values when followed by quick notes (ex. 14.6). His examples reflect the general practice of detaching equal pulse notes and longer values (chap. 11).

The instructions given by Freillon-Poncein and Hotteterre are very rudimentary. For instance, a wind player performing the melody in the first two measures of Saint-Lambert's menuet (ex. 14.2) would surely articulate it |*tu tu ru* |*tu tu ru*, instead of the |*tu ru tu* |*tu ru tu* taught by Freillon-Poncein or the |*tu tu tu* |*tu tu tu* implied by Hotteterre. In fact, a still greater variety of syllables was probably used in many concert pieces, where sophisticated players might render the instrumental counterpart of "|EST-ON |sa-ge |DANS le bel |a-ge" (app. ex. 1, mm. 1–4) something like "|TU TU |tu ru |TU ru du |tu du" (as described in chap. 13).

ARTICULATION SILENCES THAT GROUP NOTES

The silence created by two strokes being taken in the same direction on the guitar, violin, or viol implies that the second of the two notes begins a group, however small. In Visée's allemande for guitar (ex. 14.1c), the first three notes make up an introductory gesture, yet the repeated upward strum initiates an up-down pair of the second and third notes. In Marais's sarabande for viol (ex. 14.1f), the viol's repeated down-bow (m. 7)—equivalent to the violin's repeated up-bow—pairs the penultimate and final notes of the piece. Repeating a downward strum (ex. 14.1c, mm. 5, 6, and 12) allows one melodic unit to end on the first pulse of a measure and the next to start on the second.

A string of woodwind syllables is made up of units articulated *tu* or *tu-ru*. The double hyphen indicates the inseparability of *tu* and *ru*. Several *tu-ru*'s are often strung together: *tu-ru-tu-ru*. The single hyphen shows the flowing motion produced by alternated syllables. Two consecutive *tu*'s however break the flow: *tu-ru-tu-ru-tu tu-ru-tu tu* (Freillon-Poncein's first sample melody in ex. 14.6) or *tu tu-ru* (his last). Except when the second note of a measure is long, Freillon-Poncein's sample syllables only break the flow before an occasional good note or upbeat note.

In fact, woodwind syllables were probably grouped so as to imitate the textual cells and hemistiches of songs. The normal scansion of example 14.6b would be: *tu |tu tu tu |tu// tu tu |tu/ tu tu-ru-tu |tu*. (Chap. 16 gives further information on the grouping of quick notes.)

The principal advice that tutors for all instruments offered advanced players was "Let [good] taste decide." When asked if the bowing rules must always be observed, Dupont answered:

> Yes, when learning them, because this helps you acquire the style of the [different] airs; but once you are acquainted with the style, you can take whatever license and liberty you judge to be appropriate.[3] (1718b, p. 8)

The problem for modern singers and players is to acquire the knowledge of this style of an earlier age, in order to perform its music with the appropriate taste. To some extent the instructions and music for instruments other than one's own can fill in the gaps in knowledge. For instance, wind players, string players, and those who realize figured basses can observe the locations of thick chords, rolled or strummed chords, long notes, ornaments, and slurs in music for lute, guitar, harpsichord, and viol and so learn where to bring out downbeats, rhythmic movements, and the important notes at musical reposes. And wind, string, and keyboard players can learn from one another where to separate notes.

Perhaps most helpful are the instructions for articulating the dance rhythms that are sometimes written directly into instrumental music. Pieces in *style brisé* give considerable information and also attest to the great variety of stresses in the dances of any one type. Also, viol pieces by Marais—which he said could be played successfully on a number of instruments—include many performance directions.

15

Ornamenting Dance Rhythms

The graces are to the voice and to instruments
what ornaments are to a building, and like the
ornaments are not necessary to the existence
of the building, but serve only to make it
more agreeable to the view.[1]

—Jean Rousseau (1687, p. 74)

It is true that there are monosyllables that are
long and short in a first couplet . . . ; yet if in
the second there are different ones that can
never be short, it is up to the singer to rem-
edy this impropriety by his industry [in orna-
mentation], retaining as much as possible the
measure and movement of the air, which is
much easier (and consequently indispensable)
in songs that have no regular meter, than in
those subject to a particular one.[2]

—Bénigne de Bacilly (1668, pp. 350–51)

Although the ornaments in dance pieces are certainly not essential to the existence of the music, they often highlight the dance rhythms or at least mark the
meter; and, in songs and instrumental pieces ornamented in the style of *airs de
cour*, they bring out the important syllables of real or imaginary lyrics. These
goals are achieved by performing idiomatically the so-called stereotyped ornaments, such as trills and mordents, and by choosing well the less structured
embellishments. Both types of decoration may be written in by the composer
or added extemporaneously by the performer.

Until fairly recently, most modern performers of Baroque music believed
that it was authentic to begin all trills on the upper auxiliary note and "on the
beat" (at the start of the note bearing the trill), and to play *ports de voix* and

coulés—the French versions of the lower and upper appoggiaturas respectively—as ornaments that absorbed at least one-half the value of the ornamented note. However, Frederick Neumann (1978) makes a strong case for beginning many trills early and/or on the pitch of the trilled note, and for performing many *ports de voix* and most *coulés* early. These methods seem particularly well suited to dance music in lively tempos, and especially to Lully's dances.

Musicologist and harpsichordist Sven Hansell contends that to perform trills, *ports de voix*, and *coulés* before their indicated time aids the flow of the melodic line, whereas on-beat performance interrupts the flow (personal communication). For instance, when a *coulé* or the upper auxiliary of a trill fills the interval of a descending third and thus joins melodically the two notes of the interval, early performance is usually desirable. But for a trill at a hemiola or a cadence, on-beat performance provides the necessary accent.

PERFORMANCE OF TRILLS

Early manuscript and printed copies of Lully's stage works show that no more than an occasional trill or pair of quick notes decorates most of Lully's dance pieces. The evidence of his day suggests that only a few of these trills should start on the upper auxiliary. For instance, most trills in lute pieces and songs of the early and mid-seventeenth century begin on the main pitch; Borjon's musette tutor of 1672 indicates only main-pitch starts for trills; and, according to Jean Rousseau's singing tutor (1678, p. 56) and viol tutor (1687, p. 84), the trills "in all possible situations in gay pieces such as menuets" begin on the main pitch. If a trill is begun on the upper auxiliary, Rousseau stated that the auxiliary must be very light (*léger*).

All the trills in example 15.1 should therefore start on the main pitch or at most with a very light auxiliary. The trill in m. 1 ornaments the first note of the piece and so best begins on the main pitch. The one in m. 2 starts perhaps with a very light auxiliary, since the approach is from the upper neighbor. The one in m. 4 starts on the main pitch because it is directly preceded by its lower neighbor.

Jean Rousseau demonstrated the use of main-pitch trills for the viol in example 15.2. Although this example is not specifically a dance piece, it has rhythms and melodic patterns that occur often in such music. Except for the last two trilled notes, all those bearing trill signs are either quick notes or are approached from the lower neighbor.

Among Lully's contemporaries also, trills that start with a light auxiliary were begun early. In Rousseau's example of trills with auxiliary starts (ex. 15.3), the

EXAMPLE 15.1.
Lully, menuet, from *Amadis*, 1684.

EXAMPLE 15.2.
Trills with main-pitch start. J. Rousseau, 1687, p. 84. Only
the trill marked *, which ornaments a pulse value and is approached from the upper neighbor, may be started with a
"very light" auxiliary. The written pitch of the long cadential
trill marked ** takes up the first half of the note's value, and
the rest of the note is trilled.

EXAMPLE 15.3.
Early and on-beat starts for trills begun with the auxiliary.
J. Rousseau, 1687, pp. 78–79.

first five begin early. Only the last three begin on the beat, and their initial
auxiliary is held for part of the value of the written note. In other words, as the
music approaches its ending, a greater number of auxiliary and on-beat starts—
with increased lengthening of the initial auxiliary—brings the motion to a gradual halt. The upper auxiliary at the end of example 15.3 is held for half the
value of the written note.

In short, trills during at least the first half of a musical period tend to start
early or on the main pitch. Only as the melody prepares for a full cadence do
the trills noticeably hold back the progress by starting on and gradually lengthening the upper auxiliary, played on the beat.

EXAMPLE 15.4.
Boismortier, "Bourrée en rondeau," from Suite for flute,
op. 35/5, 1731.

Tutors and ornament tables of the early eighteenth century show almost all trills beginning on the upper auxiliary. However, the upper auxiliary can be very light; and a few trills may start on the main pitch.

Some early eighteenth-century composers used two trill signs in simple dance tunes. Joseph Bodin de Boismortier, for instance, indicated certain trills with the symbol ⌄, or chevron; others with + (ex. 15.4). These signs perplex many modern performers.

However, Boismortier's chevron occurs mainly in the course of a melody, often on relatively short note values, and would seem to indicate a trill begun with a very light auxiliary (perhaps sounded early) or sometimes on the main pitch. Often there is room for only one or two shakes; at other times, this brief trill may be concluded by dwelling briefly on the main pitch. Perhaps a turn can be substituted for the first trill in example 15.4, since the melody ascends.

Boismortier's + in these pieces occurs chiefly over the penultimate note or over the final one at a melodic cadence. Its performance thus seems to require an initial auxiliary performed on the beat and held long enough to be clearly heard. If time allows, the trilling probably continues through undotted notes but stops where a dot occurs. Only if the written note is very short might the initial auxiliary start early.

Composers of keyboard solos and of dance songs in the style of *airs de cour* tended to be more specific than others in indicating how to perform trills. For instance, D'Anglebert's table of ornaments for his harpsichord pieces of 1689 includes signs for seven kinds of trill, a substitution for a trill, and a "detachment" (articulation silence) before a trill. Although D'Anglebert's table indicates that all his trills start on the beat and on the upper auxiliary, Neumann argues that at least certain ones require an early start (1978, pp. 260–62).

PERFORMANCE OF CERTAIN OTHER
STEREOTYPED ORNAMENTS

The timing of *ports de voix* and *coulés* resembles that of the start of trills. According to Saint-Lambert (1702, pp. 42–43), harpsichordists disagreed as to whether these ornaments should be performed early or on the beat. He contested the on-beat starts in D'Anglebert's table, preferring early ones.

Mordents in concert dances are usually performed at the time of the written note, to make a rhythmic accent. Yet Neumann cites a few mordents that would sound better played early (1978, pp. 423, 428). Mordents are usually approached from one or more steps below the written note.

According to Saint-Lambert, D'Anglebert's "detachment" is needed before trills and mordents in pieces with a gay tempo (which include most dance pieces). It is particularly necessary in cases where the written note before a trill is the upper neighbor or the one before a mordent is the lower one (1702, p. 56).

François Couperin mentioned that earlier harpsichordists had used the same finger for a *port de voix* as for the previous note (1717, p. 20), creating a significant articulation silence before the ornament. But Couperin himself prepared the ornament more subtly and smoothly by employing an adjacent finger; some silence remains however because the previous note is on the same pitch as the ornament and is thus played with the same key.

Other performers of the *grand siècle* also employed articulation silences to usher in many ornaments. Rousseau's viol tutor says that an "aspiration" (articulation silence) must be made at the end of the note preceding a trill that begins on the upper auxiliary (1687, p. 90); and Hotteterre's articulation syllables for woodwind instruments reveal that a similar silence, needed to produce the *t* of the syllable *tu*, precedes all tongued ornaments (1707, pp. 27). In example 15.5 articulation silences (marked ○) occur before all ornaments as well as before each *tu*.

Dupuit's fingerings for the *vielle à roue*, or hurdy-gurdy, also demonstrate the practice of pointing up ornaments with a preceding silence (1741, p. 2). This folk instrument, equipped with two sets of strings, a keyboard, and a wheel, became popular among the aristocracy during the reign of Louis XV. The bass strings produce a drone that sounds as long as the wheel is turned. The melody strings, tuned in unison, are sounded when the player depresses a key with the left hand, thus stopping a string, while turning the wheel with the right.

An articulation silence is created in the melody when the finger is lifted. When no melody string is stopped, no melody note is produced. Repeating a finger or a note, or crossing one finger over another, creates such a silence. In

EXAMPLE 15.5.
Articulation silences before tongued ornaments. Hotteterre, 1707. a. cadential trill, p. 27; b. *port de voix*, p. 32; c. *coulements (coulés)*, p. 33. ○ indicates articulation silence.

EXAMPLE 15.6.
Articulation silences before hurdy-gurdy ornaments. Dupuit,
1741, p. 2.

example 15.6, silences are produced in one of these three ways before every ornament. In m. 1, the subtler "new style" fingering recommended by Couperin is used (see above). At the first (○), the fingering creates a silence only if the trill starts with the upper auxiliary; at the second (○), only if the trill begins on the main pitch.

Dance songs, however, exhibit no preponderance of crisp consonants at the start of ornamented syllables. The trilled second syllable of "Est-on sa-ge" (app. ex. 1, m. 1), pronounced *ton* because French syllables tend to begin with consonants, is quite sharply prepared; but the trilled fourth syllable of "Dans le bel a-ge" (m. 4), pronounced *la*, is not prepared at all.

FREE ORNAMENTATION OF DANCE RHYTHMS

Concert pieces with dance titles contain not only stereotyped ornaments but often some kind of less structured embellishment. The latter may decorate one or two notes, the repetition of a whole reprise, the second or third stanza of a song, or the repetition of a whole piece. The ornamentation of a whole piece, and sometimes that of the second or third stanza of a song, was called a *diminution* or a *division* in the late sixteenth and early seventeenth centuries and a *double* in the late seventeenth and early eighteenth. All three terms were also used for the embellishment of a single note.

Free ornamentation in French dance music embraces two styles of decoration. The first divides the notes of the melody into more or less continuous quick notes and, occasionally, into very quick ones. This style descended from the instrumental diminutions of the sixteenth century and is the usual one for French dance music in a rather lively tempo. The second was developed to enhance the long syllables and bring out the important words in the *airs de cour* of the early and mid-seventeenth century. It is the normal one for slow pieces.

An early instrumental piece using the diminution technique is Nicolas Vallet's arrangement for lute of an allemande song whose words have unfortunately been lost (ex. 15.7). The song has four stanzas, each composed of a four-measure period and an ornamented, or divided, repeat of that period. Not only are the repeats divided, but each stanza is more divided than the one before.

The first period of the first stanza (mm. 1–4) presents the melody with a simple chordal accompaniment. In the second period (mm. 5–8), the chords are abandoned and the melody is decorated with quick-note divisions—the

EXAMPLE 15.7.
Instrumental-style ornamentation. Vallet, allemande "Fortune helas pourquoy," for lute, 1615 (transcription by André Souris, in Nicolas Vallet, *Le secret de muses*, vol. 1, reproduced by permission of Éditions du Centre National de la Recherche Scientifique).

EXAMPLE 15.7.
Continued

commonest style of division in post-Lullian quick dances and their *doubles*.
The second stanza (mm. 25–32) has more quick notes in the bass, a usage also
found in some post-Lullian dances in slow and fast tempos. The fourth stanza
(mm. 73–80) features successions of very quick notes in the melody or the bass,
a technique seldom used during Lully's day.

In dance songs and pieces for the theater, divisions into quick or very quick
notes occur only on isolated pulses, but they may be more or less continuous in
concert dances or their *doubles* (see ex. 16.10). Divisions move chiefly by step
in French-style pieces; yet leaps are common in Italian-style dances written by
French composers.

The rhythms in the free embellishments of *airs de cour* are highly varied
since they reflect the length of syllables and the meaning of words. Singers have
a particular problem when the second or third stanza of a dance song is set to
the same music as the first, and short syllables fall where long ones fell before,
or vice versa. To rectify the mismatch of syllables and note lengths that naturally arises, Bacilly found it "absolutely necessary" for singers to add corrective
embellishments (1668, p. 392).

Although Lully largely avoided free ornamentation in his operas, he would
occasionally ask his father-in-law, the great singer Michel Lambert, to prepare a
double as a favor for another singer (Mattheson, 1722–25, II, p. 50). The
anonymous *double* shown in example 15.8 for Lully's menuet song from *Psyché*
(app. ex. 1) is certainly similar to those Lambert wrote for his own *airs de cour*,
but this ornamentation may have been added some years after Lully's and Lambert's deaths. The opera *Psyché* was performed in 1678 but not published until
1720, and no earlier manuscript exists.

The embroideries in this menuet *double* include *ports de voix*, *coulés*, trills,
and *passages* of quick and very quick notes. Though they alter the rhythms

EXAMPLE 15.8.
Ornamented second stanza for a dance song. Anonymous, for
Lully, "Est-on sage," from *Psyché*, 1678 (1720 publication).

EXAMPLE 15.9.
Ornamented refrain couplets set to a chaconne bass. Bousset,
Printemps," from *Second receüil . . .* , 1700, pp. 273–75.

slightly to accommodate the music to the syllable lengths, the original anti-
spastic (SLLS), hegemeolian (SSSLS), and most other rhythms remain.

In Jean-Baptiste de Bousset's song "Printemps," ornamented repeats of the
rondeau refrain are set to a chaconne bass (ex. 15.9). Of the eight measures in
the refrain, Bousset decorated only one for the first repeat and three for the
second.

A flute arrangement by Hotteterre le Romain of the anonymous "brunette,"
"Le beau berger Tircis" (set by D'Anglebert for harpsichord [ex. 13.2]), includes a *double* for the first stanza and a highly decorated second stanza. (Brunettes were rustic love songs popular among the French aristocracy.) In example 15.10, Hotteterre's version of the second stanza and of the final two

EXAMPLE 15.10.
Flute arrangement of a traditional gavotte song. Hotteterre,
"Le beau berger Tircis," from *Airs et brunettes*, ca. 1723,
p. 79.

measures of its repetition appear directly under the first to facilitate comparison of the textual cells, syllable lengths, and note values.

Hotteterre's elongation of the penultimate measure of the second stanza and
its repeat illustrates the distortion of the meter Bacilly sanctioned in "certain
older gavottes" that were performed "with more tenderness" than usual (1668,

p. 106). One of the poetic lines whose meter Bacilly said might be corrupted is in fact "Ah! petite Brunette" (p. 107). In the Tircis brunette, this line combines with the final one in an especially passionate utterance, which Hotteterre inflected differently in each repetition. First his singer declaims, "AH YOU/ MAKE me DIE"; then, "AH/ you MAKE me DIE"; and finally, "AH/ you MAKE me DIE." Each time, the exclamation "Ah" is longer, and in the final repetition the emphasis is on "me."

Bacilly justified such corruption of a measure in lengthening an exclamatory word:

> The dance meter [may be] disturbed to give more magnificence, and to adorn [the melody] in a hundred more and more agreeable ways, according to the art and all the techniques of good singing, to better express certain exclamations, and [give] more grace.[3] (1668, p. 107)

He made clear, however, that dance songs other than tender gavottes like that in example 15.10 "must always preserve their proportions, so that a menuet or sarabande does not become a song in free meter" (p. 108).

Some years after Lully's death, Montéclair supported Lully's distaste for the elaborate embellishment of *doubles*:

> The incomparable Lully, that superior genius whose works will always be esteemed by true connoisseurs, preferred melody, beautiful modulation, agreeable harmony, judiciousness of expression, naturalness, and, lastly, noble simplicity to the absurdity of the *doubles*. . . . Nevertheless, *doubles* continue to be imposed on untrained ears.[4] (1739, pp. 86–87)

Yet Montéclair himself wrote out decorations for the repetitions of many dance reprises and created *doubles* for many brunettes. Example 15.11 gives several composers' *doubles* for the first reprise of the first stanza of the Tircis gavotte, all arranged for flute. The embellishments in these *doubles* follow the syllable lengths to a great extent, though the triplets that start the first (ex. 15.11a) are more instrumental than vocal.

Often the reprises of concert dances—especially those of sarabandes, gavottes, and some menuets—are ornamented as elaborately in their first playing as others are in their repeats. A typical instance is D'Anglebert's version of the Tircis gavotte (ex. 13.2). In such pieces, modern players should search out the skeleton melody, articulate the dance rhythms appropriately, and perform other notes as expressive ornaments.

Clarity and an understanding of an ornament's function are the important factors in performing and composing embellishments of all kinds. To learn the proper use and performance of the French graces, modern performers should practice the pieces for all instruments and voice for which Baroque ornamentation exists. Only in this way can the indispensable "good taste" be developed.

Further information on executing the stereotyped ornaments is given in Neumann (1978), and some guidance on their affect and use appears in Mather (1973). Additional examples of ornamented brunettes and French dances ap-

EXAMPLE 15.11.
Flute *doubles* for "Le beau berger Tircis." a. Montéclair, 1720,
pp. 2–3; b. Hotteterre, 1723, p. 79. M: R (Jean-Jacques
Rippert?), 1725, p. 41: c. first *double*; d. second *double*.

pear in Mather and Lasocki (1976), in Hans-Peter Schmitz (1965), and in David
Lasocki's edition of Hotteterre (1723). Still other examples employing embellishments of both types can be found in modern editions of concert pieces by,
for instance, Louis Couperin, Marin Marais, Michel de La Barre, Caix d'Her-
velois, Hotteterre, and Montéclair.

16

Grouping Unslurred Quick Notes

To make the playing more agreeable, and to avoid too much uniformity in the tongue strokes, they are varied in several ways. For example, two principal articulations are used, namely *tu* and *ru*. The *tu* . . . is employed . . . on most eighth notes; because, when the notes are on the same line, or when they leap, you pronounce *tu*. When they ascend or descend by steps, you again use *tu*, but always alternate it with *ru*. . . .

You must note that *tu* and *ru* are ruled by the number of eighths [in a pulse, beat, or measure]. When the number is odd, you pronounce *tu ru* immediately. . . . When it is even, you pronounce *tu* on the first two eighths, then alternate *ru* [with *tu*]. . . .

You must also observe that eighth notes should not be performed equally, and in certain measures you must make one long and the next short; this too depends on the number [of quick notes]. When the number is equal, you make the first note long, the second short, and so on for the others. When it is unequal, you do the opposite. . . . The measures in which this is most commonly practiced are those of 2, 3, and $\frac{6}{4}$ meter.[1]

Although these rules are general, they however admit some exceptions. . . .[2]

—Jacques Hotteterre le Romain
(1707, pp. 27–28, 30)

With these instructions, the flutist Hotteterre taught woodwind players to articulate unslurred, stepwise-moving quick notes from bad to good. A few French

EXAMPLE 16.1.
Articulation of an ascending and descending scale passage.
Violin bowing by Muffat (1698t, p. 225); right-hand harpsichord fingering by Saint-Lambert (1702, p. 42) and F. Couperin
(1717, p. 29); woodwind tonguing by Hotteterre (1707, p. 27).
Editorial brackets supplied by the present authors group the
notes of the ascending and descending scales.

keyboard fingerings and several violin bowing instructions also seem to support
the bad-good flow as standard for unslurred eighth notes in the common French
meters. On the other hand, the syllables set to a succession of quick notes in
dance songs and pieces are grouped by their meaning and pronunciation into
larger textual cells.

The techniques that couple unslurred quick notes are very different on
woodwind, string, and keyboard instruments. The fingerings used by a harpsichordist to link quick values in fact slur the notes, whereas the alternated syllables of wind players and alternated bow strokes of string players produce an
effect quite different from slurs on their instruments. Also, while woodwind
players normally use their secondary syllable, *ru*, for good quick notes, string
players are more inclined to use their primary stroke—the down-bow on violin
and up-bow on viol. Harpsichordists, on the other hand, employ primary fingers—1, 3, 5—for both good and bad quick notes.

Example 16.1 gives three performance versions of an ascending and descending scale passage begun on a bad note: Muffat's bowings (for the first four notes);
Hotteterre's woodwind syllables; and the right-hand harpsichord fingerings that
both Michel de Saint-Lambert and François Couperin gave for essentially the
same rhythm and pitches (which contain no accidentals). Both Saint-Lambert
and Couperin omitted the initial rest, a common practice of the day; and Saint-
Lambert omitted the bar lines, began on A instead of G, and made the last note
of the ascent as well as the descent a whole note.

STANDARD AND ALTERNATIVE FLOW
OF WOODWIND SYLLABLES

As explained in chapter 14, the woodwind syllables *tu* and *ru* are inseparable.
The *t* is prepared by a small articulation silence, while the *r* is pronounced
into the flowing air stream. The simplest coupling of woodwind syllables occurs
on the two notes following a dotted quarter note. In Freillon-Poncein's tutor
(1700, p. 16) these notes are pronounced *tu* and *ru*, making a bad-good pair

EXAMPLE 16.2.
Woodwind syllables for dotted figures in simple-duple meter.
Freillon-Poncein, 1700, p. 16

EXAMPLE 16.3.
Woodwind syllables that articulate ternary anapests (SSL).
a. Freillon-Poncein, 1700, p. 16. Hotteterre, 1707, p. 28:
b. example with the sign 3; c. example with the sign $\frac{6}{4}$.

(ex. 16.2). We write this coupling as *tu-ru*. When the two notes are on the
same pitch, however, Hotteterre used *tu* for both (p. 27), as at the end of example 16.4.

Woodwind syllables for the three notes that usually follow a dotted note
in gigue-like pieces group the notes as an anapest (SSL), recalling the end-
accented textual cells that begin Lully's gigue song from *Amadis* (app. ex. 4).
Each trio of syllables starts with the very quick note of one beat and ends with
the dotted one on the next: *tu-ru-|tu* (ex. 16.3). The square brackets added to
examples 16.3b and c show a larger phrasing, or scansion, that sometimes includes two such anapests and imitates the hemistiches of dance lyrics.

For a long succession of unslurred quick notes, Freillon-Poncein and Hotteterre alternated the syllables. As was shown in example 16.1, Hotteterre placed
tu on the first (bad) eighth note after an eighth rest and *ru* on the following
(good) one, and then alternated *tu* and *ru* on bad and good notes respectively
until a longer value, a repeated note, or a leaping melodic interval interrupted
the succession. The last note in the example is preceded by an articulation silence that emphasizes the note's finality. On the other hand, for an even number

EXAMPLE 16.4.
Woodwind syllables for an even number of quick notes.
Hotteterre, 1707, p. 27.

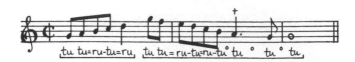

EXAMPLE 16.5.
Woodwind syllables for a rhythm commonly found in menuets.
Freillon-Poncein, 1700, p. 16 bis.

EXAMPLE 16.6.
Good-bad coupling of woodwind syllables. a. Hotteterre, 1707,
p. 30; b. Freillon-Poncein, 1700, p. 17.

of quick notes in a pulse, beat, or measure, each of the first two notes is articulated *tu* and the third, *ru*, undoubtedly to ensure that the bad-good pairing is maintained (ex. 16.4). The brackets in the example again group the notes of an ascending and a descending scale passage. Articulation silences point up the cadential trill, the anticipation of the final note, and the final note.

To show how the standard woodwind pattern relates to dance music, example 16.5 gives Freillon-Poncein's syllables for a rhythm often found in menuets. These syllables are the only ones we found for a specific dance. As usual, each bad quick note clings to the following good note, whether an eighth or a quarter.

Besides the standard, bad-good arrangement of unslurred quick notes, Hotteterre offered an alternative, good-bad one to be used for "a greater sweetening." Although good taste should decide which syllables to choose, the alternative pattern is often suitable when a pair of quick notes falls between two longer values (1707, pp. 30–31). Example 16.6 shows the alternative pattern for two, four, six, and eight such quick notes.

In the quotation that begins this chapter, Hotteterre implied that the standard coupling of the syllables is especially suitable for quick notes performed unequally. But even if the notes are performed as equally as possible, the standard (bad-good) articulation makes the notes sound more unequal than the alternative (good-bad) one.

PAIRED FINGERINGS ON HARPSICHORD

For several reasons, specific pairings of keyboard fingerings are often difficult to establish. To begin with, most fingered scale passages in François Couperin's pieces start with the primary finger 1 or 5, regardless of whether the first note is bad or good. Thus the scales in examples 16.1 and 16.4 would both begin 1-2-3-4-5. Next, the fingering sequence 1-2-3-4-5 may be grouped 1=2=3=4=5, 1=2=3=4=5, or 1=2=3=4=5, simply by lifting the hand and replacing it for a new pair. Finally, fingerings that appear to be coupled in one way may in fact be coupled in the opposite way. For instance, the right-hand fingerings in example 16.1 are probably articulated: 1=2(?)3=4-3=4-3=4/ 5=4(?)3=2-3=2-3=2, with a lift and replacement of the hand after each ascending 4 (and perhaps 2) and each descending 2 (and perhaps 4). Here the notes of an ascending 3=4 or a descending 3=2 are inseparable. However, these same fingerings *can* be executed with smoother 4=3 or 2=3 (good-bad) pairs, if the shorter finger (4 ascending, 2 descending) is brushed toward the palm to allow the longer finger (3) to cross over it: 1(?)2=3(?)4=3-4=3-4/ 5(?)4=3(?)2=3-2=3-2. Hansell suggests turning the right wrist slightly outward or moving the right elbow a little away from the body to facilitate the third finger cross-overs (1985, p. 152). In this way, either coupling can also serve scale passages begun with a primary finger on a good note.

Although Couperin's fingerings for isolated passages in his pieces are presumably intended to shed light on unusual situations, a few help to establish the usual quick-note flow in dance pieces. For instance, his right-hand fingering for thirds in example 16.7 clearly groups quick notes from bad to good. This passage is particularly interesting because it includes two ways of fingering bad-good note pairs. In the first, bad notes are played with secondary fingers, and some silence separates the pairs while the hand moves to each new position (mm. 6–9). But, as the passage continues and the passion mounts, bad notes are played with primary fingers (mm. 10–11), probably in part to avoid placing the thumb on the F-sharp in m. 10. As a result, all enforced silences disappear. To ensure that these bad notes performed with primary fingers are not perceived as good ones, Couperin took the precaution of notating the first bad one in m. 10 as a very quick note.

EXAMPLE 16.7.
Right-hand harpsichord fingerings for consecutive thirds.
F. Couperin, passacaille, 1717, livre 2, ordre 8, p. 68,
couplet 4, mm. 6–15. Brackets suggest the scansion of
lyrics; ○ indicates articulation silence within bracketed
groups.

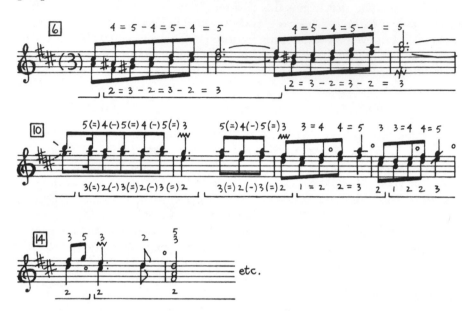

PAIRED BOW STROKES

Muffat's statement that the good notes of French dance music played on the violin "give the ear a little repose" while the bad ones "leave a desire to go on" (see chap. 11) and his practice of playing good notes with primary bow strokes (see chap. 12) extend to quick notes. Primary, reposeful bow strokes—down-bows on violin and up-bows on viol—are the ones normally used for good quick notes. Secondary, restless strokes are employed for bad ones (1698t, p. 239).

Dupont agreed with Muffat, saying that the player "gives weight to" or "reposes upon" good quick notes and "passes quickly over" bad ones (1718a, p. 9). Example 16.8 shows the relationship of these notes; below Dupont's music we have placed his explanatory words and added single or double hyphens to indicate the grouping of the notes. For the ternary dotted figures in gigues, the player passes quickly over the quick note of one beat and reposes on the dotted note of the next (Dupont, 1718a, p. 36). To show that the eighth note in these figures functions as both the repose of the previous quick note and the elan of the dotted note, we have placed the "re-" of "repose" beneath the eighth notes in the example.

Except for Muffat's and Dupont's rather general advice on the relative repose

EXAMPLE 16.8.
Performance of quick notes. Dupont, 1718a. a. in simple-
duple meter, p. 9; b. in ternary dotted figures. Brackets
show the scansion of imaginary lyrics.

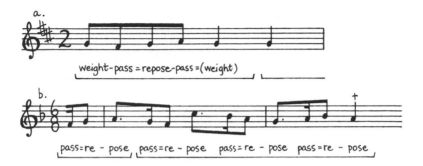

EXAMPLE 16.9.
Bad-good bow strokes for unequal quick notes. Brijon, "Mouvement de menuet," 1763, section "Principes de musique," p. 4.

and restlessness of good and bad notes, we found no mention of Baroque string
players' grouping of quick notes. Nevertheless, dividing a bow stroke for the
two quick notes of a pulse unit automatically separates the bad note from the
previous good one and groups it with the following note, whatever its value.

Although alternated bow strokes do not by themselves group notes in any
particular way, the somewhat later description (1763) by the French violinist
C. R. Brijon of how to bow unequally performed quick notes with alternated
strokes in effect groups the notes from bad to good. Whether violinists of the
grand siècle also used Brijon's method is not known, though they probably did
so when they wanted the standard, bad-good flow.

To alternate the strokes for unequally performed quick notes, the bow is
lifted after playing a good quick note with the down-bow, and replaced closer
to the frog to start the following bad one with the up-bow (Brijon, pp. 21–24).
In m. 1 of example 16.9, for instance, the slightly shorter (bad) quick note
played with the up-bow employs only two-thirds as much bow as the slightly
longer (good) one played with the down-bow. In m. 3, two-thirds of the divided
stroke is used for the good note and one-third for the bad one. In both cases,
the resulting silence between the good and bad quick notes makes the good
one finish a group and the bad one start the next. Brijon's bowing method in

EXAMPLE 16.10.
Mixture of slurred and unslurred pairs of quick notes. F. Cou-
perin, gavotte, for unspecified instruments, from *Les nations:
La françoise*, 1726.

m. 1 makes leaping notes unequal in length; his grouping of four quick notes in
m. 3 is exactly the same as that produced by the standard woodwind syllables
tu-tu-ru-tu.

François Couperin's gavotte for unspecified instruments (ex. 16.10) contrasts
runs of slurred (good-bad) and unslurred (probably bad-good) pairs of quick
notes. For the quick notes at the start of this piece, Couperin used a succession
of two-note slurs, which he notated with square brackets. But after the two
measures of the first rhythmic subject, he changed to a succession of unslurred
quick notes, most likely articulated with the standard bad-good flow. Similar
successions of good-bad and then bad-good articulations continue throughout
the piece. In the example we have placed the standard violin bow strokes above
the notes and suggested the probable woodwind syllables below them. If the
reversed inequality is employed for the slurred notes and the standard inequality for the unslurred ones, the two articulations are especially contrasted.

SINGERS' SMALL GROUPS OF SYLLABLES

The syllables set to quick notes in the dance songs of the *grand siècle* are articulated far more diversely than is implied by the woodwind syllables of Freillon-
Poncein and Hotteterre and by the violin bowings of Muffat, Dupont, and Brijon. Yet the many similarities indicate that singers' syllables can serve as models
for instrumentalists.

Even the simplest bad-good pair of quick notes may be set to a variety of
syllable lengths in dance lyrics. The syllable set to the single quick note after a
dotted quarter commonly begins a two-syllable word or a tightly knit pair of
monosyllables. As such, it and the following syllable resemble the woodwind
player's bad-good *tu-ru*: "beau-té," "pi-tié," "tour-ment" (app, ex. 2); "par-
lons," "cha-grin" (app. ex. 5); "van-ger," "est prêt," "rem-plir," "mes voeux"
(app. ex. 3). At the same time, the first syllable of such words is not necessarily
short. Of the above, "beau-," "van-," "rem-," "est," and "mes" are long in any
context; and "tour-" and "par-" are always somewhat long.

Occasionally, a dotted quarter note and its following quick note are set instead to a monosyllable with feminine ending. In this case, the ending normally

separates itself from its word and begins the next textual cell: "L'on-/de |se . . ." (app. ex. 2, mm. 12–14). An exception of course is the feminine ending at the end of a line: "a-|lar-mes" (app. ex. 4, mm. 4–5).

A two-syllable word or a pair of monosyllables that follows a dotted quarter rarely fills a complete textual cell. One or two previous syllables are almost always included in its syntax and pronunciation: "La beau-té," "la plus sé-vè-re," "Prends pi-tié," "d'un long tour-ment" (app. ex. 2, mm. 1–4); "Ne par-lons plus," "de cha-grin" (app. ex. 5, mm. 2–4); "Pour me van-ger," "de l'in-grat-te Cli-me-ne," "Ba-chus est prêt," "à rem-plir," "tous mes voeux" (app. ex. 3, mm. 1–8). In these textual cells, the dotted quarter creates a declamatory pause, during which the listener is aroused to wonder what will follow: "The -?-," "the most -?-," "Takes -?-," "on a long -?-." The delay makes the last two-syllable word or pair of monosyllables all the more forceful when it finally appears.

Three syllables set to an anapestic grouping of two quick notes and a following longer value (SSL) are also more varied than Hotteterre's standard and alternative articulations would lead one to believe. This grouping is often employed for a single three-syllable word: in simple-duple meter, "re-non-çons," "Ban-nis-sons" (app. ex. 5); in compound-duple meter, "dé-sor-mais," "Les plai-sirs," "Il est temps" (app. ex. 4). Besides the long syllable at the end of the cell, either the first ("Ban-," "Les"), second ("-non-," "-sor-,"), or both ("Il est") are long, regardless of the musical rhythm. Again, such a group may be part of a larger textual cell: "Ban-nis-sons l'en-nuy."

In dance songs of the *grand siècle*, four or more syllables are rarely set to consecutive quick notes and a longer value. But when they are, Ranum (1985) says they usually make up a long textual cell; sometimes a repose within the group momentarily interrupts the flow. The lines in example 16.11, which begin the second reprise of Lully's song, are typical of the few having many quick notes. The first five consecutive quick notes (mm. 10–11) divide at the caesura of the line. The next ten (mm. 13–14) divide three times—after two feminine cadences and after a one-syllable textual cell.

Example 16.11 shows too that syllables set to good quick notes are normally long, at least by symmetry (see chap. 13), and that syllables set to bad ones are usually short. On the other hand, a syllable on a bad note may be in Bacilly's "always long" category, especially if it begins an important word or textual cell: "grand" (m. 9), "ser-" (m. 11).

Thus the difference between the articulations of unslurred quick notes described in instrumental tutors and those found in the lyrics of dance songs is not as great as may appear at first. The undulating symmetry of the mainly alternating long and short syllables on quick notes in dance lyrics parallels that of the alternating good and bad notes to which they are fitted. Also, the fact that a short syllable naturally "yields to" or "is thrown onto" the following long one (see chap. 13) reveals a fundamental arsic-thetic, bad-good relationship of syllables set to quick notes.

EXAMPLE 16.11.
Syllables set to quick notes in a dance song. Lully, gavotte,
from *Bellérophon*, 1679, second reprise, first five lines.

Certainly the tutors of Freillon-Poncein and Hotteterre were meant only for
beginners; and French Baroque woodwind virtuosi, like opera singers, can be
presumed to have used a far greater variety of syllables and syllable groupings
than is given in the rather brief instruction books. In most cases a continuous
sing-song of *tu-ru*'s is inappropriate for a succession of quick notes, or of *tu-ru-tu*'s
for the ternary dotted figures in gigues. Indeed, the woodwind artists of the
day may have imitated singers' varied consonants more closely and used *tu* for
hard consonants (*t, d, k, g, p, b*), *ru* for soft ones (*r, l*), and *du* or *lu* for those
in between (*m, n, s, v, f, z*, etc.). In this case, "PAR l'é-CLAT/ de la |gloi-re"
(ex. 16.11, mm. 12–13) would be played "TU=ru-TU/ tu=ru-|tu=ru"; and "Qui
sui-vit ta vic-|toi-re" (mm. 13–14), perhaps "tu=lu-du-tu=lu-|tu=ru."

In any case, the main point to remember in performing the quick notes of dance music is to preserve the pulse movement while also implying the end-accents of lyrics. With the normally short-long articulation of bad-good notes, the pulse is revealed by the slight extra length of each good note. With the alternate (good-bad) grouping, the pulse is revealed by the articulation silence that prepares the good note. Bringing out the pulse is certainly necessary for long successions of quick notes, as in Couperin's gavotte (ex. 16.10), but a sing-song rendition with no attention to the reposes of the music is in very poor taste.

17

Summing Up — The Many Aspects of Movement

Many confuse movement with measure, and believe that, because we usually say *air de mouvement* to distinguish [a lively piece] from a very slow air, all movement in vocal music consists only of a certain bouncing proper to gigues, menuets, and other similar pieces.

Movement is however quite different from what these people imagine; I hold that it is a certain quality that gives soul to a melody, and that it is called movement because it moves [the feelings], that is, because it excites the attention of listeners.[1]

    —Bénigne de Bacilly (1668, pp. 199–200)

It is not enough to know how to beat the measure according to the various time signatures; it is also necessary to enter into the spirit of the composer—that is to say, into the different movements that the expression of the piece demands.[2]

    —Jean Rousseau (1710?e, p. 86)

I find that we confuse measure with what is called rhythmic fall [*cadence*] or movement. Measure refers to the length and equality of the pulses [*temps*], and rhythmic fall [or movement] is really the spirit and the soul that must be joined to it.[3]

    —François Couperin (1717, p. 40)

Composers, librettists, choreographers, and performers of the *grand siècle* used the word *mouvement* for many different aspects of dance rhythms. Follow-

ing the tenets of ancient Greece, they balanced the "five real and natural qualities of beauty"—uniformity, variety, regularity, order, and proportion"—with a
mixture of passionate expressions called "movements of the animal spirits."
During the late sixteenth and the early seventeenth centuries, Arbeau's dancers
moved to specified step-units and floor patterns; guitar accompanists used certain patterns of downward and upward hand motions and particular progressions
of tonic to dominant harmonies; and Mersenne employed abstract patterns of
"long" and "short" note values, which he named "rhythmic movements," to
identify the many dance rhythms.

During the *grand siècle*, pieces in duple meter were recognized to have
a movement different from those in triple meter (Furetière, 1690, article,
"Mouvement"); the reposes of poetic caesuras and rhymes moved to the rhythmic fall of the dance; and the movement of rhetorical periods and parts united
the rhythms of an entire dance piece. *Belle danse* choreographies adapted the
traditional dance rhythms to new notions about movement; and almost all
dance measures began with a bend-rise, or *mouvement*. In fact, Furetière defined movement in part as "various motions the body makes to move agreeably
in cadence" (1690, article, "Mouvement").

Tempo and affect were perhaps related most directly to the movement of the
music. Furetière recognized one aspect of movement to be "the way of beating
the measure to hasten or slow the time of the pronunciation of words, or of the
playing marked by the notes." But in the quotations that begin this chapter,
Rousseau, Couperin, and Bacilly identified movement chiefly with the sentiment, spirit, and soul of the music. And Richelet used the term to mean "everything that touches and moves the heart" (1680, article, "Mouvement"). Although Bacilly believed that variations in tempo contribute greatly to the
expressiveness of a song, he recognized a "purer and more spiritual" quality of
movement,

> which inspires in [listeners'] hearts whatever passion the song wishes to arouse. . . .
> [This quality] holds the listener in suspense and makes the melody more inter-
> esting, [causing] a mediocre voice to be worth more than a very beautiful one that
> lacks expression.[4] (1668, pp. 200–201)

According to François Couperin, the influence of movement on the sentiment of the music applied mainly to French pieces:

> The sonatas of the Italians are hardly affected by this rhythmic fall [i.e., move-
> ment]. But all our airs for the violin [which are mainly dance pieces] and our pieces
> for harpsichord, viols, etc. [also mainly dance pieces], designate and seem to wish
> to express some [particular] sentiment. Thus, not having invented signs or charac-
> ters to communicate our particular ideas, we try to remedy this by marking at the
> beginning of our pieces some words, like *tendrement*, *vivement*, etc., that approxi-
> mate what we would like heard.[5] (1717, pp. 40–41)

It is the articulation of the dance rhythms that brings out all aspects of movement in a performance. According to *Le Dictionnaire de l'Academie Françoise*,
to sing or play *en mouvement* is "to heed the measure carefully, to make it very
clear" (1694, article, "Mouvement"). To mark the meter, performers of the

grand siècle employed strong physical motions: violinists accompanying dances used primary bow-strokes for the most reposeful notes and secondary strokes for the most transitory ones; instrumentalists playing concert dances brought out important notes with their most forceful strumming, bowing, fingering, or tonguing strokes; and singers stressed not only the most thetic syllables but often the previous one or two, so as to underline the final movement toward an important repose. In addition, musicians chose and performed ornaments so as to enhance the movement, and they tended to group quick notes in bad-good pairs that furnished an underlying wavelike motion.

By combining all the above aspects of movement, French composers and performers were able to express the spirit and soul of every measure, phrase, and piece of dance music. For it is the various combinations of these aspects that differentiate one dance from another—the courante and sarabande from the gavotte, bourrée, chaconne, and other dances (Furetière, 1694, article, "Mouvement")—and distinguishes between two sarabandes and between one phrase and the next.

Readers will of course be able to follow the instructions in this book more easily if they perform in a resonant hall of small to moderate size and play instruments of early designs, preferably French ones tuned at least a half step below modern pitch. But even without authentic halls, instruments, and tunings, performers can recover a large measure of the spirit and soul of French Baroque dance music if they focus on the various aspects of movement that form the basis for the different instructions. By comparing the aspects of movement in each piece with the most typical ones for the dance type (given in Part II) and then adapting the interpretation to the piece's individual features, modern performers cannot fail to arrive at the soul of the music.

II

Rhythmic Characteristics of Fifteen Dance Types

Part II is devoted to the fifteen character dances most often found in French choreographies and concert music of the *grand siècle*. Some of them have more than one characteristic form. For instance, several kinds of menuet music are found in Lully's operas; and many dances have an early version and one or more later ones.

During the late sixteenth and early seventeenth centuries, the musical forms of some dances were about the same in Italy as in France, and some dance melodies appeared in a number of arrangements by different composers for various combinations of instruments and voice. Pieces written in the early style during the *grand siècle* were sometimes headed by such words as *dans le style ancien* (in the early style).

Most dances that were introduced at the French court during the seventeenth century retained their original homophonic textures and simple melodic lines, even in their concert versions. However, the concert versions of allemandes, courantes, and gigues developed from the *style brisé* of lutenists, so that these pieces have a mildly polyphonic texture overlaid with many stereotyped ornaments.

During the late Baroque, many concert dances employed elements of the Italian style that came to maturity in the string music of Arcangelo Corelli. This music features melodic and harmonic sequences, eighth-note pulses, leaping and detached pulse notes, and occasionally large numbers of quick notes. Corelli's music was introduced in France in the late seventeenth century and instantly became fashionable there. Such composers as François Couperin, Hotteterre le Romain, and Marin Marais used elements of the Italian style, often fusing the French and Italian idioms.

Each chapter of Part II gives general information on a particular dance, followed by its most typical step rhythms, guitar rhythms, rhythmic movements, and so on. Most such rhythms appear at the start of a piece; and to a somewhat lesser extent, they may dominate the remainder. Our use of certain sources, procedures, and signs are explained below. In most examples, we have included only the highest voice and the bass line.

Arbeau's Dance Motions and Step Rhythms. Although we have based our discussions of Arbeau's treatise chiefly on Julia Sutton's edition of Mary Stuart Evans's translation, we have returned to the original French names for the dances. For instance, we use "allemande" instead of "alman," "courante" instead of "coranto."

As in chapter 2, we employ L and R for weighted steps onto the left and right foot respectively, and (l) and (r) to show unweighted steps. Other dance motions are indicated with words below the steps.

Early Guitar Rhythms. As in chapter 3, strumming patterns are notated as in the original tablatures or described with words, such as down–down–up or down–up–down. For the original *alfabeto* indications, which in fact produce chords in all inversions, we have substituted modern chord symbols in root position.

Rhythmic Movements. As in chapter 4, L and S stand for a long and a short value respectively. In Mersenne's music, L's are.whole notes or halves; S's are halves or quarters. In the dance music of the *grand siècle*, L's are usually halves; S's, quarters.

Rhythmic Subjects. The dance songs of Patricia M. Ranum's largely unpublished collection have furnished most of our examples. They have also served as the basis of the typical rhythmic subjects cited.

As in chapter 6, arabic numerals above the notes indicate the syllables of a line of lyrics. A single slash shows the principal break in a line of seven or fewer syllables; a double slash, that in a line of eight or more.

As in chapter 7, we use the following symbols below the notes:

⌐⌐	harmonic repose weaker than a musical half-member
⌐·⌐	weak cadence at the end of a musical member
⌐·⌐	strong cadence at the end of a musical period
⌐·⌐	final cadence of a musical reprise
⌐ , ⌐· , ⌐·⌐ , ⌐·⌐	interrupted or extended repose or cadence

As in chapter 13, where syllable lengths are designated, the end-accents of masculine lines, hemistiches, and textual cells are written in capital letters;

those of feminine lines, in bold-faced print. Syllables that are long because of symmetry are underlined.

Dance Motions and Step Rhythms of the belle danse *Choreographies.* The signs for left and right steps are those described under "Arbeau's Step Rhythms." In addition, as in chapter 8, (L) or (R) shows that the weight remains on the standing (left or right) foot while the change of weight to the opposite foot is delayed. A curved arrow indicates the "bend" and "rise" of a *mouvement*.

Tempos and Affects. The general affect of a dance is described in many sources, but our information comes chiefly from Furetière's dictionary (1690), Brossard's dictionary (1705e), Dupont's general music tutor (1718a), and the descriptive words most commonly used for that dance type. Many sources not cited corroborate this evidence.

The instructions for beating time come mainly from treatises, tutors, and dictionaries by Corneille (1694–95), Loulié (1696t), Masson (1697), Freillon-Poncein (1700), Saint-Lambert (1702), and Hotteterre (1719). Where no conducting pattern is given, two equal beats for each measure should be assumed.

As in chapter 10, numerals following the letters MM give the metronomic equivalent of a pendulum or other early marking. Pendulum markings come from the writings of L'Affilard (1705e), d'Onzembray (1732), La Chapelle (1736), and Choquel (1759). We have translated the markings called *pouces* into modern metronomic equivalents by means of the *pouce du Roi* (2.71 cm., or 1.07 inches) and the acceleration due to gravity at Paris (981 cm., or 32.11 feet, per sec. per sec.). When a theatrical work cited by d'Onzembray includes two or three dances of a particular type, we have included at least two of the examples. The symbol "c" on the bottom line of the staff in many of L'Affilard's examples represents a breath mark.

Bowing Patterns. Bowed examples come chiefly from pedagogical writings for the violin by Muffat (1698), Montéclair (1711–12), and Dupont (1718b) and from concert pieces for the viol by De Machy (1685), Marais (1701, 1711, 1717, 1725), and Morel (1709). We have included the complete music of most violin examples, but our rhythmic diagrams of viol pieces show only a few of the many patterns.

As in chapter 12, violin bowings are shown above the music, viol bowings below. Equivalent viol or violin bowings are given in parentheses, the viol's up-bow being equivalent to the violin's down-bow. For the violin strokes, modern bowing signs are substituted for the old, except that Muffat's dot represents the second divided stroke in his examples. We have added in parentheses those violin strokes not written but implied in the original. For some measures, Montéclair included two violin bowings. The one closer to the notes is the one he recommended; the other was practiced by "some other players."

The old signs are kept for the viol strokes: for the down-bow, t, for *tirer* (to pull); for the up-bow, p, for *pousser* (to push). Viol bowings are marked as in the original, that is, only where the flow of alternating strokes is broken. When the first stroke is not given in the original, it is added in parentheses.

Muffat was the only Baroque writer who gave examples of bowed dances and at the same time explained why he chose the bowing. Thus discussions other than Muffat's are our own inferences.

18

Allemandes

Many examples of the French allemande and the Italian *alemana* appeared in the mid-sixteenth century. Both words mean "German," and the dance is thought to have originated in Germany. Arbeau (1589) and Negri (1602) described steps for the allemande and *alemana* respectively, but Mersenne (1636) said the allemande was no longer danced but only played. It became one of the standard pieces in instrumental suites of the *grand siècle*.

At least three kinds of allemande were composed in France: processional dances and concert pieces of the early Baroque, concert pieces of the *grand siècle*, and folklike pieces of the early eighteenth century that again were danced. Most late Baroque sources that mention allemandes refer to the pieces of the *grand siècle*.

Allemande rhythms of the late sixteenth century resemble bourrée and gavotte rhythms of the early seventeenth. In early concert allemandes, repetitions of phrases, reprises, and whole pieces are often ornamented with divisions into quick notes and sometimes very quick ones.

Concert allemandes of the *grand siècle* are more elaborate and contrapuntal. Their rhythms are stylized divisions of the earlier ones. The two reprises of these pieces are about the same in length, often differing by one measure. Although the music is divided throughout into quick notes and seems to allow little extra embellishment, Marais wrote a *double* for at least one concert allemande (1711, #15) and an ornamented *petite reprise* for many others. Many examples from the early eighteenth century include the leaping pulses and running quick notes of Italian violin music.

The music of the danced allemande of the early eighteenth century again resembles that of the bourrée. The folklike nature of this allemande is shown by the title of Pécour's choreography of 1702, "Le branle allemande." It is the only kind of allemande included in *belle danse* choreographies.

Arbeau's Dance Motions and Step Rhythms. Arbeau's allemande (ex. 18.1) is a two-part processional dance in which partners join hands and fall in line, one couple behind the other. As the musicians play part A, the dancers proceed

EXAMPLE 18.1.
Arbeau, allemande, 1589t, pp. 126–27.

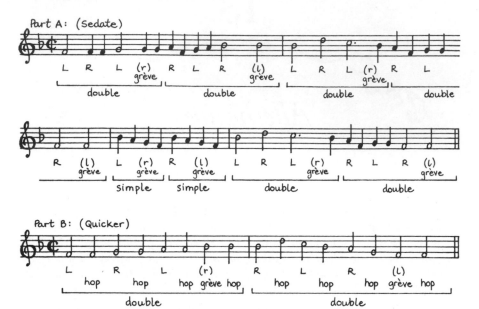

from one end of the hall to the other. The musicians then stop playing, and the dancers engage in light conversation. The musicians again play part A, and the dancers return to the end from which they started. To complete the dance, the musicians play part B to "a quicker, more lively duple time," but Arbeau did not say whether the dancers proceed again or dance in place. Parts A and B have the same melodic skeleton.

Most step-units of Arbeau's part A are closed doubles whose individual steps are set to minims, or half notes, and whose "close" is performed with a *grève*, or simulated kick. That the third "measure" of example 18.1 contains two simples instead of the usual two doubles agrees with the ambiguity of phrasing found in many concert allemandes of the *grand siècle*.

In part B, the dancers perform the same doubles but, because of the faster tempo, they place their steps to semibreves (whole notes) instead of to minims; they also make little springs (probably hops) between the steps.

In both parts of Arbeau's allemande, the weighted step before each *grève* has some feeling of repose, because the dancers' travel halts. A similar repose often occurs in the middle of a measure in concert allemandes of the *grand siècle*.

Guitar Rhythms. No single chord progression or stroke pattern characterizes the *alemana* in early guitar books. Most pulse notes are strummed downward, and the good pulse or good quick note of a pair is always strummed downward. Example 18.2 shows a typical piece.

EXAMPLE 18.2.
Typical *alemana* from an early guitar book. Sanseverino, 1622,
p. 25.

EXAMPLE 18.3.
"M.ᵣ Martin's" allemande for guitar. Mersenne, 1636t, p. 97.
Reprinted from Marin Mersenne, *Harmonie universelle/ The
Books on Instruments* (The Hague, Martinus Nijkoff, 1957),
by permission of the translator, Roger Chapman.

A piece in *punteado* notation by a "M.ᵣ Martin," cited by Mersenne, is the
only French allemande we found for the Spanish guitar. The downward-pointing
tails on the notes in example 18.3 show all pulses to be strummed downward.

Rhythmic Movements. According to Mersenne, the rhythmic movement of allemandes is the choreobacchius (LSSLL, or LSSSSL). But only early allemandes
clearly exhibit this movement, and, even in these pieces, most L's are divided.
Example 18.4 relates the allemande rhythms in examples 18.1 and 18.3 to
choreobacchii.

Metrical Proportions. Some early allemandes have the sign C and four half-note
pulses in each measure, grouped 2 + 2. Others have the sign ₵ and four
quarter-note pulses, again grouped 2 + 2. Most concert allemandes of the
grand siècle are marked C or ₵ and contain eight eighth-note pulses in each
measure. These pulses are grouped 4 + 4 because these eighth notes are in fact
divisions of the earlier four quarter-note pulses, grouped 2 + 2.
  A few concert allemandes of the early eighteenth century are marked 2; they

EXAMPLE 18.4.
Choreobacchii in two early allemandes. a. choreobacchius;
b. Arbeau's allemande; c. "M.ʳ Martin's" allemande (time
values are half those of a. and b.).

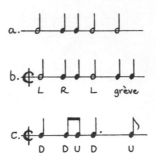

EXAMPLE 18.5.
An allemande with the sign 2. Hotteterre, "La royalle," for
flute, op. 2/1, 1708.

contain four quarter-note pulses in each measure, again grouped in fours
(ex. 18.5). Two such measures make the equivalent of one marked **C**, but with
doubled note values.

Most folklike allemandes of the early eighteenth century are marked 2; their
measures contain four quarter-note pulses, grouped 2 + 2. Others have the
sign $\frac{2}{4}$ and four eighth-note pulses, also grouped 2 + 2.

Inequality of Quick Notes. Some twentieth-century scholars have believed that
Marin Marais's statement that concert allemandes of the *grand siècle* have equal
eighth notes (1701, preface) means that sixteenth notes are also played equally.
However, many French writers of the early eighteenth century proclaimed the
inequality of sixteenth notes in pieces in **C** and **¢** meters having equal eighths;
and Saint-Lambert, who attributed the equality of eighths and inequality of sixteenths in **C** to the slowness of the tempo, cited allemandes as an example
(1702, p. 26). Further corroboration comes from Corrette's violin tutor (1738,
p. 4), which includes allemandes among the four-beat pieces whose sixteenths
are played unequally.

Rhythmic Subjects. Early allemandes normally start on the downbeat, but two upbeat quick notes begin Vallet's lute arrangement of the allemande "Fortune helas pourquoy" (ex. 7.1). Reposes in Arbeau's allemande (ex. 18.1) fall mid-measure; those in "Fortune," on downbeats.

The music of many concert allemandes of the *grand siècle* begins with an initial figure, or musical rhyme, of one to three upbeat quick notes followed by a note on the downbeat. The downbeat note is often a dotted value, namely, a division of the first L of the choreobacchius (LSSLL). Some other examples, however, start on the downbeat, at mid-measure, or with an upbeat pulse note. The initial rhyme is repeated to announce the second reprise, and sometimes earlier.

Even in the first measure of most concert allemandes of the *grand siècle*, pulses are divided into quick notes. At least one dotted figure and perhaps some very quick notes are commonly included.

Concert allemandes of the *grand siècle* normally contain two to four independent voices, one of which comes to a repose on the second downbeat of the music. Other voices usually continue through that downbeat and rest on the next downbeat or the one after that. Only at full cadences, which tend to occur at irregular intervals and are often delayed until the end of the reprise, do all voices repose together. The final repose of each reprise may fall mid-measure. In François Couperin's trios *Les nations*, a rest or a comma indicates the end of a rhythmic subject; these subjects differ in length, but all follow the above principles.

The folklike allemandes of the late Baroque have two-measure rhythmic subjects that begin with an upbeat pulse, as in a bourrée. Leaping pitches are common.

Dance Motions and Step Rhythms of belle danse *Choreographies.* Springing steps predominate in Pécour's choreography of 1702; and pictures beside the choreographic tracts show partners interlocking hands and later, after separating, putting their fists on their hips. Such pictures, normally associated with folk dancing, are not found in other *belle danse* choreographies, but the actions depicted occur in danced allemandes of the later eighteenth century.

Tempos and Affects. Arbeau (1589) described the allemande of his day as a simple, rather sedate dance. Allemandes of the *grand siècle* could be slow or quick.

Late seventeenth- and early eighteenth-century writers characterized (concert) allemandes as slow and solemn pieces. Corneille counted these pieces in four slow beats; Furetière and Brossard called them "serious" pieces; and Grassineau (1740) described them as "a sort of grave, solemn music, whose measure is full and moving." But some concert allemandes of the early eighteenth century have the word "gay" at their start; these pieces often employ features of the Italian style or of the folklike allemande of the early eighteenth century, which was a rapid dance.

EXAMPLE 18.6.
Pendulum marking. La Chapelle, allemande, 1736. ♩ = 9
pouces, or MM 120.

EXAMPLE 18.7.
Viol bowings and their violin equivalents. a. De Machy, 1685,
p. 35; b. Marais, 1701, #63; c. Marais, 1701, #61; d. Marais,
1725, #93; e. Marais, 1725, #59, "Gay"; f. Marais, "Allemande du goût des anciens," 1725, #60; g. Marais, 1725,
#93; h. Marais, 1701, #38.

Only La Chapelle gave a pendulum marking for an allemande: MM 120 for
half notes (ex. 18.6). This folklike piece resembles a bourrée in its rhythm and
tempo.

Bowing Patterns. Although we found no violin bowings for allemandes, viol
bowings are plentiful. Some typical measures are shown in example 18.7, in
which excerpts a-f are beginnings of pieces and excerpts g and h are conclusions
of reprises.

Most good pulses in the viol allemandes are played with primary strokes
(exx. 18.7a, b). In a measure with an unequal number of strokes, a secondary
stroke is divided so that the bowing comes out "right" (ex. 18.7c). Slurs do not
alter the need to follow the rule of the down-bow and indeed may facilitate

it (exx. 18.7d, e). "Gay" allemandes (ex. 18.7e) and those "in the old style" (ex. 18.7f) are bowed in the same way as stylized ones.

Examples 18.7g and h show bowing practices that may occur at the end of a reprise whose final repose falls mid-measure. In example 18.7g, a primary stroke is retaken to start the second reprise. In example 18.7h, slurs in the penultimate measure cause a secondary stroke to fall on the final downbeat. The latter practice is allowed because the repose in the final measure falls mid-measure instead of on the downbeat.

Bourrées

The bourrée is a French folk dance whose court version may have descended from the second and third of three pieces called "La bouree" [*sic*], arranged for four parts in Michael Praetorius' *Terpsichore* of 1612. The first of the three dances begins with a six-measure period, a feature not found in later examples and therefore not discussed here. The second and most typical piece starts with an upbeat quarter note to a four-measure period, set to a 1, 7, 1–6, 5 bass line (ex. 19.1a). The melody of the third piece is similar except that it begins on the downbeat and is set to a simple descending bass line: 1, 7, 6, 5 (ex. 19.1b).

Another similar melody is the song "La bouree" [*sic*] in Jacques Mangeant's collection of unaccompanied melodies and lyrics (ex. 19.1c). One difference is the single half note in m. 2, which replaces the two quarters in Praetorius's prototypes. A bad half note in the second measure characterizes many bourrée melodies of the *grand siècle*.

Each of Nicholas de Vallet's two collections of lute pieces (1615 and 1616) includes a bourrée whose melody resembles Praetorius' except that the upbeat is divided into two eighths. In example 19.1d, the bass progression is 1, 7, 1, 5 (these bass progressions are not found in later bourrées). In both of Vallet's arrangements, written-out repeats are ornamented with almost continuous eighths (as here, mm. 5–8).

Jean-Jacques Rousseau (1768) reported that the bourrée as a dance type came from the province of the Auvergne, but Vallet's title "Bourée [*sic*] d'avignon" seems to indicate that the prototypes in example 19.1 originated somewhat further to the southeast, in the papal state of Avignon.

The texture of bourrées is homophonic, and their form is binary. Repetitions of phrases, reprises, or whole dances are often ornamented with divisions into quick notes, as in mm. 5–8 of example 19.1d. According to Johann Mattheson, the bourrée melody is "more flowing, smooth, gliding, and connected than that of the gavotte" (1739, II, chap. 13, para. 90). These words also describe the difference between the *belle danse* step-units for these two dances.

EXAMPLE 19.1.

The prototype bourrée. Praetorius, 1612, #32: a. "La bouree"
(2); b. "La bouree" (3). c. Mangeant, "La bouree," 1615 (Paris
BN Res Ye 2633 fol 52vº); d. Vallet, "Bourée d'avignon," 1615
(transcription by André Souris, in Nicolas Vallet, *Le secret
de muses*, vol. 1, reproduced by permission of Éditions du
Centre National de la Recherche Scientifique).

EXAMPLE 19.2.
Arbeau, *fleuret*, 1589t, p. 107.

EXAMPLE 19.3.
Rhythmic movements in example 19.1b.

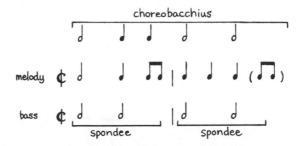

Arbeau's Dance Motions and Step Rhythms. Arbeau did not mention the bourrée; but he did show the timing of the *fleuret*, the predecessor of the *pas de bourrée*. In a variation of the basic step-unit of the galliard, the first of the *cinq pas* (five steps) may be replaced by a pair of quicker steps, which then combine with the second of the five steps to make a *fleuret* (ex. 19.2).

Rhythmic Movement. Although Mersenne did not mention the bourrée, the melodic rhythm of the first two measures of example 19.1b divides a choreobacchius (LSSLL), the movement Mersenne associated with allemandes and gavottes. Each measure of Praetorius' bass line moves to a spondee (LL). Example 19.3 shows how these two rhythmic movements relate to Praetorius' music. The initial upbeat and further rhythmic variations in the other three pieces in example 19.1 mask the underlying rhythmic movements.

Metrical Proportions. The earliest bourrées are marked C or ₵. Most French examples of the 1670s and later have the sign 2, and their measures contain four quarter-note pulses, grouped 2 + 2. Some French bourrées of the early eighteenth century are marked $\frac{2}{4}$ and have four eighth-note pulses, grouped 2 + 2.

Rhythmic Subjects. Rhythmic subjects in bourrées are two measures long. The first in a piece normally begins with an upbeat pulse and often finishes with a feminine ending. The final "mute" *e* may be set to a bad long note (ex. 19.4a) or to a bad pulse note (ex. 19.4b).

The first line of a bourrée song usually has six syllables. Such short lines have no formal caesura and only one musical repose. The repose of the first line is rather weak (app. ex. 5, mm. 1–2).

EXAMPLE 19.4.
Six-syllable rhythmic subjects for bourrées. a. feminine ending with long note; b. feminine ending with rest; c. masculine
ending.

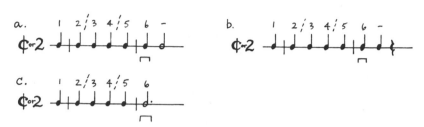

EXAMPLE 19.5.
Opening lines of three bourrée songs.

		1	2	3	4	5	6
a. Mangeant (ex. 19.1b)		Veux-tu	/ donc-ques	/ ma bel-le			
		Will you/ then		/ my pretty			
b. Lully, from *Phaeton*		Plai-sirs	/ ve-nez	/ sans crain-te			
		Pleasures,/ come		/ without fear			
c. Lully (app. ex. 5)		Mon-trons/ no-tre_al-le-gres-se					
		Let's show/ our	happiness				

Two-syllable textual cells that cross the musical beat are common in the first line of bourrée songs (ex. 19.5). The first two and the last two syllables in a line tend especially to be grouped by their syntax (exx. 19.5a and b).

Many bourrée lines, notably after the first one, have seven syllables. Then the interior break is more obvious and the final musical repose more con-clusive. The second and third lines of one of Lully's bourrée songs (app. ex. 5) are good examples. The feminine ending of the first rhythmic subject is short-ened to two pulses to allow a seven-syllable gavotte rhythm to follow; and the first pulse of the third subject is divided into quick notes to accommodate an-other seven-syllable line. Gavotte subjects are common in bourrées, where they may occur at almost any place—though rarely at the start.

The half note of a feminine ending should probably fade out in instrumental pieces, as in songs. Dupont's advice to "double the sound" (*redoubler la voix*) in the middle of that half note in bourrées, "to show that the second beat of the measure falls there" (1718a, pp. 34 and 13), goes counter to normal French pronunciation.

Dance Motions and Step Rhythms of belle danse *Choreographies.* The *pas de bourrée* (ex. 19.6), a Renaissance *fleuret* initiated with a *mouvement*, typifies this dance. Half the step-units in bourrée choreographies are *pas de bourrée*, which move to anapests (SSL). A sequence of two or four of these step-units is com-mon and creates a smoothly flowing and rapidly moving effect (exx. 9.4 and 9.8).

EXAMPLE 19.6.
Pas de bourrée.

EXAMPLE 19.7.
Pendulum markings. a. ○ (?) = 30 *tierces*, or MM 120 (L'Affilard, 1717e); b. ♩ = 32 *tierces*, or MM 112, for Lully, "Bourrée
pour les suivants de Saturne et les suivantes d'Astrée," from
Phaeton, 1683 (d'Onzembray, 1732); c. ♩ = 30 *tierces*, or
MM 120, for Destouches, Bourrée, from *Omphale*, 1701
(d'Onzembray, 1732); d. ♩ = 9 *pouces*, or MM 121 (La Chapelle, 1736).

Tempos and Affects. Dupont said that bourrées are performed "very lightly";
and Masson beat them "very quickly." Most pendulum indications are extremely brisk, though L'Affilard's very fast MM 120 for whole measures (ex.
19.7a) is probably a mistake. This marking, which was omitted from the 1705
edition and added posthumously to the 1717 one, is twice as fast as those of
d'Onzembray and La Chapelle (exs. 19.7b, c, d). Even if L'Affilard's marking
was meant for half notes, the words could hardly be articulated clearly nor
could the passion of the text be declaimed: "Love makes tears flow."

Bowing Patterns. We found only violin bowings for bourrées (ex. 19.8). They
agree with one another in most regards, though the Montéclair example is notated with an eighth-note instead of a quarter-note pulse. Several small differences in bowing occur: Muffat alternated most bow strokes, because of the
quick tempo; whereas Montéclair and Dupont used primary strokes on all good
pulses. Also, Montéclair slurred some quick notes in pairs, while Dupont alternated or divided strokes for all quick notes.

These three violin pedagogues agreed on the need for a secondary stroke on
the bad long note of a feminine ending and also on the bad pulse-note start of
the next rhythmic subject (see ex. 19.8a, m. 2). Muffat's dot indicates dividing
these two strokes, rather than retaking the second. The resulting silence or decay of sound between the two notes is indicated by editorial commas.

EXAMPLE 19.8.
Violin bowings and their viol equivalents. a. Muffat, 1698t,
p. 229; b. Montéclair, 1711–12, p. 12; c. Dupont, 1718b,
p. 6.

When two quick notes start a new rhythmic subject, Montéclair and Dupont followed slightly different practices. Montéclair alternated strokes (ex. 19.8b, m. 6); this course does not force a separation of the rhythmic subjects, but in all probability the bow would be lifted at the end of the long note, setting off the end of one subject from the start of the next. Dupont used a secondary stroke for all three notes (ex. 19.8c, m. 14); perhaps he would retake the bow for the first quick note.

20

Canaries

The Italian *canario* and the French canarie originated in the Canary Islands, a Spanish-owned archipelago. Examples in early Italian guitar books are mainly plucked rather than strummed, and several early pieces have essentially the same melody (for instance, exx. 20.1 and 20.2). Michael Praetorius' canarie (ex. 20.1) is a set of variations on two distinct melodies (mm. 1–2 and 3–4), each composed to the same two-measure bass progression. Examples from the *grand siècle* have homophonic texture, are in binary or rondeau form, and are often compared with gigues.

Early Dance Motions and Step Rhythms. Arbeau's dance motions for the canarie may be related to later flamenco dancing. Arbeau described the dance as gay, but also as "strange and fantastic, with a strong barbaric flavor." Each of Arbeau's step-units includes three steps: The main one is a weight change made by stamping; two weightless steps are then taken by what Arbeau calls "marking" the free heel and then the free toe against the side of the foot that has just stamped (1589t, p. 85). Each stamp–heel–toe movement produces the LSS rhythm of a dactyl. These foot movements fit equally well Arbeau's binary dactyls in example 20.2 and Praetorius' ternary ones in example 20.1.

By 1636 Mersenne reported that the canarie was very difficult to dance and was thus performed "only by those who are very well trained in this exercise, and whose foot is very fast." He identified the steps as principally *entrechats* (leaps in which the legs cross repeatedly and sometimes beat together), *cabrioles* (leaps in which the legs cross), and *pirouettes* (turns). In short, the canarie had already become a theatrical dance, which it remained in *belle danse* choreographies.

Early Guitar Rhythms. Praetorius' canarie (ex. 20.1) has the harmonic progression I, IV, I, V, I. By the *grand siècle*, this progression was abandoned.

Rhythmic Movement. According to Mersenne, the dactyl (LSS) is the movement of the canarie. Canaries of the *grand siècle* typically move to ternary dactyls.

EXAMPLE 20.1.
Melody and bass of a prototype canarie. Praetorius, "La canarie," 1612.

EXAMPLE 20.2.
Arbeau, canarie, 1589t, p. 180.

EXAMPLE 20.3.
Rhythmic subject of canarie song in example 20.4a.

Metrical Proportions. Praetorius' example is marked $\frac{6}{4}$; Arbeau's, ¢. Canaries by Lully and later composers have a 3, $\frac{6}{4}$, $\frac{3}{8}$, or $\frac{6}{8}$ sign. With $\frac{6}{4}$ and $\frac{6}{8}$, pulses are grouped in threes.

Rhythmic Subjects. During the *grand siècle*, canaries in $\frac{6}{8}$ or $\frac{6}{4}$ meter usually began on the second beat, as in examples 20.3, 20.4a and b, and 20.5a and b. A few, like many gigues, began with one or two upbeat notes. The rhythmic subject of the only canarie song we found, L'Affilard's in example 20.4a, seems also to fit many canaries without text. This subject begins on the second beat and covers the equivalent of two measures in compound-duple meter (ex. 20.3). The caesura falls on the first downbeat and the rhyme on the second.

Belle danse *Choreographies.* Choreographies of the eighteenth century are theatrical dances often calling for virtuosic springs and fast footwork. Between stationary flourishes, the dancers move rapidly through a floor pattern.

Tempos and Affects. Arbeau called canaries "gay"; Masson beat them a little more quickly than gigues; and rapid pendulum markings show that musical per-

EXAMPLE 20.4.
Pendulum markings. a. ♩. = 34 *tierces*, or MM 108 (L'Affilard,
1705e); b. ♩ = 8 *pouces*, or MM 129, for "Canaries en rondeau" (La Chapelle, 1736).

Viens a-vec moi re-po-ser sur l'her-bet - te,

EXAMPLE 20.5.
Violin bowings and their viol equivalents. a. Montéclair,
1711–12, p. 16; b. Dupont, 1718b, p. 8.

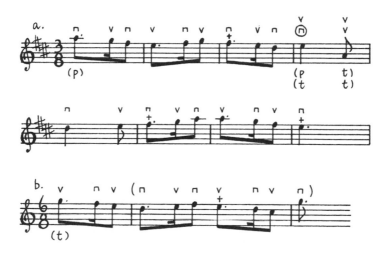

formers were pushed to the limit. Although L'Affilard's song (ex. 20.4a) expresses
excited and joyful anticipation—"Come lie with me in the short grass"—his
tempo would require extremely rapid diction.

Bowing Patterns. Because of the great speed of canaries, bow strokes are
chiefly alternated (ex. 20.5). At first glance, the only two bowed examples we
found—both for violin—seem to show that primary and secondary strokes are
equally suited to all notes. For instance, the two examples begin with the same
rhythmic subject but with opposite bow strokes. This discrepancy may occur
because Montéclair's example begins on the downbeat in $\frac{3}{8}$ meter and Dupont's
on the upbeat in $\frac{6}{8}$. In each case, the bowing chosen by the composer causes
primary strokes to fall on the most important and reposeful notes.

Montéclair's canarie in $\frac{3}{8}$ starts with a primary stroke on the downbeat (ex. 20.5a). The primary stroke is repeated for the melodic cadence of the first rhythmic subject (m. 4), probably so that the resulting separation will highlight the downbeat note of the feminine cadence. Montéclair wrote that some violinists instead divided a secondary stroke in that measure, which would make that ending masculine and cause the next rhythmic subject to begin with an upbeat eighth note.

Dupont used the piece quoted in example 20.5b also to demonstrate the bowing of gigues. Starting this piece with a secondary stroke on the second half of a $\frac{6}{8}$ measure causes all the downbeats to be played with primary strokes.

21

Chaconnes

Chaconnes are dances in triple meter that probably came to Spain from the New World. From Spain they spread to Italy in the late sixteenth century, and to France in the early seventeenth. Chaconne pieces are written as continuous variations or as chaconne-rondeaux. They are usually in the major mode, and their texture is homophonic. Several Baroque sources compare chaconnes with passacailles.

Early Guitar Rhythms. The Italian *ciaccona* of early guitar books is built on the four-measure harmonic progression I, V, vi, V or a variation of it. The progression may begin on the first or second pulse of the measure (see exx. 3.6c, 3.7b, and 21.1). When begun on the second pulse, often the downbeat of the third measure and sometimes also that of the fourth are emphasized by a change of harmony. In addition, the second pulse of the second, third, and fourth measures is frequently highlighted by a harmonic change.

Regardless of where the harmonies change, each measure is strummed down–down–up or, occasionally, down–up–down. Example 21.1 shows the most frequent harmonic progressions and strumming patterns in early chaconnes.

Bass Line Progressions. Bass lines of *grand siècle* chaconnes follow one of several scale sequences in a major key: 1, 5, 6, 5; 1, 7, 6, 5; 1, 5, 2, 5; 1, 2, 3, 4–5 (see ex. 3.8, app. ex. 6, and exx. 21.2 and 21.5a, b). Two statements of a progression make up most couplets. Contrasting couplets are set to other bass lines.

Rhythmic Movements. The melodic rhythm of chaconnes is too varied to reveal a typical rhythmic movement, but usually at least one measure of the first bass line progression of a piece has an iambic rhythm (SL).

Metrical Proportions. Most chaconnes are marked 3, and their measures contain three quarter-note pulses.

EXAMPLE 21.1.
Common harmonic progressions and strumming patterns.
Hudson, *The New Grove*, article "Chaconne."

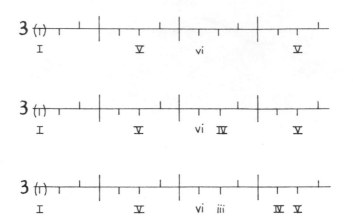

EXAMPLE 21.2.
Lully, chaconne, from *Phaeton*, 1683.

Inequality of Quick Notes. According to Corrette (1741, p. 5), eighth notes are
normally performed unequally in chaconnes; as an example he gave the chaconne from Lully's *Phaeton* (ex. 21.2). But he pointed out that eighth notes are
played equally in chaconne and passacaille couplets having sixteenths, and referred to a couplet from the passacaille from Lully's *Armide* (this piece was also
cited by Hotteterre, see ex. 29.1).

Rhythmic Subjects. The lines of chaconne songs of the *grand siècle* begin after
the first downbeat of the harmonic progression. This causes the caesura to fall
on the third downbeat and the rhyme of one line to fall on the downbeat of the
next progression, as in Lully's chaconne song from *Cadmus* (app. ex. 6). As a
result, the harmonic reposes in the second and fourth measures of early guitar
progressions are often replaced in chaconne songs and pieces of the *grand
siècle* by harmonic reposes on the third and fifth downbeats. François Couperin's commas show this later phrasing in the chaconnes of *Les nations* (1726).
Example 21.3 gives a typical rhythmic subject for a chaconne song.

EXAMPLE 21.3.
Typical rhythmic subject for a chaconne song (app. ex. 6,
mm. 1–5).

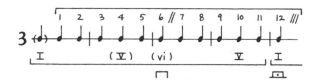

EXAMPLE 21.4.
Timing of two chaconne step-units. a. *contretemps de chaconne*;
b. Tomlinson's "chaconne or passacaille step."

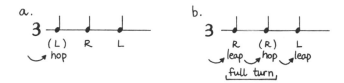

Line lengths in chaconne songs and pieces vary greatly, and the phrasing of contrasting couplets in chaconne-rondeaux is usually irregular. The final note of a chaconne song or piece is held, often extending the final progression to five measures.

Dance Motions and Step Rhythms of belle danse *Choreographies.* During the early eighteenth century, chaconnes were danced only in the theater. Their choreographies are virtuosic, highly ornamented, and similar to those of passacailles, sarabandes, and folies. Feuillet included a castanet rhythm for an untitled piece (1700a, p. 101, first brace) that is in fact the chaconne from Lully's *Phaeton.*

Two step-units are named for the chaconne, but neither actually characterizes the dance. The *contretemps de chaconne* (chaconne hop) is one of several common step-units containing a hop. The "chaconne or passacaille step," described by the English dancing master Kellom Tomlinson (1735, p. 83), occurs only occasionally.

Both the *contretemps de chaconne* and the "chaconne or passacaille step" mark the three pulses of the measure with a spring or a weighted step or both. The *contretemps de chaconne* can be fitted to 2 (exx. 8.1 and 8.4b), 3 (ex. 21.4a), or $\frac{6}{4}$ meter. The "chaconne or passacaille step" is a complete turn executed to the first two of three springing steps, each set to one pulse of triple meter (ex. 21.4b).

Chaconne choreographies, like those of passacailles, folies, and sarabandes, begin with a four-measure dance phrase. The first two measures are normally

EXAMPLE 21.5.
Pendulum markings. a. ♩ = 23 *tierces*, or MM 157 (L'Affilard, 1705e); b. ♩. = 68 *tierces*, or ♩ = MM 159, for Lully, "La chaconne des arlequins," from *Fêtes de Bacchus & de l'Amour,* 1672 (d'Onzembray, 1732); c. ♩ = 9 *pouces*, or MM 121 (La Chapelle, 1736).

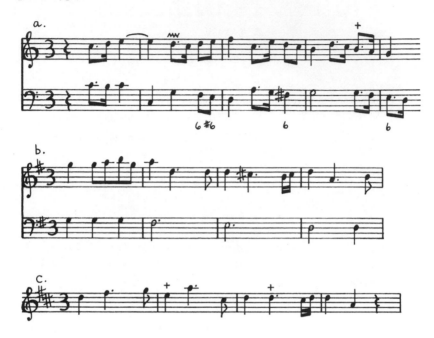

EXAMPLE 21.6.
Viol bowings and their violin equivalents. Marais: a. 1711, #56; b. 1725, #56; c. "Chaconne en rondeau," 1701, #82; d. 1725, #31.

relatively tranquil, the third more active and thus climactic, and the last again tranquil for the repose.

Tempos and Affects. Hotteterre (1719) characterized the chaconne from Lully's *Phaeton* as "gay"; Masson beat chaconnes quickly, and he and Freillon-Poncein conducted them in either three equal or two unequal beats to the measure. According to Jean-Jacques Rousseau (1768), the tempos of contrasting sections in long chaconne pieces should be the same. Apparently he meant that only the affect should change. Two of the pendulum markings for chaconnes range from MM 157 to 159 for quarter notes, while La Chapelle's considerably slower marking of MM 121 probably reflects the later date of his music.

Bowing Patterns. We found only viol bowings for chaconnes. Initial couplets that begin on the downbeat (exx. 21.6a, b) have primary strokes on all downbeats. Those that start on the second pulse of the measure (exx. 21.6c, d) tend to have secondary strokes on the downbeat of the second and perhaps the fourth measure, so that the third and especially the fifth measure can start with a primary stroke.

Slurs in the initial couplets of Marais's chaconnes commonly begin on and thereby emphasize the first and second pulses of the measure. These accents recall the downward strums in early guitar accompaniments. Later couplets in Marais's pieces have more varied rhythms and slurring, making their bowing also more varied.

22

Courantes

The French word *courante* and the Italian word *corrente* mean "running" or "flowing." In the sixteenth century, the French and Italian dances with these titles resembled one another, but by the end of the seventeenth century, the rhythms of the French examples had become more flowing, while the Italian had come to contain more running notes. Features of both dances appear in French music of the late Baroque. A courante or a *corrente* follows the allemande that starts many instrumental suites of the early eighteenth century.

The courante reigned as queen of the ballroom dances for the first 70 years of the seventeenth century. During that time it was danced so much at balls and in the theater that its step-units were often "figured" (ornamented) for variety. Changes gradually took place in the basic dance step, the length of the typical rhythmic movement, the meter sign, the organization of note values within the measure, and the tempo and the general affect.

The earliest courantes and *correnti* have simple melodies, somewhat similar rhythms, and homophonic texture. But French lutenists and harpsichordists of the early seventeenth century composed many examples with somewhat diverse rhythms, mildly polyphonic texture, and voices that come together for a repose only at the final downbeat of a reprise.

Concert pieces of the late Baroque are in binary form, with the second reprise usually one or two measures longer than the first. The texture is at least somewhat polyphonic, and free ornamentation is rare.

By the end of the seventeenth century, the Italian *corrente* had become a truly "running" piece for the violin. Examples have homophonic texture, only a few contrary rhythms, and long passages of running eighth or sixteenth notes. Some French composers of the early eighteenth century wrote out and ornamented the reprises of their Italian-style courantes.

Early Dance Motions and Step Rhythms. The courante of Arbeau's youth was a "kind of game or mime" played by three young men and three girls: Each young man in turn led his girl to the other end of the room and left her there; then each in turn, "playing the fool and making amorous grimaces and gestures while

EXAMPLE 22.1.
Arbeau, courante, 1589t, p. 124.

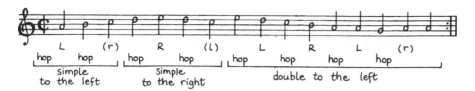

EXAMPLE 22.2.
Typical *corrente* for guitar. Sanseverino, 1622, p. 45.

pulling up his hose and adjusting his shirt," went off to bring back his girl, who turned her back on him until he started to return without her; then she feigned despair (1589t, pp. 123–24).

Early Italian and French dance steps are essentially alike. In Arbeau's example, two simples are followed by a double, and little springs (probably hops) apparently precede the steps (ex. 22.1). In Negri's Italian version (1602, p. 265, as interpreted by Little and Cusick in *The New Grove*), doubles occur at the start. Little springs precede the first three steps, and the fourth step is divided.

Through the 1630s, the courante continued to be danced in lively fashion. Mersenne described it as "a bobbing flow [*course sautelante*] of goings and comings from the beginning to the end" (1636, IIa, p. 165). However, he and de Lauze showed that the little springs of Arbeau's dance had been softened to the later *mouvements* of *belle danse* choreographies. According to Mersenne, each individual step of this dance covers one (three-pulse) measure of music and consists of "a bend, a rise, and a pose" (1636, IIa, p. 165). Mersenne gave no further timing for these actions, but they resemble those of Feuillet's *temps de courante*.

Early Guitar Rhythms. No harmonic progression characterizes the *correnti* in early guitar books; but the strumming pattern is down–down–up in each measure or half measure, usually after an initial upbeat strummed upward, as in example 22.2. Some later examples have down–up–down patterns.

Rhythmic Movements. Mersenne said the courante "is measured by the iambic foot" (SL). But trochees (LS) are the only rhythmic feet in the Italian song in example 22.3a, and trochees are mixed with iambs in most early *corrente* songs (e.g., ex. 22.3b). A choriamb (LSSL) characterizes many measures of the courantes and *correnti* of the mid-sixteenth century.

EXAMPLE 22.3.
Opening line of two early *corrente* songs. Brunelli, 1616:
a. "Balleto à 5," p. 28; b. "Corrente à 5," p. 20.

Metrical Proportions. Arbeau's courante is marked ₵, but most pieces have a 3, C ⁶₄, or ³₂ sign and three or six quarter notes in the measure. The six quarter notes are usually grouped 3 + 3. Almost all French-style courantes of the late Baroque are marked ³₂ and contain six quarter-note pulses in the measure. The pulses are grouped 2 + 1 + 1 + 2 or 2 + 2 + 2 in most measures, but return to the old 3 + 3 grouping in a few.

French courantes written in imitation of Italian *correnti* of the late Baroque are marked 3 or ³₄. When these pieces have more than a few sixteenth notes, the eighth notes are equal. In Italian-style pieces with running eighth notes, the eighth notes may be unequal, as in example 22.7, where the words *pointé-coulé* indicate a "dotted-slurred" performance.

Rhythmic Subjects. Most *corrente* songs of the early seventeenth century are set to eight-syllable lines. (Unlike the French "mute" *e*, the Italian weak syllable after the final strong one is counted as a separate syllable.) The simplest song rhythm we found, shown in example 22.3a, resembles the rhythm of Arbeau's dance (ex. 22.1) except that the song is written in long-short instead of equal values. The stressed syllables of the Italian caesura and rhyme (*vag-*, *bion-*) are preceded in the example by the bar lines of later courantes, though the weighted steps of Arbeau's dancers would fall a half measure earlier.

The commonest rhythm in Italian songs of the mid-seventeenth century, given in example 22.3b, differs from that in 22.3a in ways that set up the two reposes of the line: the delay of the first syllable makes the caesura on the third syllable more evident; and the anticipation of the sixth syllable prepares the cadence on the seventh. Features of this song found also in many courantes of the *grand siècle* are the upbeat start; the choriambic movement (LSSL) in the central measure; and the principal stress on the next downbeat, with a feminine cadence.

The early courante songs in Ranum's collection begin with a single upbeat eighth note or quarter note and have fewer long notes, making their rhythms more flowing. In the earliest of these songs (ex. 22.4a), the stress of the first

EXAMPLE 22.4.

Opening rhythmic subjects of three early courante songs.

a. from *3ᵉ livre d'Airs, et de differentes autheurs*, 1619;

b. "Belle Philis," from *Clef de chansonniers* I, 1635 (?), p. 26;

c. Boyer, "Courante pour danser," 1642, fol. 334°, p. 34.

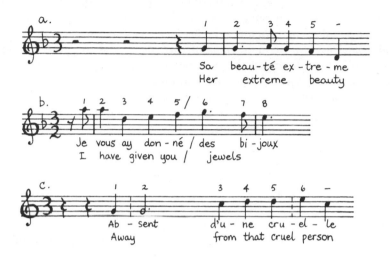

EXAMPLE 22.5.

First reprise of a courante parody. "Courante de Mme. La Dauphine," *Troisième livre d'airs*, 1689.

rhyme (-*tre*-) falls mid-measure. In slightly later examples (exx. 22.4b, c), it falls on the second downbeat.

Most French-style courantes of the late Baroque begin with an upbeat eighth or quarter note, a choriambic measure (LSSL) having L's divided into dotted figures or equal pulses, and a masculine or feminine repose on the second downbeat. This rhythmic subject begins the late seventeenth-century parody shown in example 22.5. (We found no original courante songs composed during the late Baroque.) Subsequent lines of this song, as of the other parodies in Ranum's collection, rhyme at the next downbeat or the one thereafter. Many lines are short, and many rhymes are feminine.

François Couperin's commas in his trios *Les nations* (1726) show that numerous feminine endings also conclude the rhythmic subjects in instrumental courantes. In Example 22.6 parenthetical commas (added by the present authors) indicate similar feminine endings. Examples 22.6 and 22.7 contrast the starts of courantes in the French and Italian styles by Couperin. The running eighth notes in the Italian-style first measure look rather like an ornamentation of the standard rhythm in the French-style piece.

Dance Motions and Step Rhythms of belle danse *Choreographies.* By the early eighteenth century, the courante was danced mainly as instruction for beginners. Pécour's choreography from *La Bourgogne* (ex. 22.8) is one of the few French examples in Feuillet notation. Its footwork is characterized by two step-units: the *temps de courante* (courante count) and the *pas de courante* (courante step). Only the latter takes the equivalent of a whole measure. The individual steps of both units are timed to half notes. In contrast, according to the German dancing master Gottfried Taubert, the dancer's arms move to half measures (1717, p. 552).

Tempos and Affects. Early courantes and *correnti* were presumably performed quickly, as their names indicate. Toward the end of the *grand siècle*, a moderate to slow tempo and corresponding affect were more often prescribed for courantes, in contrast to the quicker tempos of *correnti*. Dupont reported that courantes were performed "solemnly"; Masson conducted them "in three slow

EXAMPLE 22.6.
Courante in the French style. F. Couperin, *Concert royale*
IV, 1714.

EXAMPLE 22.7.
F. Couperin, "Courante a l'italiènne," from *Concert royale*
IV, 1714.

EXAMPLE 22.8.
Opening of a courante choreography. Pécour, Courante, from
"La Bourgogne," 1700.

beats"; and many examples have such words as "stately," "serious," or "gallant" at their start.

The difference between the early and late courantes may lie less in the speed of the pulse than in the length of the basic step-unit and of the typical rhythmic movement. The pulse of the two known pendulum markings (MM 164 and 180) is only somewhat slower than that of the commonest marking for menuets (MM 213). But Mersenne's step-unit—a bend, rise, and pose—and the rhythmic movements of early courantes—trochees (LS) and iambs (SL)—take up only three pulses; whereas Feuillet's *pas de courante* and the choriambs (LSSL) of late examples take up six. Naturally, a step-unit or rhythmic movement to every three pulses is perceived as quicker than one to every six, if the pulses are approximately the same tempo.

Indeed, pendulum markings reveal that courante measures with the $\frac{3}{2}$ sign have the tempo of a pair of healthy heart beats (MM 28–30). In other words,

EXAMPLE 22.9.
Pendulum marking. ♩ = 40 *tierces*, or MM 90 (L'Affilard, 1705e).

Non, non, je n'aim-er - ai   ja - mais.

EXAMPLE 22.10.
Violin bowing and its viol equivalent. Muffat, 1698t, p. 228.

EXAMPLE 22.11.
Viol bowings and their violin equivalents for the starts of
courantes. a. De Machy, 1685, p. 37; b. Marais, 1701, #52;
c. Morel, "La dacier," 1709, p. 12; d. Marais, 1701, #23.

their half measures (MM 56–60) are slightly slower than the commonest menuet measures (MM 71) and move to the standard one-second beat of the early seventeenth century.

The relationships of courante half measures to menuet measures and to healthy heartbeats is perceived less readily in terms of the half-note beats cited by the pendulum markings. D'Onzembray gave MM 82 for each of three presumably half-note beats in a courante by Mato (which we were unable to locate); L'Affilard's courante song (ex. 22.9) is slightly quicker (MM 90 for half notes).

Bowing Patterns. A further indication of the relatively quick pulse of courantes of the late Baroque are the bowing patterns taught during this period. Despite the sign 3, Muffat alternated the violin's bow strokes, "because of the speed of these dances," making primary strokes fall on odd-numbered quarter notes (ex. 22.10). A secondary stroke was divided only for a pair of quick notes (m. 5). Neither Montéclair nor Dupont gave bowings for a courante, but Dupont's general music tutor says that all quarter notes in these pieces should be detached (1718a, p. 43).

Courantes for viol alternate most bow strokes, regardless of the meter sign. Of the four starts of pieces cited in example 22.11, only the last has a rhythm that calls for a change from the normal alternating pattern.

23

Folies

The French word *folie* and the Italian *folia* are related to the English word *folly* and mean "insane" or "empty-headed." Portuguese sources of the late fifteenth century report the frenzied motions of this dance; and, throughout its more than 200 years of popularity, this music exhibited a certain extravagance in its harmonic progressions, melodic rhythms, lyrics, and instrumental variations.

The dance probably came to Portugal from the New World in the late fifteenth century. From there it spread to Spain in the sixteenth, to Italy in the early seventeenth, and to France in the mid-seventeenth century.

Richard Hudson (*The New Grove*, article "Folia") points out that there are essentially two versions of this dance: the Italian *folia* of the early seventeenth century, and the French folie of the late seventeenth and early eighteenth centuries. The early *folia* is far more varied in its melodies and bass progressions than the later folie, though some features of certain *folias* survive in the folie. During the seventeenth century the Italian *folia* was favored in Germany; at the end of that century the French folie was popular in England, where it was called "Farinel's [spelled in various ways] ground": perhaps the French violinist Michel Farinel introduced it there.

Both the folie and the *folia* are sectional variations on a two-part bass progression. Each half of the progression covers four measures of six quarter notes, or eight measures of three, and has two equal members. Each member resembles the four-measure progressions of early passacailles, chaconnes, and sarabandes. Because each variation is considered a separate *folia* or folie, the plural forms, *folias* (or sometimes, *folia*) and folies (or *couplets de folies*) are often employed.

The texture of this music is homophonic. The songs have many verses. The varied couplets in the instrumental pieces are highly diverse, each evoking a different passion.

By the late seventeenth century, at least the first half of the first couplet of all French folies had essentially the same melody, rhythm, harmony, and bass line. The origin of this standard form is unknown. The first parody words that Ranum found are four highly satirical stanzas written in 1664 about the extreme inso-

EXAMPLE 23.1.
Strumming patterns for *folias* in early guitar books.

EXAMPLE 23.2.
The start of an early *folia*. Sanseverino, 1622, p. 29.

EXAMPLE 23.3.
Early *folia* set to the later folie progression. Calvi, 1646.

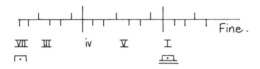

lence of flatulence perpetrated in the presence of the anonymous author. Example 23.8 gives the melody and the words of this first stanza (only mm. 1–8 follow the later instrumental form); no bass line was included for any of the parodies. Perhaps it was the ribald nature of the first folie parody, along with the political satires on the same tune in the next few years, that led to the standardization of the first couplet. The earliest instrumental couplet with the standard form is the one that starts Lully's arrangement of 1670 for Louis XIV's outdoor wind band (ex. 23.5, mm. 1–16).

Early Guitar Rhythms. Most early *folias* begin with the second quarter note of the measure or half measure (ex. 23.1). This note is strummed downward; the next, upward; and those of succeeding half measures, down–down–up.

No complete harmonic progression characterizes early *folias*, whose mode may be major or minor, but most begin with i, V, i, VII or, as in example 23.2, with I, V, I, VII. The first half of the standard French progression—i, V, i, VII; III, VII, i, V—is found in a few early Italian examples. A *folia* by Carlo Calvi (ex. 23.3) begins with this sequence of chords distributed over four measures of six pulses; the start of each half measure is marked by a new chord. The second

EXAMPLE 23.4.
Stefani, "Aria della folia," from *Scherzo amorosi*, 1622.

half of Calvi's progression, starting with the last two strums of the fourth full measure, begins the same way as the first but finishes on the tonic major.

Bass Line Progressions. Each half of a *folia* song by Agostino Stefani (1622; ex. 23.4) begins with the bass line of the later French form—1, 5, 1, 7. In m. 8 the bass line reposes on 5, in m. 16, on 1. The bass pitches are the roots of the chords in the harmonic progression.

The bass line for the first half of Lully's wind band arrangement of the standard couplet (ex. 23.5, mm. 1–8) moves along similar scale degrees in D minor—1, 5, 1, 7; 3, 7, 1, 5. Again these pitches form the roots of chords. Measures 9–16 repeat the beginning of the bass line—1, 5, 1, 7—but end on the first degree of D major.

The standard progression has three levels of harmonic motion (ex. 23.6). Each two-measure unit includes what is nowadays called a movement from a tonic- to a dominant-function chord, namely from i or III to V or VII. Each four-measure member alternates between the minor and the relative major. The first eight measures end on today's dominant (V), the second eight on the major tonic (I). A fascinating ambiguity results from the constant oscillation between tonic and dominant functions, minor and major modes, and half and full cadences.

Metrical Proportions. The sign 3 is used for early *folias*, whether they cover sixteen measures of three quarter notes or eight measures of six. The standard *folies* are in 3 meter and have three quarter-note pulses in each measure.

EXAMPLE 23.5.
Wind band arrangement. Lully, "Les folies d'Espagne," 1670.

EXAMPLE 23.6.
Harmonic motion in the standard folie progression.

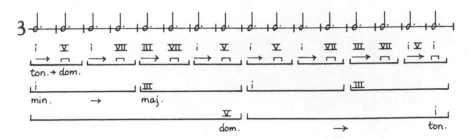

EXAMPLE 23.7.
Folie rhythms. a. antispast; b, c, and d. divisions; e. soldiers'
steps.

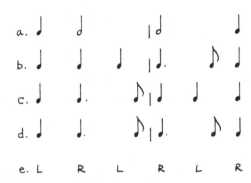

Rhythmic Movements. The standard couplet moves to two-measure antispasts
(|SL|LS) having the L's divided into dotted figures or into pairs of quarter notes
(exx. 23.7a–d). Marchers step with the right foot to the divided L's and the final S
(ex. 23.7e).

Rhythms Based on the Standard Drumbeat. The background rhythm of Lully's
triple-meter march is the drumbeat "March of the King's Regiment" (ex. 23.5). In
mm. 1–8 of the standard couplet this drumbeat accompanies four wind parts
playing a rhythm that is only slightly different: three quarter notes replace the
dotted figure in each second measure. In mm. 9–16 the drum rhythm quickens
to alternating measures of eighth and sixteenth notes. The second of Lully's
couplets features eighth-note motion in the melody, the standard rhythm and
progression in the bass, and an eighth note followed by sixteenth notes in each
measure of the drum part. In the third couplet, the standard rhythm and melody return to the treble; eighth-note motion appears in the bass; a solo drummer plays a slight variation of the standard drumbeat; and the other drummers
beat single, one-measure strokes. All these rhythms foreshadow similar rhythms

in the varied couplets of later folies. (The complete score of this piece may be seen in Sandman [1974, pp. 54–59].)

Rhythmic Subjects. Stefani's *folia* melody (ex.23.4) is similar in many ways to that of the first folie parodies of the *grand siècle*. A poetic line is set to every four measures of music, and the general shape of the melody in mm. 1–8 is the same except that Stefani's begins on the third degree of the scale, while those of the later French folies begin on the first (Hudson, 1973).

Although a few French parodies begin on the second pulse of the measure, most start on the downbeat. The first line of the earliest parody (ex. 23.8)

EXAMPLE 23.8.
French parody words to the tune of "Folies d'Espagne,"
1664, Paris BN, ms. fr. 12667, p. 229.

EXAMPLE 23.9.
Dotted rhythm in an English parody. D'Urfey, "The King's
Health, sung to Farrinel's Ground," 1682, third strain (i.e.,
couplet).

Let To - ries guard the King, let Whigs in Hal - ters swing;

breaks into equal hemistiches in agreement with the standard, two-measure
drumbeat. The hemistiches of the three other lines are unequal and break after
the first note of the second measure. The first rhyme is feminine (mm. 4 and
12); the second, masculine (mm. 8 and 16). The melody of mm. 9–16 differs
from the usual eighteenth-century instrumental form.

Of particular interest in *folia* and folie songs is the important syllable on the
second pulse of the first measure: *Al-* in example 23.4 and *Vous* in example
23.8. This bad-note stress recalls the downward strum on this note in the early
guitar pieces.

Performance of Quick Notes. The unequal performance of running eighth notes
is substantiated in Thomas D'Urfey's English drinking song set to "Farrinel's
[*sic*] Ground" (ex. 23.9). In D'Urfey's third strain, the melody begins as in
Lully's second couplet, but the first eighth note of each pulse unit is dotted and
the second is shortened to a sixteenth note—probably to show the English musicians the French practice of playing quick notes unequally. In contrast, Marais
places dots over eighth notes performed equally in some of his "Couplets de
folies" for viol (1701, #2).

Dance Motions and Step Rhythms of belle danse *Choreographies.* Folies in
eighteenth-century choreographies are solo theatrical dances for a lady or a
gentleman. These pieces use steps similar to those of virtuosic passacailles,
chaconnes, and sarabandes. Swirling *pirouettes* are common, and castanets are
added in one short example for a gentleman. Folies for ladies have mainly
smooth steps, such as *temps de courante, coupés,* and *pas de bourrée.* Those
for gentlemen include many springing steps.

Feuillet's example with a castanet part (1700a, p. 102) begins with a four-
measure dance phrase (ex. 23.10). Each of the first two step-units has a hop and
a leap; the third, the three steps of a *pas de bourrée;* the fourth, the single but
delayed weight change of a *temps de courante.* The dancer thus steps to the
rhythm LS|LS|SSS|LS while sounding the castanets to L|L|SSS|L; each L of
the castanets has the length of three S's. The S's of the steps and the castanets
create a climax in the third measure of the phrase. Feuillet's folie choreography
in the 1700 *Recueil,* for a lady, begins with smooth and sliding steps: two *temps*

EXAMPLE 23.10.
Folie choreography with castanets. Feuillet, 1700a, p. 102.

EXAMPLE 23.11.
Start of a standard couplet for viol. Marais, "Couplets de
folies," 1701, #20.

de courante, a *coupé battu*, and another *temps de courante*. (In the *coupé battu*, the foot making the second step of a *coupé* strikes the standing foot and then drops backward.) Again, the phrase climaxes in the third measure.

Tempos and Affects. The satirical innuendos of the seventeenth-century parodies suggest a moderately quick tempo, and Freillon-Poncein conducted folies with three "light" beats. Eighteenth-century parodies are drinking songs for unrequited lovers, and probably have a somewhat slower tempo. Perhaps the increased number of quick and very quick notes in the varied couplets of many instrumental folies of the late seventeenth and early eighteenth centuries slowed the tempo of these pieces. No pendulum markings have been found.

Bowing Patterns. Marais's "Couplets de folies" for viol (ex. 23.11) is the only bowed example we located. In the standard couplet Marais used the secondary stroke on the first of every two downbeats and then alternated the strokes. This allows the chords of his arrangement, on the second and fourth pulses of the pattern, to be played with primary strokes. The unbroken succession of secondary-primary pairs of bow strokes agrees with the secondary-primary (left-right) succession of steps by Lully's marchers in example 23.5. At the same time, the primary strokes on the fourth and sixth pulses coincide with the caesural and cadential reposes of possible lyrics—whether the imagined hemistiches are equal or unequal in length.

Marais's bowing of the standard couplet differed from the way that he and others bowed essentially the same melodic rhythm in sarabandes (see chap. 32). The sarabande bowing confirms triple meter in its first measure, whereas the folie bowing at first denies it. The other 31 couplets of Marais's folie are extremely diverse in their rhythms and slurring, and thus also in their bowing patterns.

24

Forlanes

The forlane is a gigue-like dance that seems to have originated among the chiefly Slavic population of the Italian province of Friullia. It came to France from Venice, where it was danced in the street to the accompaniment of mandolins, castanets, and drums. André Campra was the first to use the forlane in a French opera, *L'Europe galante* of 1697 (ex. 24.1). The two forlanes in his *Carneval de Venise* of 1699 are performed by dancers portraying Slavs, Armenians, and gypsies. A refrain of usually eight measures is heard at the beginning and end of Campra's forlanes and also in the middle of the forlane in François Couperin's *Concert Royale* IV (1714–15), which is in rondeau form. These pieces have homophonic texture.

Rhythmic Movements. Examples by Campra and later French composers move to double iambs having the first S before the bar line: S|LSL. At least one iamb in every pair of measures is usually divided into a ternary (dotted) anapest (SS|L).

Metrical Proportions. The first French forlanes are marked $\frac{6}{4}$ and contain six quarter-note pulses in the measure, grouped 3 + 3. Some later examples have a $\frac{6}{8}$ sign and six eighth-note pulses.

Rhythmic Subjects. We found no forlane songs written during the Baroque period, but Campra's instrumental examples consist of a variety of two-measure rhythmic subjects, each repeated without ornamentation, as in example 24.1. Most of these subjects start with an upbeat pulse note and, unlike rhythmic subjects based on French lyrics, end with a three-note repose. (Such reposes are natural in the Italian language.) Example 24.2 shows the skeleton rhythm of these subjects.

Later French composers sometimes altered the basic rhythmic skeleton and the length of repeated sections. For instance, the forlane in François Couperin's *Concert Royale* IV (ex. 24.3) is similar to Campra's pieces except that the note values are reduced, the bar lines are moved a half measure, and the repetitions occur after only four measures. (Couperin's repetition of mm. 1–4, not shown

EXAMPLE 24.1.
A forlane refrain. Campra, from *L'Europe galante*, 1697.

EXAMPLE 24.2.
Skeleton rhythm of forlanes.

EXAMPLE 24.3.
F. Couperin, "Forlane rondeau," from *Concert royale* IV,
1714–15.

here, is like its first statement except for a masculine cadence in the melody.)
The commas following the first, second, and fourth downbeats were inserted by
Couperin to show the phrasing.

Dance Motions and Step Rhythms of belle danse *Choreographies.* Choreographies are virtuosic theatrical dances with a variety of step-units, including

EXAMPLE 24.4.
Measures paired by their step-units. Campra, "La forlana,"
from *L'Europe galante*, 1697 (Pécour, 1700).

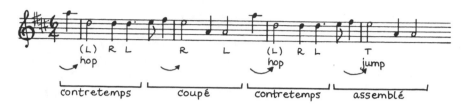

EXAMPLE 24.5.
Violin bowing and its viol equivalent. Corrette, "Forlanne,"
1738, p. 19. t above a note represents a trill, not a down-bow,
or *tirer*.

many hops and leaps. Pécour's of 1700 for the forlane in *L'Europe galante* begins with pairs of two-measure dance phrases that match the pairs of two-
measure musical phrases. Example 24.4 shows the first two such pairs. The
contretemps de gavotte in m. 1 is taken forwards; the conclusive *coupé* in m. 2 is
ornamented with a quarter turn on the first step and a "beat" (*battu*) on the
second. The *contretemps de gavotte* in m. 3 is taken backwards; the landing on
both feet of the *assemblé* in m. 4 is even more final than the ornamented *coupé* in
m. 2. Such pairs of two-measure phrases predominate in forlane choreographies.

Tempos and Affects. No pendulum markings have been found, but it is known
that Venetian forlanes were lively dances. By the middle of the eighteenth century, however, d'Alembert (1752) described the tempo as moderate and halfway
between those of loures and gigues.

Bowing Patterns. Michel Corrette (1738) gives the only bowing we found. As
with the menuets in this violin tutor, almost all the strokes are alternated—
even though some secondary ones then fall on good and long notes, and some
primary ones on bad and short ones. The bracket in example 24.5 embraces
strokes that do not follow the "rule of the down-bow." Earlier forlanes may have
observed that rule more closely than did this late example.

25

Gavottes

The gavotte is a French dance that first appeared in the late sixteenth century. Eighteenth-century sources often compare it with the bourrée and the rigaudon. Gavottes have homophonic texture and are in binary or rondeau form.

Three kinds of gavotte can be differentiated in France: the early examples for dancing, the tender and highly decorated songs mentioned by Bacilly in 1668, and those pieces that were sung and danced in the theater during the *grand siècle*. Instrumental gavottes of the early eighteenth century imitate the second or the third type.

A characteristic of some early gavotte melodies is a repeated note at reposes, as in example 25.1. This feature occurs also in some later gavottes (ex. 25.5a and app. ex. 2).

The earliest gavotte songs of the kind described by Bacilly that we found are a few *airs anciens*, or traditional airs, published in the very late seventeenth century and the early eighteenth. These pieces are often arranged for instruments and richly ornamented, for example, "Le beau berger Tirsis" (sometimes spelled "Tircis") discussed in chapters 13 and 15.

Lully's gavottes have few ornaments and are set chiefly to pulse notes and dotted figures (app. ex. 2). His gavotte melodies include more leaps than do his bourrées.

Ornamentation in instrumental pieces of the *grand siècle* may be present in the first statement of the music, in the repetition of a reprise, or in one or more *doubles*. It may imitate the divisions of sixteenth-century instrumental dances or the embellishments of *airs de cour*.

Arbeau's Dance Motions and Step Rhythms. Arbeau described the gavotte as "a miscellany of double branles," divided by passages chosen at will from the galliard. That is, it is danced in the round but with divisions of its doubles. The divisions are left to the discretion of the dancers and change with each repetition of the melody. In the middle of a dance, each couple takes a few turns alone, and then the lead gentleman and lady kiss all the dancers of the opposite sex (1589t, p. 175).

EXAMPLE 25.1.
Two divided doubles for a gavotte. Arbeau, 1589t, p. 176.

Example 25.1 gives the opening of a gavotte melody and also some choreographic divisions that might be danced to it—a divided double to the left and one to the right. Some features of Arbeau's suggested divisions are preserved in the eighteenth-century *pas de gavotte*.

Arbeau's divided double to the left includes four steps, each followed by a little spring (probably a hop). For the first step, the only one with a change of weight, the dancer steps to the left and onto the left foot. For the second step, he places his right foot next to the left but does not shift his weight onto it. For the third, the right foot crosses over the left and the right toe touches the floor. The fourth is a simulated kick with the right foot, which is still crossed over the left.

Arbeau's divided double to the right includes five steps, three of them weighted and two followed by little springs. For the first step, the dancer brings the right foot next to the left and shifts his weight onto it. For the second, the left foot crosses over the right and the left toe touches the floor. For the third, the dancer steps onto the left foot, crosses the right foot over the left, and touches the floor with the right toe. The fourth is a simulated kick with the right foot, which is still crossed over the left. The fifth is a *capriole*, a large spring during which the feet move quickly backward and forward in the air (see ex. 2.8).

Rhythmic Movements. The four steps of Arbeau's first divided double move to the rhythm of a double spondee (LLLL), and the five steps of his second to a choreobacchius (LSSLL). According to Mersenne, the gavotte moves to the choreobacchius (whose rhythm he said was LSSLL or LSSSSL). Semibreves (whole notes) are L's in Arbeau's divided LSSLL melody (ex. 25.1). Half notes are L's in Chancy's gavotte song, in which the bar lines enclose divided choreobacchii and poetic lines (ex. 25.2). Half notes are also L's in the traditional air, "Le beau berger Tirsis," which begins with an LSSSSL rhythm (ex. 15.10). In the gavotte songs of the *grand siècle*, syllables are set to choreobacchii whose half-note L's are divided into S's (ex. 25.3). In *belle danse* choreographies, the steps of the *pas de gavotte* move to the undivided LSSLL rhythm (ex. 25.4).

Metrical Proportions. Most early gavottes have the sign ₵, though arrangements of "Le beau berger Tirsis" are marked C, ₵, or 2. Gavottes of the early years of the *grand siècle* have the sign ₵ and contain four quarter-note pulses in the measure, grouped 2 + 2. During the 1670s, Lully replaced the ₵ with 2. Some gavottes of the eighteenth century have the sign $\frac{2}{4}$ and four eighth-note pulses, again grouped 2 + 2.

Rhythmic Subjects. Early Italian *gavottas* and early French gavottes began on the downbeat. During the late seventeenth and early eighteenth centuries, Italian *gavottas* retained the downbeat start or began with an upbeat eighth note; whereas French gavottes started on the second half of the measure. In Chancy's gavotte song (ex. 25.2), the only one we know that antedates those of Lully, each line begins on the downbeat. D'Anglebert's harpsichord arrangement (1689) of "Le beau berger Tirsis" also begins on the downbeat (ex. 13.2), but the highly ornamented flute arrangements of the eighteenth century start on the upbeat (exx. 15.10, 15.11).

Lully moved the bar line half a measure in his gavottes, thus allowing the reposes of lyrics to fall on downbeats. Two-measure rhythmic subjects begin with an upbeat half note or its equivalent and finish with a downbeat half note or two quarter notes (app. ex. 2). François Couperin marked the ends of such rhythmic subjects with commas throughout his gavotte in *Les nations: L'Espagnole.*

The usual poetic line in Lullian gavotte songs has seven syllables, normally divided 3 + 4. The third syllable falls on the first downbeat, and the rhyme falls on the second. The first rhyme of a song is often feminine (ex. 25.3).

All but the last pair of quarter notes in the rhythmic subject is often replaced by other values. The most usual substitution is a dotted quarter and an eighth (see app. ex. 2). Continuous eighths are found only in instrumental gavottes or their *doubles.*

EXAMPLE 25.2.
Chancy, "Gavotte pour boire." from *Chansons*, livre 6, 1651.

EXAMPLE 25.3.
Simplest rhythmic subject for a Lullian gavotte song.

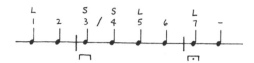

EXAMPLE 25.4.
Pas de gavotte.

Dance Motions and Step Rhythms of the belle danse *Choreographies.* By the early eighteenth century, most gavottes were danced as contredanses; only a few were choreographed as *danses à deux.* Feuillet (1706) wrote that the *pas de gavotte* was the customary step for forward and backward motion in contredanses.

We found no eighteenth-century description of the *pas de gavotte.* However, the commonest step-unit in the few gavotte choreographies is a division of a double that includes a hop and large spring reminiscent of Arbeau's divisions for a gavotte: we call this unit the *pas de gavotte.*

Like the typical rhythmic subject of the gavotte music of the *grand siècle,* the *pas de gavotte* straddles two bar lines (ex. 25.4). It begins with an upbeat half note and finishes with a half note on the second downbeat (L|SSL|L). A hop marks the first downbeat, and a jump onto both feet (an *assemblé*) marks the second. The first step, on the upbeat half note, is omitted in some dance phrases, turning the rhythm of the step-unit into that of a *pas de rigaudon.*

Tempos and Affects. The complexity of the steps that divide the doubles of early gavottes suggests a moderate tempo for the L's of these pieces. The division of most L's and some S's in early melodies would also require a certain deliberateness of tempo (exx. 25.1, 25.2).

To accommodate expressive ornamentation in the style of *airs de cour,* Bacilly allowed a slower tempo for "tender older gavotte songs" than for danced examples. As discussed in chapter 15, he even permitted some distortion of the meter in these pieces.

Gavotte pieces of the *grand siècle* have a variety of tempos and affects. According to Furetière and Richelet, the gavotte is a gay dance; Masson beat it "lightly"; Choquel said it is very fast. But Dupont reported that gavottes move "graciously" and a little slower than a [presumably processional] march, which moves "solemnly." Freillon-Poncein beat gavottes "very slowly," because he found them "more grave and serious" than bourrées and rigaudons and to have

EXAMPLE 25.5.
Pendulum markings. a. ♩ = 30 *tierces*, or MM 120 (L'Affilard,
1705e); b. ♩ = 37 *tierces*, of MM 97, for Lully, gavottes, from
Roland, 1685 (d'Onzembray, 1732); c. ♩ = 6 *pouces*, or MM 148
(La Chapelle, 1736).

EXAMPLE 25.6.
Viol bowings and their violin equivalents for four rhythmic
subjects by Marais. a. 1711, #49; b. "Gavotte singuliere,"
1725, #96; c. 1725, #39; d. "La favorite," 1717, #12.

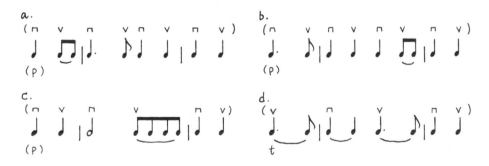

"a more touching expression." Probably the gay, light, and fast pieces recalled
the ballroom or the theater; whereas the slow, gracious, touching, and serious
ones imitated the tender older songs mentioned by Bacilly.

Pendulum markings also reveal a large range of tempos, namely, MM 97 to
148 for half notes with the sign 2 (ex. 25.5). L'Affilard's MM 120 for half notes,
for a gavotte song whose second pulse is divided (ex. 25.5a), seems too fast to
accommodate either the syllables or the sentiment of the text: "What? you pretend to be able without pain. . . ."

Bowing Patterns. We found no violin bowings for gavottes. Probably the pedagogical writers thought that these dances adhered so closely to the "rule of the

down-bow" that no instructions or examples were needed. Bowed gavottes for viol certainly follow this rule, most measures having two or four bow strokes. The opening rhythmic subjects from four of Marais's gavottes are typical (ex. 25.6). The first two have four strokes in a measure, whereas slurs in the central measures of the last two reduce the number of strokes to two. Most viol gavottes begin with a primary stroke, but the slurred note-pair that starts example 25.6d is played with a secondary stroke so that the coming downbeat can be performed with a primary one.

26

Gigues

Meredith Ellis Little (*The New Grove*, article "Gigue") shows that the jig (with variant spellings) goes back to the fifteenth century in the British Isles. The English word may have come from the old French *giquer*, to "frolic," "leap," or "gambol." English literary works of the sixteenth century suggest that jigs are fast dances with virtuoso footwork, and a few English country dances of the seventeenth century are called jigs.

The gigue appeared in French lute and harpsichord music early in the seventeenth century and developed in the *style brisé* used by these instruments. During the mid-seventeenth century, it became popular in Germany, and by the *grand siècle*, it was characterized by ternary dotted rhythms. Examples from the *grand siècle* are in binary or occasionally rondeau form, and imitation between voices at the start of a musical period or reprise is common.

Late in the seventeenth century, the *giga* appeared in Italy. This music had evidently developed from the earlier English form rather than from the French. It had homophonic texture and a particularly violinistic character that often included passages of fairly continuous quick notes. In the early eighteenth century, the Italian *giga* became popular in France.

The term *gigue anglaise* is somewhat ambiguous. French writers and composers of the Baroque period used it for examples not in the French style, but German writers and composers used it for those not in the Italian style.

Rhythmic Movements. Dactyls (LSS), in either binary or ternary (dotted) form, fill many beats. On the other hand, the syntax of gigue songs usually groups these notes as dotted anapests (SS|L) (ex. 26.2 and app. ex. 4).

Metrical Proportions. Some early English, French, German, and Italian examples use the signs C or ¢. Others are marked 3. Perhaps, as with early canaries, binary and ternary (dotted) dactyls performed at the quick tempo of these pieces sounded almost the same.

EXAMPLE 26.1.
Mixed rhythms in a gigue for harpsichord. Chambonnières,
"La Madelainette," 1670, livre premier, #17.

EXAMPLE 26.2.
Typical rhythmic subject.

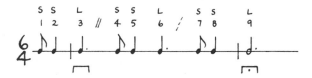

Most French-style gigues of the *grand siècle* are marked 3 or $\frac{6}{4}$, and their measures contain three or six quarter-note pulses, the latter grouped in threes. Some examples by Lully and later composers have the sign $\frac{6}{8}$ and six eighth-note pulses. Gigues in the Italian style are marked $\frac{3}{4}$, $\frac{3}{8}$, $\frac{6}{8}$, $\frac{9}{8}$, or $\frac{12}{8}$.

The rhythm of some measures in examples for lute or harpsichord implies $\frac{3}{2}$ rather than $\frac{6}{4}$ meter. In the harpsichord gigue by Chambonnières, shown in example 26.1, mm. 2 and 4 are closer to $\frac{3}{2}$ than to $\frac{6}{4}$ meter.

Rhythmic Subjects. The most typical rhythmic subject of the *grand siècle* is a $\frac{6}{4}$ or $\frac{6}{8}$ measure of ternary dotted figures, preceded by two upbeat notes and followed by one or two notes of repose (ex. 26.2). Most reposes of gigue lyrics fall on downbeats, and most textual cells end on musical beats, as in the first line of Lully's gigue song from *Amadis* (app. ex. 4). Later lines often vary in length, and sometimes in their division into textual cells.

A different rhythmic subject is found at the start of some concert pieces for instruments; François Couperin's "Gigue lourée" is typical (ex. 26.3). In these pieces, the bar line is moved a half measure, and certain dotted figures are replaced with equal pulse notes. Despite the new location of the bar lines,

EXAMPLE 26.3.
F. Couperin, "Gigue lourée," from *Les nations: L'Espagnole*
(1726).

however, Couperin showed with commas that reposes fall on intermittent downbeats.

A few bad-note accents may be featured in French gigues. Example 26.3 includes syncopations (mm. 7 and 13) and hemiolas (mm. 8 and 14), and Lully's gigue song (app. ex. 4) employs SL rhythms in certain half measures, namely, the word "Tout" occurs four times on an offbeat half note at a high pitch.

Most examples in the Italian style begin with an upbeat pulse and have few if any dotted rhythms.

Belle danse *Choreographies*. Choreographed gigues of the early eighteenth century are virtuosic theatrical pieces. They have no special step-unit but, like canaries, are characterized by flourishes of fast footwork done more or less in place. Hops and leaps are also common.

Tempos and Affects. Gigues are usually described as gay dances. According to Muffat they are extremely fast, and Dupont beat them "very lightly." But Loulié thought they should not be too quick, and Freillon-Poncein conducted them in two slow beats. This apparent disagreement probably arose because beats composed of ternary dotted figures can only be moderately fast even when the very quick notes of the dotted figures are performed as rapidly as possible.

Pendulum markings are similar to those for canaries. The rapid pace needed for the skips and leaps of dancers pushes the instrumentalists and singers to the limits of their abilities. On the other hand, L'Affilard's "serious gigue" (ex. 26.4a)

EXAMPLE 26.4.
Pendulum markings. a. ♩. = 31 *tierces*, or MM 116, for "Gigue serieux" (L'Affilard, 1705e); b. ♩. = 36 *tierces*, or MM 100, for "Gigue à boire" (L'Affilard 1705e); c. ♩. = 32 *tierces*, or MM 112, for Lully, gigue, from *Amadis*, 1684 (d'Onzembray, 1732); d. ♩. = 9 *pouces*, or MM 121 (La Chapelle, 1736); e. ♩. = 12 *pouces*, or MM 105, for "Air de rondeau," adapted from Lully, *Thesée*, 1675 (Choquel, 1759).

a. Quand l'A - mour nous pre - sen - te ses chaî - nes

b. Mes a - mis, il faut boi - re à longs traits,

c.

d.

Gay. (mouvement de Gigue).

e. Pour le peu de bon temps qui nous res-te. Rien n'est plus fu-nes-te qu'un noir cha-grin.

seems too fast for its message: "When love presents us its chains." Even his "gigue for drinking," which is slightly slower, becomes a patter song at the tempo given. Choquel's song "in the movement of a gigue" also seems too quick for its disheartening text: "For the little time that remains to us, Nothing is more deadly than black grief."

The German musician Mattheson said that examples in the Italian syle, being "not for dancing, but for fiddling, . . . force themselves to extreme speed and volatility" (1739, II, chap. 13, para. 102).

Bowing Patterns. Jean Rousseau and the violin pedagogues recommended alternating the strokes for gigues. Muffat attributed this practice to the quick tempo, implying that a more sophisticated bowing would be unmanageable. However, Muffat's gigue (ex. 26.5a) and the two by Montéclair (ex. 26.5c, d) include occasional adjustments that divide secondary strokes or repeat primary ones. Dupont's gigue (ex. 26.5c) is the same piece he used for canaries.

Muffat and Dupont began their gigues in such a way that, by alternating the

EXAMPLE 26.5.
Violin bowings and their viol equivalents. a. Muffat, 1698t,
p. 229; b. Dupont, 1718b, p. 8. Montéclair, 1711–12: c. p. 18;
d. pp. 22–23.

EXAMPLE 26.5.
Continued

strokes, primary ones fall on all downbeats and all reposes. Example 26.5a starts with a primary stroke on a bad quick note and, for the fourth rhythmic subject (end of m. 6, a repeat of the first), begins again with a primary stroke— even though this requires repeating a primary one. Example 26.5b starts with a secondary stroke on a dotted note and continues with a primary one on a bad quick note.

Montéclair's two bowed gigues (exx. 26.5c, d) begin with essentially the same rhythm as Muffat's example, but with the opposite bow stroke, probably because Montéclair preferred a secondary stroke for the bad quick notes that start these pieces. In example 26.5c, he repeated a primary stroke for the initial downbeat of both reprises (mm. 1, 9). In the last phrase (mm. 13–17), he divided a secondary stroke (m. 14) to begin the final rhythmic subject as before, even though this makes the piece end with a secondary stroke. Montéclair showed that some other players of his day would have alternated the strokes throughout example 26.5c, making no adjustment at all, although some secondary strokes would thereby be played on downbeats.

EXAMPLE 26.6.
Viol bowings and their violin equivalents. Marais: a. 1701, #32; b. "La badine," 1701, #82; c. "La piquante," 1717, #49; d. "Le bout entrain," 1717, #37; e. 1725, #50; f. "La precieuse," 1725, #77.

In example 26.5d, even Montéclair allowed secondary strokes to fall on downbeats. In most measures, the first pulse is played with a secondary stroke and the fourth with a primary one. This breaking of the "rule of the down-bow" is presumably tolerated because in effect it shifts the bar lines of the piece to the middle of the measure.

Concert gigues for viol (ex. 26.6) have a greater variety of rhythms and far fewer dotted figures than do the pedagogical examples for violin. When dotted figures do occur, the first two or all three notes of the beat are often slurred. Most measures of these pieces have two, four, or six alternating bow strokes. When there is an odd number of strokes, a secondary stroke is divided to start a new rhythmic subject or musical member, or to ensure that a note of repose is played with a primary stroke. We found primary strokes repeated only to start a second reprise.

Loures

The musical instrument called *loure* belongs to the bagpipe family. The musical form of the same name first appeared in the 1670s and may have derived from peasant songs and dances accompanied by bagpipes. The probability of this ancestry is substantiated by Hotteterre's tutor of 1738 for musette (a sophisticated kind of bagpipe), which contains several anonymous brunettes with rhythms remarkably similar to those of Lully's loure from *Alceste* (ex. 27.1b), which it also includes. (As mentioned in chap. 15, brunettes are rustic love songs that were popular among cultivated people in the mid-eighteenth century.) Loures are in binary form, and many have extended phrases and contrapuntal texture. Concert loures often include a few ternary dotted figures and are often compared with gigues.

Rhythmic Movements. The anonymous loure in example 27.1a and the *Alceste* loure (ex. 27.1b) move to antispasts that straddle a bar line (SL|LS). The downbeat L is often divided into a dotted figure; and, at the end of a reprise, the upbeat L may be divided in the same way. Sometimes the initial antispast in a loure is altered so much by abbreviating or expanding the first SL that the SL|LS movement is difficult to recognize. In example 27.2a the first SL is reduced to a single pulse; in example 27.2b it is preceded by the upbeat pulse of another measure; and in example 27.2c its time value is halved.

Metrical Proportions. Most loures are marked $\frac{6}{4}$, and each measure contains six quarter-note pulses, grouped 3 + 3. A few have the sign 3 and three quarter-note pulses.

Rhythmic Subjects. In many ways, the lyrics of the loure songs of the *grand siècle* in example 27.2 resemble those of the anonymous brunette in example 27.1a. The rhymes of all four fall on the downbeat L of the second antispast (SL|LS), which is the second downbeat in pieces marked $\frac{6}{4}$ and the fourth in

EXAMPLE 27.1.

A brunette for musette and a theatrical loure. a. anonymous
brunette, Hotteterre, 1738, p. 46; b. Lully, "Loure pour les
pécheurs," from *Alceste*, 1674 (cited in Hotteterre, 1738,
p. 42).

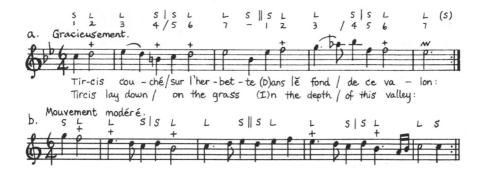

EXAMPLE 27.2.

Initial rhythmic subject of three songs. a. De la Guerre, from
Cephale et Procris, 1694; b. Campra, from *L'Europe galante*,
1698; c. La Barre, from *Triomphe des arts*, 1700.

EXAMPLE 27.3.
Hemiola at the end of a first reprise. La Barre, from *Le triomphe des arts*, 1700.

EXAMPLE 27.4.
Pendulum markings. a. ♩. = 32 *tierces*, or MM 112, for Colasse, "Danse des divinities de la mer," from *Thetis & Pelée*, 1689 (d'Onzembray, 1732); b. ♩. = 48 *pouces*, or MM 52 (La Chapelle, 1736).

those marked 3. The first lines of the loure songs, like the second line of that brunette, divide after the downbeat L of the initial antispast.

Although "mute" *e*'s are unstressed in French, they are often set to offbeat undivided L's in loure songs, and these notes tend to be trilled. For this reason, instrumentalists should not swell half notes in loures, even where they are trilled. In examples 27.1, 27.2, and 27.3, "mute" *e*'s on "longs" are indicated by a "short" sign to show their lack of stress.

A hemiola is likely to occur at the end of a loure reprise. For instance, the melody and words that conclude the first reprise in example 27.3 clearly articulate a $\frac{3}{2}$ pattern.

Belle danse *Choreographies*. Loure choreographies of the eighteenth century, like those of canaries and gigues, are theatrical pieces that include a great variety of step-units. But loures differ from the other two dances in having smoother step-units and more flowing floor patterns.

Tempos and Affects. Loures are slow or moderate in tempo and are sometimes called "slow gigues." Dupont performed loures "solemnly"; many examples are

EXAMPLE 27.5.
Violin bowings and their viol equivalents. Montéclair, 1711–12,
p. 17.

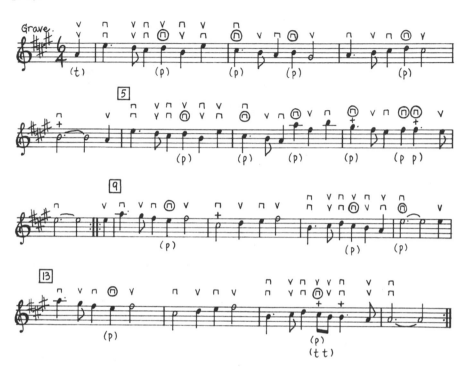

marked *grave*; and Hotteterre (1738) added the words *mouvement modéré* to
Lully's loure in example 27.1b. Masson conducted loures with two slow beats,
but Hotteterre conducted four unequal beats in each measure.

The two existing pendulum markings for loures differ greatly, though the
rhythms of the two pieces in example 27.4 are almost identical. D'Onzembray
prescribed the same quick tempo that he employed for a gigue, but La Chapelle's tempo is only half as fast.

Bowing Patterns. The only bowed example we found was given by Montéclair
(ex. 27.5). Although his example shows that some players alternated almost all
the strokes in loures, as in gigues, he himself repeated primary strokes—making
an articulation silence—at the start of many measures and half measures.

Menuets

According to Brossard's dictionary (1703), the menuet came from Poitou, a province in southwestern France. Two branles in triple meter that came earlier from that province—the "branle double de Poitou" and the "branle à mener de Poitou"—closely resemble the earliest menuets in their rhythmic subjects and formal structures; and some aspects of the step-units and floor patterns of Arbeau's duple-meter "branle double" and triple-meter "branle de Poitou" anticipate those of the menuet. Arbeau described only the duple-meter "branle double," and only the "branle de Poitou," not the "branle à mener de Poitou" that later writers sometimes called simply the "branle de Poitou" or the "branle à mener."

Late seventeenth- and early eighteenth-century writers differed on the origin of the term *menuet*. Some said that it came from an alternative form of the French adjective *menu*, meaning "small" or "fine," and referred to the small, elegant steps of the dance. Others stated that the word came from the French verb *mener* (to lead) and thus from the "branle à mener."

The menuet first appeared at the French court around 1660. Louis Couperin's three menuets in the Bauyn manuscript (ca. 1660) are the earliest music we found. Two of these (one called the "Menuet de Poitou" [ex. 7.2]) have the six-measure members of the "branle à mener." The third has the four-measure members of the "branle double de Poitou."

The early menuet also had a Spanish flavor. Dancers portraying two Spanish couples performed the first example to appear in a stage production, Lully's *Mariage forcé* of 1664. The music for this menuet (see ex. 4.12) is based on the hegemeole (SSSLS), which Mersenne associated with sarabandes. Perhaps Du Manoir, addressing the members of the newly founded Academy of Dance in 1664, was referring to Lully's Spanish menuet when he complained that the Academy did not properly observe the differences between the menuet and the Spanish dances:

> Is it not an established fact that you have applied menuet steps to an air in the movement of the sarabande or chaconne, under the pretext that the [meter] sign is

the same [for all three dances], whereas the notes of a menuet should be phrased [*coupées*] differently from those of a sarabande?[1] (1664, pp. 28–29)

Despite Du Manoir's complaint, many menuets continued to be set to hegemeoles (SSSLS), and Feuillet gave castanet rhythms for an unidentified piece (1700a, p. 101, second and third braces) called "Menuet" in the Menetou manuscript of harpsichord transcriptions (p. 109).

For a quarter century after its introduction at court, the menuet enjoyed great popularity as a theatrical and a ballroom dance: examples to be sung and danced were featured in all musical stage works and were choreographed for all court occasions. The menuet rapidly spread to other European courts and soon replaced the courante as the most popular dance at balls. The German dancing master Taubert called the menuet "a [younger] sister of the courante" (1717, p. 615) and also related it to the passepied. All three dances have both simple and "figured" (ornamented) steps; all are normally performed as *danses à deux*; and their step rhythms are the same or nearly so.

By the eighteenth century, menuets had lost favor to the newer dances. Some were choreographed as contredanses, but few new *belle danse* choreographies were created. Older, well-established choreographies were used to start the court balls: menuets had replaced the branles as the traditional dances of the day. During this period, menuets were extremely popular as concert pieces and were included in most instrumental suites and many sonatas.

Because menuets have such a long history and are related to so many other dances, examples vary greatly. Most are in binary form, though a few are set as rondeaux; and almost all have homophonic texture. Embellishments may be stereotyped ornaments, vocal-style decorations, or fairly continuous quick notes. Menuets often appear in groups of two or more.

Early Dance Motions and Step Rhythms. Arbeau's "branle double" and "branle de Poitou" are characterized by a divided double for their second step-unit. Four of the steps in each of these divided doubles suggest the footwork in one of the later menuet step-units.

The last four steps of the divided closed double in Arbeau's "branle double" (exx. 2.7 and 28.1a) move to the rhythm of the choriamb (LSSL): except for Arbeau's start on the left foot and his lack of *mouvements*, these steps are identical with those of Rameau's *pas de menuet* (exx. 28.6b,c). The first four steps of the divided open double in Arbeau's "branle de Poitou" (ex. 28.1b) begin on the right foot and move to the rhythm of the first paeon (LSSS), whose L is as long as three S's. In Arbeau's youth, the young women of Poitou stamped their feet on the divided steps, creating an "agreeable noise" with their wooden shoes (1589t, p. 147). The first four steps are the same as those of Taubert's *pas de menuet en fleuret* (ornamented menuet step; ex. 28.6e) (1717, pp. 634–35).

The dancers of Arbeau's "branle de Poitou" moved only to the left around the circle. De Lauze (1623) and Mersenne (1636) described the "branle à mener de Poitou" as a round dance whose ring is broken by each dancer in turn. The head dancer leads the others in a snakelike chain and then takes the hand of the last

EXAMPLE 28.1.
Second (dance) measure of two branles. Arbeau, 1589t. a. branle
double (divided closed double), p. 130; b. branle de Poitou
(divided open double), p. 147.

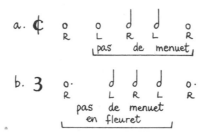

dancer to close the circle again. The serpentine path is retained in the reversed
"S" and later the "Z" figures of menuets.

Rhythmic Movements. According to Mersenne, the "branle double de Poitou"
is characterized by the iamb (SL); the "branle à mener de Poitou" by the paeon
(LSSS or SSSL), though "some relate the movement of this [latter] dance to the
blacksmith's beat" (*battement du Mareschal*)—also an iamb.

Various combinations of iambs (SL) and their opposites, trochees (LS), and
two versions of the paeon (LSSS and SSSL) appear often in menuets. Antispasts
(SLLS) begin many menuet melodies, and dancers step to choriambs (LSSL) or
first paeons (LSSS). Hegemeoles, a division of the fourth paeon (SSSL), start
many menuet songs.

Metrical Proportions. Most menuets are marked 3, and their measures contain
three quarter-note pulses. Some examples of the early eighteenth century have
the sign $\frac{3}{4}$ and again three quarter-note pulses. A few pieces marked $\frac{6}{4}$ or $\frac{6}{8}$ combine two measures of 3 or $\frac{3}{8}$ meter and begin on the downbeat or the upbeat; the
downbeat start suits the dance steps, whereas the upbeat start suits the dance
lyrics. Perhaps the rhythmic conflict between steps and lyrics is the reason
French composers wrote few menuets in compound-duple meter.

Rhythmic Subjects. Because of the great popularity and long life of the menuet,
composers experimented considerably with rhythmic subjects. The lines of
songs and the rhythmic subjects of pieces are set to two, three, four, or five
measures. Most lines and subjects start on the downbeat, but many three-
measure ones and a few others begin with an upbeat quarter note. Musical
members encompass a single line or subject of three, four, or five measures, or a
pair of two-measure lines or subjects.

As discussed in chapter 6, a few two-measure menuet lines and their corresponding rhythmic subjects are fitted to a single rhythmic movement. The lines
set to antispasts (SLLS) at the start of Lully's menuet song (app. ex. 1) are typi-

EXAMPLE 28.2.
Four-measure lines set to two rhythmic movements. a. two
antispasts (SLLS|SLLS), in Lully, Menuet, from *Atys*, 1676;
b. double trochee plus hegemeole (LSLS|SSSLS), in Lully,
Menuet, from *Persée*, 1682.

EXAMPLE 28.3.
Usual skeleton structure for a four-measure rhythmic subject.

cal. But many more four-measure lines cover two rhythmic movements and
break into hemistiches after the second downbeat, not between the two rhythmic movements (ex. 28.2). Some four-measure lines of menuet songs, like those
of L'Affilard's drinking song (app. ex. 3), are set mainly to pulse notes. Again,
the lines break after the second downbeat. Example 28.3 shows the usual skeleton structure for a four-measure rhythmic subject in a menuet. Rhythmic values
between the reposes are too varied to be generalized.

Musical members of three measures have a different structure (ex. 28.4).
They often begin with an upbeat pulse and are usually composed of SL and LS
rhythms arranged in a number of ways, with some L's divided into dotted figures. The rather weak first repose often falls on the first downbeat.

Lully and his followers also experimented with menuets whose musical mem-

EXAMPLE 28.4.
Menuet lines set to three-measure members. Lully, menuet
"Le satyr," from *Ballet des muses*, 1666.

EXAMPLE 28.5.
Pairs of lines set to five-measure members. Lully, song following "Menuet pour les pastres," from *Alceste*, 1674.

bers have five measures. We found no song with this phrasing specifically la-
beled as a menuet, but the untitled song that follows Lully's instrumental "Menuet pour les pastres" in the finale of *Alceste* has rhythms almost identical to it
(ex. 28.5). In this song, a musical member covers two lines of lyrics. The first
line takes up most of three measures, with the poetic and musical reposes falling together on the downbeat of the third measure; the second line starts with
the last quarter note of that measure. In this particular song, the rhyme of the
second line occurs on the fifth downbeat, but the corresponding musical cadence is completed only on the last pulse of that measure.

Dance Motions and Step Rhythms of belle danse *Choreographies.* In the standard choreography for the menuet (Rameau, 1725b), the dancers make their opening bows, approach the "presence," retreat on the diagonal to opposite corners of the room, and make one or more "Z" figures. Taking right hands, they circle each other one or more times; taking left hands, they circle in the opposite direction one or more times. They continue with one or more "Z" figures and, taking both hands, again circle once or twice. To end the dance, they return to their starting place and make their final bows.

The principal step-unit, the *pas de menuet,* has a variety of *mouvements* but always begins with the right foot and has only one timing of its steps (LSSL). The *pas de menuet en fleuret* has the same footwork but different timing (LSSS). In the several versions of Rameau's *pas de menuet,* a *mouvement* precedes the first step and often the second or fourth steps, or all three.

Feuillet's *pas de menuet bohémienne,* or gypsy menuet step, is the one that Dufort (1728) called the earliest menuet step (ex. 28.6a). According to his timing, the two *mouvements* of this step-unit initiate both L's of the choriamb (LSSL).

The *pas de menuet avec trois* [with three] *mouvements* was popular in the early *belle danse* choreographies. Its *mouvements* initiate both L's and the first S of the choriamb (LSSL), making a molossus (LLL), or hemiola rhythm (ex. 28.6b).

The *pas de menuet avec deux* [with two] *mouvements* differs from the bohemian version. Its *mouvements* initiate the first L and first S of the choriamb (LSSL; ex. 28.6c). This step-unit was perhaps more favored in late than in early *belle danse* choreographies.

The *pas de menuet avec un* [with one] *mouvement* occurs infrequently in the choreographies. Its *mouvement* initiates only the first L of the choriamb (LSSL; ex. 28.6d). Taubert recommended this step-unit for courtiers too old or corpulent to bend their knees more often (1717, pp. 633–34).

Two other step-units help decorate the "figured" menuets of the *belle danse* choreographies: the four steps of the *pas de menuet en fleuret* are set to the rhythm of a paeon (LSSS) (ex. 28.6e); and, according to Rameau, the *con-*

EXAMPLE 28.6.
Principal step-units of the menuet. a. *pas de menuet bohé-mienne;* b. with three *mouvements;* c. with two *mouvements;* d. with one *mouvement;* e. *pas de menuet en fleuret;* f. *con-tretemps de menuet* (Rameau).

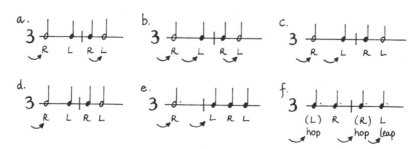

tretemps de menuet (menuet hop) moves to the rhythm of a double spondee (LLLL), in which L's are dotted pulse values (ex. 28.6f). Because the *mouvements* of these two step-units emphasize both downbeats, they contrast well with the choriamb (LSSL) or molossus (LLL) of the *pas de menuet.*

The timing of steps to three- and five-measure rhythmic subjects is not known. Perhaps subjects of three measures were danced with a *pas de menuet en fleuret* plus a *temps de courante*—the *belle danse* equivalent of the divided double in Arbeau's "branle de Poitou." Or perhaps two-measure step-units were repeated throughout a six- or ten-measure dance phrase, in order to come out right at the end.

Tempos and Affects. Many writers, including Muffat, Masson, Saint-Lambert, Brossard, Taubert, and Hotteterre (1719), mentioned the menuet's quick tempo and its gay character, or both. Richelet described the menuet as "a kind of flowing dance." Furetière and Corneille cited its small, quick steps.

Less agreement is found on the conducting pattern. Masson and Freillon-Poncein made two unequal beats in each measure; Saint-Lambert counted two beats in each pair of measures; and, according to Masson and Dufort, dancing masters conducted three equal beats in two measures, as for one $\frac{3}{2}$ measure.

Most pendulum markings range from MM 71 to 78 for dotted half notes. Only La Chapelle called for a much slower tempo, namely, MM 129 for quarter notes (MM 43 for measures). His tempo anticipated that of the court menuet at the

EXAMPLE 28.7.
Pendulum markings. a. ♩. = 51 *tierces*, or MM 71, for "Menuet à boire" (L'Affilard, 1705e); b. ♩. = 48 *tierces*, or MM 75, for "Menuet serieux" (L'Affilard, 1705e); c. ♩. = 51 *tierces*, or MM 71, for Campra, menuet, from *L'Europe galante*, 1697 (d'Onzembray, 1732); d. ♩. = 51 *tierces*, or MM 71, for Destouches, menuet, from *Marthésie*, 1699 (d'Onzembray, 1732); e. ♩ = 8 *pouces*, or MM 129 (La Chapelle, 1736); f. ♩. = 22 *pouces*, or MM 78 (Choquel, 1759).

EXAMPLE 28.8.
Menuet timed to the heartbeat. $\downarrow$. = MM 60 (Marquet, 1747).

EXAMPLE 28.9.
Timings for barrel organ. Engramelle, 1775. a. $\downarrow$. = MM 73, for #6; b. $\downarrow$ = MM 160, for "Menuet de Zelindor," #4; c. $\downarrow$ = MM 144–160 for "Menuet du Roy de Prusse," #11.

end of the eighteenth century. Choquel's MM 78 for dotted halves, on the other hand, anticipated the very quick menuets that led to Beethoven's scherzi.

Some modern musicians, dancers, and scholars question the validity of the pendulum markings for menuets, believing them to be too quick for the natural grace of the dance and its music. Indeed, all but La Chapelle's markings do seem to be more quick than gay. Nevertheless, several later sources indirectly corroborate the pendulum markings and also testify to the gradual slowing of the court menuet.

In 1747 Dr. François-Nicolas Marquet wrote in a medical treatise that a healthy heart beats at the tempo of a menuet measure, or once per second: MM 60. The menuet music that he cited (ex. 28.8) is typical for his day. His tempo is slightly slower than any with pendulum rates except La Chapelle's and probably reflects the relaxation of the menuet tempo by the middle of the century.

In 1768 Jean-Jacques Rousseau described one menuet as "very lively and very gay" and another as "elegant, noble, a little gay, but the least gay of all the dances at the ball." The latter was the old court dance still further moderated.

In 1775 Père Engramelle explained how to prick an organ barrel for the notes of various pieces, including three menuets. In the process, he showed the exact tempo of each piece (ex. 28.9). One menuet moves to the very lively tempo of

EXAMPLE 28.10.
Violin bowings before 1738. a. Muffat, 1689t, p. 230; b. Montéclair, 1711–12, p. 15; c. Dupont, 1718b, p. 7.

the earlier pendulum markings: MM 73 for measures. The other two, which are slower than Marquet's menuet, bear witness to the continued slackening of tempo for the court dance: MM 160 and 144–160 for quarter notes.

The court menuet of the late eighteenth century is the one best known today. That is probably why many modern musicians and dancers are reluctant to accept the lively tempo and gay affect given by the pendulum rates for the earlier menuet.

Bowing Patterns. Until the late 1730s, pedagogical examples of menuets for violin used primary strokes on almost all downbeats. These bowings commonly grouped measures in pairs. (The pairing of measures and the pairing of pairs of measures show that the section of a menuet cited by Muffat in ex. 28.10a must begin on the second measure of an eight-measure period.)

The bowings of Muffat and Dupont are identical in principle (exx. 28.10a and c). They divide a secondary stroke to play the second and third quarter notes in the first of two measures, so that the second measure can start with a primary stroke; if needed, they retake the bow to start each new pair of measures with a primary stroke. In this way, the violinist's retaken down-bow reinforces the dancer's "rise" at the start of every two-measure menuet step.

The bowing preferred by Montéclair (ex. 28.10b) differs. After three quarter notes in the first measure, a primary stroke is retaken for the second downbeat. In all the menuets cited in French violin tutors before 1738, we found an up-bow on the first of a pair of measures only once—in m. 11 of this example. In this second reprise, after firmly establishing the 2 + 2 grouping of measures, Montéclair alternated strokes through the two middle measures of a four-measure member, thereby suggesting a hemiola (mm. 10–11).

Primary and secondary strokes are alternated for quick notes in all pedagogical examples unless a bad note would thereby be played with a primary stroke. In this case, a secondary stroke is divided. See for instance mm. 2, 11, and 19 of example 28.10c.

As mentioned in chapter 12, Muffat accused "some German and Italian orchestras" of going counter to the Lullian practice and alternating strokes continuously throughout menuets (ex. 28.11). Nevertheless, the rhythm of the music Muffat cited is such that the longest notes and the final repose are played with primary strokes. Corrette's violin tutor of 1738 is the first French source we found that alternates strokes for pulses and longer values throughout a menuet (ex. 28.12). Even so, a secondary stroke is divided in m. 4 to avoid playing bad quick notes with the primary stroke.

In the bowed dance pieces for viol, the pulses and quick notes are generally

EXAMPLE 28.11.
Bowing practice attributed to some Germans and Italians.
Muffat, 1698t, p. 230.

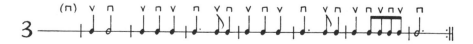

EXAMPLE 28.12.
Corrette's violin bowing, 1738, p. 14.

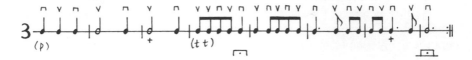

EXAMPLE 28.13.
Typical viol bowings and their violin equivalents. a. De Machy, 1685, p. 43; b. Marais, 1711, #35; c. Marais, 1711, #23.

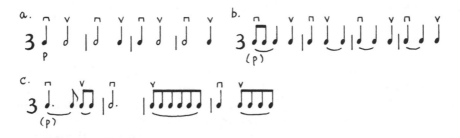

EXAMPLE 28.14.
Irregular viol bowings and their violin equivalents. Marais, "2ᵉ menuet," second reprise, 1725, #100.

slurred so that each measure has one primary and one secondary stroke, which often articulate rhythmic movements. De Machy's bowing for the start of a menuet (28.13a) articulates two antispasts (SLLS), and the slurs of Marais's first example (28.13b) make a choriamb (LSSL) and a double trochee (LSLS). The downbeat following a measure having only one (primary) stroke is normally played with a secondary stroke (ex. 28.13c). In later measures, as in example 28.14, a primary stroke may be retaken either to start a new musical period (m. 7) or to make the bowing come out right at a final cadence (m. 11).

Woodwind Syllables. The only woodwind syllables specified for a particular character dance are Freillon-Poncein's for one measure of a menuet, given in example 16.5. These syllables group quick notes from bad to good.

29

Passacailles

The *passacalli* in early guitar books are interludes in major or minor mode rather than dance pieces. The Italian guitarist Francesco Corbetta brought this music to France in the mid-seventeenth century. Most examples from the *grand siècle* are in minor.

Passacailles were not usually danced at balls, and the first included in a stage work is the one in Lully's *Persée* of 1682. The earliest French lyrics appear in Destouches's operas of the 1690s as part of larger passacailles for instruments and dancers. Keyboard pieces and songs are shaped as chaconne-rondeaux, while pieces for dancing are continuous variations. Baroque writers often compared passacailles with chaconnes.

Early Guitar Rhythms. Passacalli in early guitar books follow the chord progression I, IV, V, I or i, iv, V, i. Most chords change on bar lines. Strums are usually performed down–down–up. Chapter 3 gives several early examples, some of which begin on the second pulse of the measure.

Bass Line Progressions. Bass lines in passacailles of the *grand siècle* often move to the scale degrees 1, 7, 6, 5, a progression also common among chaconnes of this era. Two statements of a progression usually make up a musical couplet. Contrasting couplets move to other bass lines and may end in related keys.

Rhythmic Movements. The melodic rhythms of passacailles are too varied to reveal a typical rhythmic movement. But at least one measure of the first bass line progression of a piece tends to have an iambic (SL) rhythm.

Metrical Proportions. Most *passacalli* in early guitar books are marked 3, though a few have the sign **C**. All passacailles of the *grand siècle* are marked 3; measures contain three quarter-note pulses.

Performance of Quick Notes. Both Hotteterre (1719) and Corrette (1741) cited the passacaille from Lully's *Armide* as an example in which eighth notes are per-

EXAMPLE 29.1.
Unequal and equal eighth notes. Lully, passacaille, from
Armide, 1686. a. unequal eighth notes in a first couplet;
b. equal eighth notes in a later couplet.

EXAMPLE 29.2.
Pendulum markings. a. ♩ = 34 *tierces*, or MM 106 (L'Affilard,
1705e); b. ♩ = 38 *tierces*, or MM 95, for Lully, passacaille,
from *Persée*, 1682 (d'Onzembray, 1732); c. ♩ = 33 *pouces*, or
MM 63 (La Chapelle, 1736).

formed unequally in the first couplet (ex. 29.1a) but equally in a later one (ex. 29.1b). The reason is that the later eighths leap or are mixed with sixteenths.

Rhythmic Subjects. Because the bass progression is the identifying feature of passacailles, the melodies are extremely diverse and may begin on any pulse of the measure. Too few songs are available to allow any generalizations about them.

Dance Motions and Step Rhythms of belle danse *Choreographies.* Pécour's choreography to Lully's passacaille from *Persée* (ex. 9.10) lies within the abilities of most ballroom dancers, but other passacaille choreographies feature a large number of virtuosic steps. As with the chaconne, folie, and sarabande, passacaille choreographies begin with four-measure dance phrases. The first two step-units are relatively tranquil; the third is more active and climactic; the last is often a *temps de courante*, again tranquil.

Tempos and Affects. According to Brossard, passacailles have a "more tender" expression than chaconnes; Hotteterre (1719) used the word *grave* to describe the passacaille from Lully's *Armide*; and Masson conducted passacailles in three slow beats. The minor mode of most passacailles of the *grand siècle* probably contributes to their tender or solemn affect. Jean-Jacques Rousseau (1768) believed that the tempo of long passacailles should not change, despite contrasts in affect between the sections.

The three pendulum markings in example 29.2 vary widely, from MM 63 to 106 for quarter notes. The earliest markings, given by L'Affilard and d'Onzembray, are considerably quicker than the latest one, given by La Chapelle. L'Affilard's tempo seems well chosen to declaim his lyrics: "It's too much to complain, and to suffer from your charms," and d'Onzembray's tempo for Lully's dance music is certainly right for the eighteenth-century choreography described in chapter 9. La Chapelle's tempo shows the passacaille of his day to have slowed considerably.

30

Passepieds

The passepied originated in Brittany. According to the German composer and scholar Michael Praetorius, the name *passepiedz* [*sic*] (pass-feet) means that the dancer beats one foot against the other and then sets it down (1612, preface). This is the only known reference to the early footwork. More than a hundred years later, Friedrich Erhardt Niedt wrote that the name *passe-pied* [*sic*] shows that the feet in this dance move "as quickly as if greased" (1721, p. 101). These pieces are often compared with menuets.

Passepieds of the *grand siècle* are typically in binary form and have homophonic texture. Free ornamentation of repeats is uncommon, perhaps because of the many quick notes. Passepieds sometimes appear in pairs; and, in stage works, a pair of passepieds often follows a pair of rigaudons.

Metrical Proportions. Passepieds of the early seventeenth century are marked ¢, but their rhythms would fit triple meter if bar lines were arranged to mark off every three instead of every four pulses. In example 30.1a, for instance, the sign ¢ of the original notation implies that the music is arranged in measures of four quarter notes; whereas a ⅜ sign, with halved note values and an upbeat start (ex. 30.1b), would create the three-pulse measures, rhythmic subjects, and hemiola rhythms typical of the *grand siècle*.

Some passepieds of the *grand siècle* are marked 3, and their measures contain three quarter-note pulses. But most have the sign ⅜ and three eighth-note pulses. A few are marked ⁶⁄₈, and one measure is equivalent to two of ⅜.

Rhythmic Subjects. The rhythmic subjects of passepied songs vary in the course of a reprise. The first line almost always starts with an upbeat eighth note and ends with a feminine rhyme (ex. 30.2a). Usually a later line ends with a masculine rhyme (ex. 30.2b), which causes the one after that to start with the second pulse of the measure (ex. 30.2c).

Musical members are four measures long and usually cover a pair of poetic lines. L'Affilard's passepied (ex. 30.5a) is typical. However, members that include a true or softened hemiola often cover only one line (ex. 30.3, mm. 29–32).

EXAMPLE 30.1.
Mersenne, passepied, 1636, IIa, p. 169. a. original notation
in ¢ meter; b. the present authors' notation in $\frac{3}{8}$ meter, with
note values halved.

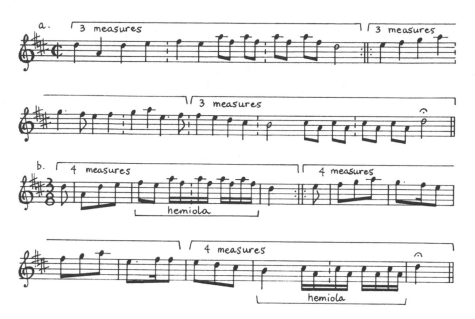

EXAMPLE 30.2.
Typical rhythmic subjects. a. first subject of a reprise; b. often
a later subject; c. the one after that.

EXAMPLE 30.3.
True and softened hemiola. Lully, passepied, from *Persée*,
1682, mm. 27–32.

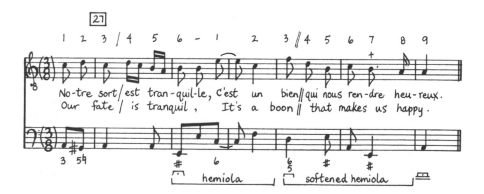

No-tre sort/est tran-quil-le, c'est un bien‖qui nous ren-dre heu-reux.
Our fate / is tranquil , It's a boon‖ that makes us happy .

EXAMPLE 30.4.
Rhythmic counterpoint. Pécour, plate 5 (period 4) of "Le
passepied," *Recueil*, 1700.

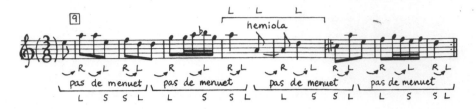

EXAMPLE 30.5.
Pendulum markings. a. ♩. = 42 *tierces*, or MM 86 (L'Affilard,
1705e); b. ♩. = 36 *tierces*, or MM 100, for Campra, "Premier
passepied," from *L'Europe galante*, 1697 (d'Onzembray, 1732);
c. ♩ = 6 *pouces*, or MM 148 (La Chapelle, 1736); d. ♩. = 15
pouces, or MM 94 (Choquel, 1759).

Some lines of passepied songs, such as the first in example 30.3 (mm. 27–28),
contain one or two pair of running sixteenth notes. Most instrumental pieces
have a greater number of paired sixteenths.

Dance Motions and Step Rhythms of belle danse *Choreographies.* Passepieds
were danced in many stage works of the *grand siècle*, yet most existing choreographies are *danses à deux* for the ballroom and use the several versions of the
pas de menuet as their basic step-units. The dancers move so quickly that viewers are more aware of the floor patterns than of the footwork.

The individual steps of the *pas de menuet* often make counterpoint with a hemiola in passepied music. Example 30.4 shows a hemiola in the last dance period of the second of a pair of these dances. Only *pas de menuet* with three *mouvements*, whose steps are timed to a choriamb (LSSL), are set to this musical reprise and its repetition. The rhythmic counterpoint arises because the hemiola in mm. 12–13 of the music (LLL) embraces the last measure of one step-unit (SL) and the first measure of the next (LS).

Tempos and Affects. Passepieds are very fast and lively dances, and were often said to be livelier and gayer than menuets. Conducting patterns and pendulum markings confirm this description. Masson and Freillon-Poncein conducted two

EXAMPLE 30.6.
Pedagogical violin bowings and their viol equivalents. a. Montéclair, 1711–12, p. 15; b. Dupont, 1718b, p. 6.

unequal beats in each measure, while Hotteterre beat only one. According to Masson, dancing masters counted only one beat in each pair of measures.

Most pendulum markings are very quick and range from MM 86 to 100 for measures. At the slowest of these markings, L'Affilard's lyrics are expressed furiously: "Fickle shepherdess, you've cheated me too much." La Chapelle's tempos for his somewhat later music are markedly slower, namely, MM 148 for quarter notes in 3 meter. Even so, his passepied is more rapid than his menuet.

Bowing Patterns. Pedagogical bowings for passepieds, as for menuets, group measures in pairs and use primary strokes on almost all downbeats. Probably because of the quicker tempo of passepieds, Montéclair divided a secondary stroke more often and repeated a primary one less often in his passepied (ex. 30.6a) than in his menuet (ex. 28.10b). In m. 2 of the passepied a primary stroke is repeated and then a secondary one is divided. The bowing shapes the music to match imaginary lyrics: the feminine cadence of the first imaginary line falls on the first two pulses of m. 2; the third pulse starts the next line.

According to Montéclair, some players divided a secondary stroke in the first measure, alternated strokes in the second, and repeated a primary one for the downbeat of the third. This method would appeal to dancing masters, because the repeated stroke marks the first downbeat of each two-measure step-unit.

The quick notes in example 30.6b allowed Dupont to avoid repeating any primary strokes. He too divided a secondary stroke in the first of every pair of measures.

We found no bowings for viol.

31

Rigaudons

Rigaudons are French provincial dances that Corneille called "rustic" and Mattheson said were danced in Provence by sailors and peasants. A letter by Mme de Sévigné (1673) provides the first evidence we found of the rigaudon at the French court: "Mme Santa Cruz triumphs in the rigaudon." Rigaudons first appeared in French stage works in the 1690s.

Rigaudons are binary in form, have homophonic texture, and often occur in pairs; free ornamentation of repeats is rare. These pieces are often compared with bourrées, and their melodies are sometimes indistinguishable from bourrée melodies. Instrumental suites seldom include both rigaudons and bourrées.

Rhythmic Movements. The rigaudon's most characteristic rhythmic subject moves to the epitrite (SLLL).

Metrical Proportions. Most rigaudons are marked 2 (or occasionally ¢); their measures contain four quarter-note pulses, grouped 2 + 2. A few have the $\frac{2}{4}$ or $\frac{4}{8}$ sign and four eighth-note pulses, again grouped 2 + 2.

Rhythmic Subjects. Many rigaudon songs begin with a line of four syllables set to the epitrite with bar lines before the first and last L's; that is, an upbeat pulse note is followed by three long notes (S|LL|L). The second line is longer and moves chiefly in pulse notes. A musical member embraces each pair of lines, which together have no more than twelve syllables. The first member of Campra's song from *L'Europe galante* (ex. 31.1a) is typical.

Sometimes, as in the final member of Campra's song (ex. 31.1b), the epitrite concludes a musical member. In this case, one or more syllables almost always precede it, so that the last two lines are somewhat equal in length. The concluding epitrite is perhaps most usual at the end of a reprise.

Regardless of the location of the epitrite, the harmony in the first line of a rigaudon member tends to be relatively static (Little, *The New Grove*, article "Rigaudon"). For instance, the first three notes of the first line in example

EXAMPLE 31.1.
Typical opening and closing members. Campra, from *L'Eu-rope galante*, 1697. a. first member; b. final member.

31.1a, which is set to an epitrite, are part of a G-minor chord; whereas the notes of the first line of the final member (ex. 31.1b, mm. 21–22), though not set to an epitrite, also form part of that chord.

Some rigaudons do not use the epitrite at all but move mainly in pulse notes. These pieces may begin with a rhythmic subject similar to that of the bourrée.

Dance Motions and Step Rhythms in belle danse *Choreographies.* Most choreographed rigaudons are *danses à deux* for the ball. The step-unit named for this dance, the *pas de rigaudon*, never starts the dance and is used only occasionally in a choreography. The *pas de rigaudon* is a *pas de gavotte* taken in place and without the beginning *pas marché* (walking step). The timing of the *pas de rigaudon* resembles the rhythm of a divided epitrite (ex. 31.2). However, the step-unit is usually set to continuous pulse notes rather than to an epitrite in the music.

Tempos and Affects. Rigaudons are very quick dances. Dupont recommended they be played gaily; Choquel said they are very fast; and Masson beat them very quickly. Pendulum markings are also very fast, from MM 116 to 148 for half notes in 2 meter (ex. 31.3).

Corneille pointed out that the second of a pair of rigaudons is a little gayer

EXAMPLE 31.2.
Pas de rigaudon as an epitrite (SLLL).

EXAMPLE 31.3.
Pendulum markings. a. ♩ = 30 *tierces*, or MM 120 (L'Affilard, 1705e); ♩ = 31 *tierces*, or MM 116, for Campra, "Premier rigaudon," from *L'Europe galante*, 1697 (d'Onzembray, 1732); c. ♩ = 6 *pouces*, or MM 148 (La Chapelle, 1736); d. ♩ = 8 *pouces*, MM 129, for rigaudon de provence, "Les Capuchins de Meudon" (Choquel, 1759).

EXAMPLE 31.4.
Pedagogical violin bowings and their viol equivalents. a. Montéclair, 1711–12; b. Corrette, 1738, p. 18.

than the first. In many concert suites, however, the first rigaudon is in the major mode, the second in minor; and then the first is repeated. Because a minor key normally expresses a more subdued feeling than a major one, the rigaudon in minor would naturally be the less gay of the two. Perhaps the first rigaudon might be played a little more gaily when it is repeated than at its first appearance.

Bowing Patterns. Pedagogical bowings for the violin are extremely straightforward (ex. 31.4); even Corrette's example of 1738 strictly follows the rule of the down-bow. According to Dupont's general music tutor, all pulse notes in rigaudons are detached (1718a, p. 37). We found no bowings for the viol.

32

Sarabandes

The *sarabanda* was brought from the New World to Spain and then introduced into Italy and France along with the Spanish guitar. Praetorius (1612) included several sarabandes among his French dances; and, according to Mersenne (1636), these pieces were "danced to the sound of guitars and castanets."

Sarabandas and sarabandes went through a number of changes during the Baroque period. Their strumming patterns and rhythmic movements were altered to meet the requirements of metrical bar lines. Their phrasing was modified to fit the rhythms of French lyrics. Their tempo was moderated and their form changed.

The texture of sarabandes of the late Baroque is chiefly homophonic, though imitation among the voices sometimes introduces reprises or rondeau couplets. A sarabande in binary form may end with a *petite reprise*, often ornamented freely. Composers sometimes wrote out and varied the repeats of binary reprises or rondeau refrains, or added a *double* to ornament the whole piece. Embellishment of written-out repeats was usually in the style of *airs de cour*.

Early Guitar Rhythms. Sarabande accompaniments in early guitar books are set to the harmonic progression I, IV, I, V; and most pieces are strummed down–down–up in each measure. Sanseverino followed this practice (ex. 32.1a), but slightly later guitarists sometimes used other chord progressions and other strumming patterns. For instance, Martin (ex. 32.1b) begins with the progression i, V, i, iv and uses an upward strum on the second pulse of the initial measure (a dotted note value reinforces that weakened pulse). Calvi (1646) goes still further afield and uses an eight-measure progression having quite different harmonies and the down–up–down strumming pattern (ex. 32.1c shows the first four measures of one example). The harmonies of most sarabandes of the *grand siècle* are unrelated to the early harmonic progression.

Rhythmic Movements. According to Mersenne, the sarabande moves to the rhythm of the hegemeole (SSSLS); and each reprise of the sarabande melody he

EXAMPLE 32.1.
Harmonic progressions and strumming patterns. a. Sanseverino, 1622, p. 20; b. Martin, in Mersenne, 1636, III, p. 97;
c. Calvi, 1646, p. 23.

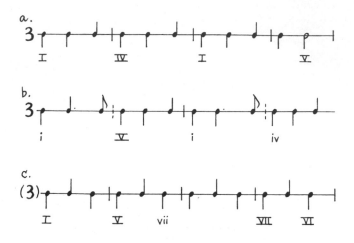

EXAMPLE 32.2.
Rhythmic movements in a sarabande melody. Mersenne,
1636, IIa, p. 166.

cites begins with two of these rhythmic movements, the L of each divided into
a dotted figure (ex. 32.2). Each reprise continues with two antispasts (SLLS) in
which some L's are divided. Martin's sarabande for guitar (ex. 32.1b), cited by
Mersenne, begins with two double iambs (SLSL) having the L's divided into
dotted figures or equal pulses.

Sarabandes also "follow the blacksmith's beat" (*battement du Mareschal*: SL),
according to Mersenne. Perhaps accompanying guitars, tambourins, or castanets would sound this rhythm against the hegemeoles (SSSLS), divided antispasts (SLLS), and divided double iambs (SLSL) of the melody. Using iambs
(SL) to accompany sarabandes would seem a natural development from the
downward strums on the first and second pulses of the measure specified by
early guitar books.

Sarabandes of the *grand siècle* also move to a variety of rhythmic movements, their L's often divided into dotted figures (ex. 32.3).

EXAMPLE 32.3.
Typical rhythmic movements and their common divisions in
sarabandes of the *grand siècle*. a, b. hegemeoles (SSSLS);
c, d. antispasts (SLLS); e. double iamb (SLSL); f. double
trochee (LSLS).

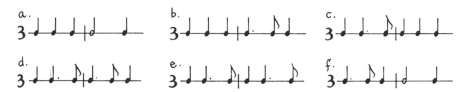

EXAMPLE 32.4.
Equal quick notes in a sarabande bass line. "Sarabande du
Sigr. Corelli," Hotteterre, 1719, p. 59.

Metrical Proportions. Early sarabandes are marked 3. The guitar pieces in example 32.1 have quarter-note pulses; the sarabande melody in ex. 32.2 has half-
note pulses. Most examples of the *grand siècle* have the sign 3 and three
quarter-note pulses or the sign $\frac{3}{2}$ and three half-note pulses; a few are marked $\frac{6}{4}$
and have six quarter-note pulses, grouped 3 + 3.

Performance of Quick Notes. Although eighth notes are normally played unequally, Hotteterre noted that those in the bass of Italian-style sarabandes
should be performed equally, as in an example by Corelli (ex. 32.4).

Rhythmic Subjects. The lines of early sarabande songs are set to two, four, or
five measures. The earliest sarabande song in Patricia Ranum's collection (by
Richard, 1637) has only five-measure lines, and Boyer's "Cloris" (1642; ex. 4.7)
has only two-measure lines. The first reprise of his "Belle riviere" (1642; ex. 4.8)
has two lines of two measures each and one of four; the second reprise, two lines
of two measures each and one of five. Lully's very early and only sarabande song
(from *Ballet de la raillerie*, 1659), a "sarabande in canon," begins with the same
two-measure rhythm as Boyer's "Cloris."

Almost all the sarabande songs of the *grand siècle* in Ranum's collection begin
with four-measure lines, set to the notes of two hegemeoles (each SSSLS).
Often the L of the first hegemeole is divided into a dotted figure. Usually the
LS of the second is set to the feminine ending of the four-measure line.

About half these songs begin with equal hemistiches, one for each hegemeole
(ex. 32.5a). When they start with unequal hemistiches (ex. 32.5b), the caesural

Example 32.5.
Basic skeleton structures of rhythmic subjects. a. equal hemistich; b. unequal hemistich.

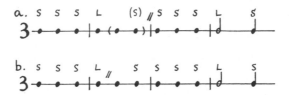

Example 32.6.
Equal and unequal hemistiches. a. Lully, "Sarabande des con-
trefeseurs," from *Ballet de la raillerie*, 1659; b. Destouches,
from *Venus et Adonis*, 1697.

repose on the second downbeat makes the second hemistich longer than the
first. Example 32.6 shows the equal hemistiches of Lully's first line and the unequal ones of a later song. Sarabande songs that start with equal hemistiches
almost always end with unequal ones, while those that begin with unequal
hemistiches may include a few equal ones.

In recognition of the downward strum on the second pulse of the measure in early guitar pieces, this note is usually intensified in pieces of the *grand siècle*—at least in the first and third measures. It may be dotted and the following value shortened to a quick note (exx. 32.6b, m. 3; 32.8; 32.10). Or it may be trilled (ex. 32.9b, m. 1; ex. 32.10a, m. 1) or set to a long syllable, such as "-FIN/" (ex. 32.6a, m. 1) and "-<u>reux</u>" (ex. 32.6b, m. 1).

In recognition of the L of the traditional hegemeole (SSSLS), the first pulse of the second measure is often dotted (exx. 32.6; 32.9b, c, d; 32.10). In sarabande lines having a shorter first hemistich (ex. 32.6b), the dotted note corresponds to the caesural repose. In the middle two measures of many sarabande members, a lengthened first pulse of the second measure and a lengthened second pulse of the third suggest a true or softened hemiola (see ex. 32.9a, mm. 2–3; ex. 32.9d, mm. 2–3; and ex. 32.10a, mm. 14–15).

The only sarabande songs we know with the sign $\frac{3}{2}$ begin with an upbeat note (e.g., ex. 32.9a). A few sarabande pieces start with the second pulse of the measure, perhaps in imitation of chaconne songs.

Dance Motions and Step Rhythms of belle danse *Choreographies.* With the exception of the ballroom sarabande in Pécour's "La Bourgogne," most *belle danse* choreographies are theatrical solos or duets similar to those for passacailles, chaconnes, and folies. No single step-unit characterizes these choreographies, and a large variety of steps and quick changes of affect are common. Some examples have chiefly smooth steps; others, many springing ones. Choreographies often begin with a four-measure dance phrase having relatively tranquil steps in the first two measures. The third measure is more active, with quicker steps, springing steps, or turns. The phrase ends with its most tranquil step, usually a *temps de courante*.

Tempos and Affects. Sarabandas and sarabandes of the early seventeenth century are gay and lively: Furetière called sarabandes "gay" and "amorous," and Bacilly (1668) considered them quick dances but allowed sarabande songs to be performed more slowly. The Italian *sarabanda* and the English "saraband" remained quick through most of the seventeenth century; a few French instrumental pieces of the eighteenth century are marked "gay" (ex. 32.7).

EXAMPLE 32.7.
Gay dance for violin. Duval, Sarabande "Les castagnettes,"
from Sonatas, livre VI/6, 1716.

EXAMPLE 32.8.
Corbetta, Sarabande "Tombeau de Madame," words by Mlle
des Jardins, 1671.

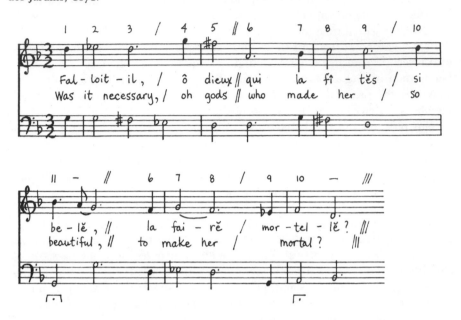

A sarabande song by the guitarist Francesco Corbetta may be the first example with a truly slow tempo (ex. 32.8). It mourns the death in 1670 of
"Madame," sister-in-law of Louis XIV. The many "mute" *e*'s on dotted half notes
in this song display grief as they die away over each of these long values. Corbetta probably used the sign $\frac{3}{2}$ to indicate a tempo slower than the usual one.

By the end of the seventeenth century, most French sarabandes were slow.
Dupont said they are performed solemnly; Masson conducted them in three
slow beats; and composers marked them "slow," "solemn," "moderate," or
"tender." Hotteterre (1719, p. 58) employed the word *lent* (slow) for the sarabande from Destouches's *Issé*.

Of the pendulum markings shown in example 32.9, La Chapelle's MM 64 for
quarter notes is the slowest. D'Onzembray's MM 73 for quarter notes and L'Affilard's MM 72 for half notes marked $\frac{3}{2}$ may represent the standard pace of
French sarabandes of the early eighteenth century. This tempo suits L'Affilard's
tender and happy text: "Let's taste the sweet pleasures // That a tender love
inspires," and it is appropriate for the eighteenth-century choreography for
Destouches's music. In the opera, while the sarabande is danced, the beautiful
Issé lays her troubles aside and sleeps.

L'Affilard's sarabande "en rondeau" has a slightly quicker tempo and a somewhat less tranquil text: "If you seek a heart that is faithful. . . ." His example
with the sign $\frac{6}{4}$ has a far quicker tempo and even more agitated lyrics: "It is too
much to suffer for Celimene."

EXAMPLE 32.9.

Pendulum markings. a. ♩ = 50 *tierces*, or MM 72, for "Sarabande tendre" (L'Affilard, 1705e); b. ♩ = 42 *tierces*, or MM 86, for "Sarabande en rondeau" (L'Affilard, 1705e); c. ♩ = 27 *tierces*, or MM 133, for "Sarabande" (L'Affilard, 1705e); d. ♩ = 49 *tierces*, or MM 73, for Destouches, sarabande, from *Issé*, 1699 (d'Onzembray, 1732); e. ♩ = 32 *pouces*, or MM 64 (La Chapelle, 1736).

Bowing Patterns. Because sarabandes have a number of rhythms, a variety of bowing patterns are used. Most sarabande measures begin with a primary stroke but, unlike the early strumming pattern (down–down–up), the second pulse of the measure is usually played with a secondary stroke.

Pedagogical examples by Montéclair and Dupont (ex. 32.10) begin with a rhythm also found in folies—an antispast (SLLS) having both L's replaced by dotted figures. For this rhythm, the two writers divided a secondary stroke for the second and third notes of m. 1; alternated the strokes in m. 2; and retook a primary stroke to start m. 3. In this way, they paired the first and second measures.

EXAMPLE 32.10.
Pedagogical violin bowings and their viol equivalents. a. Montéclair, 1711–12, p. 15; b. Dupont, 1718b, p. 6.

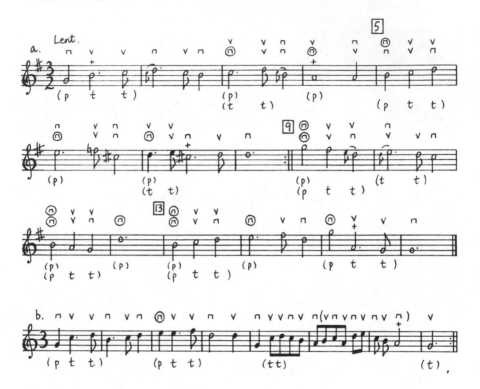

EXAMPLE 32.11.
Violin bowings for two-measure rhythms. a. Montéclair and
Dupont, mm. 1–2; b. Montéclair, mm. 3–4, and Dupont,
mm. 3–4; c. Montéclair, mm. 5–6, 13–14, and Montéclair,
mm. 9–10; d. Montéclair, mm. 7–8; e. Dupont, mm. 7–8;
f. Montéclair, mm. 11–12; g. Montéclair, mm. 15–16; h. Dupont, mm. 5–6.

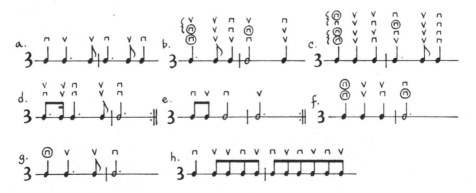

EXAMPLE 32.12.
Viol bowings and their violin equivalents. a. Morel, 1709,
#22; b. Marais, 1701, #28; c. Marais, 1711, #44; d. Marais,
1701, #53; e. Marais, 1701, #54.

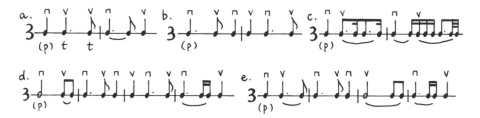

The great variety of bowings cited by Montéclair and Dupont for two-measure units is shown in example 32.11. To facilitate comparison, we have halved Montéclair's note values. Dupont's reprise (ex. 32.11e) ends with an unconventional secondary stroke, probably because any other practice—such as dividing a primary stroke for the two quick notes or retaking a primary one for the final downbeat—would separate the notes unduly.

Viol composers usually slurred a few notes in each pair of sarabande measures. Examples 14.1e and f cite the first reprises of two sarabandes whose notes are slurred to fit rhythmic movements. Example 32.12a, b, and c show a few other viol bowings for the first two measures of sarabandes. In examples 32.12d and e, a secondary stroke falls on the downbeat of the third measure of a four-measure member, but the bowing comes out right at the end so that the next member can start with a primary stroke on the downbeat.

APPENDIX

Six Complete Dance Songs

APPENDIX EXAMPLE 1.
Lully, menuet song from *Psyché*, 1678.

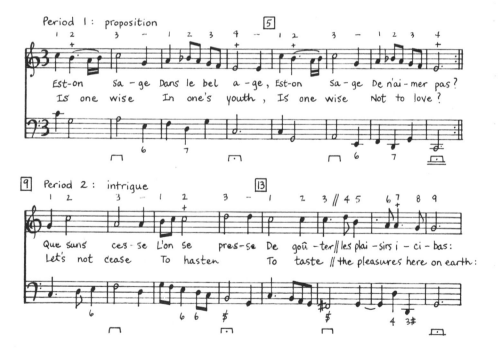

APPENDIX EXAMPLE 1.
Continued

APPENDIX EXAMPLE 2.
Lully, gavotte song from *Atys*, 1689.

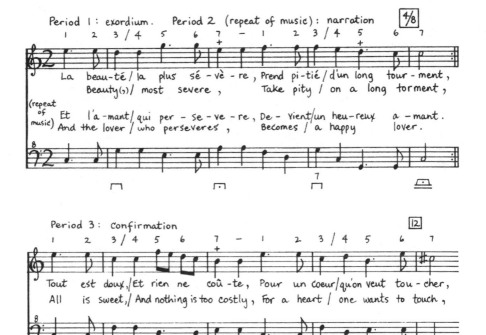

APPENDIX EXAMPLE 2.
Continued

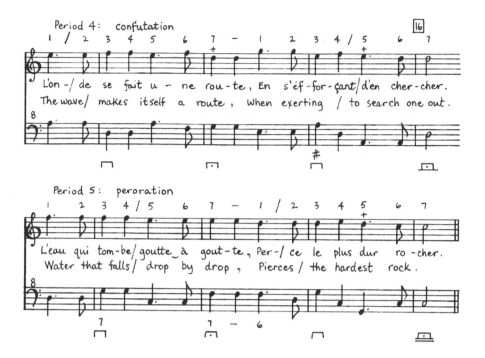

APPENDIX EXAMPLE 3.
L'Affilard, menuet song from *Principes très faciles*, 1705e,
p. 98.

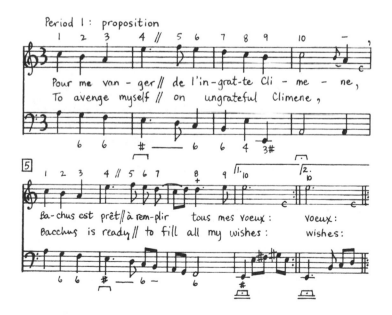

APPENDIX EXAMPLE 3.
Continued

Period 2: intrigue

Cru- el A - mour, ‖ je suis las de ta chaî - ne,
Cruel Cupid, ‖ I am tired of your chain,

Le Dieu du vin ‖ Va rom - pre tous mes noeuds;
The God of wine ‖ is going to break all my bonds;

Period 3: denouement

Il fait cou - ler ‖ son jus à tas - se plei - ne,
He makes his juice ‖ flow into a full cup,

J'en boi - ra tant ‖ que j'é - tein - drai mes feux.   feux.
I'll drink so much ‖ that I'll extinguish my fires.   fires.

APPENDIX EXAMPLE 4.
Lully, song following a gigue in *Amadis*, 1684.

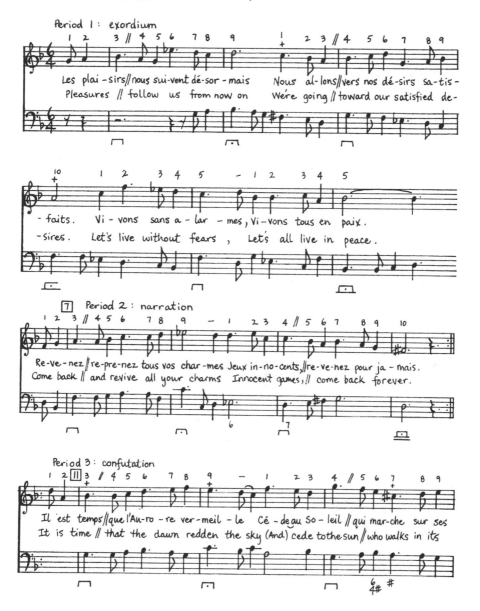

APPENDIX EXAMPLE 4.
Continued

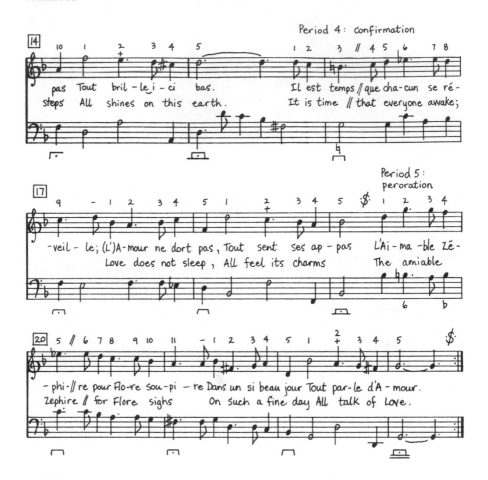

APPENDIX EXAMPLE 5.
Lully, bourrée song from *Bellérophon*, 1679.

APPENDIX EXAMPLE 5.
Continued

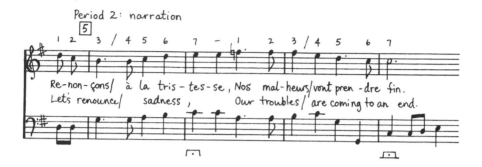

Period 2: narration

Re-non-çons/ à la tris-tes-se, Nos mal-heurs/vont pren-dre fin.
Let's renounce/ sadness, Our troubles/ are coming to an end.

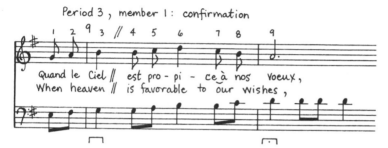

Period 3, member 1: confirmation

Quand le Ciel ‖ est pro-pi-ce à nos voeux,
When heaven ‖ is favorable to our wishes,

Period 3, member 2: confutation

Ban-nis-sons l'en-nuy Ban-nis-sons l'en-nuy‖ qui nous pres-se,
Let's banish the ennui Let's banish the ennui ‖ that presses us,

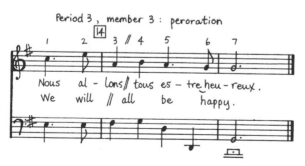

Period 3, member 3: peroration

Nous al-lons‖ tous es-tre heu-reux.
We will ‖ all be happy.

APPENDIX EXAMPLE 6.

Lully, chaconne song from *Cadmus et Hermione*, 1673.

APPENDIX EXAMPLE 6.
Continued

BIBLIOGRAPHY

PRIMARY SOURCES

Alberti, Leone Battista. *Ten Books on Architecture*. Original Latin text, Florence, 1485. Translated into Italian by Cosimo Bartoli and into English by James Leoni, edited by Joseph Rykwert, New York: Transatlantic Arts, 1966.

Alembert, Jean Lerond d'. *Elémens de musique, théorique et pratique*. Paris, 1752. Facsimile, New York: Broude, [1966].

Anglebert, Jean-Henry d'. See D'Anglebert, Jean-Henry.

Anon. *Nouvelles parodies bachiques*, Vol. III. Paris, 1702.

Arbeau, Thoinot [Jehan Tabourot, pseud.]. *Orchésographie, et traicte en forme de dialogue, par lequel toutes personnes peuvent facilement apprendre & practiquer l'honneste exercice des danses*. Langres, 1588; 2d ed., 1589. Resetting of type, with "Notice sur les danses du XVI siècle" by Laure Fonta, Paris: Vieweg, 1888. Translated by Mary Stewart Evans and reprinted with corrections, new introduction, and notes by Julia Sutton; and with Labanotation by Mireille Backer and Julia Sutton, New York: Dover, 1967.

Aristotle. *Poetics*. Reprint in Greek with English translation in S. H. Butcher, *Aristotle's Theory of Poetry and Fine Art with a Critical Text and Translation of the Poetics*, 4th ed., London: Macmillan, 1927.

———. *Politics*. Reprint in Greek with English translation by H. Rackham, Cambridge: Harvard University Press, 1959.

———. *The Metaphysics*. Reprint in Greek with English translation by Hugh Tredennick, Cambridge: Harvard University Press, 1961.

———. *Problems*. Reprint in Greek with English translation by W. S. Hett, Cambridge: Harvard University Press, 1961.

Augustine, Aurelius, Saint. *De musica*. German translation by Johann Perl, 3d ed., Paderborn: F. Schöningh, 1962. Synopsis by W. F. Jackson Knight, London: The Orthological Institute, ca. 1946.

Bacilly, Bénigne de. *Remarques curieuses sur l'art de bien chanter*. Paris, 1668. Facsimile, Geneva: Minkoff, 1974. Translated and edited by Austin B. Caswell, Jr., as *A Commentary upon the Art of Proper Singing*, [Brooklyn]: Institute of Mediaeval Music, 1968.

Balon, Jean. See Dezais, and [Jean] Balon.

Beaujoyeulx, Baltasar de. Preface to *Circé ou Le balet comique de la Royne*. Paris, 1581.

Bérard, Jean-Antoine. *L'art du chant*. Paris, 1755. Facsimile, New York: Broude, 1967. Facsimile, Geneva: Minkoff, 1972. Translated and edited by Sidney Murray, Milwaukee: Pro Musica, 1969.

Boileau-Despreaux, Nicholas. *L'art poétique*. Paris, 1673. Reprinted in Jacques Charpier and Pierre Seghers, eds., *L'Art poétique*, Paris: Éditions Seghers, 1956. Reprinted with translation by Sir William Soame (1683) as *Boileau's Art of Poetry*, in A.S. Cook, ed., *The Art of Poetry*, Boston: Ginn, 1892; reprint, New York: G.E. Stechert, 1926.

Bonin, Louis. *Die neueste Art zur galanten und theatralischen Tantz-Kunst*. Frankfurt and Leipzig, 1711.

Borjon, Charles Emmanuel. *Traité de la musette, avec une nouvelle methode, pour ap-

prendre de soy-mesme à jouer de cet instrument facilement, & en peu de temps. Lyon, 1672.

Bourdelot, Pierre, and Pierre Bonnet. *Histoire de la musique et des ses effets.* Paris, 1715; Amsterdam, 1725. Facsimile, edited by Othmar Wessely, Graz: Akademische Druck- und Verlagsanstalt, 1966.

Bousset, Jean-Baptiste. *Second recüeil . . . contenant une eglogue bachique et 20 livres d'airs serieux et à boire.* Paris, 1700.

Boyer, Jean. *IIme livre des chansons à danser et à boire.* Paris, 1642.

Brijon, C. R. *Réflexions sur la musique, et la vraie manière de l'exécuter sur le violon.* Paris, 1763. Facsimile, Geneva: Minkoff, 1972.

Brossard, Sebastien de. *Dictionaire de musique, contenant une explication des terms grecs, latins, italiens & françois les plus usitez dans la musique.* Paris, 1703. Facsimile, Amsterdam: Antiqua, 1964. Facsimile of 2d (1705) ed., edited by Harald Heckmann, Hilversum: Frits Knuf, 1965.

Brunelli, Antonio. *Scherzi, arie, canzonette, e madrigali. Libro terzo.* Venice, 1676.

Caccini, Giulio. *Nuove musiche e nuova maniera di scriverle.* Florence, 1601. Facsimile, edited by H. Wiley Hitchcock, Madison: A-R Editions, 1970.

Calvi, Carlo. *Intavolatura di chitarra, e chitarriglia.* Bologna, 1646.

Campra, André. *Les festes venitiennes.* Paris, 1710. Reprint, Paris: Heugel, 1971.

———. *L'Europe galante.* Paris, 1724. Facsimile, Farnborough: Gregg Press, 1967.

Chambonnières, Jacques Champion de. *Les pièces de clavessin. Premier livre.* Paris, 1670. Reprint, New York: Broude, 1967.

Chancy, François de. *IVe livre des chansons du Sieur de Chancy.* Paris, 1651.

Charpentier, Marc-Antoine. "Règles de composition" (ca. 1693). Paris, Bibliothèque Nationale, Ms. n.a. fr. 6355, f. 13. Translated by Jon Quentin Kuyper as "Marc-Antoine Charpentier's 'Règles de composition': A Translation and Commentary," M.A. thesis, The University of Iowa, 1971.

Choquel, Henry-Louis. *La musique rendue sensible par la méchanique, ou nouveau systeme pour apprendre facilement la musique soi-meme.* Paris, 1759; new ed., 1762.

Cicero. *Orator.* Reprint in Latin with English translation by H. M. Hubell. Cambridge: Harvard University Press, 1962.

Corbetta, Francesco. Transcription of Corbetta's works in Richard T. Pinnell, *Francesco Corbetta and the Baroque Guitar: With a Transcription of His Works,* Vol. II. Ann Arbor: UMI Research Press, 1980.

Corneille, Thomas. *Le dictionnaire des arts et des sciences.* Paris, 1694–95. Facsimile, Geneva: Slatkine Reprints, 1968.

Corrette, Michel. *L'Ecole d'Orphée: Méthode pour apprendre facilement a jouer du violon dans le goût françois et italien avec les principes de musique et beaucoup de leçons a I, et II violons.* Paris, 1738.

———. *Méthode pour apprendre aisément à jouer de la flute traversière.* Paris and Lyon, ca. 1739. Facsimile, edited by Mirjam Nastasi, Buren: Frits Knuf, 1978. Translated by Carol Reglin Farrar as *Michel Corrette and Flute Playing in the Eighteenth Century,* Brooklyn: Institute of Mediaeval Music, 1970.

———. *Méthode théorique et pratique, pour apprendre en peu de temps le violoncelle dans sa perfection.* Paris, 1741. Facsimile, Geneva: Minkoff, 1972.

Couperin, François. *Pièces de clavecin. Premier livre.* Paris, 1713. Edited by Kenneth Gilbert, *Le Pupitre* XXI, Paris: Heugel, 1972.

———. *L'Art de toucher le clavecin.* Paris, 1717. Facsimile, New York: Broude, 1969. Reprint with German translation by Anna Linde and English translation by Mevanwy Roberts, Wiesbaden: Breitkopf & Härtel, 1933.

———. *Troisième livre de pièces de clavecin . . . [et concerts royaux].* Paris, 1722.

———. *Les nations. Sonades et suites de simphonies en trio. . . .* Paris, 1726.

Couperin, Louis. *Pièces de clavecin,* edited by Paul Brunold, revised by Thurston Dart. Monaco: L'Oiseau-Lyre, 1959.

Crousaz, Jean Pierre de. *Traité du beau*. Amsterdam, 1715. Facsimile, Geneva: Slatkine Reprints, 1970.

D'Anglebert, Jean-Henry. *Pièces de clavecin*. Paris, 1689. Reprint, edited by Kenneth Gilbert, *Le Pupitre* LIV, Paris: Heugel, 1975.

Danoville, le Sieur. *L'Art de toucher le dessus et basse de viole*. Paris, 1687. Translation and commentary by Catherine Elizabeth Betts as "Danoville's 'L'Art de toucher le dessus et basse de viole,'" M.A. thesis, University of Illinois, 1957.

De Lauze. See Lauze, F[rançois] de.

De Machy. *Pièces de violle en musique et en tablature différentes les unes des autres et sur plusieurs tons*. Paris, 1685. Reprint, 1913. Reprint of "Avertissement" as Appendix D(a) in Hans Bol, *La basse de viole du temps de Marin Marais et d'Antoine Forqueray*, Bilthoven: A. B. Creyghton, 1973. Translation and commentary by Gordon J. Kinney in "Writings on the Viol by Dubuisson, De Machy, Roland Marais, and Étienne Loulié," *Journal of the Viola da Gamba Society of America* XIII (1976):20–31.

De Pure. See Pure, Michel de.

Descartes, René. *Passions of the Soul*. Amsterdam, 1649. Translated by Elizabeth S. Haldane and G. R. T. Ross in *The Philosophical Works of Descartes*, Vol. I, Cambridge: University Press, 1911, corr. 1931; reprint of 1931 ed., New York: Dover, 1955, 1967.

———. *Renati Des-cartes musicae compendium*. Utrecht, 1650. Facsimile, New York: Broude, 1968. Translated by Walter Robert, [Rome?]: American Institute of Musicology, 1961.

Dezais, and [Jean] Balon. *XI.ᴱ Recüeil de danses pour l'année 1713*, collected and notated by Dezais. Paris, 1713.

———. *XII.ᴱ Recüeil de danses pour l'année 1714*, collected and notated by Dezais. Paris, 1714[?].

———. *XIIII.ᴱ Recüeil de danses pour l'année 1716*, collected and notated by Dezais. Paris, 1716[?].

———. *XVI Recueil de danses pour l'année 1718*, collected and notated by Dezais. Paris, 1718[?].

Le Dictionnaire de l'Academie Françoise. Paris, 1694.

Du Buisson. [Untitled manuscript treatise on viola da gamba.] Library of Congress, M2.l/Book.T2 17C, ff. l–25, 67–90, dated 1666. Reprinted as Appendix A in Hans Bol, *La basse de viole du temps de Marin Marais et d'Antoine Forqueray*, Bilthoven: A. B. Creyghton, 1973. Translation and commentary by Gordon J. Kinney in "Writings on the Viol by Dubuisson, De Machy, Roland Marais, and Étienne Loulié," *Journal of the Viola da Gamba Society of America* XIII (1976):17–19.

Dufort, Giovanni Battista. *Trattato del ballo nobile*. Naples, 1728.

Du Manoir, Guillaume. *Le mariage de la musique avec la dance, contenant la réponce au livre des treize protendus Academistes, touchant ces deux arts*. Paris, 1664.

Dupont, Pierre. *Principes de musique par demande et par reponce, par lequel toutes personnes, pouront aprendre deux même a connoitre toutte la musique*. Paris, 1718a.

———. *Principes de violon par demandez et par réponce par le quel toutes personnes, pourant aprendre deux memes a jouer du dit instrument*. Paris, 1718b.

Dupuit, Jean-Baptiste. *Principes pour toucher de la viele avec six sonates pour cet instrument qui conviennent aux violons, flutes, clavessin, etc.*, Oeuvre 1. Paris, 1741.

D'Urfey, Thomas. *The Songs of Thomas D'Urfey*, edited by Cyrus Lawrence Day. Cambridge: Harvard University Press, 1933.

Écorcheville, Jules. *Vingt suites d'orchestre du XVIIᵉ siècle français*. Berlin: Liepmannssohn; Paris: Fortin, 1906.

Feuillet, Raoul-Auger. *Chorégraphie; ou l'art de décrire la dance, par caractères, figures et signes démonstratifs*. Paris, 1700a. Facsimile, New York: Broude, 1968 [bound with Feuillet, *Recueil de dances*, 1700, and Pécour, *Recueil de dances*].

Facsimile of 1701 ed., Bologna: Forni, 1970. Translated by John Weaver as *Orchesography or the Art of Dancing, by Characters and Demonstrative Figures*, London, 1706.

―――. *Recueil de dances*. Paris, 1700b. Facsimile, New York: Broude, 1968 [bound with Feuillet, *Chorégraphie*, and Pécour, *Recueil de dances*, 1700].

―――. Preface and "Traité de la Cadance" in Louis Guillaume Pécour, *Recueil de ·dances*, Paris, 1704. (See full entry under Pécour, Louis Guillaume.) "Traité" translated by John Weaver as *A Small Treatise of Time and Cadence in Dancing*, London, 1706.

―――. *Recüeil de contredanses*. Paris, 1706. Facsimile, New York: Broude, 1968. Translated by John Essex as *For the Furthur Improvement of Dancing. A Treatis of Chorography of ye Art of Dancing Country Dances after a New Character*, London, 1710. Facsimile, Farnborough: Gregg International, 1970.

Feuillet, Raoul-Auger, and Louis Guillaume Pécour. *VIIIme Recüeil de danses pour l'année 1710*, collected and notated by Feuillet. Paris, 1709. See also Pécour, Louis Guillaume, and Raoul-Auger Feuillet.

Freillon-Poncein, Jean-Pierre. *La véritable manière d'apprendre à jouer en perfection du haut-bois, de la flute et du flageolet*. Paris, 1700. Facsimile, Geneva: Minkoff, 1971.

Furetière, Antoine. *Dictionaire universel, contenant generalement tous les mots françois tant vieux que modernes, et les termes de toutes les sciences et des arts*. The Hague, 1690.

Grassineau, James. *A Musical Dictionary*. London, 1740. Facsimile, New York: Broude, [1966].

Grimarest, Jean Léonor Le Gallois de. *Traité du recitatif*. Paris, 1707. Facsimile of 1760 ed., New York: AMS Press, 1978.

Hotteterre, Jacques, dit le Romain. *Principes de la flute traversière ou flute d'Allemagne, de la flute a bec ou flute douce, et du haut-bois, divisez par traitez*. Paris, 1707. Facsimile of [1710] Amsterdam ed. with German translation by H. J. Hellwig, Kassel: Bärenreiter, 1941. English translation by David Lasocki as *Principles of the Flute, Recorder and Oboe*, London: Barrie & Rockliff; New York: Praeger, 1968. English translation by Paul Marshall Douglas as *Rudiments of the Flute, Recorder and Oboe*, New York: Dover, 1968.

―――. *L'Art de préluder sur la flute traversière, sur la flute-à-bec, sur le haubois, et autres instruments de dessus*. Paris, 1719. Reprint ed., Michel Sanvoisin, Paris: Zurfluh, 1966. Facsimile, Geneva: Minkoff, 1978.

―――. *Airs et brunettes a deux et trois dessus pour les flutes traversieres . . . les plus convenables a la flute traversiere seule, ornez d'agrements par M^r. Hotteterre le Romain*. Paris, ca. 1723. The ornamented unaccompanied pieces edited by David Lasocki as *Ornamented Airs and Brunettes*, London: Nova Music, 1980.

―――. *Methode pour la musette, contenant des principes, par le moyen desquels on peut apprendre à jouer de cet instrument, de soy-meme au défaut de maître*, Oeuvre X. Paris, 1738. Facsimile, Geneva: Minkoff, 1977.

Kirnberger, Johann Philipp. *Recueil d'airs de danses caractéristiques, pour servir de modèle aux jeunes compositeurs, et d'exercice à ceux qui touchent du clavecin*. Berlin, 1778.

La Chapelle, Jacques-Alexandre de. *Les vrais principes de la musique exposé par une gradation de leçons distribuéez d'une manière facile et sûre pour arriver a une connaissance parfaite et pratique de cet art. . . .* Paris, 1736.

La Croix, A. Phérotée de. *Art de la poésie françoise et latine, avec une idée de la musique sous une nouvelle méthode*. Lyon, 1694.

L'Affilard, Michel. *Principes très faciles pour bien apprendre la musique*. Paris, 1694; Amsterdam, 1717. Facsimile of 5th (1705) ed., Geneva: Minkoff, 1971.

Lambranzi, Gregorio. *Neue und curieuse theatralische Tantz-Schul*. Nürnberg, 1716. Translated by Derra de Moroda as *New and Curious School of Theatrical Dancing*, with original plates by Johann Georg Puschner and preface by Cyril W. Beaumont, Brooklyn: Dance Horizons, 1966. Facsimile of original drawings, New York: Dance Horizons, 1972.

Lamy, Bernard. *Nouvelles réflexions sur l'art poétique*. Paris, 1668. Reprint, Geneva: Slatkine, 1973.

————. *De l'art de parler*. Paris, 1675. Translated as *The Art of Speaking, written in French by Messieurs du Port Royal*, London, 1676. 4th French ed., rev. and aug., published as *La rhetorique ou; L'art de parler*, Paris, 1701. 2d English ed., corr., London, 1708.

Lauze, F[rançois] de. *Apologie de la danse et la parfaicte methode de l'enseigner tant aux cavaliers quaux dames*. Paris, 1623. Reprint with translation by Joan Wildeblood as *Apologie de la danse: A Treatise of Instruction in Dancing and Deportment*, London: Frederick Muller, 1952.

Le Blanc, Hubert. *Défense de la basse de viole contre les entreprises du violon et les prétentions du violoncel*. Amsterdam, 1740.

Loulié, Étienne. *Elémens ou principes de musique*. Paris, 1696. Translated and edited by Albert Cohen as *Elements or Principles of Music*, [Brooklyn]: Institute of Mediaeval Music, 1965.

————. "Methode pour apprendre a jouer la violle," ca. 1690s. Paris, Bibliothèque Nationale, fonds fr. n.a. 6355, ff. 210–22. Digest and partial translation by Albert Cohen, *Journal of the Viola de Gamba Society of America* III (1966):17–23. Reprinted as Appendix B in Hans Bol, *La basse de viole du temps de Marin Marais et d'Antoine Forqueray*, Bilthoven: A. B. Creyghton, 1973. Translation and commentary by Gordon J. Kinney in "Writings on the Viol by Dubuisson, De Machy, Roland Marais, and Étienne Loulié," *Journal of the Viola da Gamba Society of America* XIII (1976):39–55.

————. "Methode pour apprendre a jouer de la flute douce," 2 versions, ca. 1700. Paris, Bibliothèque Nationale, fonds fr. n.a. 6355, ff. 170–209v.

Lully, Jean-Baptiste. *Persée*. Paris, 1682.

————. *Roland: tragedie mise en musique*. Paris, 1685.

————. *Armide* [1686]. Vocal score, arranged by Henri Busser, Paris: H. Lemoine, 195[?].

————. *Psyché*. Paris, 1720.

————. Operas in *Oeuvres complètes de J.-B. Lully*, edited by Henry Prunières. New York: Broude, ca. 1930–. Ser. A: v. 1 (1930), *Cadmus et Hermione*; v. 2 (1932), *Alceste*; v. 3 (1939), *Amadis*. Ser. B: v. 1 (1931), *Ballet du temps*; *Ballet des plaisirs*; *Ballet de l'amour malade*; v. 2 (1933), *Ballet d'Alcidiane*; *Ballet des gardes*; *Ballet de Xerxès*. Ser. D: v. 1 (1931), *Le mariage forcé*; *L'amour médecin*; v. 2 (1933), *Les plaisirs de l'ile enchantée*; *Pastorale comique*; *Le sicilien*; *George Dandin, ou Le grand divertissement royal de Versailles*; v. 3 (1938), *Le divertissement royal de Chambord*; *Le bourgeois gentilhomme*; *Ballet des nations*; *Le divertissement royal: Les amants magnifiques*.

————. Operas in *Chefs-d'oeuvre classiques de l'opéra français*, vocal score. New York: Broude, 1971. *Alceste* (v. 16), *Atys* (v. 18), *Bellérophon* (v. 19), *Cadmus et Hermione* (v. 20), *Isis* (v. 21), *Phaeton* (v. 23), *Proserpine* (v. 24), *Psyché* (v. 25), *Thésée* (v. 26).

Mangeant, Jacques. *Recueil des plus belles chansons de dances de ce temps*. Caen, 1615.

Manuscript Menetou. See Secondary Sources under Curtis, Alan.

Marais, Marin. *The Instrumental Works, Vol. I "Pièces à une et à deux violes (1686–89)*," edited by John Hsu. New York: Broude, 1980.

————. *Pièces de violes . . . 2e livre*. Paris, 1701. Facsimile, Basil: Ruedy Ebner, 1977[?].

————. Reprint of "Avertissements" from *Pièces* of 1686, 1689, 1701, 1711, 1717, 1725 as Appendix D(b) in Hans Bol, *La basse de viole du temps de Marin Marais et d'Antoine Forqueray*, Bilthoven: A. B. Creyghton, 1973.

————. *Six Suites for Viol and Thoroughbass* [*Pièces* of 1701, 1711], edited by Gordon J.

Kinney. Recent Researches in the Music of the Baroque Era XXI/XXII. Madison: A-R Editions, 1976.

Marquet, François-Nicolas. *Nouvelle méthode facile et curieuse, pour apprendre par les notes de musique à connoitre le pous de l'homme et les différens changemens qui lui arrivent, depuis sa naissance jusqu'à sa mort.* Nancy, 1747; 2d ed., Amsterdam and Paris, 1769.

Masson, Charles. *Nouveau traité des regles pour la composition de la musique.* Paris, 1697. Facsimile of 2d (1699) ed., edited by Imogene Horsley, New York: Da Capo Press, 1967. English translation of 2d ed. in Gary Thomas Hoiseth, "Charles Masson's 'Nouveau traité des règles pour la composition de la musique' and 'Divers traitez sur la composition de la musique': A Translation and Commentary," M.A. thesis, The University of Iowa, 1972.

Mattheson, Johann. *Critica musica.* Hamburg, 1722–25. Facsimile, Amsterdam: Frits Knuf, 1964.

———. *Der vollkommene Capellmeister.* Hamburg, 1739. Facsimile, edited by Margarete Reimann, Kassel: Bärenreiter, 1954. English translation in Ernest C. Harriss, *Johann Mattheson's "Der vollkommene Capellmeister": A Revised Translation with Critical Commentary,* Ann Arbor: UMI Research Press, 1981.

Ménestrier, Claude François. *Remarques pour la conduite des bals.* Lyon, 1668.

———. *Des ballets anciens et modernes selon les regles du theatre.* Paris, 1682.

Mersenne, Marin. *Harmonie universelle, contenant la théorie et la pratique de la musique.* Paris, 1636. Facsimile, 3 vols., edited by François Lesure, Paris: Éditions du Centre National de la Recherche Scientifique, 1963. The books on instruments translated by Roger E. Chapman as *Harmonie Universelle: The Books on Instruments,* The Hague: Martinus Nijhoff, 1957. [Of the facsimile, we cite only Vols. II and III. Vol. II is divided into two large sections, each with its own pagination. What we call section IIa includes "Traitez de la voix, et des chants," pp. 1–180; what we call section IIb includes "Traitez des consonances, des dissonances, de genres, des modes, & de composition," pp. 1–330, and "De l'art de bien chanter," pp. 331–442. Page numbers 334–40 of IIb are mistakenly shown as 134–40.]

Mesangeau, René. *Oeuvres de René Mesangeau.* Edited and translated by André Souris. Paris: Éditions du Centre National de la Recherche Scientifique, 1971.

Millet, Jean. *La belle methode, ou l'art de bien chanter.* Lyon, 1666. Reprint, edited by Albert Cohen, New York: Da Capo Press, 1973.

Montéclair, Michel Pignolet de. *Nouvelle méthode pour apprendre la musique par démonstrations faciles.* Paris, 1709.

———. *Méthode facile pour aprendre a jouer du violon avec un abregé des principes de musique necessaires pour cet instrument.* Paris, 1711–12.

———. *Brunettes anciènes et modernes, apropriées à la flûte traversière avec une basse d'accompagnement, premier recüeil.* Paris, ca. 1720.

———. *Menuets tant anciens que nouveaux qui se dansent aux bals de l'opera. Deuxième recueil contenant cent & un menuets.* Paris, 1725.

———. *Principes de musique divisez en quatre parties.* Paris, 1739.

Morel, Jacques. *1.ʳ livre de pièces de violle avec une chaconne en trio pour une flute traversière, une violle et la basse-continue.* Paris, 1709.

Muffat, Georg. *Florilegium primum,* preface. Augsburg, 1695. Edited by Heinrich Rietsch in *Denkmäler der Tonkunst in Oesterreich* I/2 [2], Vienna, 1894. Translation in Oliver Strunk, *Source Readings in Music History,* New York: Norton, 1950, pp. 442–44.

———. *Florilegium secundum,* preface. Passau, 1698. Edited by Heinrich Rietsch in *Denkmäler der Tonkunst in Oesterreich* II/2 [4], Vienna, 1895; reprint, Graz: Akademische Druck- und Verlagsanstalt, 1959. Beginning of translation in Strunk, *Source Readings,* pp. 445–47; remainder in "Georg Muffat's Observations on the Lully Style of Performance," translated by Kenneth Cooper and Julius Zsako, *Musical Quarterly* LIII/2 (April 1967):220–45.

Negri, Cesare. *Le gratie d'amore.* Milan, 1602. Facsimile, New York: Broude, [1969].

Niedt, Friedrich Erhardt. *Musicalische Handleitung, Die Zweyte Auflage verbessert, vermehret mit verschiedenen Grundrichtigen Anmerkungen und einem Anhang von mehr als 60. Orgelwerchen versehen durch J. Mattheson.* Hamburg, 1721. Facsimile, Buren: Frits Knuf, 1976.

Onzembray, comte d' (Chevalier Louis-Léon Pajot). "Description et usage d'un métro-metre ou machine pour battre les mesures & les temps de toutes sortes d'airs," *Histoire de l'Academie Royale des Sciences avec les mémoires de mathématique et physique, Année 1732,* Paris, 1735, pp. 182–95.

Pajot, Louis-Léon, Chevalier, comte d'Onzembray: see Onzembray.

Pécour, Louis Guillaume. "Le passepied nouveau." Separate publication, notated by Feuillet. Paris, 1700a.

———. *Recueil de dances,* collected and notated by Feuillet. Paris, 1700b. Facsimile, New York: Broude, 1968 [bound with Feuillet, *Chorégraphie* and *Recueil de dances,* 1700].

———. *P[remi]er receüil de danses de bal pour l'année 1703,* collected and notated by Feuillet. Paris, 1702.

———. *II.ᵐᵉ Recüeil de danses de bal pour l'année 1704,* collected and notated by Feuillet. Paris, 1703.

———. *Recueil de dances contenant un tres grand nombres, des meillieures entrées de ballet . . . tant pour homme que pour femmes, dont la plus grande partie ont été dancées à l'opera,* collected and notated by Feuillet. Paris, 1704. (See also under Feuillet, Raoul-Auger, Preface and "Traité . . . .")

———. *VI.ᵐᵉ Recüeil de danses et de contredanses pour l'année 1708,* collected and notated by Feuillet. Paris, 1707.

———. *Nouveau recüeil de dance de bal et celle de ballet contenant un tres grand nombres des meillieures entrées de ballet . . . tant pour hommes que pour femmes qui ont été dancées a l'opera[. O]uvrage tres utile aux maitres et a toutes les personnes qui s'apliquent a la dance,* collected and notated by Gaudrau. Paris, 1712.

Pécour, Louis Guillaume, and Raoul-Auger Feuillet. *V.ᵐᵉ Recüeil de danses de bal pour l'année 1707,* collected and notated by Feuillet. Paris, 1706. See also Feuillet, Raoul-Auger, and Louis Guillaume Pécour.

Philidor, Pierre Danican. *Premier oeuvre contenant III. suittes a II. flutes traversieres seule avec III. autres suittes dessus et basse, pour les hautbois, flutes, violons, ec.* Paris, 1717. Facsimile, Florence: Studio per Edizioni Scelte, 1980.

———. *Deuxième oeuvre contenant II. suittes a 2. flutes-traversières seules avec II. autres suittes dess. et basse, pour les hautbois, flutes, violons, ec.* Paris, 1718. Facsimile, Florence: Studio per Edizioni Scelte, 1980.

Piani, Giovanni Antonio. *Sonatas for Violin Solo and Violoncello with Cembalo [XII Sonato, Opus 1, Paris, 1712],* edited by Barbara Garvey Jackson. Recent Researches in the Music of the Baroque Era XX. Madison: A-R Editions, 1975.

Plutarch. *Les oevres morales E meslees de Plutarque,* French translation by Jacques Amyot, Paris, 1572. Reprint with introduction by M. A. Screech, [The Hague]: Mouton; [New York]: Johnson Reprint, 1971.

Praetorius, Michael. *Terpsichore.* Wolfenbüttel, 1612. Günther Oberst, ed., *Gesamtausgabe der musikalischen Werke von Michael Praetorius XV,* Wolfenbüttel and Berlin: Georg Kallmeyer, 1929.

Printz, Wolfgang Caspar. *Compendium musicae signatoriae et modulatoriae vocalis, oder Kurtzes Begriff aller derjenigen Dingen so einem der die vocal-Music lernen will, zu wissen.* Dresden, 1689.

———. *Wolfgang Caspar Printzens von Waldthurn Phrynis Mitilenaeus, oder Satyrischer componist.* Dresden and Leipzig, 1696.

Pure, Michel de. *Idée des spectacles anciens et nouveaux.* Paris, 1668.

Mʳ R [Jean-Jacques Rippert?]. *Brunettes ou petits airs à deux dessus, à l'usage de ceux qui veulent apprendre à jouer de la flûte traversière.* Paris, 1725.

Raguenet, François. *Parallèle des italiens et des françois en ce que regarde la musique et les opéras*, 1702. Facsimile, Geneva: Minkoff, 1976. Reprint of English translation attributed to J. E. Galliard (1709), with spelling and punctuation modernized by Oliver Strunk, as "A Comparison between the French and Italian Music," *Musical Quarterly* XXXII/3 (July 1946):411–36.

Raison, André. *Livre d'orgue*, 1688. Reprint as *Premier livre d'orgue*, Paris: Éditions musicales de la Schola Cantorum, ca. 1963.

Rameau, Pierre. *Abbrégé de la nouvelle méthode dans l'art d'écrire ou de tracer toutes sortes de danses de ville*. Paris, 1725a. Facsimile, Farnborough: Gregg International, 1972.

———. *Le maitre à danser*. Paris, 1725b. Facsimile, New York: Broude, 1967. Translated by Cyril W. Beaumont as *The Dancing Master*, London: C. W. Beaumont, 1931.

Richelet, César Pierre. *La versification françoise*. Paris, 1677.

———. *Dictionnaire françois*. Geneva: Widerhold, 1680. Rev. ed. as *Nouveau dictionaire françois, contenant generalement tous les mots, anciens et modernes de la langue françoise*, Geneva: G. de Tournes, Cramer, Perachon, Ritter, & S. de Tournes, 1710.

Rousseau, Jean. *Méthode claire, certaine et facile, pour apprendre à chanter la musique*. Paris, 1678. 5th ed., rev. and aug., Amsterdam, ca. 1710.

———. *Traité de la viole*. Paris, 1687. Facsimile, Amsterdam: Antiqua, 1965.

Rousseau, Jean-Jacques. *Dictionnaire de musique*. Paris, 1768. Facsimile, Hildesheim: Georg Olms; New York: Johnson Reprint, 1969.

Saint-Lambert, Michel de. *Les principes du clavecin*. Paris, 1702. Facsimile, Geneva: Minkoff, 1974.

Sanseverino, Benedetto. *Intavolatura facile delli passacetti*. Milan, 1620.

———. *Il primo libro d'intavolatura per la chitarra alla spagnuola*. Milan, 1622.

Sanz y Celma, Gaspar Francisco Bartolomé. *Instruccion de musica sobre la guitarra espanola*, 3d ed. Zaragoza, 1674. Facsimile of books 1 and 2 with book 3 of 8th (1697) ed., edited by Luis Garcia-Abrines, Zaragoza: Institucion "Fernando el Catolico" de la Excma. Diputacion Provincial (C.S.I.C.), 1952.

Sol, C. *Methode tres facile, et fort necessaire, pour montrer à la jeunesse de l'un & l'autre sexe la maniere de bien dancer*. The Hague, 1725.

Spinoza, Baruch. *Earlier Philosophical Writings: The Cartesian Principles and Thoughts on Metaphysics*. Translated by Frank A. Hayes with introduction by David Bidney. Indianapolis and New York: Bobbs-Merrill, 1963.

Taubert, Gottfried. *Rechtschaffener Tanzmeister oder, gründliche Erklärung der frantzösischen Tantz-Kunst*. Leipzig, 1717. Includes German translation of Feuillet's *Chorégraphie*, pp. 745–915. Facsimile, Munich: Heimeran, 1976.

Tomlinson, Kellom. *The Art of Dancing*. London, 1735.

Vallet, Nicolas. *Le secret des muses. Premier livre (1615), second livre (1616)*. Edited and transcribed by André Souris, Paris: Éditions du Centre National de la Recherche Scientifique, 1970.

Visée, Robert de. *Livre de pièces pour la guittarre*. Paris, 1686. Edited by Robert W. Strizich in *Oeuvres complètes pour guitare*, Le Pupitre XV, Paris: Heugel, 1969.

Weaver, John. See Feuillet, Raoul-Auger.

SECONDARY SOURCES

Aldrich, Putnam. *Rhythm in Seventeenth-Century Italian Monody*. New York: Norton, 1966.

Anthony, James R. *French Baroque Music from Beaujoyeulx to Rameau*. London: Batsford, 1973; New York: Norton, 1974. Rev. ed., New York: Norton, 1978.

Bank, J. A. *Tactus, Tempo and Notation in Mensural Music from the 13th to the 17th Century*. Amsterdam: Annie Bank, 1972.

Barnett, Dene. "French Bowing Rules and the Minuet," *Musicology [Journal of the Musicological Society of Australia]* II (1965–67):22–34.

Beardsley, Monroe C. *Aesthetics from Classical Greece to the Present.* New York: Macmillan, 1966.

Borrel, Eugène. "Les indications métronomiques laissés par les auteurs français du XVIIIe siècle," *Revue de musicologie* IX (1928):149–53.

Boyden, David D. *The History of Violin Playing from Its Origins to 1761.* London: Oxford University Press, 1965.

Brainard, Ingrid. *The Art of Courtly Dancing in the Early Renaissance.* Part II: *The Practice of Courtly Dancing.* West Newton, Mass.: Author, 1981.

Buch, David Joseph. "The Influence of the *Ballet de cour* in the Genesis of the French Baroque Suite," *Acta musicologica* LVII/1 (Jan.-June 1985):94–109.

Buelow, George J. "Rhetoric and Music," *The New Grove* XV, pp. 793–803.

Burford, Freda. "Contredanse," *The New Grove* IV, pp. 703–705.

Butler, Gregory G. "The Projection of Affect in Baroque Dance Music," *Early Music* XII/2 (May 1984):200–207.

Caswell, Austin Baldwin, Jr. "The Development of the 17th-Century French Vocal Ornamentation and its Influence upon Late Baroque Ornamentation." Ph.D. diss., University of Minnesota, 1964. (Vol. 1 is a translation of Bénigne de Bacilly's *A Commentary upon the Art of Proper Singing* [q.v.].)

Caswell, Judith Eleanor Carls. "Rhythmic Inequality and Tempo in French Music between 1650 and 1740." Ph.D. diss., University of Minnesota, 1973.

Cohen, Albert. "Early French Dictionaries as Musical Sources," in *A Musical Offering: Essays in Honor of Martin Bernstein,* edited by Edward H. Clinkscale and Claire Brook. New York: Pendragon Press, 1977, pp. 97–112.

Cohen, Selma Jeanne. *Dance as a Theatre Art: Source Readings in Dance History from 1581 to the Present.* New York: Dodd, Mead; Harper & Row, 1974.

Conté, Pierre. *Danses anciennes de cour et de théatre en France: éléments de composition.* Paris: Dessain & Tolra, 1974.

Croce, Benedetto. *Aesthetic as Science of Expression and General Linguistic.* Translated from the Italian by Douglas Ainslie. Rev. ed. New York: Noonday Press, 1922.

Curtis, Alan. "Musique classique française à Berkeley: pièces inédites de Louis Couperin, Lebègue, La Barre, etc.," *Revue de musicologie* LVI/2 (1970):123–64. (Includes inventory of Manuscript Menetou.)

Cusick, Suzanne G. See Little, Meredith Ellis, and Suzanne G. Cusick.

Delattre, Pierre. *Principes de phonétique française à l'usage des étudiants anglo-saxons.* Middlebury, Vermont: College Store, 1951.

Devoto, Daniel. "La folle sarabande," *Revue de musicologie* XLV/1 (July 1960):3–43; XLVI/2 (December 1960):146–80.

———. "De la zarabanda à la sarabande," *Recherches sur la musique française classique* VI (1966):27–72.

Ellis, Meredith. "The Sources of Jean-Baptiste Lully's Secular Music," *Recherches sur la musique française classique* VIII (1968):89–130.

———. "Inventory of the Dances of Jean-Baptiste Lully," *Recherches sur la musique française classique* IX (1969):21–55. See also Little, Meredith Ellis.

Eppelsheim, Jurgen. *Das Orchester in den Werken Jean-Baptiste Lullys.* Münchner Veröffentlichungen zur Musikgeschichte VII. Tutzing: Hans Schneider, 1961.

Geoffroy-Dechaume, Antoine. *Les "secrets" de la musique ancienne: recherches sur l'interpretation, XVIe-XVIIe-XVIIIe siècles.* Paris: Fasquelle, 1964.

Gilbert, Katharine, and Helmut Kuhn. *A History of Esthetics.* Rev. and enl. ed. Bloomington: Indiana University Press, 1953.

Guilcher, Jean-Michel. *La tradition populaire de danse en Basse-Bretagne.* Paris and The Hague: Mouton, 1963.

———. *La contredanse et les renouvellements de la danse française.* Paris and The Hague: Mouton, 1969.

Gustafson, Bruce. *French Harpsichord Music of the Seventeenth Century: A Thematic Catalog of the Sources, with Commentary.* Ann Arbor: UMI Research Press, 1979.

Hampshire, Stuart. *The Age of Reason: The 17th Century Philosophers.* New York: Mentor Books, 1956.

Hansell, Sven H. "Folk Fiddling in Sweden: Ornamentation and Irregular Rhythm and Its Relation to Seventeenth-Century French Keyboard Music." Paper read at Annual Meeting, American Musicological Society, Denver, Colorado, 8 November 1980.

————. "François Couperin's Comparison of French and Italian Music," in *Analytica: Studies in the Description and Analysis of Music in Honour of Ingmar Bengtsson.* Publications, No. 47. Stockholm: Royal Swedish Academy of Music, 1985, pp. 149–62.

Harding, Rosamund E. M. *Origins of Musical Time and Expression.* London, New York and Toronto: Oxford University Press, 1938.

Highet, Gilbert. *The Classical Tradition: Greek and Roman Influences on Western Literature.* New York and London: Oxford University Press, 1949.

Hilton, Wendy. *Dance of Court and Theater: The French Noble Style, 1690–1725.* Princeton: Princeton Book Co., 1981.

Holliday, Kent. "The Origin and Evolution of the Sarabande." *Divisions* I/4 (1980):23–31.

Houle, George L. "The Musical Measure as Discussed by Theorists from 1650 to 1800." Ph.D. diss., Stanford University, 1961.

————. *Meter in Music, 1600–1800: Performance, Perception, and Notation.* Bloomington: Indiana University Press, 1987.

Hsu, John. *A Handbook of French Baroque Viol Techniques.* New York: Broude, 1981.

Hudson, Richard. "Chordal Aspects of the Italian Dance Style 1500–1650," *Journal of the Lute Society of America* III (1970):35–52.

————. "Further Remarks on the Passacaglia and Ciaconna," *Journal of the American Musicological Society* XXIII/2 (1970):302–14.

————. "The *Zarabanda* and *Zarabanda Francese* in Italian Guitar Music of the Early 17th Century," *Musica Disciplina* XXIV (1970):125–49.

————. "The *Folia* Dance and the *Folia* Formula in 17th Century Guitar Music," *Musica Disciplina* XXV (1971):199–221.

————. "The Music in Italian Tablatures for the Five-Course Spanish Guitar," *Journal of the Lute Society of America* IV (1971):21–42.

————. "The Folia Melodies," *Acta Musicologica* XLV/1 (Jan.-June 1973):98–119.

————. Articles in *The New Grove*: "Canary" (III, pp. 676–78), "Chaconne" (IV, pp. 100–102), "Folia" (VI, pp. 690–92), "Passacaglia" (XIV, pp. 267–70), "Sarabande" (XVI, pp. 489–93).

————. *Passacaglia and Ciaccona: From Guitar Music to Italian Keyboard Variations in the 17th Century.* Ann Arbor: UMI Research Press, 1981.

————. *The Folia, the Saraband, the Passacaglia, and the Chaconne: The Historical Evolution of Four Forms that Originated in Music for the Five-course Spanish Guitar.* 4 vols. Compiled and introduced [by Richard Hudson]. Neuhausen-Stuttgart: Hännsler-Verlag, ca. 1982.

————. *The Allemande, the Balletto, and the Tanz.* 2 vols. Cambridge: University Press, 1986.

Isherwood, Robert N. *Music in the Service of the King: France in the Seventeenth Century.* Ithaca: Cornell University Press, 1973.

Lancelot, Francine. "Écriture de la danse. Le système Feuillet," *Ethnologie française* I/1 (1971):29–50.

Lesure, François. *L'Opéra classique français. XVIIe et XVIIIe siècles. Iconographie musicale* I. Geneva: Minkoff, 1972.

Little, Meredith Ellis. Articles in *The New Grove:* "Bourrée" (III, pp. 116–17), "Forlana" (VI, pp. 708–709), "Gavotte" (VII, pp. 199–202), "Gigue" (VII, pp. 368–71),

"Loure" (XI, pp. 256–57), "Minuet" (XII, pp. 353–58), "Passepied" (XIV, pp. 273–74), "Rigaudon" (XVI, pp. 15–16). See also Ellis, Meredith.

Little, Meredith, and Suzanne G. Cusick. Articles in *The New Grove:* "Allemande" (I, pp. 276–80), "Courante" (IV, pp. 875–78).

McGowan, Margaret M. *L'art du ballet de cour en France, 1581–1643.* Paris: Editions du Centre de la Recherche Scientifique, 1963.

Maland, David. *Europe in the Seventeenth Century.* New York: St. Martin's Press, 1966.

Massip, Catherine. *La vie des musiciens de Paris au temps de Mazarin, 1643–1661: Essai d'étude sociale.* Paris: A. & J. Picard, 1976.

Mather, Betty Bang. *The Interpretation of French Music from 1675 to 1775 for Woodwind and Other Performers.* New York: McGinnis & Marx, 1973.

Mather, Betty Bang, and David Lasocki. *Free Ornamentation in Woodwind Music: 1700–1775.* New York: McGinnis & Marx, 1976.

Mohr, Ernst. *Die Allemande, eine Untersuchung ihrer Entwicklung von den Anfangen bis zu Bach und Händel.* Leipzig and Zurich: Kommissionsverlag von gebr. Hug, 1932.

Morier, Henri. *Dictionnaire de poétique et de rhétorique.* Paris: Presses Universitaires de France, 1961.

Neumann, Frederick. *Ornamentation in Baroque and Post-Baroque Music: With Special Emphasis on J. S. Bach.* Princeton: Princeton University Press, 1978.

The New Grove Dictionary of Music and Musicians, edited by Stanley Sadie. 20 vols. London: Macmillan; Washington, D. C.: Grove's Dictionaries of Music, 1980.

Newman, Joyce Enith Watkins. *Jean Baptiste de Lully and His Tragédies lyriques.* Ann Arbor: UMI Research Press, 1979.

Pinnell, Richard T. *Francesco Corbetta and the Baroque Guitar: With a Transcription of His Works.* 2 vols. Ann Arbor: UMI Research Press, 1980.

Powell, Newman Wilson. "Rhythmic Freedom in the Performance of French Music from 1650 to 1735." Ph. D. diss., Stanford University, 1958.

———. "Kirnberger on Dance Rhythms, Fugues, and Characterization," in *Festschrift Theodore Hoelty-Nickel.* Valparaiso, Indiana: Valparaiso University, 1967, pp. 65–76.

Ranum, Patricia M. "Prototype of a Glossary of French Terms of Movement." Unpublished manuscript, copyright 1981.

———. "Le phrasé des danses baroques selon les paroles," *La Danse. Actes du 1ᵉʳ Colloque International sur la danse ancienne, Besançon, September 1982,* pp. 100–112.

———. "Les caractères des danses françaises," *Recherches sur la musique française classique* XXIII (1985):45–70.

———. "Audible Rhetoric and Mute Rhetoric: The Seventeenth-Century French Sarabande," *Early Music* XXIV/1 (Feb. 1986):22–39.

Riley, Maurice Winton. "The Teaching of Bowed Instruments from 1511 to 1756." Ph. D. diss., University of Michigan, 1954.

Ritcheson, Shirley Spackman. "Feuillet's 'Chorégraphie' and Its Implications in the Society of France and England, 1700." M.A. thesis, The Ohio State University, 1965.

Rosow, Lois. "French Baroque Recitative as an Expression of Tragic Declamation," *Early Music* XI/4 (Oct. 1983):468–79.

Saint-Arroman, *L'interprétation de la musique française 1661–1789. I: Dictionnaire d'interprétation (Initiation).* Paris: Librairie Honoré Champion, 1983.

Sandman, Susan Goertzel. "Wind Band Music under Louis XIV: The Philidor Collection, Music for the Military and the Court." Ph.D. diss., Stanford University, 1974.

———. "The Wind Band at Louis XIV's Court," *Early Music* V/1 (Jan. 1977):27–37.

Schmitz, Hans-Peter. *Die Tontechnik des Père Engramelle: ein Beitrag zur Lehre von der musikalischen Vortragskunst im 18. Jahrhundert.* Kassel: Bärenreiter, 1953.

———. *Die Kunst der Verzierung im 18. Jahrhundert.* Kassel: Bärenreiter, 1965.

Scholfield, P. H. *The Theory of Proportion in Architecture.* Cambridge: University Press, 1958.

Schwandt, Erich. "L'Affilard on the French Court Dances," *Musical Quarterly* LX/3 (July 1974):389–400.

Scott, Clive. *French Verse-Art: A Study.* Cambridge and New York: Cambridge University Press, ca. 1980.

Seagrave, Barbara Ann Garvey. "The French Style of Violin Bowing and Phrasing from Lully to Jacques Aubert, 1650–1730, as Illustrated in Dances from Ballets and Dance Movements from Violin Sonatas of Representative Composers." Ph.D. diss., Stanford University, 1958.

Somville, Marilyn Elizabeth Feller. "Vowels and Consonants as Factors in Early Singing Style and Technique." Ph.D. diss., Stanford University, 1967.

Taubert, Karl Heinz. *Hofische Tänze: ihre Geschichte und Choreographie.* Mainz: Schott, 1968.

Tyler, James. *The Early Guitar: A History and Handbook.* Early Music Series IV. London: Oxford University Press, 1980.

Veilhan, Jean-Claude. *The Rules of Musical Interpretation in the Baroque Era (17th-18th Centuries), Common to All Instruments.* Paris: Leduc, 1979 [original French version 1977].

Walker, D. P. "Musical Humanism in the 16th and Early 17th Centuries," *Music Review* II/1 (1941):1–13; II/2 (1941):111–21; II/3 (1941):288–308; III/1 (1942):55–71.

———. "The Aims of Baïf's *Académie de Poésie et de Musique,*" *Journal of Renaissance and Baroque Music* I/2 (June 1946):91–100.

———. "The Influence of *Musique mesurée à l'antique,* Particularly on the *Airs de Cour* of the Early Seventeenth Century," *Musica Disciplina* II/1–2 (1948):141–63.

———. "Some Aspects and Problems of Musique Mesurée à l'Antique. The Rhythm and Notation of Musique Mesurée," *Musica Disciplina* IV (1950):163–86.

Walker, D. P., and François Lesure. "Claude Le Jeune and *Musique Mesurée,*" *Musica Disciplina* III/2–4 (1949):151–70.

Williams, Charles Francis Abdy. *The Aristoxenian Theory of Musical Rhythm.* Cambridge: University Press, 1911.

Witherell, Anne L. *Louis Pécour's 1700 "Recueil de danses."* Ann Arbor: UMI Research Press, 1982.

Wolff, Hellmuth Christian. "Das Metronom des Louis-Léon Pajot 1735," in *Festskrift Jens Peter Larsen.* Copenhagen: Wilhelm Hansen, 1972, pp. 205–17.

Wood, Melusine. *Some Historical Dances, Twelfth to Nineteenth Century, Their Manner of Performance and Their Place in the Social Life of the Time.* London: Imperial Society of Teachers of Dancing, 1952; 2d ed., 1972 [omitting "Some" from title].

———. *More Historical Dances Comprising the Technical Part of the Elementary Syllabus and the Intermediate Syllabus, the Latter Section Including Such Dances as Appertain but not Previously Described.* London: Imperial Society of Teachers of Dancing, 1956.

Zaslaw, Neal Alexander. "Materials for the Life and Works of Jean-Marie Leclair, l'aîné." Ph.D. diss., Columbia University, 1970.

———. "Mozart's Tempo Conventions," *International Musical Society: Report of the Eleventh Congress, Copenhagen 1972.* Copenhagen: Wilhelm Hansen, 1974, pp. 720–33.

NOTES

INTRODUCTION

1. Et la façon tant estimée
De nos poètes anciens,
Les Vers avecques la musique,
Le Balet confus mesuré,
Démonstrant du ciel azuré
L'accord par un effect mystique.

2. Um die zum guten Vortrag nothwendigen Eigenschaften zu erlangen, kann der Tonkünstler nichts bessers thun, als fleissig allerhand *characteristische Tänze* spielen. Jede dieser Tanzmusiken hat ihren eignen Rhythmus, ihre Einschnitte von gleicher Länge, ihre Accente auf einerley Stelle in jedem Saz; man erkennet sie also leicht, und durch das öftere Executiren gewohnt man sich unvermerkt, den einer jeden eigenen Rhythmus zu unterscheiden, und dessen Säze und Accente zu bezeichnen, so dass man endlich leicht in einem langen Musikstücke die noch so verschiednen und durch einander gemischten Rhythmen, Einschnitte und Accente erkennet. Man gewöhnt sich ferner jedem Stücke den eigenthümlichen Ausdruck zu geben, weil jede Art dieser Tanzmelodien ihren eignen charakteristischen Tact und Wehrt der Noten hat.

3. Vornemlich ist es unmöglich, eine Fuge gut zu komponiren oder zu executiren, wenn man nicht alle verschiednen Rhythmen kent; und eben daher, weil heut zu Tage dieses Studium versäumt wird, ist die Music von ihrer alten Würde herabgesunken, und man kann keine Fugen mehr aushalten, weil sie, durch die elende Execution die weder Einschnitt noch Accente bezeichnet, ein blosses Chaos von Tönen geworden sind.

PROLOGUE

1. J'ay cru ne pouvoir donner une description plus capable d'inspirer de l'attention pour les cérémonies, & les regles des Bals particuliers, que de faire d'abord une petite relation du grand Bal du Roy; comme étant celui qui occupe le premier rang, & auquel on doit se conformer pour les autres Bals particuliers; tant par l'ordre qui s'y garde, que par le respect & la politesse que l'on y observe.

2. Il faut sçavoir d'abord, qu'il n'y a personne admis dans le Cercle, que les Princes & Princesses du Sang, ensuite les Ducs & Pairs, & les Duchesses: & après les autres Seigneurs & Dames de la Cour, chacun selon le rang qu'ils doivent occuper; mais les Dames sont assises sur le devant, & les Seigneurs aussi assis derriere les Dames. . . .

Ainsi chacun étant placé dans le même ordre, lorsque Sa Majesté souhaite de commencer, elle se leve, & toute la Cour en fait de même.

Le Roy se place à l'endroit de l'appartement où l'on doit commencer de danser (qui est du côté de l'Orchestre). Du tems du feu Roy, c'étoit la Reine avec qui Sa Majesté figuroit, au deffaut, c'étoit la premiere Princess du Sang que *Sa Majesté* prenoit, & se plaçoient les premiers, & chacun se venoit placer derriere leurs Majestez à la file, chacun selon leur rang. . . . Les Seigneurs sont d'un côté à la gauche, & les Dames à la droite: & dans ce même ordre on se fait la reverence l'un devant l'autre, ensuite Sa Majesté & sa Dame mene le branle, qui étoit la danse par où les Bals de la Cour se commençoient, tous les Seigneurs & Dames suivent leurs Majestez, chacun de leur côté. . . . Après quoy ils dansent la Gavotte, . . . on se fait de pareilles reverences en se quittant, que celles que l'on a fait avant de danser.

3. C'est pourquoi après que le Roy a dansé le premier menuet, il va se placer, & tout le monde pour lors s'asseoit, d'autant que lorsque Sa Majesté danse tout le monde est debout; après quoy le Prince qui doit danser lorsque Sa Majesté est placée, il lui fait une très-profonde reverence, ensuite il vient à l'endroit où est la Reine, ou premiere Princess, & font ensemble les reverences que l'on fait avant de danser, & de suite ils dansent le menuet, & après le menuet on fait de pareilles reverences que celles que l'on a fait devant. Ensuite ce Seigneur fait une reverence très-profonde à cette Princess en la quittant. . . .

Du même instant il fait deux ou trois pas en avant, pour adresser une autre reverence à la Princess ou Dame qui doit danser à son tour. . . .

4. Mais si *Sa Majesté* souhaite que l'on danse quelqu'autre danse, c'est un des premiers Gentilhommes de la Chambre qui le dit, ce qui n'empêche pas que l'on n'observe toujours les pareilles reverences.

5. Il est vrai, qu'il y en a plusieurs qui n'ont aucuns desseins, ni aucuns goûts, puisque c'est toûjours les mêmes figures, sans aucuns pas assurez, toute la plus grande perfection de ces contre-danses, est de se bien tourmenter le corps, de se tirer en tournent, de taper des pieds comme des Sabotiers, & de faire plusieurs attitudes qui ne sont point dans la bien-séance: . . . .

6. Je recommande sur tout à cette Jeunesse, pour qui très-souvent l'on fait ces sortes d'assemblées, d'observer les regles que leurs Maitres doivent leur avoir enseigné, afin de se faire honneur de l'éducation qu'ils reçoivent.

1. REASON AND THE PASSIONS

1. L'idée qu'on attache au mot de Beau est double. . . . Je distingue deux sortes de perceptions; j'appelle les unes *Idées* & les autres *Sentimens*. . . .

Les idées occupent l'Esprit, les sentimens interessent le Coeur. . . .

2. La Musique Vocale est une espece de langue, dont les hommes sont convenus, pour se communiquer avec plus de plaisir leurs pensées, & leurs sentimens. Ainsi celui qui compose de cette sorte de Musique, doit se considérer comme un Traducteur, qui en observant les regles de son art, exprime ces mêmes pensées, & ces mêmes sentimens.

3. On apelle nombre, dans l'Art de parler et de chanter, tout ce que les oreilles aperçoivent de proportionné . . . , soit suivant la proportion des mesures du tems, soit selon une juste distribution des intervalles de la respiration; c'est ce que les Latins apellent, *Numerosa oratio*; & les François, *Discours harmonieux*. Saint Augustin remarque qu'il y a une alliance merveilleuse de nôtre esprit avec les nombres. . . . Et Ciceron . . . dit que les nombres sont merveilleusement propres à faire agir les passions.

4. Aller par ordre, ce n'est pas sauter tout d'un coup d'une extremité à une autre, c'est s'avancer d'une difference accompagnée de beaucoup d'égalité, à une troisiéme fort approchante de la seconde, mais un peu plus éloignée de la premiere.

5. [T]out y est si vif, si aigu, si perçant, si impétueux & si remuant, que l'imagination, les sens, l'ame, & le corps même en sont entrainez d'un commun transport; . . . le Joüeur de violon . . . tourmente son violon, son corps, . . . il s'agite comme un possédé. . . .

6. Ce sont des piéces régulieres & suivies; . . . l'amour, la jalousie, la fureur, & les autres passions y sont traitées avec un art & une délicatesse infinie. . . .

7. La Rythmique est un Art qui considere les mouvemens, & qui regle leur suite & leur mélange pour exciter les passions, & pour les entretenir, ou pour les augmenter, diminuer, ou appaiser.

8. Ceux qui en usent sur les Tambours & les Trompettes, aux dances & balets, dans les Chants, & dans les vers, &c. n'ont point d'autre intention que de plaire aux auditeurs & aux spectateurs, ou de les exciter à quelque passion ou affection, soit de joye ou de tristesse, & d'amour, ou de haine, &c.

9. Les périodes égales ne doivent pas se suivre de fort prés; il est bon que le discours coule avec plus de liberté. Une égalité trop exacte des intervalles de la respiration,

pourroit devenir ennuyeux. . . . Un discours également périodique ne peut se prononcer qu'avec froideur. Les périodes . . . ne sont bonnes que lorsque l'on veut parler avec majesté, ou plaire aux oreilles. On ne peut pas courir, & en même temps marcher en cadence.

2. ARBEAU'S DANCE RHYTHMS

1. Dance vient de dancer que l'on dit en latin *Saltare*: Dancer c'est à dire saulter, saulteloter, caroler, baler, treper, trepiner, mouvoir & remuer les piedz, mains, & corps de certaines cadances, mesures & mouvementz, consistans en saultz, pliement de corps, divarications, claudications, ingeniculations, elevations, iactations de piedz, permutations & aultres contenances . . . (Arbeau, 1888 ed., p. 4).

2. La dance ou saltation est un art plaisant & proffitable, qui rend & conserve la santé, convenable aux jeusnes, aggreable aux vieux, & bien séant a tous, pourveu qu'on en use modestement en temps & lieu, sans affectation vicieuse: . . . (Ibid., p. 5).

3. DANCE RHYTHMS FROM EARLY GUITAR SOURCES

1. La *Sarabande* . . . se dance au son de la Guiterre, ou des Castaignettes, & ce par plusieurs couplets sans nombre.

2. Due castagnette di sonoro basso tien nele man la giovinetta ardita. . . . Regge un timpano l'altro, ilqual percosso con sonaglietti ad atteggiar l'invita. . . . Quanti moti a lascivia e quanti gesti provocar ponno i più pudici affetti. . . . Cenni e baci disegna or quella or questi, fanno i fianchi ondeggiar, scontarsi i petti, socchiudon gli occhi e quasi infra sestessi vengon danzando agli ultimi complessi (XX: 85–86).

4. RHYTHMIC MOVEMENTS IN MERSENNE'S AND LATER DANCE MUSIC

1. Quant aux danceries, il y a plusieurs especes qui appartiennent à la Musique Metrique, dautant qu'elles sont sujettes à de certaines mesures, ou pieds reglez & contez.

2. . . . les plus excellens pieds metriques, qui ont donné le nom & la naissance à la Rhythmique des Grecs, sont pratiquez dans les airs de Balet, dans les chansons à dancer, & dans toutes les autres actions qui servent aux recréations publiques ou particuliers, comme l'on advoüera quand on aura reduit les pieds qui suivent aux airs que l'on récite, ou que l'on joue sur les Violons, sur le Luth, sur la Guiterre et sur les autres instrumens.

Or ces pieds, peuvent estre appellez mouvemens afin de s'accommoder à la maniere de parler de nos Practiciens, & compositeurs d'airs; c'est pourquoy je me servirez désormais de ce terme, pour joindre la Théorie à la Pratique.

3. Il se divisoit, ainsi qu'eux, en deux Tems, l'un frappé, l'autre levé; l'on en comptoit trois Genres, même quatre et plus, selon les divers rapports de ces Tems. Ces Genres étoient l'*Egal*, qu'ils appelloient aussi Dactylique, ou le *rhythme* étoit divisé en deux Tems égaux; *double*, Trochaique ou iambique, dans lequel la durée de l'un des deux Tems étoit double de celle de l'autre; le *Sesquialtère*, qu'ils appelloient aussi *Péonique*, dont la durée de l'un des deux Tems étoient à celle de l'autre en rapport de 3 à 2; et enfin l'*Epitrite*, moins usité, où le rapport des deux Tems étoit de 3 à 4.

5. THE MUSICAL MEASURE

1. On se sert de plusieurs manieres de battre la Mesure pour diversifier les Pièces de Musique, comme aussi pour s'accommoder à la quantité des paroles, qui demande tantost une Mesure à quatre temps, tantost à deux, tantost à trois, &c.

2. La Mesure est ce que nous avons de plus beau dans la Musique, ou plutôt la Musique n'est rien sans la Mesure: car c'est par elle que l'on peut conduire quatre, cinq &

six parties à cent executeurs chacune, sans que les uns arrivent plutôt à la fin que les autres.

3. Les bonnes sont celles qui semblent naturellement permettre à l'oreille comme un peu de repos. . . . Les chetives . . . ne satisfaisant pas si bien l'oreille laissent apres soy le desir de passer outre (DTO, p. 50).

Die edle seynd, welche nathürlicher Weise in dem Gehör scheinen zu verweilen; . . . . Die schlechte . . . den Ohren nicht also genugthun, sondern als weiter gehende ein Verlangen nach sich lassen (DTO, p. 26).

4. La Mesure est l'âme de la Musique, puis qu'elle fait agir avec tant de justesse un grand nombre de Personnes, & que par la variété de ses mouvements elle peut encours émouvoir tant de differentes passions, pouvant calmer les unes & exciter les autres, ainsi qu'on l'a toujours remarqué.

5. Mesure a 2. temps. Cette Mesure se marque par un 2. simple, Elle est composée de 2 blanches ou de l'equivalent; elle se bat a 2 temps eqaux. Elle est ordinairement vive et piquée. On l'employe dans le debut des Ouvertures d'Opera, dans les Entrées de Ballet, les marches, les bourées, gavottes, rigaudons, branles, cotillons &c. les croches y sont pointées. On ne la connoit point dans les Musiques Italiennes.

6. CORRESPONDENCE OF MELODIC AND POETIC RHYTHMS

1. Il est aussi nécessaire d'éxaminer une piéce avant que d'entreprendre de l'éxécuter pour deux raisons, la premiére pour tâcher de deviner son caractére, et développer l'intention de l'auteur, la seconde pour trouver sa cadence; La cadence d'un air est un certain nombre de mesures qui déterminent un chant: plusieurs de ces chants qui sont de deux, de trois, ou de quatre mesures quelquefois plus, déterminent une reprise d'Air, ou un air entier; ensorte si l'air commence soit à la premiére, la seconde, la troisiéme, à la quatriéme partie d'une mesure,—il faut que chaque période de cet air commence de même, ainsi il faut lever tous les doigts arrêter la roüe pour distinguer chacune de ces parties: Ce qui est aisé à concevoir dans les airs mesurés, comme Menuets, Bourées, Rigaudons, Chacones, Contredanses et autres, où l'on voit que de deux ou de quatre mesures il y a une terminaison de chant sensible, aprés laquelle ou on répéte le commencement du même chant, ou on commence une autre phrase: c'est à ces chûtes que peu de personnes font d'attention, et d'où dépend cependant la perfection de l'exécution.

2. L'expression du Chant pour répondre à celle des paroles, dépend de l'invention & du juste discernement du Compositeur; Cette expression étant soûtenue & perfectionnée par une judicieuse diversité du mouvement de la mesure, a la force & la vertu de faire passer l'ame d'une passion à une autre; ce qui est une preuve naturelle de la perfection d'un Ouvrage.

7. RHETORICAL PROPORTIONS

1. Chantes, [qui] doivent en quelque façon imiter les Harangues, afin d'avoir des membres, des parties, & des periodes, & d'user de toutes sortes de figures & de passages harmoniques, comme l'Orateur, & que l'Art de composer des Airs, & le Contrepoint ne cede rien à la Rhetorique.

2. Car il est malaisé que la memoire retienne les diverses choses & le nombre infiny de Parties qui entrent dans une longue Harangue, si elle n'est soûlagée par quelque chose . . . qui les y arreste & les luy fasse retenir.

8. STEP-UNITS OF *LA BELLE DANSE*

1. Ce raisonnement de Platon nous apprend que la Dance n'est pas seulement un divertissement honnête, mais qu'elle est une espece d'étude & d'application, absolu-

ment necessaire pour regler nos mouvemens. C'est en effet elle qui donne un air noble & degagé à toutes les actions, & une certaine grace qu'on voit rarement en ceux qui n'ont pas appris à danser. Les actions des Orateurs, les ceremonies publiques, & l'exercice des armes demandent cette application pour acquerir cette souplesse de corps, cette addresse de mouvemens, & cette éloquence exterieure, que Ciceron & Quintillien ont si fort recommandée.

2. . . . la belle Dance est une certaine finesse dans le mouvement, au port, au pas, & dans toute la personne, qui ne se peut ny exprimer ny enseigner par les paroles. Il faut les yeux, les beaux exemples & de bons Maistres; & quelquefois mesme avoce toutes ces aydes, on a bien de la peine à la bien concevoir, & encore plus à l'executer.

9. SYMMETRICAL, POETIC, AND RHETORICAL PROPORTIONS OF *LA BELLE DANSE*

1. . . . la dance est une espece de Rhetorique muette, . . . (Arbeau 1888 ed., p. 5 bis).

2. La figure reguliere est quand deux ou plusieurs Danceurs vont par mouvement contraire, c'est à dire que tandis que l'un va à droit, l'autre va à gauche.

La figure irreguliere est quand les deux Danceurs qui figurent ensemble vont tous deux d'un même côté.

10. TEMPOS AND GENERAL AFFECTS

1. Il est pourtant generallement parlant un certain mouvement qu'on est obligé de garder dans tous les airs de Balet, & dans tous ceux de toute sorte de dance, & sur tout Françoise. Je dis Françoise, parce que j'ay remarqué parmy les Étrangers des mouvements bien plus lents & plus chantables. . . . [L]'air de Balet ne soit pas si suspensif, ni si languissant qu'on pourroit le faire, s'il ne s'agissoit que de chanter. Il faut aller encor un peu plus loin que les agrémens de la voix, & qu'il donne jusqu'à ceux d'une passion bien exprimée, d'une vivacité particuliere, & qu'il ait toûjours quelque chose d'eslevé & de gay: . . . .

11. MARKING THE MUSICAL METER

1. Mesure Marquée, c'est celle dont les Temps etaient fort marqués comme dans les Airs de danse (PBN, Fr. nouv. acq. 6355, p. 139).

2. [La Cadence de la Pièce] consiste à passer les Notes d'une même valeur avec une grand égalité de mouvement, & toutes les Notes en général avec égalité de proportion: car soit qu'on joûe une Pièce vite, ou qu'on la joûe lentement, on doit toûjours luy donner la cadence qui en est l'amc, & la chose dont elle peut le moins se passer.

12. LULLIAN BOWING OF DANCE RHYTHMS

1. La maniere de Jouer les airs de Balets sur les Violons selon le genie de feu Monsieur Battiste de Lully, prise icy en sa pureté, & si recommandable par l'approbation des meilleurs Musiciens de l'Europe, est d'une recherche si exquise, qu'on ne sçauroit rien trouver de plus exact, de plus beau, ny de plus agreable (DTO, p. 44).

Es ist die Weise der Balleten nach der Manier dess berühmtesten Johann Baptist Lulli auf der Geigen zuspihlen (welche wir in ihrer Reinigkeit allhier wollen verstanden haben, und von denen trefflichsten Meistern der Welt bewundert und gelobt worden) einer so sinreichen Nachsuchung, dass schwerlich was lieblichers, oder schöners möge erdacht werden (DTO, p. 20).

2. Les Italiens ont encore, pour les Instrumens & pour ceux qui les touchent, le même avantage qu'ils ont sur nous, pour les voix & pour les personnes qui chantent. Leurs violons sont montez de cordes plus grosses que les nôtres, ils ont des archets

beaucoup plus longs, & ils savent tirer de leurs Instrumens une fois plus de son, que nous. Pour moi, la premiére fois que j'entendis l'Orchestre de notre Opéra à mon retour d'Italie, l'idée de la force de ces sons qui m'étoit encore présente, me fit trouver ceux de nos violons si foibles, que je crus qu'ils avoient tous des sourdines (pp. 103–104).

3. . . . ou l'archet par le tiré et le poussé, unis et liés, sans qu'on apperçoive leur succession, produit des roulades de sons multipliés à l'infini, qui n'en paroissent qu'une continuité, tels qu'en formoient les gosiers de Cossoni et de Faustina.

13. FORCEFUL ARTICULATION OF LULLIAN DANCE LYRICS

1. . . . le Langage familier, & celuy du Chant, sont bien differens, mesme à l'égard de la simple Prononciation; car pour ce qui regard celle qui se fait avec poids, je veux dire avec la force necessaire à l'expression du sens des Paroles, il y a encore une tres-grande difference de celle que l'on practique dans le commun Langage, . . . dans le Chant qui est une espece de *Declamation*, il y a bien de la difference d'une *m*, ou d'une *r*, à une autre pour faire valoir les Paroles, & leur donner la fermeté & la vigueur qui fait que le Chant en a plus de varieté, & n'ennuye point à la longue, comme seroit celuy qui reciteroit simplement des Vers sur le Theatre, au lieu de les declamer.

14. ARTICULATION OF DANCE RHYTHMS IN CONCERT PIECES

1. . . . l'Archet en est l'ame, puisque c'est luy qui l'anime, & qui exprime toutes les passions qui conviennent avec la Voix, & qui marque les differents mouvemens du Chant; . . . .

2. A propos de marquer & d'adoucir, ... Cela est bon sur le Luth, le Theorbe, la Viole, & autres Instrumens, dont les cordes se peuvent fraper tant & si peu que l'on veut, pour marquer leur difference avec le Clavessin, de laquelle ceux qui les touchent tirent un grand avantage, pretendant que par ce moyen ils font parler leurs Instrumens, & leur font mesme exprimer les passions de tendresse, ou de colere, par le moyen du son, ou plus fort, ou plus foible, ce qui se fait en touchant legerement les cordes, ou bien en les frappant avec force, ...

3. Ouy, lorsque l'on aprend par ce que cela vous facilite de trouver le gout des Airs, mais quand l'on sçait, l'on prend t'elle lissence et liberter que l'on juge apropos.

15. ORNAMENTING DANCE RHYTHMS

1. Les Agrémens sont à la Voix & aux Instruments ce que les Ornements sont à un Edifice, & comme les Ornements ne sont pas necessaires pour la subsistance du Bastiment, mais qu'ils servent seulement à le rendre plus agreable à la veue; . . .

2. Il est donc vray qu'il se trouve des Monosyllabes qui sont longs & brefs dans un premier Couplet . . . ; & cependant s'il se trouve que dans le second il y en ait d'autres qui ne puissent jamais estre brefs, c'est à celuy qui chante à remedier par son industrie à cet inconvenient, & conserver autant que faire se peut la mesure & le mouvement de l'Air, ce qui est bien plus aisé (& par consequent indispensable) dans les Chants qui n'ont point leur mesure reglée, que dans les autres qui sont assujettis à une certaine mesure.

3. . . . on rompt la Mesure de la Danse, afin de leur donner plus d'éclat, & les tourner de cent manieres l'une plus agreable que l'autre, & selon tout l'Art & toute la Methode de bien Chanter, mesme pour mieux exprimer certaines Exclamations, & avec plus d'agrément.

4. L'incomparable Lulli, ce genie superieur dont les ouvrages seront toujours estimés des vrais connoisseurs, a preferé la melodie, la belle modulation, l'agréable harmonie, la justesse de l'expression, le naturel et enfin la noble simplicité, au ridicule des Doubles . . . et cependant ils ne laissent pas d'en imposer aux oreilles ignorantes.

16. GROUPING UNSLURRED QUICK NOTES

1. Pour rendre le jeu plus agréable, & pour éviter trop d'uniformité dans les coups de Langue, on les varie en plusieurs manieres; Par exemple on se sert de deux articulations principales; Sçavoir, *Tu* & *Ru*. Le *Tu* est le plus en usage, . . . & sur la plus grande partie des Croches: car lorsque ces dernieres sont sur la même ligne, ou qu'elles sautent, on prononce *Tu*. Lorsqu'elles montent ou descendent par degrez conjoints, on se sert aussi du *Tu*, mais on l'entremêle toûjours avec le *Ru*, ...

On doit remarquer que le *Tu*, *Ru*, se reglent par le nombre des Croches. Quand le nombre est impair on prononce *Tu Ru*, tout de suite. . . . Quand il est pair on prononce *Tu*, sur les deux premières Croches, ensuite *Ru* alternativement, ...

On fera bien d'observer que l'on ne doit pas toûjours passer les Croches également & qu'on doit dans certaines Mesures, en faire une longue & une breve; ce qui se regle aussi par le nombre. Quand il est pair on fait la premiére longue, la seconde breve, & ainsi des autres. Quand il est impair on fait tout le contraire; . . . . Les Mesures dans lesquelles cela se pratique le plus ordinairement, sont celle à Deux-temps, celle du triple simple, & celle de six pour quatre.

2. Quoique ces Regles soient générales, elles admettent cependant quelques exceptions, ...

17. SUMMING UP—THE MANY ASPECTS OF MOVEMENT

1. Plusieurs confondent le Mouvement avec la Mesure, & croyent que parce qu'on dit d'ordinaire un Air de mouvement, pour le distinguer d'un Air fort lent, tout le Mouvement du Chant ne consiste que dans un certain sautillement propre aux Gigues, aux Menuets, & autres semblables.

Le Mouvement est donc tout autre que ce qu'ils s'imaginent; & pour moy je tiens que c'est une certaine qualité qui donne l'ame au Chant, & qui est appellée Mouvement, parce qu'elle émeut, je veux dire elle excite l'attention des Auditeurs, ...

2. . . . il ne suffit pas pour conduite une Musique de sçavoir battre la Mesure suivant les differens Signes, il faut encore entrer dans l'esprit de l'Autheur, c'est a dire dans les differens mouvemens que demande l'expression de la Piéce, ...

3. Je trouve que nous confondons la Mesure avec ce qu'on nomme Cadence ou Mouvement. *Mesure* définit la quantité et l'égalité des temps; et *Cadence* est proprement l'esprit et l'âme qu'il y faut joindre.

4. . . . qu'elle inspire dans les coeurs telle passion que le Chantra voudra faire naître. . . .

. . . qui tient toûjours l'Auditeur en haleine, & fait que le Chant en est moins ennuyeux, . . . qui fait valoir une Voix mediocre, plus qu'un fort belle Voix qui manquera d'Expression.

5. Les *Sonades* des Italiens ne sont gueres susceptibles de cette Cadence. Mais tous nos airs de violons, nos Pièces de clavecin, de violes, &c. dèsignent, et semblent vouloir exprimer quelque sentiment. Ainsi, n'ayant point imaginé de signes, ou caractères pour communiquer nos idées particulières, nous tâchons d'y remèdier en marquant au commencement de nos pièces par quelques mots, comme *Tendrement, Vivement,* &c., à-peu-près ce que nous voudrions faire entendre.

28. MENUETS

1. . . . n'est-il point constant à l'égard des pas, que vous en avez appliqué de menuets sur un air en mouvement de Sarabande, ou de Iaconne? sous prétexte que le signe est dénoté par une mesme marque, au lieu que les notes d'un menuet doivent estre autrement coupées que celles d'une Sarabande. . . .

INDEX

(Chiefly from Part I)

Editor: Natalie Wrubel
Book designer: Joan Cavanagh
Jacket designer: Joan Cavanagh
Music manuscript: Mark Johnson
Production coordinator: Harriet S. Curry
Typeface: Caledonia, Cochin Display
Printer: Haddon Craftsmen, Inc.
Binder: Haddon Craftsmen, Inc.

BETTY BANG MATHER is Professor of Music at the University of Iowa. She conducts workshops on performance practice and is author of several books and articles on music of the Baroque period. DEAN M. KARNS is Registrar and Director of Institutional Research at Coe College. He has appeared as a harpsichordist and as a performer of court dances from the period of Louis XIV.